ALSO BY JIM COLLINS

Built to Last (with Jerry I. Porras)
Good to Great
Good to Great and the Social Sectors
How the Mighty Fall
Great by Choice (with Morten T. Hansen)
Turning the Flywheel
Beyond Entrepreneurship 2.0 (with Bill Lazier)

What to Make of a Life

CLIFFS, FOG, FIRE AND THE SELF-KNOWLEDGE IMPERATIVE

Jim Collins

Cornerstone Press

CORNERSTONE PRESS

UK | USA | Canada | Ireland | Australia
India | New Zealand | South Africa

Cornerstone Press is part of the Penguin Random House group of companies whose addresses can be found at global.penguinrandomhouse.com

Penguin Random House UK,
One Embassy Gardens, 8 Viaduct Gardens, London SW11 7BW

penguin.co.uk

First published in the US by Harper Edge, an imprint of HarperCollins Publishers 2026
First published in the UK by Cornerstone Press 2026
001

Copyright © Jim Collins, 2026

The moral right of the author has been asserted

Penguin Random House values and supports copyright. Copyright fuels creativity, encourages diverse voices, promotes freedom of expression and supports a vibrant culture. Thank you for purchasing an authorised edition of this book and for respecting intellectual property laws by not reproducing, scanning or distributing any part of it by any means without permission. You are supporting authors and enabling Penguin Random House to continue to publish books for everyone. No part of this book may be used or reproduced in any manner for the purpose of training artificial intelligence technologies or systems. In accordance with Article 4(3) of the DSM Directive 2019/790, Penguin Random House expressly reserves this work from the text and data mining exception.

Designed by Bonni Leon-Berman

Printed and bound in Great Britain by Clays Ltd, Elcograf S.p.A.

The authorised representative in the EEA is Penguin Random House Ireland,
Morrison Chambers, 32 Nassau Street, Dublin D02 YH68

A CIP catalogue record for this book is available from the British Library

ISBN: 978–1–529–97975–6

Penguin Random House is committed to a sustainable future
for our business, our readers and our planet. This book is made from
Forest Stewardship Council® certified paper.

For my grandmother Delores
Who stood strong for me when I was most vulnerable

For Joanne
Always

Contents

1	A Life Transformed	1

PART I: COMING INTO FRAME

2	One Big Thing	17
3	A Constellation of Encodings	49
4	Flipping the Arrow of Money	90
5	Focus the Fire	113

PART II: NAVIGATING CLIFFS AND FOG

6	Cliffs	139
7	Fog	156
8	Simplex Stepping	185
9	The Roulette Wheel of Life	209

PART III: FEEDING THE INNER FIRE LONG AND LATE

10	Extend Out/Circle Back	243
11	Choosing Responsibilities	267
12	Feeding the Inner Fire (and Doing Great Work Late)	290
13	Questions Are Better Than Answers	317

Acknowledgments	329
Appendixes	337
Sources	353
Index	383

What to Make of a Life

1

A Life Transformed

My first big cliff in life came quite young, when I lost my father while he was still alive.

My parents had split up in steps, starting when my mom left my father in San Francisco and took me and my brother back to Boulder, Colorado. My father, a beatnik artist, had taken us to live just a few houses down from Haight Street on Ashbury in the mid-1960s. The Summer of Love happened a couple of blocks from our front steps, though my main emotional memory of being a grade-school kid in Haight-Ashbury in 1967 is not love but fear. Haight-Ashbury was ground zero for the counterculture, a kaleidoscopic street scene that felt like growing up in some sort of bizarre theme park for lost flower children, but with a hidden undercurrent of violence. At one point, I started my daily walk to school stepping over the chalked outline of a man who had been shot dead in front of our house. My mom finally said, "That's it!" and left with us kids.

We moved into an ice-box-cold basement with three sleeping cots and a hot plate for a stove, my mom heroically keeping us afloat on a low-paying job and small sums sent by my father. We could not afford a Christmas tree, so my brother and I rolled a rock into the basement, painted it green and red with paint I "borrowed" from school art class, and called it our "Christmas rock."

I desperately hoped my father would return to us and *be* a father. After a year of largely silent absence, he returned. Within two years my parents divorced, leaving my mom to do her best yet again, alone with two sons. My mom said to me at age 13, "You're the man of the house now." I had no idea how to be that, having no male guidance, no role models.

In early high school, I gave one last try with my father, hoping for a dad. He'd gone off to live in an adobe hut with a dirt floor, about 30 miles north of Albuquerque, New Mexico. I rode the Greyhound bus to see him, carrying a packaged turkey to cook in a woodstove for Thanksgiving, an offering we might share together. Over that weekend, he asked almost nothing about me, but talked mainly about himself and how unfairly his mother had treated him. He also sought to elicit my assistance to get his mother to send him money. When I boarded the bus going back north, I knew once and for all, "There will never be a father there."

And that was the true fracture point. My father would live another few years before succumbing to bladder cancer that should have been curable, but to me he'd already died the instant I boarded the return bus from New Mexico.

That tearing moment with my father planted the first of multiple seeds that would germinate and ultimately sprout forth in the research project that led to this book. I left New Mexico without a father, and full of questions. How to get through the befuddling terrain of youth? How to find a path? How to become an adult? What to do with this one amazing gift of a single life to live? I didn't know, and I didn't know how to know.

Life: A Systematic Study

What to make of a life?

That is the question.

It's a question that can assert itself multiple times across the long arc of our lives. It's a question many of us face when young, as we try to first find our way in the world. It's a question we can face again, when life fractures under our feet and we realize that we must evolve or even radically change our answer. And it's a question that we can revisit yet again, when we know we're well past midlife, trying to figure out how to renew ourselves and keep the fire within burning long and late.

The purpose of this book is to share with you what I learned in a ten-year research project into a set of remarkable lives. I set out to learn how the people I studied addressed the Big Question of what to make of a life, and how they addressed it again at different phases of life. My principal objective was to discern common elements across the vast differences of people in this study. I translated those commonalities into the chapter structure of this book, which can serve as a conceptual scaffolding as you wrestle with your own questions of life.

Let me be clear right up front: It is *not* my intention to direct or advise you on what to make of *your* life. I promise no prescriptions or recipes or directives. Indeed, one of the conclusions of this entire effort is that no one can tell you what to do with your life or how specifically to lead your life. And if they do, they're almost certainly wrong. This is decidedly *not* a self-help book. But it is a self-knowledge book. By getting to know the lives in this study through the concepts that follow, you might come a bit closer to the ancient precept, the imperative inscribed on the Temple of Apollo at Delphi: "Know Thyself."

As I began the research for this book, I confronted a fundamental problem: how to construct a *systematic* study that might yield new insights on the timeless questions of life. I needed a *structured method*. I love doing research in a systematic way, then going from observations to insights and concepts and frameworks. I finally settled upon constructing pairs of people matched at cliffs, then studying their lives up to the cliff, through the cliff, then after the cliff. A cliff is a significant event that alters the trajectory of life and forces choices about what's next. The big cliffs can radically change a life, requiring people to reconstitute their lives and reenvision the years to come.

To quickly illustrate the method, here are four pairs from the study:

Robert Plant and Jimmy Page stood side by side as lead singer and lead guitarist of Led Zeppelin. Then their drummer, John Bonham, died. Robert Plant could not imagine continuing without his best friend on drums, so Led Zeppelin also had to die. Plant and Page went over the cliff, both facing the question, Who am I without Led Zeppelin? What then became of Plant and Page, and how did they reorient their lives? What do their lives, together and divergent, teach about finding a path in life and then having to reconceive of that life when the path as they knew it ended?

Cardiss Collins and Maryon Pittman Allen had their lives ripped in half by a tragic cliff, when they lost their husbands, one to a plane crash, the other to a heart attack. Reeling in grief, they faced a second shock: Their husbands had served in Congress, and these two women inherited their seats, sending them off to a role for which they'd never prepared. How did they reconstruct their lives, and why did they take such divergent paths?

Alan Page and Carl Eller played side by side as NFL superstars, No. 88 and No. 81 on the Minnesota Vikings' famed "Purple People Eaters" defensive line. They played in the same four Super Bowls, shared six Pro Bowls together, and entered the Pro Football Hall of Fame. What did they do to create meaningful lives after their athlete identities died, and what can we learn from how they tackled this existential question in such strikingly different ways?

Alice Paul and Lucy Burns fought side by side, dedicating their lives to the achievement of women's suffrage. Ever since they'd first met in jail as young women, their lives had been woven together in pursuit of one epic goal. And then it was done. The 19th Amendment passed. Paul and Burns faced the question of the rest of their lives: *We won! Now what?*

These are but eight of the lives in the study. In total, the project consisted of 2,809 years of people lives systematically studied, across 34 remarkable life cases that we carefully selected from an original list of 500 possibilities. They came from a range of socioeconomic backgrounds and engaged in a wide array of human endeavors, including music, acting, science, writing, athletics, test piloting, politics, business, entrepreneurship, parenting, social cause, law, medicine, military, global affairs, architecture, and fashion design.

I chose cliffs as a primary lens in this study for three principal reasons. First, cliffs are a powerful way to glean insight into the question of what to make of a life because *life-altering cliffs force people to reconsider the question anew.* While I learned (and will share) valuable lessons by looking at how the people in our study found their initial paths in life, the fracture point of cliffs dramatically sharpened the lens. It's one thing to iterate through our teens and twenties, getting a foothold on life; it's another to have your life upended (or even totally shattered) by a major cliff that dramatically alters (or even outright ends) life as you knew it before. The stark reality of cliff events proved exceptionally powerful for gleaning insight into how they navigated. Second, I hypothesized that we could learn valuable lessons about what makes people tick by paying particular attention to how they handled cliffs and not just how they handled life when it hummed along between cliffs. Third, I was deeply curious about how people handle the question of self-renewal and keeping the inner fire burning bright over the long course of a life. Examining how different people handled the challenge of reconstituting their lives after hitting life-altering cliffs would be a powerful way to satisfy my curiosity.

Along the way, at a pivotal point in the research that I'll get to in a later chapter, I realized that the odds any of us will complete a life without cliffs are close to zero. Some cliffs are bigger than others, but life is punctuated by cliffs. They could be personal cliffs or professional cliffs, success cliffs or failure cliffs, graduation cliffs or retirement cliffs, planned cliffs or shockingly unexpected cliffs, bad luck cliffs or good luck cliffs, cliffs of life-defining wins or cliffs of tragic loss that split a life in two. Cliffs are us.

Cliffs also became the ideal juncture point to match people into *pairs*. The idea behind a matched pair is to select two study subjects in the same or very similar situation (in this case, experiencing a similar cliff), then compare and contrast their decisions and actions to yield deeper insights. It's a little like putting twin bugs into the same lab dish and seeing how each responds to its conditions. As you will see in the coming chapters, using the matched-pair method yielded vital insights that would not have been clear without pairs.

Now, I want to make one important clarification about the role of matched pairs in this study. One day, as I was getting deep into this research, my wife, Joanne, said to me, "Remember, Jim, *people are not stock returns!*" In my prior research for books like *Good to Great* and *Built to Last*, my research colleagues and I could use metrics of performance, like cumulative investment returns and other measures of corporate success. This simply *does not apply to lives*. The range of criteria people use to assess the quality of their lives varies widely, and there are no justifiable universal criteria analogous to stock returns. This study does not frame some people and their lives as "better" than others; there are no absolute "winners" and "losers" among the research subjects, relative to each other. Who is to say what makes one life "better" than another? To assert my own definitions of what makes a "better" life would corrupt the research by letting my own values and biases drive the interpretation of results. I didn't want to proclaim what to make of a life based on my own idiosyncratic views; I wanted to *discover* common elements and patterns that vastly different people and lives had in common.

The research behind this book consumed the better part of a decade to complete. I hired teams of research assistants to help me with what became the largest project I'd ever done; 28 people joined the research effort at various points. Across the entire effort, including the process of selecting and discarding candidates for study, we assembled more than 20,000 articles and source documents and more than 400 books (consisting of more than 100,000 pages), along with a variety of ancillary sources such as recorded lectures, interviews, video footage, documentary films, and audio recordings. I particularly enjoyed engaging directly with the study subjects' actual work when possible, reading writers' books in sequence, listening to musicians' discographies across decades of their work, and watching actors' films one by one as they aged into different types of roles.

We limited the study to people who were deceased or whose lives were already largely in the record books, enabling me to assess how life unfolds from youth, through midlife, to later in life. We found many of the most illuminating quotations and vivid details in materials that came from the actual time of events, going back many decades. These sources gave me invaluable perspective on how their lives unfolded in real time, when they didn't entirely know their own futures. We constructed detailed life chronologies and categorical coding documents, synthesizing the vast amounts of information we gathered.

Which leads me to an important point about the study subjects, and their relevance to you and me. It's an impressive group, even intimidating. We have Nobel Prize recipients, award-winning actors, two of the first astronauts to orbit Earth, presidents and congressional leaders, world champion athletes, people who have naval ships named after them, famous musicians, supreme court justices, groundbreaking business visionaries, world-shaping cause leaders, and even people who helped found a nation. This is not a random sample of the population! The famous nature of the people in this study is an artifact of the research: To do the study, I needed copious amounts of information. I selected luminaries, many of them famous, for a simple reason: *That's where the data is.*

It is not my goal to help you become as successful or as famous as they were. In fact, most of the people in our study were not trying to become famous; they were just leading their lives, and it just so happened that their lives ended up being famous. Furthermore, it turns out that some of the people in our study deliberately chose to shift away from highly visible success as their lives progressed, taking a more private path, which proved just as interesting and useful for gaining insight. As the pages of this book unfold, you will see how they struggled with many of the same issues and challenges that you and I struggle with. Their lives unfolded imperfectly. They made mistakes. They endured pain and loss. They wandered at times. They were, like you and me, quite human.

Three Books in One

I've broken this book into three parts.

PART I: COMING INTO FRAME

This part has to do with how the people in the study found and committed to a path that met three tests: (1) They were deeply encoded for it, (2) they made the economics work to pursue it, and (3) it ignited their inner fire and they *focused* that fire into doing it. Every person in the study came fully into frame with all three tests at least once in life, and for many this was their path out of the fog of youth. Half of the study subjects did it more than once, shifting from one path to an entirely new path that also met the tests.

PART II: NAVIGATING CLIFFS AND FOG

I expected cliffs to be prominent in their lives (that was, after all, the study design), but I didn't expect the pervasiveness of fog. Episodes of fog—when people find themselves feeling lost or confused or befuddled or disoriented—can roll in at any point in life, but they are particularly prevalent in the wake of cliffs. This study taught me that even the most accomplished people can land in a major fog funk. Fog is not a defect. It is an artifact of life. The question is, How did they get past the cliffs and through the fog?

PART III: FEEDING THE INNER FIRE LONG AND LATE

These lives devastate the myth that our younger selves must tower over our older selves, that our best, most creative phase of life necessarily comes in the first half. One of my favorite findings is how many of them did some of their most significant and groundbreaking work well past the midpoint of their lives, sometimes well into their sixth, seventh, even eighth and ninth decades. Though this section is not just about their visible output (some took a very personal or private turn later in life) but about keeping the fire burning long and late, even growing hotter and brighter as the decades click by.

I came to see this work not as one book but as three books in one. The entire work might read differently to you at different times of life, depending on which of the three parts most resonate when you are reading it. If you're in search of a meaningful path, perhaps the first will speak most loudly. If reeling from a cliff and feeling lost in the fog, perhaps the second will take center stage. If principally struggling with the question of restoking and sustaining the fire long and late, perhaps the third will command more of your attention. Though, as you'll discover, you cannot entirely separate each part (or even each chapter) from all the others; each part of the book contains elements of all the others. This reflects a basic truth: Life does not happen in nice neatly prepackaged stages. Life is not linear; it is unfolding, layered, and organic.

My Life Transformed

Fortunately, I found my own way through the fog after getting on that Greyhound bus in New Mexico, largely due to coming across people who helped me become me. The biggest turning point came when Joanne and I got engaged four days after our first date on the Stanford campus where we attended on scholarship. We got married a few months later, me at 22 and Joanne at 21, and I began a conscious effort to try to become a person worthy of being married to her. We're still tightly bonded, now 45 years later. Also at Stanford, while in graduate school, I met the closest thing to a father I ever had, the late Professor Bill Lazier. At age 30, through Bill's championing me to the deans, I landed a position teaching at the Stanford Graduate School of Business; that's the moment I stepped out of the fog of youth and settled upon a life of research, writing, and teaching. Yet I'd never fully rid myself of the questions of life, not just my own, but overall questions that confront many of us. Those questions ultimately led to doing this book.

There were times when I felt overwhelmed by the magnitude of this project, wondering if I'd taken on something bigger than I could do. After I finished systematically digesting the first couple of pairs of lives, exhausted from the deep dive, I realized that I'd worked through only about 306 years of people lives across the two pairs. Looking ahead, I calculated that I had more than 2,000 years of people lives yet to go. I thought to myself, "This is too big! I can't possibly do this." But each pair of lives became so compelling, and the learning became so fascinating, that I could not stop. My friends began to wonder if I'd gotten lost somewhere, or whether maybe something had happened to me, because my correspondence atrophied to a trickle. No, I would tell them, I'm just hunkered down in the creative cave. The total effort filled some of the best years of my life to date; I began the early sketching of this project at age 55, and I'm now writing these words at age 67.

It all proved worthwhile, not just because there is now this book to share with you, but because doing this project transformed me in profound ways. By working through all the lives in this study, step by step as their lives unfolded, I feel as if I've almost lived alongside them. I was creating for myself the most marvelous collection of interesting friends whose stories held me in endless fascination. Gradually at first, then in cascading waves, I noticed that the research was not just changing my brain; it was changing *me*. The sign of good research is that you end up in places you never expected. If after years of research all you do is reconfirm your own preconceptions, then what is the point of doing research? The whole point is to discover, to be surprised, to come to see the world and how it works differently than you did before.

After this study, I will never look at life the same ever again, and I will never look at other people the way I used to. I am a different person, and many of my previous ways of thinking, and even my emotions, have evolved or fundamentally changed. My relationship to my lost father even changed, softening and allowing me to forgive and reconcile even though he is long gone from this earth. I titled this chapter "A Life Transformed" because by studying the transformations of the people in this book over the long arc of their lives, *it is I who became transformed.*

Full Set of Study Subjects—Alphabetical by Last Name

Tenley Albright	Figure skater and surgeon.
Maryon Pittman Allen	Columnist, U.S. senator, and vintage restorative artist.
Lucy Burns	Suffragist.
Jimmy Carter	U.S. president and human rights advocate.
Cardiss Collins	Civil servant and U.S. representative.
Charles Colson	Political operative and founder of Prison Fellowship.
Gordon Cooper	Fighter pilot, test pilot, and astronaut.
John Ehrlichman	Political operative and writer.
Carl Eller	Football player and substance abuse prevention advocate.
Gerald R. Ford	U.S. representative, U.S. president, and statesman.
Michael J. Fox	Actor and Parkinson's activist.
Benjamin Franklin	Entrepreneur, writer, scientist, and U.S. Founding Father.
Georgia Frontiere	Stage performer and CEO of the Los Angeles Rams.
John Glenn	Fighter pilot, test pilot, astronaut, and U.S. senator.
Katharine Graham	CEO of The Washington Post Company.
Grace Hopper	Pioneering computer scientist and U.S. Navy officer.
Dolores Huerta	Labor activist.

Carol Heiss Jenkins	Figure skater and coach.
George C. Marshall	Military officer and U.S. secretary of state.
Barbara McClintock	Pioneering geneticist.
Toni Morrison	Novelist.
Sandra Day O'Connor	U.S. Supreme Court justice.
Alan Page	Football player and Minnesota Supreme Court justice.
Jimmy Page	Guitarist of Led Zeppelin and music producer.
Alice Paul	Suffragist and women's rights activist.
I. M. Pei	Modern architect.
Robert Plant	Vocalist of Led Zeppelin and musical adventurer.
Carlos Santana	Guitarist.
Roger Sherman	Entrepreneur, lawyer, and U.S. Founding Father.
Meryl Streep	Actor.
Barbara Tuchman	Historian and author.
Vera Wang	Fashion designer.
Maurice White	Leading musician of Earth, Wind & Fire.
Debra Winger	Actor.

Part I

Coming into Frame

2

One Big Thing

Young Barbara McClintock had no idea she would become a geneticist with insights so revolutionary that she would be cast into the scientific wilderness and later recognized with a Nobel Prize. She knew only that she loved to lose herself in thought, becoming so utterly absorbed that she could forget even herself.

Once during a college geology exam, McClintock found herself enraptured, the answers flowing from her brain into the exam booklet. She finished early and was getting ready to turn in her exam when she encountered a problem: She could not remember her own name.

In her excitement to dig into the exam questions, she'd flipped right past the space to write her name. Sitting there as seconds, then minutes, ticked by, she hoped her name would come to her. It did not.

Five minutes passed. No name.

Ten minutes, no name.

Fifteen minutes, still no name.

McClintock began to worry. What would happen if time ran out and she could not recall her name? She felt too embarrassed to interrupt one of her classmates to ask, "Excuse me, sorry to bother, but can you tell me who I am?"

So, she just sat there, trying to conjure her name.

Finally, after about 20 minutes, she remembered her name and turned in her exam before the clock ran out.

McClintock described herself as being entranced with the joy of study and learning. But where to channel this unusual ability to focus so intently that she could forget her own name?

Along the way, she took a genetics course and so impressed the professor that he invited McClintock, then aged 19, to enroll in his graduate genetics course. Bang! In genetics, she found a perfect arena to deploy her brain as an organic decryption machine. She found that she enjoyed working with maize (another word for corn) to construct genetics experiments and lose herself in deciphering the results.

She kept taking one step after another with no clear plan in mind, finishing her undergraduate degree in botany, a master's degree, then a PhD, all the while getting deeper into research with maize. She began writing scientific articles, first one, then another, then a third, fourth, fifth, drawn inexorably forward by each little puzzle. "I don't remember having any [professional] aspirations," she reflected to the biographer Evelyn Fox Keller, author of *A Feeling for the Organism*. "I suddenly realized that I had gotten myself into this position [of being a research scientist] without recognizing that that was where I was going."

The more she did her genetics work, the more she found herself well constructed for it. She discovered that she had the ability to mentally transport herself into a cell, almost like walking around the interior of a house, directly observing its inner workings and making friends with the chromosomes. McClintock drew upon her unusual capabilities when she traveled to Stanford to help solve a difficult genetics puzzle related to *Neurospora* (a form of mold). After a few days of working in the lab, peering through a microscope, she hit a wall, unable to crack the riddle of the chromosomes. She wandered out onto the Stanford campus and settled onto a bench shaded by eucalyptus trees, and activated the organic decryption machine in her head. Less than an hour later, her mental tumblers snap-clicked into place, and she hurried back to the lab. "And suddenly I knew everything was going to be just fine," she said of this moment. One of her colleagues later reflected that McClintock's short visit had done "more to clean up the cytology of *Neurospora* than all other cytological geneticists had done in all previous time on all forms of mold."

She could become so consumed with a puzzle that life itself could seem less important than solving the problem at hand. While driving across the country after visiting colleagues at Caltech, McClintock had a curious reaction to recent news about car crashes: She didn't fear dying in a car crash so much as dying in a car crash *before* she'd solved the puzzle on her mind. "I was just so interested in what I was doing I could hardly wait to get up in the morning and get at it," said McClintock. "One of my friends, a geneticist, said I was a child, because only children can't wait to get up in the morning to get at what they want to do."

In her early 30s, McClintock survived on research fellowships and a modest salary at Cornell. By her mid-30s, she'd accepted an assistant professorship at the University of Missouri, which led straight to a major cliff. McClintock hit the wall of limited opportunities for women in science in traditional academia in the early 1940s. She could theoretically stay in academia and acquiesce to more junior teaching roles without substantial research support, but Barbara McClintock was not made for that type of faculty position. For one thing, she found herself ill-constructed for and drained by lecture-style teaching. For another, McClintock cared more about doing her research and solving genetics puzzles than being socially accepted in the stuffy confines of the faculty lounge.

In one incident, McClintock wanted to continue her lab work on a Sunday, but found the door locked and she'd not brought her keys. She could go back to her residence to get her keys, but that would delay getting to the puzzle at hand in the lab. So, she found a way to climb up the side of the building and through a window, her antics causing quite a buzz on campus. "I had no chance of being promoted, I was excluded from faculty meetings and things like that," said McClintock. She'd been politically protected by a mentor and colleague named Lewis Stadler, but the dean told her that if Stadler left, she'd probably be fired. McClintock concluded that "there was no hope for a maverick like me to ever be at a university."

For Barbara McClintock, the path of traditional academia as a platform for doing her scientific work had crumbled away. She decided to abandon the whole idea of being a professor, asked for a leave without pay, and cast about for a different platform to pursue her research. She didn't seek a lot of money; she simply sought the resources and freedom to continue with her research, writing to one friend that she would be willing to make a smaller salary if needed. Fortunately, McClintock eventually landed a full-time position at a Carnegie-funded research institution at Cold Spring Harbor, about 30 miles outside New York City on Long Island. At Cold Spring Harbor, which remained her intellectual home for the rest of her life, she did her most groundbreaking work.

In her fifth decade of life, McClintock made and published a radical and seminal discovery. Following her belief that one must let the evidence shape thinking, rather than bringing a preformed answer to impose upon the evidence, she saw something quite contrary to conventional theory: "mobile genetic elements" (sometimes called transposable genetic elements or jumping genes). In essence, she discovered that segments of DNA can jump, moving from one place along a segment of DNA to another.

The response from members of the scientific community ranged from incomprehension to indifference. When she first presented her seminal finding on mobile genetic elements, many of those in attendance failed to grasp her work. She tried again at a few more symposia, but she became too exasperated to keep trying. "It was just a surprise that I couldn't communicate," McClintock later said. "I was being ridiculed, or being told that I was really mad." McClintock never doubted she was right—the mountain of meticulous evidence she'd assembled proved her discovery beyond any reasonable doubt—and she believed that the scientific community would eventually catch up. Even so, it would take decades for McClintock's revolutionary insight to be fully accepted. As one scientific colleague put it, "She felt she had crossed a desert alone and no one had followed her."

What sustained Barbara McClintock across the desert when no one followed? She turned being ignored into an opportunity for more of what she valued most, namely the freedom to do her work, following her curiosity, constructing her experiments, letting the maize speak to her. She so loved the freedom to work without intrusion that she refused to get a telephone for most of her life. When the Nobel Assembly of the Karolinska Institute decided to award McClintock the Nobel Prize (more than three decades after her discovery), they could not reach her directly. McClintock later said she learned about it on the radio. As the news of her winning the prize began to swirl around Cold Spring Harbor, a colleague went rushing off to locate McClintock; he found her alone on a morning stroll picking walnuts. When asked at a press conference pulled together at Cold Spring Harbor, "What do you think of big to-dos like this? With all the attention that's being heaped on you?" McClintock responded in an endearing tone that elicited laughter and applause: "You put up with it."

In her Nobel Banquet speech, she commented on her desert years: "In the interim I was not invited to give lectures or seminars, except on rare occasions, or to serve on committees or panels, or to perform other scientists' duties. Instead of causing personal difficulties, this long interval proved to be a delight. It allowed complete freedom to continue investigations without interruption, and for the pure joy they provided." For McClintock, it wasn't about being in love with the *idea* of being a prizewinning geneticist but about being in love with the actual *doing* of the daily tasks of being a geneticist. While McClintock acknowledged the prize as "an extraordinary honor," she added, "It might seem unfair, however, to reward a person for having so much pleasure over the years."

McClintock continued to live the same simple life. Her wardrobe consisted mainly of unadorned clothes—khakis, simple collared shirts, and sweaters. She lived in a small cottage a short walk from her laboratory. She worked through each day with joyful intensity, showing no particular interest in taking time to cook elaborate meals; she kept herself fueled in part by feeding her sweet tooth, especially with handfuls of jelly beans. She remained focused on the work itself, not on the money that might come from the work. At the press conference upon the news of her Nobel Prize, someone asked what she would do with the prize money. McClintock responded, "I don't even know what the award brings in." When told it was $190,000 (quite a lot in the early 1980s), she seemed almost befuddled. "Oh, it *is*? I didn't know. I'll just have to get to one side and think about this." I found no evidence that her lifestyle and work routine changed in any significant way after the Nobel Prize. McClintock remained intellectually engaged, fascinated by genetics puzzles right until she entered the hospital. She passed away at age 90, just a few miles from her maize fields.

Three Elements of One Big Thing

Barbara McClintock's life beautifully illustrates one of the most essential findings that showed up across the entire set of lives in the study. She answered the question of what to make of a life partly by bringing together a triad of mutually reinforcing elements:

1. She discovered and deployed a set of her encodings.
2. She flipped the arrow of money.
3. She focused the inner fire.

I'm going to briefly introduce these three elements below, to fix them in your mind. In the subsequent three chapters, we will extensively explore and illustrate each of these elements. These elements will show up repeatedly in the lives of the people you'll meet throughout the book as they exit the fog of youth, work through the cliffs of life, and sustain continuous self-renewal well into their latest decades.

DISCOVER AND DEPLOY ENCODINGS

Encodings are durable capacities of a person's intrinsic construction that lie within, awaiting discovery through the experiences of life.

Barbara McClintock discovered a set of natural encodings that she trusted and followed, even without knowing exactly where they would lead. She didn't *learn* how to lose herself in thought; she was encoded to lose herself in thought. She didn't learn how to make her brain into an organic decryption machine; she *discovered* that she came pre-packaged with that encoding and then used it. No one taught her to mentally transport herself into a cell and walk around inside that cell making friends with the chromosomes; that was just an idiosyncratic encoding specific to Barbara McClintock.

Before going any further, I want to be clear to not confuse the concept of encodings with the rare phenomenon of intellectual genius. The point is not that McClintock was a genius (though she was that) but that she instinctively played to deeply encoded ways of operating that suited *her* exceptionally well. A colleague said of McClintock after her death, "The fact that she is gone makes me think of an extinct species or a miraculous creation that will never again be seen in the world." *This very same sentiment could apply just as well to every single person in our study,* not because of their "genius," but because of how they played exquisitely to their unique constellation of encodings.

Each constellation of encodings is its own category-of-one distinctive blend. There was just one Barbara McClintock, one John Glenn, one Alice Paul, one Toni Morrison, one Benjamin Franklin. Just as there is only one of you, and only one of me. The thing that set them apart is their ability to play so consistently to their own individual (and sometimes quite peculiar) package of encodings.

This study leads me to conclude that each of us likely has a vast and spectacular constellation of encodings within, more than we will *ever* be able to discover in a single lifetime. You don't create encodings; you discover them. You don't add encodings from without; you find them within.

> The question is not whether a person has encodings. *Everyone* has encodings. The question is this: Which encodings will the journey of life lead you to discover, and will you trust them enough to align your life around them?

Throughout this book, you will see case after case of people doing exactly that. Even if they didn't have the language for it, they answered the question of what to make of a life in large part by discovering, trusting, and following their encodings.

FLIP THE ARROW OF MONEY

None of the people in our study measured their lives primarily by the amount of money they made. *Not one.* Yet equally true, they all understood that they needed to make the economics of their lives work. Recall how Barbara McClintock never saw her genetics work principally as a means to making money, and how flummoxed she was in learning of the Nobel Prize money. Yet also, especially in the wake of leaving traditional academia, she faced the very practical question of how to sustain herself and fund her work. Landing at Cold Spring Harbor provided her a lab, ample fields for her maize experiments, and a salary that kept her well stocked in the basics of life (including plenty of jelly beans). For McClintock, money and resources became the *means* to do her research, rather than her research being a means to make money. Every person in our study made this flip at some point in their lives, from seeing money principally as the output of their efforts ("I work to make money") to seeing money as *an input to fuel their efforts* ("I need money to do what I'm encoded for").

Few of the people in our study came from substantial family wealth. In fact, more of them had to overcome significant economic scarcity somewhere along the path of their lives. Whatever their starting economic circumstances, whether easy or difficult, they made the flip.

FOCUS THE INNER FIRE

Imagine being so intrinsically compelled by what you do that it feels almost unfair to receive rewards and recognition for doing it. Imagine being so compulsively engaged that you wish there were more hours in the day, and more days in a life, so that you could do even more of it. Imagine the thing you are doing feels almost more important than life itself. *(I didn't worry so much about dying in a car crash as dying in a car crash before I'd solved the puzzle!)* Imagine doing something you love so much that no amount of money could entice you to give up doing it. Imagine having such an unquenchable enthusiasm for what you do that you might seem childlike to those around you. Imagine that focusing the inner fire with great intensity does the exact opposite of causing burnout: It *feeds* the fire. Imagine you are able to sustain the fire for days, weeks, months, years, decades, maybe even the rest of your entire life. Like Barbara McClintock, all the people in this study had extended phases of life where they not just felt the inner fire but *focused* it. They didn't just focus in some random direction; they focused their energies *in alignment with their encodings*.

All Three Together into One Big Thing: Finding a Personal Hedgehog

An ancient Greek poet crafted the kernel of a useful parable, later popularized by the philosopher Isaiah Berlin: The fox knows many things, but the hedgehog knows one big thing. (The hedgehog has one big defense of rolling into a ball with sharp spikes pointed outward to defeat the crafty fox that knows a multitude of attack strategies rather than one big one.) Throughout this book, I will sometimes use the phraseology of being "in a hedgehog" or "in hedgehog mode" to wrap the idea of these three specific elements integrated together into the pursuit of One Big Thing.

> *To find a personal hedgehog* means that you've found an arena of activity that meets three tests: (1) You're encoded for it; (2) you flip the arrow of money in doing it; and (3) it focuses the inner fire. *To be in hedgehog mode* means you've committed to organize your life and channel a huge chunk of your energy toward the pursuit of this One Big Thing. The point here is not that the people in this study *are* hedgehogs (or foxes) as a personality type, but that they went into hedgehog mode for extended periods of time.

Mark Twain once quipped that the difference between the almost right word and the right word is the difference between the lightning bug and lightning. I kept thinking about that when looking at the people in our study. When they met all three tests and clicked into hedgehog mode they lit up like lightning. Only, it wasn't just a single flashing bolt. It was a full-on lightning storm that lasted for years to decades. The invitation to join the graduate genetics course at Cornell "cast the die for my future," said McClintock, who then applied herself to genetics puzzles for the next seven decades. Hedgehog mode indeed!

Grace Hopper: An Expansive Life Within One Big Thing

To further illustrate and explore the above concepts, let's turn now to Barbara McClintock's matched-pair companion in the study, Grace Hopper.

Young Grace Hopper had no life plan to become a seminal pioneer in computer science, laying foundations for the software revolution that would make computers widely useful. She knew only that she loved gadgets and figuring out how they worked. On one trip to a summer cottage, young Hopper became fascinated by the alarm clocks, and she disassembled all seven alarm clocks in the bedrooms. I picture little Grace moving from room to room, creating mountains of screws, wheels, gears, cogs, bells, springs, or whatever else might be inside. After that, her mother limited Grace to just one clock to playfully explore. "I took everything apart to find out how it worked," said Hopper, "because that is what I liked to do."

Born less than five years apart, Grace Hopper and Barbara McClintock had remarkable similarities in their early lives. Hopper earned a PhD in her 20s (in mathematics) and became an assistant professor in a traditional academic setting (at Vassar).

Then, at age 36, recently separated from her husband and inspired to serve in World War II, Hopper joined the U.S. Navy Reserve. Upon graduation from Naval Reserve Midshipmen's School, commissioned as a lieutenant junior grade, she received a wartime assignment that would shape the rest of her life. The Navy assigned her to a secret computation project at Harvard, under the leadership of Commander Howard Aiken, a Harvard professor who also served in the Navy.

When Hopper walked into Harvard's Cruft Laboratory, Commander Aiken pointed her to a gigantic machine, as long as a four-story building is high, named the Mark I. Hopper flat-out gadget geeked. "I'd always loved a good gadget," Hopper later recalled. "And I'm afraid that in my heart, when I first saw Mark I, my first thought was . . . gee, that's the prettiest gadget I ever saw."

Hopper was staring at one of the very first computers ever built. "I walked into a room and Prof. Howard Aiken said, 'Lieutenant, that is a calculating machine.' I looked at a monstrous device stretching 51 feet across a large room. It was Mark I and I was stepping into history."

Working on the Mark I, Hopper had a profound realization: The key to making computers pervasive and useful lay not in the hardware but in the software. As one of the first computer programmers in all of human history, Hopper saw firsthand just how inefficient and error-prone programming could be. Suppose you had to write actual software code every time you wanted to do a spreadsheet analysis, rather than being able to access a predesigned spreadsheet application. You'd make mistakes and spend all your time programming rather than thinking about the problem you're trying to solve. Instead of writing 100 one-off programs, Hopper and her colleagues sought to create a catalog of prepackaged routines that could be called upon repeatedly. They essentially invented the modern concept of subroutines, the precursor to standard programs, repeatable algorithms, and easy-to-use applications.

On the Mark I project, Grace Hopper's natural encodings for working with gadgets came alive, and she deployed them to get the most out of a computer. She instinctively shifted from being a problem solver to being a tool builder—*don't just solve the problem, use the problem to build a tool!* Right from the get-go, Hopper displayed a penchant for making computers more accessible, and Commander Aiken asked her to create the first-ever manual of operations for a computer. On the Harvard computation team, Hopper also discovered previously untapped leadership encodings. She proved so adept at keeping people unified and focused on the Mark I project that Commander Aiken essentially turned leading the team over to her.

By the end of the war, Hopper knew where she wanted to focus her inner fire. She could have returned to Vassar as a respected professor of mathematics and had a perfectly fine career, but with computers and software she'd found the One Big Thing she wanted to dedicate herself to for the rest of her life.

But then, as with McClintock, Hopper hit the ceiling of limited opportunity to continue her scientific work within the confines of a traditional academic institution. A few years after the war, Hopper's three-year contract as a faculty research fellow at Harvard expired. "They didn't promote women at Harvard at that point," said Hopper, "so at the end of three years my time was up." Hopper, like McClintock, did not confuse a position ("being at Harvard" or "being a professor") with her life's work, and she decided to recast herself on a different platform outside the strictures and constraints of traditional academia.

Hopper joined one of the early computer companies, where she would rise to become head of all systems research and lead visionary efforts to democratize computers through software. She developed the first compiler in history and worked toward making it possible to write software using English words. She perceived the need for tools to make it easier for people to write software across a variety of computers. Without standard languages, the widespread use of computers would have been unlikely, perhaps impossible, and without Grace Hopper the widespread adoption of standard languages would have been slower, likely much slower. The next time you turn on your computer and enjoy how seamlessly all the applications function, say a little thank-you to Grace Hopper. (To go deeper into Hopper's story and how it merged with the early history of computers and software, see Kurt W. Beyer's superb book, *Grace Hopper and the Invention of the Information Age*.)

Hopper had a gift for creating team cultures of altruistic pirates. When she first began developing the compiler, she had no approval, no budget, no giant corporate initiative. Instead of trying to convince the finance-minded corporate types of her idea, she simply started recruiting programmers to work on her compiler project, *and to do so on their own time*. She got the first three revisions of the compiler completed with her unpaid pirate crew. She then made the argument to corporate: *Well, you already have a team invested in the project, and we've already made a working prototype, so you might as well make it official and fund a department to fully develop the compiler.* Hopper got her funding.

Later, after she returned to active duty in the Navy (*at age 60*), Hopper kept a Jolly Roger flag in her office at the Pentagon, a visible symbol of getting her teams swept up in the excitement of pirating for the work at hand. She and her team went on a furniture-scavenging mission, foraging around the Pentagon in the middle of the night, removing what they needed from other offices. When found out, she pointed out that, well, the furniture they took wasn't bolted down!

Hopper discovered and deployed quite different encodings for teaching and communication from McClintock, Hopper being naturally adept at giving inspired presentations and interesting interviews. She reveled in crafting vivid analogies and metaphors. "I like analogies," said Hopper. "I watched some lumbering up in Maine. . . . [A]nd when they get a great big log and one ox can't budge the darn thing, they don't try to grow a bigger ox and they don't import an elephant—they use two oxen." Hopper used this oxen analogy to convey the idea that a network of smaller computers would be better than having one ever-bigger computer—a prescient point she made before the personal computer industry had even been born and more than two decades before the internet boom. In another vivid teaching moment, Hopper used cut wires to convey the increasing power of computers, and how a computation that used to take a microsecond (a millionth of a second) had dropped to require only a nanosecond (a billionth of a second). But how did she help people viscerally grasp the difference? She'd hold up a little wire cut to the distance electricity could travel in a nanosecond, 11.8 inches: *This is a nanosecond*. Then for the sake of dramatic comparison, she'd bring out a coiled wire 984 feet long: *This is a microsecond*. Her point made vivid: Just think of the computing efficiencies when programmers need only 11.8 inches versus 984 feet (metaphorically) to accomplish the same task due to increased computer processing power.

Throughout Hopper's post-Harvard life, she showed shrewd instincts for how to create leverage within bureaucracies and across industry ecosystems to get big things done. Think for a moment: How would you go about getting the emerging computer industry to adopt standard languages? Hopper figured that if she could get the Navy to require Navy-certified standard languages, then companies would respond to the sheer purchasing power of the Department of Defense.

She positioned herself to become director of the Navy Programming Languages Group and helped lead the effort to ensure the adoption of COBOL (Common Business Oriented Language) as a standard across the Navy. COBOL became so pervasive that more than 200 billion lines of COBOL ran on computing devices worldwide by the end of the 20th century.

Like McClintock, Hopper saw money as a necessary condition for doing her work, and so long as she could do her work the way she wanted, she showed little interest in making ever more money. When an interviewer noted that she could have become very wealthy had she become a business entrepreneur, she replied, "I've already received the highest award I'll ever receive, no matter how long I live, no matter how many more jobs I may have, and that has been the privilege and the responsibility of serving very proudly in the United States Navy."

As with Barbara McClintock, the fire within Grace Hopper kept burning bright for decade upon decade. Even in her 70s, she bounded out of bed by 5 a.m. on many days and traveled up to 200 days per year. She never tired of teaching anyone and everyone about her beloved computer gadgets, about the wonders of compilers, about tools for better programming, about the power of standard languages. She even went on *Late Night with David Letterman* at age 79, sparkling the segment with humor and charm, still exuding a childlike enthusiasm for sharing her love of computers and software. She pulled a bundle of 11.8-inch cut wires out of her purse, gleefully telling Letterman that these were visual nanoseconds and letting him pick one from the bundle for himself of whatever color he wanted. If you want to see what a fully on fire nearly 80-year-old in hedgehog mode is like, I encourage watching it.

In another interview conducted late in her life, Hopper reflected on the joys of her life: "I've had a wonderful time. I've had tremendous opportunities. I've had tremendous luck. Just think, if the Navy had not ordered me to that first computer, I might not have had anything of what I have today." The interviewer then asked Hopper if she was living her present life to her absolute fullest, to which she replied, "Oh, I am having a wonderful time."

Hopper remained on active duty in the U.S. Navy until age 79, rising to the rank of rear admiral. Even after retiring as the then-oldest serving officer in the Navy, she continued to proselytize for her beloved computer gadgets as a consultant for Digital Equipment Corporation. She died at age 85, having happily focused the fire in alignment with her encodings for nearly five decades since first falling in love with the Mark I. While Hopper did not receive a Nobel Prize like McClintock (there was no Nobel for computer science in Hopper's time), she did receive the National Medal of Technology and Innovation for her seminal contributions to the field of computer science. And somewhere in the world, as I write these words, sails a guided-missile destroyer named in her honor, the USS *Hopper* (DDG 70). Of all the impressive forms of recognition accumulated by the people in this study, Grace Hopper's namesake destroyer might just be my favorite.

Commonalities Across Vast Differences

The power of this research comes not just from studying a plethora of interesting people but from constructing matched pairs of lives examined side by side to sharpen, deepen, amplify, and add nuance to the concepts. The basic method of the study involves pairing two lives together at a similar or identical cliff event and then studying their entire lives up to the cliff, through the cliff, and after the cliff. For an overview of Barbara McClintock and Grace Hopper as a pair, see the nearby side-by-side life chronologies, "Barbara McClintock and Grace Hopper Side by Side."

Barbara McClintock and Grace Hopper Side by Side

	BARBARA MCCLINTOCK		GRACE HOPPER
Early Life	Born in 1902. Grew up principally in the New York area. Graduated from high school at age 16.	Early Life	Born in 1906. Grew up principally in the New York area. Graduated from high school at age 17.
Ages 17–24	Age 17: Entered college at Cornell. Age 21: Bachelor's degree in botany. Age 22: Master's degree in botany. Age 24: PhD in botany.	Ages 17–27	Age 17: Entered college at Vassar. Age 21: Bachelor's degree in mathematics and physics. Age 23: Master's degree in mathematics. Age 27: PhD in mathematics.
Ages 24–33	Held academic and teaching position at Cornell. Awarded several research fellowships.	Ages 27–36	Held academic and teaching position at Vassar. Joined the Navy after U.S. entry into World War II.
Ages 34–38	Held position as assistant professor at the University of Missouri.	Ages 37–42	Assigned by the Navy to work on computers at Harvard. Continued at the Harvard Computation Laboratory after the war.
Age 38	Hit the ceiling of opportunity in traditional academia; abandoned academic platform to prioritize her work in genetics research. "I had no chance of being promoted," said McClintock. "There was no hope for a maverick like me to ever be at a university."	Age 42	Hit the ceiling of opportunity in traditional academia; abandoned academic platform to prioritize her work in computer science. "They didn't promote women at Harvard at that point," said Hopper of when her postwar contract ended at Harvard, "my time was up."
Age 39	Joined Cold Spring Harbor Laboratory, an independent research entity funded by the Carnegie Institute.	Age 42	Joined Eckert-Mauchly Computer Corporation, while retaining commission in the U.S. Navy Reserve.

Continued

Ages 40–50	Did seminal work on the control of genes and discovered mobile genetic elements.	Age 43–53	Did seminal work on standard programming languages and creation of the first compiler.
Ages 51–80	Continued work on questions related to the control of genes. Became a distinguished service member at Cold Spring Harbor at age 65. Remained active in the genetics community as her life's work became widely accepted.	Ages 54–79	Continued work related to software and standard languages. Returned to active duty in the U.S. Navy at age 60 as director of the Navy Programming Languages Group. Remained on active duty until age 79, rising to the rank of rear admiral.
Ages 81–90	Awarded Nobel Prize at age 81 for her discovery of mobile genetic elements. Continued her work at Cold Spring Harbor Laboratory until her death at age 90.	Ages 80–85	Awarded National Medal of Technology and Innovation at age 84 for her work on computer languages. Consulted for Digital Equipment Corporation until her death at age 85.

Note: Due to ambiguity in the sources as to some of the precise dates (month and day) relative to birthdays, cited ages in these chronologies may vary by +/-1 year.

Setting Grace Hopper and Barbara McClintock next to each other illustrates one of the most important lessons from this research and the lives in this study. There are common elements in how they answered the question of what to make of a life, but the individual specifics varied greatly from person to person. There is no standard recipe book.

Both Hopper and McClintock discovered and deployed a set of encodings. Both Hopper and McClintock flipped the arrow of money. Both Hopper and McClintock focused the inner fire. Both Hopper and McClintock integrated their encodings, their economics, and their inner fire into a personal hedgehog. Both Hopper and McClintock went into hedgehog mode for decades. But they did so *in very different ways because they were very different people with very different encodings.*

Whereas McClintock thrived on being a solitary scientist who carefully protected her privacy, Hopper thrived on working with and through people and institutions. I find it hard to imagine Barbara McClintock being happy building teams, navigating corporate politics, or serving in the U.S. Navy, whereas Hopper seemed perfectly constructed for these roles. But equally, I find it hard to imagine Grace Hopper operating as a solo scientist, burrowing away in a private laboratory for years on end, toiling away in her maize fields.

Let's do a little thought experiment. Try to imagine a young Barbara McClintock listening to a commencement speech by Grace Hopper. In this thought experiment, imagine the commencement organizers asked Hopper to address the question of how to be successful and happy in life. Hopper then regales her audience with stories of leading software teams, of finding paths to influence, of focusing on changing the world (in her case through software), of being able to lead across sectors from business to military, of the importance of serving in uniform, of getting on influential committees, of forging like-minded pirates into inspired teams taking on the bureaucracy, of the importance of going on shows like *Late Night with David Letterman*, of giving inspiring lectures and being in the public eye, and so forth. Now, what would likely happen if the young McClintock took all the lessons to heart and tried valiantly to live them in her own path? *Disaster!* Barbara McClintock likely would not have become the Barbara McClintock who discovered mobile genetic elements.

Now let's flip the experiment around and envision Barbara McClintock giving a commencement speech to a young Grace Hopper. Imagine McClintock addressing the same question about success and happiness in life, but with a focus on such things as the importance of seeking freedom to work alone above all else, of being disconnected from the world while spending endless hours lost in a trancelike state so deep that you might forget your own name, of living without a phone or other easy way to be reached, of posting Do Not Enter signs to preserve privacy, of going ever deeper into a singular line of inquiry, of being driven by the urgent need to solve a puzzle without regard as to whether it might have social utility in the world, and so forth. What would likely happen if the young Hopper took all the McClintock lessons to heart and tried valiantly to live them in her own path? *Disaster!* Grace Hopper likely would not have become the Grace Hopper who played such a massively impactful role in the advancement of computer software.

> This has profound implications for people finding their way in life, especially young people seeking to exit the fog of youth: Be wary of advice based on other people's specific experience. The advice might be well meaning, and perhaps even inspiring, but it might reflect their own encodings, which differ from *your* encodings.

Notice also that McClintock and Hopper differed in the expansiveness of activities within each of their personal hedgehogs. McClintock burrowed ever deeper into her scientific work related to the control of genes. McClintock likely had other encodings she could have discovered, but her decades of focused scientific work at Cold Spring Harbor did not unveil them. Hopper, in contrast, drew upon a much wider array of encodings, roaming across very different types of institutions and roles (though all of it within her hedgehog as a pioneering scientist and leader in computer software). As you get to know the people in this study, you will meet some who were more narrowly focused in a hedgehog (like McClintock), while others were much more expansive and multifaceted, even within a single hedgehog (like Hopper).

This study became a search for commonalities across vast differences. Just as every planet has gravity, every individual in our study shared a few important elements with the study set as a whole. Yet also, just as every planet differs from every other planet in its particulars, every individual person and life is different from every other individual person and life. If every human being is encoded differently from every other human being on this planet, then there are more than 8 billion idiosyncratic categories of *one*.

Single or Serial?

To read about Barbara McClintock and Grace Hopper, you might get the impression that the people in this study pursued one, and only one, big thing in their lives. They find a hedgehog and never leave it (even if they expand within it). However, McClintock and Hopper reflect only one of two meta-patterns in the research.

Meta-pattern No. 1, single hedgehogs: Once they found a hedgehog, these people largely stayed within it as a primary focus for the rest of their lives.

Meta-pattern No. 2, serial hedgehogs: These people discovered and moved on to a second (or even a third) hedgehog across their lives.

As it turned out, the people in this study *split right down the middle* between the single and the serial patterns.

Let's illustrate meta-pattern No. 2 with a pair of professional athletes who faced the question of what to make of their lives after the end of their athletic careers: Alan Page and Carl Eller.

Alan Page awakened to his athlete encodings when he joined the football team at Central Catholic High School in Canton, Ohio. Page had no idea this would eventually lead him to enshrinement in the Pro Football Hall of Fame, then being built just four miles from his high school football field (and where Page worked a summer job on the construction site). Page had no such grand visions when he walked onto the high school football field.

Yet once into the game, Page discovered that he had a package of physical, mental, and psychological encodings well suited to the game of football. Not merely big (Page would eventually carry more than 240 pounds on his six-foot, four-inch frame), he displayed a devastating quickness. Watching film of Page, I'm reminded not of a raging bull but of a lithe and lethal jaguar that crouches in stillness, quiet and watchful, then explodes into chase and attack mode, cutting across the field, pivoting at full speed, dragging his prey to the ground.

Page earned a scholarship at the University of Notre Dame, where he became an All-American on an undefeated national championship team. The Minnesota Vikings NFL franchise then selected Page in the first round of the draft. Page donned a purple jersey and joined a defensive line so fierce that it garnered the nickname Purple People Eaters. Though Page himself never really liked the nickname ("I wasn't purple and I didn't eat people"), he flourished alongside the other three linemen (including his matched-pair companion, Carl Eller). Recognizing Page's distinctive blend of intellect, speed, and instinct, Coach Bud Grant gave Page the freedom to roam and reposition himself on the line, trusting him to sense the best angle of attack. Page played 238 NFL games without a miss and got voted to the Pro Bowl nine consecutive times. The Associated Press named him league Most Valuable Player for 1971, the first defensive player in history to be so named.

Alan Page had found a spectacular first hedgehog, but an impending cliff loomed. Page knew that no matter how exceptional his football capabilities, his NFL career would absolutely come to an end. What would come next?

The seeds of Page's second hedgehog showed up early, before he'd even entered high school. First came the seminal U.S. Supreme Court case *Brown v. Board of Education*, handed down when Page was eight. The ruling planted a seed within Page about the power of the law as a mechanism for equal justice. Page would later reference the Supreme Court Justice Thurgood Marshall, who had argued the case, as an inspiration. Second, Page became enthralled with the television show *Perry Mason*, a courtroom drama series built around a criminal defense attorney played by Raymond Burr. Page watched adults in the neighborhood going off to work in the factories and mills, then toggled back and forth in his mind, contrasting work in the steel mills with life in the courtroom as portrayed in the show. "I watched a lot of Perry Mason on television," Page later said. "What he did seemed pretty cool to me."

While playing in the NFL, Page began to discover encodings and forms of inner fire that would eventually be elements of his second hedgehog, as a justice on the Minnesota Supreme Court. Page described himself as having an "overly developed sense of injustice" roiling below his calm, almost cerebral persona. In a 1971 game against the Detroit Lions, Page leaped across the line of scrimmage with such quickness that the referee called him offside (jumping across the line before the snap of the ball). Page, normally soft-spoken and reserved, felt the penalty unfair. He hadn't jumped offside; he just moved with such speed that it *looked* as if he'd jumped offside! His sense of injustice provoked, Page sliced through the line on a subsequent play, the Lions' quarterback seeing a flash of purple with the number 88 charging right at him before Page draped his powerful arms around him to drag him to the ground. Page then got up, strode over to the referee, and—though you can't hear his words on the film—made sure the referee knew he'd made an unfair call. For the rest of the game, Page channeled his fury into relentlessly disrupting the Lions, throwing the quarterback for multiple losses, and blocking a punt for a safety, en route to a decisive 29–10 Vikings victory.

The next year, Page became a member of the executive committee of the NFL Players Association, finding the league's restrictive policies around free agency unjustifiable. Page became one of the highest-profile players to catalyze a 42-day players' strike, at one point carrying a picket sign reading People, Not Property and wearing a shirt emblazoned with No Freedom No Football. He even persuaded the college All-Stars to cancel their annual game against the Super Bowl champions as part of exerting leverage on behalf of players' rights. Page's efforts on behalf of the players association ignited an interest in labor law.

On the cusp of age 30, while still playing in the NFL, Page enrolled in the University of Minnesota Law School. He had previously enrolled in night classes, early in his NFL career, but stopped when he felt overwhelmed by the coursework. This time, Page found himself invigorated by law school: "I loved every minute of it." He reveled in the intellectual intensity, the process of learning, the writing, the thinking, the discussions, the range of legal subjects. Law school revealed a powerful set of encodings within Page, and it fueled his inner fire for a life far beyond football. While still playing in the NFL, Page earned his doctor of jurisprudence degree and passed the bar.

At age 36, Page retired from the NFL with a distinctive flourish, underscoring that he'd fully made the shift from hedgehog No. 1 in football, where he used his head "for a battering ram or as a place to keep my helmet," toward hedgehog No. 2, where he would use his brain as a legal scholar. Picture one of the greatest defensive linemen in all of history standing on the field where he is about to play the final game of his career. He stands at a microphone arranged for him to be able to thank his fans and say a few final words. The stadium goes quiet, and Page, already showing gray in his beard, marks the occasion by invoking the poet Tennyson: "It's been a great career. I've enjoyed every moment. And when I stop and think it reminds me of a line from Tennyson's *Ulysses*: 'I am a part of all that I have met.' Thank you." The television announcers wondered aloud how many other defensive linemen quote Tennyson. "I believe he is the only one, probably ever," said one.

Page first worked at a law firm specializing in labor law, but didn't find himself drawn to selling law services, so he moved to the Minnesota attorney general's office, which required no selling. Page found himself increasingly drawn to the possibility of becoming a court justice. At age 47, he joined the Minnesota Supreme Court. He won his seat with 62% of the vote and, according to *National Journal*, had the support of every living Minnesota governor, Republican and Democrat.

It's hard to imagine two more different sets of encodings than those required to be an NFL defensive lineman and those required to be a justice. Page proved himself exceptionally well equipped to simplify complex legal questions to the crux issue. He displayed a penchant for writing clear, well-constructed, and understandable opinions. He'd sometimes even quote Dr. Seuss children's books to make his points even more accessible. Chief Justice Kathleen Blatz struggled to edit Page's opinions—not because they were turgid or unclear, but because they required so little editing. Blatz lined out extraneous or confusing language with a blue pencil, but with Page she said "there just wasn't much to put a blue pencil through. He'd already done it."

A photo of Page donned in a purple justice's robe with a pink bow tie dominates the cover of *All Rise: The Remarkable Journey of Alan Page*, Bill McGrane's delightfully informative biography of Page. An image of Page in his Vikings uniform sits smaller and in the background. It's a perfect metaphor for the fact that Page's spectacular NFL career lay in the past, superseded by his life on the court. "The majority of people don't really like their jobs, which makes me very fortunate," explained Page. "I am excited every day in my job. When I put on the robe and walk into the courtroom, I'm just as pumped as I was running onto the football field." Page's chambers at the Minnesota Supreme Court noticeably lacked ostentatious reminders of his football stardom. Whereas Page's NFL career lasted about 15 years, he would serve on the court for nearly a quarter century, happily immersed in the work, usually seven days a week, until mandatory retirement at age 70.

Then, heading into his 70s, Alan Page went full force into a *third* path in frame with his encodings and inner fire, joining his wife, Diane, in building the Page Education Foundation. As with his shift from football to law, the seeds of Page's shift from law to education had been planted early in life. His parents shaped the Page family ethos around the importance of getting a good education, even moving the family across town in search of better schools. Encoded to prepare, Page had begun setting foundations for the shift to education decades earlier.

Picture the enshrinement ceremony of Alan Page's induction into the Pro Football Hall of Fame. Page made an unusual choice in who would give his enshrinement introduction. He didn't choose anyone from the world of football, not a coach, an owner, a fellow player. He chose instead Willarene Beasley, principal of North Community High School in Minneapolis. Page then stepped to the microphone and graciously accepted enshrinement into the Pro Football Hall of Fame. "As I try to give meaning to this occasion for myself, I want to focus on what I can do for the future," said Page. "On this occasion, I ask myself, 'What contribution can I still make that would be truly worthy of the outpouring of warmth and good feelings as I have received today?' And the answer, for me, is clear: to help give other children the chance to achieve their dreams." And while Page reinforced the value of athletics to teach teamwork and discipline, he put a stake in the ground right there at the pinnacle of recognition for athletic achievement: School must come first, and "if [students] can't handle the demands of both, then maybe athletics should go." Only about 20% of Page's speech related to football or athletics.

But Page didn't *just* make a speech. He and his wife, Diane, used the Hall of Fame induction as an ideal moment to launch the Page Education Foundation, which they announced around the time of the enshrinement ceremony. The foundation would focus on students of color in the state of Minnesota, built upon the idea of granting postsecondary education scholarships *and* requiring recipients to spend time tutoring and mentoring elementary and middle school students.

By the time Page retired from the Minnesota Supreme Court, the foundation had built substantial momentum, and he rechanneled his inner fire to its work. He also began writing children's books with his daughter, partly to raise funds for the foundation. When a middle school changed its name to the Justice Page Middle School, Page called it the highest honor of his life, higher even than the Pro Football Hall of Fame and league MVP.

> The life of Alan Page shows that no matter how exciting or interesting or meaningful or accomplished the early decades of life, you simply do not need to accept the premise that life peaks early. Even if one fulfilling path comes to an end, that does not mean the best of life comes to an end. What comes next might be even *more* fulfilling.

Let's further explore the serial hedgehog pattern with Carl Eller, Alan Page's matched-pair companion in the study. Eller and Page played together on the Minnesota Vikings team for 11 seasons. Both were members of the famed "Purple People Eaters" where they went into their defensive stances within a few feet of each other for thousands of defensive plays, Page wearing No. 88 and Eller wearing No. 81. Like Page, Eller joined the Vikings as a first-round draft pick after earning All-American honors (at the University of Minnesota). Page and Eller each made multiple Pro Bowl appearances, including five times together. As with Alan Page, Carl Eller's cumulative football performance earned him induction into the Pro Football Hall of Fame, a stature attained by less than two percent of all NFL players. Both Page and Eller played their last NFL games in their 30s, Page at 36 and Eller at 37.

Like Alan Page, Carl Eller found an inspired second hedgehog after his NFL career, but his path was strikingly different.

Page and Eller had played together in the exact same four Super Bowls as Vikings, all four being losses (in 1970, 1974, 1975, and 1977). Eller, however, played what he came to call his *fifth* Super Bowl: the personal quest to achieve sobriety. "I have had a bout with alcohol and drugs, and I have overcome it without dying or ending up in jail," said Eller at a 1985 hearing before the Select Committee on

Narcotics Abuse and Control of the U.S. House of Representatives. "*That*," Eller later said of his journey to achieve sobriety, "was the Super Bowl I *won*."

Emerging from the depths of his own struggle, Eller forged a second hedgehog as a leader in his communities, with a particular focus on eradicating and preventing substance abuse in youth and athletes. "I am able to give something back to the community," said Eller to the 1985 select committee. "I am grateful for the many wonderful things that have happened to me in my life. And athletics has been one of them. I made mistakes that were very, very costly. Mistakes that I hope never to make again. . . . [B]ut it is not, however, the mistakes that are so important, but what I have learned from them that I can help other athletes . . . to avoid repeating them."

Eller turned the full force of his inner fire to doing exactly that. He earned certification as a chemical dependency practitioner. He operated a drug treatment center. He founded the United States Athletes Association to help youth and athletes prepare for life and to inspire a "chemically free lifestyle." He created a program called "Game plan II" to help professional athletes prepare for life after sports and "give them a better than average chance against drug abuse." He also made a film titled *My Fifth Super Bowl* about the challenges of addiction, which became a powerful tool in the hands of drug counselors working with young people.

The enduring theme of community runs through Eller's life like a red thread. At his Pro Football Hall of Fame induction ceremony, Eller's son, whom Eller had asked to introduce him, said, "In my dad's early years with the Vikings, he purchased a home in north Minneapolis when most of his teammates were leaving the inner city for the suburbs. . . . And if you talk to people in north Minneapolis today, you will unquestionably hear a story about how Carl Eller has helped them or someone they know and what it means to have Carl Eller as a part of their community." Like his match companion Alan Page, Eller used his induction to the Pro Football Hall of Fame to focus on the future: "I want to use this platform to help young African American males to participate fully in this society." In his 60s, he expanded his community leadership, serving as president of the Retired Players Association to support retired professional football players, most of whom had never reached superstar status. The association focused on raising awareness and funds for conditions stemming from repeated head trauma.

Then, in an exquisite twist to a creative life, Eller began a late transition into using an entirely different set of encodings: He became a ceramic artist. He set up a studio in northeast Minneapolis, where he would lose himself for hours on end, spinning pottery and crafting beautiful ceramic bowls, utterly absorbed in what one article called his "contemplative passion." When the Minnesota Vikings opened a new stadium in 2016, Eller (then 74) created a set of ceramic art pieces to be featured on its walls. In his youthful playing days, Eller had earned the nickname Moose. (Imagine being an offensive lineman trying to block a full-sized moose tearing across the line trying to get to the quarterback, and you get the idea.) But my favorite video of Eller comes not from his Moose days, not from him tossing aside offensive linemen and rampaging into the backfield, but a video of Eller in his mid-70s discussing the creation of his ceramic art installation for the Vikings' stadium. Eller still carried those huge moose hands on his powerful six-foot, six-inch frame, but he used them in flowing gestures, lovingly showing the ceramic bowls that he'd crafted to evoke the feel of Minnesota lakes. He expounded upon his work with ageless zeal. If you had no idea of his prior life, the only impression you'd get is of an artist happily sharing his work, his creative encodings shining through, and the inner fire burning bright well into his eighth decade of life.

Alan Page and Carl Eller
Football and After

ALAN PAGE		**CARL ELLER**	
Ages 14–21	High school and college football. All-American, Notre Dame.	Ages 14–21	High school and college football. All-American, University of Minnesota.
Age 21	Drafted in the first round by the Minnesota Vikings.	Age 21	Drafted in the first round by the Minnesota Vikings.
Ages 22–33	Minnesota Vikings defensive line 1967–78; played in four Super Bowls; selected into nine Pro Bowls.	Ages 22–37	Minnesota Vikings defensive line 1964–78; played in four Super Bowls; selected into six Pro Bowls.
Age 33	Left the Vikings, joined the Chicago Bears.	Age 37	Left the Vikings, joined the Seattle Seahawks.
Age 36	Final season playing in the NFL.	Age 37	Final season playing in the NFL.
Ages 37–70	Second career principally in law and the court. Served on the Minnesota Supreme Court for 23 years. Launched the Page Education Foundation with his wife, Diane. Inducted into the Pro Football Hall of Fame.	Ages 39–62	Second career principally in community leadership, focused on eradicating and preventing substance abuse in athletes and youth. Launched rehab centers and programs. Inducted into the Pro Football Hall of Fame.
Ages 71+	Shifted primary focus to building the Page Education Foundation. Co-authored children's books with his daughter.	Ages 63+	Served as president of the Retired Players Association. Became a ceramic artist.

Note: Due to ambiguity in the sources as to some of the precise dates (month and day) relative to birthdays, cited ages in these chronologies may vary by +/-1 year.

Both Alan Page and Carl Eller dealt successfully with the question of life after the end of their professional football careers. They didn't accept the premise that their most meaningful years would be relegated to their younger selves as glorified superstars. They never stopped addressing the question of what to make of a life, and they both answered it beautifully by activating different encodings and refocusing the inner fire.

> Alan Page and Carl Eller illustrate a key perspective from this research. The task in life is *not* to find the *one* thing you are made for. Some people in the study, like Barbara McClintock and Grace Hopper, stayed within a single hedgehog for the rest of their lives once they'd found it. Whereas others, such as Page and Eller, made mind-boggling transitions, discovering and deploying radically divergent sets of encodings and flourishing in wildly different arenas of activity.

As you learn about the lives in the rest of this book, you might think about the question, Are you likely to be a single hedgehog or a serial hedgehog across the long arc of your own life? Of course, it might not be entirely up to you, because you may hit a cliff that forces you into a major transition. And even if you stay in a single arena, you might also consider: Are you likely to be more narrowly focused, like McClintock burrowing ever deeper into the control of genes, or more expansive even within a single hedgehog, like Grace Hopper and her multifaceted modes in pioneering computer science?

Either way, single or serial, the same three elements apply: *discover and deploy encodings, flip the arrow of money,* and *focus the inner fire.* The lives in this study illustrate the wide range of ways people answer the question of what to make of a life, but they *all* found a way to activate all three elements and bring them together into One Big Thing that they pursued with great intensity for years to decades. Every person in the study did so at least once in life, and half did so more than once. They also illustrate that *even within the same individual life* you can continually discover encodings that lie hidden within until the frame of life shifts to bring them into view. It doesn't matter whether you are young, midstream, or in the later decades, the process of discovery and deployment can add ever more fuel to the inner fire. Expansive we are.

3

A Constellation of Encodings

I'd like you to fix an image in your mind. Picture a constellation of stars. Now imagine looking through a frame that limits how much of the constellation you can see (such as looking through the lens of a telescope or camera); stars outside the frame remain hidden, while those inside the frame shine brightly through the lens. This is how I came to think about discovering encodings. The encodings are fixed, just as the stars in the sky are largely fixed. What changes as people move through life is the positioning and size of the frame, and whether a big cluster of encodings sits brightly visible in frame.

Life worked best for the people in our study when they deployed themselves into activities that aligned with a big bright set of their encodings. I will sometimes shorthand this with the phrase "in frame." Conversely, their lives didn't work as well when they deployed themselves into activities poorly aligned with what they were encoded for. I will sometimes shorthand this with the phrase "out of frame." Even the most exceptional people can get sidetracked by going out of frame. They can also be revitalized by coming back in frame.

To vividly illustrate this idea, let's explore the lives of John Glenn and his matched-pair companion, Gordon Cooper.

John Glenn and Gordon Cooper: Coming into Frame

John Glenn got the inklings of his first hedgehog the summer he turned eight. Glenn's father, who ran a small plumbing business, had been called to a job in a nearby town. Afterward, en route back to Glenn's hometown of New Concord, Ohio, they happened to drive by a biplane landed in a field. They stopped for a look, young John enthralled by the idea that this large, somewhat gangly mechanical creature could *fly*. The pilot was selling rides, and Glenn's father asked John if he wanted to go up. What adventurous kid would say no? Soaring, roaring, swooping, gliding, banking over the fields—the *feel* of flying activated something inside John, imprinting a permanent, visceral memory that simply would not fade. Neither John nor his father fully knew it at the time, but a seed of what Glenn would make of a big portion of his life had just been sown. John watered the seed by building model airplanes, dreaming of flying, and sticking his arm outside the car window using his hand to capture the feel of lift under a wing.

Of course, lots of little kids get excited about airplanes, but few of them go on to become pilots, much less one of the greatest pioneering aviators of a generation. And it might not have happened for John Glenn either, save for a sequence of events that would put him fully in frame.

The first came at age 19. After high school, Glenn enrolled at Muskingum College, just a quarter mile from his childhood home—and found himself struggling. He dreamed of taking flying lessons, but neither he nor his family had the money to pay for them. So, he hunkered down to "practical" courses in subjects like chemistry, thinking he might try to become a physician, but he didn't take to them. Sports didn't fit his encodings either; Glenn failed to make the varsity starting teams in either basketball or football despite his can-do spirit and try-hard ethos. On the verge of changing majors and a bit lost in the fog of youth, Glenn happened to notice a posting on a bulletin board. The U.S. Department of Commerce sought applicants to a program for training pilots. John Glenn saw a way to get flight training *and* get it fully paid for by the government. His parents disapproved—*it just seems so dangerous . . . those hurtling machines crash all the time . . . we've seen newsreel footage of aircraft disintegrating in an exploding fireball . . . a college graduation sounds better than a funeral . . .* But John Glenn wouldn't let go of the idea. This most dutiful of dutiful sons would likely not outright defy his parents, but neither would he let them stifle his dream. He pressed them to relent, even enlisting his physics professor to help make his case, and they finally acquiesced. He applied, got accepted, and enrolled in the Civilian Pilot Training Program.

Then everything began to click. Glenn thrived on pilot training, learning how to handle the challenges of flying—takeoffs, landings, weather, turbulence, navigation. He thrived on preparing for what-if contingencies—what if the engine fails, what if the wing unexpectedly dips, what if you hit horrific turbulence, what if . . . He thrived on the complete attention required in the moment, moment upon moment, sustaining hyper-focused concentration for as long as needed. Unlike college chemistry and sports, where Glenn seemed to have few natural encodings, piloting and all it entailed offered increasingly well-founded hope that he'd stepped into something that fed the fire and at which, with time and training, he could become exceedingly capable.

At age 20, Glenn's life took a dramatic turn that locked him fully in frame: the United States' entry into World War II. With his newly minted pilot's license in hand, he'd positioned himself for a shot at becoming a Naval Aviator. After volunteering for military service, Glenn finagled himself into Naval Aviator training, graduating in the top ten percent of his flying class. Glenn discovered he had an instinctive feel for flying, the aircraft becoming not just a contraption he occupied but almost a natural extension of his brain, his limbs, his hands, his feet, his fingers as he operated the manual controls. He wore the aircraft like a glove.

He then leveraged his performance to become a Naval Aviator in the U.S. Marine Corps, deployed to a combat squadron in the Pacific, where he would fly more than 50 missions. To the disappointment of his father, Glenn decided to remain an aviator after the war—becoming a fighter jet pilot and test pilot—rather than return home to the family business or college preparation for medical school.

In combat missions (and later, in test flights) he discovered more rarefied encodings. Not only did Glenn have natural instincts for flying, but he also remained calm and performed well in situations when everything is falling apart and people (or your own failing aircraft) are trying to kill you. As odd as it might sound to those of us who have no idea how we'd fare in combat, Glenn loved the challenge of putting his skills to work when it counted most. When flying fighter jets in the Korean War, for instance, he expressed disappointment when a mission produced "no contact" with adversaries trying to knock him out of the sky. The greater the danger, the higher the speed, the less room for error, the more Glenn became calm, clear, functional. If you're in a situation where you might die at any moment, and you have to perform with precision to lower the odds of getting killed, and where making a single mistake might result in your instant death, getting anxious about that fact only increases the chances that you will make a mistake and die. So, the rational thing is to lower your anxiety precisely *because* the situation is so dangerous. But how many people have the wiring to actually *do* that? Later, in the space program, sensors would show that Glenn's heart rate would be about the same when seated atop a giant rocket counting down to launch as someone sitting on a couch at home watching TV.

Throughout his aviator career, Glenn navigated multiple moments that could have killed him. He barely skirted an embankment at nearly 500 miles an hour, muscling the controls by hand when a direct hit blew a shoulder-width hole in his jet's tail. He navigated a jet through a hail of shrapnel, more than 300 hits including a two-foot gash in the wing; the aircraft had to be junked. He survived a test pilot mishap when a canopy seal failed, causing his cockpit to immediately depressurize at 44,000 feet above sea level. The oxygen regulator failed. The emergency backup failed. System A had failed. System B failed. System C failed. There was no System D. Glenn's head went fuzzy, his vision blurred. With one last idea before fading out to death, Glenn activated a tiny supply of oxygen in his parachute pack, just enough to descend to breathable altitude. In another test pilot moment, an eight-pound piece of gunmetal detached and flew into a duct, destroying one of the engines and barely missing the fuel tanks. It could easily have been a cataclysmic midair explosion. Glenn's understated calm about these incidents shows throughout his memoir, *John Glenn*, almost as if he were recounting a trip to the store and having a near miss with a shopping cart in the parking lot.

Glenn embodied the test pilot code of cool, threading the needle through near-death moments while downplaying it all with a folksy voice well practiced at restrained monotone. Later, during his orbital mission as an astronaut, Glenn's space capsule sent a signal that the landing bag had been deployed, which, if true, meant the heat shield had loosened. And that, in turn, could result in the heat shield tearing off during reentry and John Glenn being incinerated in a fireball that exceeded 3,000 degrees Fahrenheit. People following Glenn's historic flight waited anxiously as seconds, then minutes, ticked by while Glenn fell through the atmosphere, ground-to-capsule communications silenced by the ionized heat layer enveloping the capsule. When Glenn regained radio contact (the heat shield had held), he responded to ground control's question, "How are you doing?" with the tone of a somewhat bored actuary having an uneventful day in an office cubicle: "Oh, pretty good."

Along the way, Glenn discovered other encodings that he deployed as personal operating modes throughout his life. He discovered a natural affinity for checklists, describing himself as "check-happy"—checking, rechecking, and rechecking again before takeoff—an encoding that lined up perfectly in frame with the unforgiving nature of being a combat aviator, test pilot, and astronaut. It also reflected another encoded trait: He absolutely reveled in the minutiae of his work. Glenn's spectacular spikes of visible performance rested on day-in-and-day-out grunt work behind the scenes, and he found himself exceptionally well suited to grunt mode.

Glenn also had an encoded mode that he drew upon to great effect: a natural instinct to volunteer himself into the thick of what's coming next. After World War II, he saw an emerging shift to jet fighters, and he noticed that the Air Force had jumped ahead of the Navy in implementing jet training. So, he proposed that the Navy send "somebody from our unit" to go through an Air Force jet training course for instructors. Then, once the Navy accepted his idea, Glenn volunteered *himself* to be the "somebody from our unit" to go get immersed in jet training. In his early 30s, Glenn volunteered himself for full-on combat duty in the Korean War, tapping yet again his calm-under-stress encodings on behalf of his country. He flew more than 60 missions in Korea and shot down three enemy MiGs. Glenn's combat experience put him in perfect position to join the next wave of elite aviators pushing the edges of what jets could do. After Korea, he volunteered as a test pilot for supersonic aircraft. At age 35, Glenn volunteered himself yet again, this time for a special mission that he conceived of and named Project Bullet to break the cross-country jet speed record. The Air Force held the record, and Glenn convinced the Navy that it could snatch the record with its advanced F8U Crusader supersonic jet. Project Bullet being Glenn's idea, he got the mission and broke the speed record by 21 minutes.

Combat aviator in the Pacific, jet fighter pilot in Korea, test pilot in the supersonic age, Project Bullet—each iteration, each step, Glenn just kept volunteering himself into the future. I did not find evidence that anyone taught him this capability; it just showed up early, and he used it repeatedly over the decades, including in the space program. NASA did not yet exist when Glenn (aged 36) volunteered himself for special assignment to be a human guinea pig for the earliest space simulators, including putting humans through g-force experiments on centrifuges. And all this put him in perfect position to volunteer yet again, when the United States launched its first manned space program. At age 37, Glenn became the only representative from the U.S. Marine Corps and the oldest person accepted into the seven original astronauts in Project Mercury. At age 40, Glenn became the first American in history to orbit Earth, for which he would be known for the rest of his life.

Let's turn now to Gordon Cooper, whose life tracked remarkably similar to John Glenn's life until their early 40s. For a quick overview, see the nearby side-by-side life chronologies of Glenn and Cooper to age 43.

John Glenn and Gordon Cooper
Similar Lives to Age 43

JOHN GLENN		**GORDON COOPER**	
Early Life	Father arranged his first flight before age ten, which ignited an interest in flying.	Early Life	Father took him on his first flight before age ten, which ignited an interest in flying.
Ages 19–32	Enlisted in the military. Became a Naval Aviator and fighter jet pilot.	Ages 17–29	Enlisted in the military. Became an Air Force pilot and fighter jet pilot.
Ages 32–37	Became a test pilot. Set transcontinental supersonic jet speed record.	Ages 29–32	Became a test pilot. Worked on advanced supersonic aircraft.
Age 37	Selected into NASA's Project Mercury, one of the original seven astronauts.	Age 32	Selected into NASA's Project Mercury, one of the original seven astronauts.

Continued

Age 40	Space capsule mission. Became the first U.S. astronaut to orbit Earth. Navigated successful reentry despite possible heat shield failure.	Age 36	Space capsule mission. Became the first U.S. astronaut to sleep in space. Navigated successful reentry despite total power systems failure.
Ages 40–42	Became a national hero, ticker-tape parade in New York. Received NASA's Distinguished Service Medal. Remained in the space program, with hopes for a Moon mission.	Ages 36–42	Became a national hero, ticker-tape parade in New York. Received NASA's Distinguished Service Medal. Returned to space on Project Gemini, with hopes for a Moon mission.
Ages 42–43	With the prospect of going back to space on a significant new mission fading away, decided to resign from NASA and the military.	Ages 42–43	With the prospect of going back to space on a significant new mission fading away, decided to resign from NASA and the military.

Note: Due to ambiguity in the sources as to some of the precise dates (month and day) relative to birthdays, cited ages in these chronologies may vary by +/-1 year.

As with John Glenn, Gordon Cooper's father introduced him to the experience of flying before the age of ten, and by age 20 he'd already had some flight training. Like Glenn, he joined the military (though World War II ended before he could test his skills in combat), and by his early 20s he'd committed himself to military flying. Like Glenn, a big set of Cooper's encodings aligned brightly in frame, Cooper later noting that flying "came as naturally as breathing and eating." Like Glenn, Cooper never let the inherent danger of his work dissuade him, not even when his first operating group assignment (at age 23) had an epidemic of engine failures and 21 pilot fatalities in two years.

Like Glenn, Cooper moved from fighter pilot to test pilot. He honed skills testing experimental aircraft. He did a stint at the fabled

Edwards Air Force Base, the very epicenter of the test pilot universe where Chuck Yeager had broken the sound barrier. Test pilots at Edwards would push aircraft to the edge of catastrophe to discover their limits, trying to come as close to that edge as possible without crossing over into oblivion. Each step—military flight school to fighter jets to test pilot—reinforced not only that Cooper had found a viable vocation at which he could make a living but that he'd found something for which he was deeply encoded and that he wanted to focus all his inner fire into doing. In one elegant phrase in his memoir, *Leap of Faith*, Cooper captured the feel of finding encodings: "I . . . discovered my truest element."

Like Glenn, Cooper earned a spot as one of the seven original astronauts in Project Mercury. Like Glenn, he displayed an encoded ability to exude calm right on the edge of launch. Sitting atop 200,000 pounds of explosive fuel, he not only had a controlled heart rate but actually fell asleep! Cooper later described waiting for all the technicians to complete their prelaunch calibrations: "I felt myself begin to nod off. . . . Knowing how busy I would soon be, it seemed like an ideal opportunity to grab a nap. So, sitting atop the fully fueled rocket, with no place to go for the time being, I fell fast asleep."

Like Glenn, Cooper maintained stoic composure in the face of potential catastrophe during his orbital flight. On his 19th of 22 orbits, a little green light lit up on the panel, a little green light that was not supposed to be on, a little green light indicating that the capsule had begun reentry. But that couldn't be! There were three more orbits to go, and Cooper knew that he'd not deviated from the orbital path. Then all the electronics began to fail. On the 20th orbit, ground control relayed to Cooper that his capsule was experiencing "a total power failure." Then the temperature control system failed. Then the gyroscopes, then the onboard clock. Cooper relayed back: electrical power, out; carbon dioxide levels, above maximum; cabin temperature, rising. Then, with dry, ironic humor, Cooper monotoned with a slight Oklahoma drawl, "Other than that, things are fine."

Cooper then did something remarkable: He manually piloted the capsule almost like an aircraft, firing retrorockets and manually controlling the angle and path of descent. He navigated the capsule partly by means of a line etched on the window relative to the horizon. Drawing upon star maps that he'd committed to memory, he selected a guide star fixed in space along the capsule's path to help him stay on course. He used his wristwatch for getting the timing just right. Small errors in angle could destroy the heat shield, send the capsule tumbling, or splash him down hundreds of miles off course in a vast ocean where no one would know exactly where he was. The result? He nailed it. Cooper brought the capsule down stunningly close to target, better than nearly all previous Mercury Seven spaceflights. When President Kennedy called him upon splashdown, Cooper said with understated test pilot cool, "Thank you, sir. It was a good flight. I enjoyed it."

Gordon Cooper's gripping orbital flight turned him into a famous national hero. He got a ticker-tape parade in New York, and an estimated 4.5 million people lined the route. He addressed a special joint session of Congress, along with justices of the Supreme Court and members of the cabinet, and got a standing ovation. He appeared on the covers of *Time* and *Life*. He received NASA's Distinguished Service Medal in a special Rose Garden ceremony, presented by President Kennedy.

Gordon Cooper had no idea as a young man that following his encodings for flying would land him in the Rose Garden. He didn't pursue cutting-edge flying because he thought that one day it would make him rich or famous. Once he found himself in frame, he knew what he wanted to make of a big portion of his life. He could no more stop himself from flying than he could stop himself from breathing. He wanted to explore the edge of aviation for as long as he could, and he gave himself over to full hedgehog mode.

Encodings Are Deeper Than Strengths

Both John Glenn and Gordon Cooper illustrate living a portion of life fully in frame with a big bright set of encodings. They also illustrate that encodings are deeper and much more powerful than mere "strengths." Pause and reflect for a moment what it must have felt like to be Glenn or Cooper in an aircraft. It's not just that they were "good" at flying. Imagine all those neurons firing down into the muscular system, the feeling of precise hand movements that made the aircraft almost an extension of their minds. Imagine the instinctive comfort of being in a piece of machinery hurtling through the sky at supersonic speed. Imagine what it must feel like to have hyperawareness that you just might die in the next few moments and to *simultaneously* feel calm and confident with your heart rate holding steady as you focus on the task at hand. Imagine feeling that your life at that moment is in the best possible hands—your own—and for that to actually be *true*.

> The point here is not that Glenn and Cooper had greater natural talents than the rest of us. Rather, the point is that they each discovered a set of encodings that made them more natural at flying than most other possible ways they could have spent that portion of their lives. It's not about finding what you can do better than others, but about finding what you can do exceptionally well *relative to other ways you could expend yourself.*

All of us have a range of strengths, activities we are reasonably good at. Some of these strengths come from superb training, hard work, extensive practice, personal discipline, cumulative experience, and/or sheer force of will. The list of things we become good enough at to call a strength can be much longer than the list of things that meet the test of deep encodings. Recall Gordon Cooper's description of discovering his "truest element" in flying. Keep in mind: Encodings lie within, waiting to be discovered, rather than being taught from without. The lives of the people in this study, like Glenn and Cooper, demonstrate that the key question is not "what are you good at?" but "what are you encoded for?" Perhaps think of this as analogous to being right-handed or left-handed. You can train yourself to be better at handwriting with your less dominant hand—maybe even turn it into a strength—yet you will likely continue to feel more natural (and likely write better) with your dominant hand.

Of course, Glenn and Cooper trained and practiced and honed their capabilities for thousands upon thousands of hours. But it is not the thousands of hours per se that made them such exquisitely designed creatures for flying. It was thousands of hours *expended directly in line with a preexisting set of encodings*. John Glenn could have trained and practiced just as intently for thousands of hours in chemistry, in pursuit of medical school, or in football, in hopes of an athletic career, but all that energy would have been spent out of frame. John Glenn would maybe have worked just as hard, trained just as much, but he wouldn't have become *John Glenn*.

In Frame, Then Out Of Frame, Then Back In Frame Again: The Senator and the Explorer

By age 42, John Glenn had spent more than two decades of his still-young life almost perfectly in frame. After Project Mercury, he tried repeatedly to volunteer himself for another mission, hoping for a shot at the Moon landing, only to find himself stymied. Glenn later reflected that President Kennedy might have intervened with NASA to keep him out of the rotation, with Kennedy believing that Glenn had simply become too valuable as a national hero to put his life at risk. Sensing that he'd never get another flight, he decided to leave the space program. A year later, he resigned his commission in the U.S. Marine Corps. At age 43, John Glenn hit the cliff.

No matter what he did with the rest of his life, no matter how many years he had yet to live (he had 52 years, as it happened), he'd already etched what would likely be the first line of his obituary: first American to orbit Earth. But he did not stop. He already had his possible next path in mind. In high school, he'd been enthralled with civics class. When stationed near Washington, D.C., during his military career, he'd spend free time sitting in the Senate gallery, utterly fascinated with the legislative process. So, when the cliff came, he'd already set his sights on becoming a U.S. senator.

It would take John Glenn more than a decade to get to Congress. In the interim, he served as an executive at Royal Crown Cola Company. While Glenn appears to have been an adequate business executive, he was out of frame relative to his earlier life—lightning bug, not lightning bolt. Despite having spent approximately ten percent of his life engaged at Royal Crown, he dedicated only about two-tenths of a percent (0.2%) of the text of his memoir to his role at the company. He didn't fail as a business executive, but there is no evidence that he significantly distinguished himself either. The inner fire still burned hot within Glenn, and he simply could not capitulate to a post-aviator life of lucrative but uninspired adequateness. At age 52, in 1973, after having had two previously unsuccessful bids for the Senate, Glenn ran again.

Political campaigns can be a form of social combat, and Glenn's combat instincts activated in one slicing moment where he shot his opponent's campaign right out of the sky. His primary opponent Howard Metzenbaum (a former entrepreneur) had repeatedly derided Glenn's military career as not being a real job. In the final debate, Glenn waited until the closing arguments for the perfect moment, locked aim, and opened fire:

Howard, I can't believe you said I have never held a job. I served 23 years in the United States Marine Corps. I served through two wars. I flew 149 missions. My plane was hit by anti-aircraft fire on 12 different occasions. I was in the space program. It wasn't my checkbook; it was my life on the line. It was not a nine-to-five job where I took time off to take the daily cash receipts to the bank.

I ask you to go with me, as I went the other day, to a Veterans Hospital and look those men, with their mangled bodies, in the eye and tell them they didn't hold a job. You go with me to any Gold Star mother and you look her in the eye and tell her that her son did not hold a job. You go with me to the space program, and go as I have gone to the widows and orphans of Ed White and Gus Grissom and Roger Chaffee, and you look those kids in the eye and tell them that their Dad didn't hold a job. You go with me on Memorial Day coming up and you stand in Arlington National Cemetery, where I have more friends than I'd like to remember, and you watch those waving flags. You stand there, and you think about this nation, and you tell me that those people didn't have a job.

I'll tell you, Howard Metzenbaum, you should be on your knees every day of your life thanking God that there were some men—some men—who held a job. And they required a dedication to purpose and a love of country and a dedication to duty that was more important than life itself. And their self-sacrifice is what made this country possible.

I have held a job, Howard!

Metzenbaum's campaign went down in flames right then and there. Glenn went on to win every single Ohio county in the general election, and he would serve nearly a quarter century in Congress.

With his move to the Senate, Glenn found himself solidly back in frame. While the Senate offered no opportunities for leveraging his ability to calmly perform in the face of imminent death (though he did keep flying his own personal airplane), it did draw upon other encodings. Recall his "check-happy" nature, his penchant for minutiae, and his capacious capability for grunt mode. In the Senate, he ran his office by checklists and focused his efforts on the behind-the-scenes grunt work of getting legislation done. As Glenn put it about some grinding work as chairman of the Governmental Affairs Committee (the parking home for some of the most unglamorous congressional work on the mechanics of government), "They're not the big press release–type items. They're the things that are what we have jokingly called around my office 'the grunt work of government.' But if somebody doesn't do them, who will do it? Who—who's going to do those things if I didn't?" As a famous national hero with a secure seat from his home state, he had no need for bloviating self-promotion, putting him perfectly in frame for the unglamorous work of legislative sausage making. Within his first two years in Congress, according to *The Washington Post*, he achieved an undefeated string of more than 35 amendments in a row gaining adoption on the Senate floor.

He also discovered superb encodings that he'd not seen before, such as a penchant for committee work and working in small legislative groups. "He's dynamite in quiet communication," said one political observer, "and it comes across, especially when he's with small groups." His liberal-leaning instinct that "government can help the people" combined with his conservative-leaning instinct for national defense and self-reliance made for a perfect blend in the liberal/conservative mix of his home state. Glenn's political encodings lay in being the consummate representative of what he called the "sensible center." Glenn spent the same number of years in the U.S. Senate (24) as he spent focused on aviating—a perfect example of a serial hedgehog.

Along the way, Glenn had one huge disappointment, when he threw himself out of frame and decided to run for president of the United

States. After his second senatorial win, where he won with nearly 69% of the vote, political chatter increased about the idea of Glenn for president. And Glenn began to listen. Combat pilot, jet fighter pilot, test pilot, astronaut, senator—why not president? When Glenn was 60, *The New York Times* ran a feature story titled "John Glenn's Presidential Countdown." The Glenn-for-President idea flowed from seeing him as the next Eisenhower, a famous war hero with a winning smile (he could "outgrin Dwight D. Eisenhower," wrote the *Times*) and a moderate who could appeal to the vast middle of America. He ran an ad evoking an Eisenhower-esque ethos, touting himself as a man "who understands war but who loves peace."

But stop and think for a moment. On the surface, the Glenn-Eisenhower analogy seems apt, both being beloved military heroes. But Glenn and Eisenhower had very different encodings. Eisenhower thrived in organizing and leading vast armies, making him well suited to building a vast campaign organization. Eisenhower also had an executive temperament that would serve him well in the Oval Office. Glenn, in contrast, had largely thrived as an individual aviator, *alone in the cockpit*, calling upon a quite different set of encodings. A presidential race calls for conveying a grand vision in simple terms, but when asked for the legacy he would like to create as president, Glenn gave a rambling 400-plus-word complex answer that touched upon international relations, free enterprise, preserving peace, raising the standard of living, the role of education and research, civil rights, women's rights, and democracy versus socialism—a mishmash with no grand, vivid, memorable, or unifying theme. He also loathed the fundraising required to mount a massive presidential campaign.

Less than a year after announcing his candidacy, Glenn terminated his formal campaign after poor showings in early primaries, with a hefty load of campaign debt. Glenn would later call his failed run for the presidency his biggest disappointment. He'd been drawn out of frame, and he languished.

Fortunately, at age 62, Glenn still had his Senate seat. He clicked back in frame and enjoyed a very successful 15 more years as the senior U.S. senator from his home state of Ohio. Oh, and he clicked even more encodings into frame when he went back to space at age 77.

Wait—back to space at age 77? Glenn never lost his love of flying or his desire to go back to space. At age 73, he had an idea: At some point, we're going to need to learn about older people in space. He activated his volunteer encodings, marched into the NASA administrator's office, and proposed the idea of sending "somebody" older up on a space shuttle mission. *You need an aged guinea pig to go up there! And if you buy the idea, well, I have the perfect candidate in mind. I volunteer!* To buttress his case, he put himself through an astronaut-level physical examination. Just like with Project Bullet, Glenn's instinct for volunteering himself for a mission of his own conception put him in Space Shuttle *Discovery*, where he would orbit Earth 134 times.

And what of Gordon Cooper?

In his early 40s, as with John Glenn, Cooper began to realize that he would not be selected to go to the Moon. At first, he thought he might continue his life as an elite pilot, even as he left NASA. Unfortunately, the Air Force had plans to promote Cooper to general officer, a potentially terrible outcome for him (despite the prestige of securing the word "General" in front of his name). He paid a visit to the chief of staff of the Air Force. "Sir, I understand there's a regulation that general officers can't fly single-seat fighters," said Cooper. "Will you grant me an exception, sir?" The response: no exceptions. So, at age 43, the exact same age that Glenn resigned his commission in the U.S. Marine Corps, Cooper resigned. After nearly a quarter century of living life with big bright encodings fully in frame, Gordon Cooper faced the question, *What's next?*

Cooper had always been more than just a fighter jock and astronaut. He'd been an *explorer* with a keen interest in pushing the edges of aviation and technology. He earned a degree in aeronautical engineering while also developing his flying skills. He gravitated to test piloting partly because he wanted to explore the outer limits of what supersonic aircraft could do. Project Mercury offered perhaps the ultimate manifestation of his explorer encodings, with Cooper becoming one of the first humans in history to see our tiny Earth from space.

After leaving NASA and the Air Force, Cooper redeployed his encodings into an array of activities, most of which fit with exploration and technology. He worked for several years as a vice president for research and development at Disney, helping the company think ahead about new technologies. He explored alternative energies, solar power, fuel cells, and electric vehicles; later in life, he championed the idea of converting to methanol for jet fuel. He served as a technical consultant to businesses ranging from automotive production to electronic systems. Over the decades, he tried multiple business ventures, in fields as far ranging as underwater treasure hunting and reconfiguring airplanes from piston engines to turbines.

He also became serious about exploring UFOs. Cooper's earnest interest in UFOs began in his fighter jet days, dating back to a specific incident in 1951. Flying a fighter jet at its maximum altitude of 45,000 feet, he spotted a set of unidentified objects soaring far above him and moving much faster than him. He remained convinced for the rest of his life that he'd seen aircraft more advanced and unlike anything in his experience. Cooper believed that this gave mankind an opportunity to make a technological leap by learning from these advanced aircraft. When he participated in a United Nations hearing on UFOs, he stressed the opportunity for learning from those "more technically advanced than we are on Earth."

Like John Glenn, Cooper made a few missteps along the way. Throughout his post-NASA life, Cooper's golden name and trusting, open-minded nature attracted people to him, not all of whom proved reliable. In 1997, *The Wall Street Journal* published a nearly 5,000-word article that featured some of Cooper's ill-fated business travails. While I do not trust a single article as a definitive source for assessing a person's character and encodings, one of its main points rings true with other materials assembled on Cooper's life: He trusted people, perhaps to a fault, making him open to opportunists. The article quoted one associate who'd done two failed ventures with Cooper: "He [Cooper] doesn't believe anybody's going to say things that are not true," and then adding, "You have to believe, if you go up into space in a pillbox."

The inevitable missteps of life did not extinguish the fire within Gordon Cooper. He kept stepping forward, extending out, exploring. He did not spend his post-NASA life looking back to his glory days as a pioneering test pilot and astronaut. "I'm not the kind of person who lives in the past," reflected Cooper years after leaving NASA, while getting involved with exploring advanced technologies. "Being an astronaut was what I wanted to do—it was great. What I'm doing now is great too. The best years are always coming."

Let's pause to consider three additional lessons about encodings, highlighted by setting Glenn and Cooper side by side.

First, while a person's encodings remain constant, the framing of those encodings can change quite substantially over the course of a life.

Some encodings show up early, such as Glenn's and Cooper's natural instincts for flying. Other encodings become visible only later in life, such as Glenn's natural effectiveness working behind the scenes to operate the levers of legislating. Some encodings fell out of frame when life changed; serving in the U.S. Senate didn't call upon Glenn's capacity to remain calm when failure to perform might result in death within the next few seconds. Some of Glenn's aviator encodings then popped back in frame when he went back to space in his late 70s.

> It's not that people "add" new encodings. Rather, it's like *discovering* stars that had always been there but were previously unseen. Some encodings stay in frame, and get used, across decades and multiple walks of life (as the frame shifts or widens), such as Glenn's check-happy nature and Cooper's impulse for exploring and pushing

the edge of technology. Other encodings drop from view when the frame shifts. It's not that these encodings cease to exist; they're simply not called upon.

Second, even highly accomplished people can languish when they operate contrary to their encodings, when they fall out of frame.

Here we have two of the most accomplished people of a generation, two of the greatest pilots of all time who became national heroes. Yet even these two remarkable individuals had episodes when they fell out of frame, such as Glenn's ill-fated run for president and some of Cooper's business ventures where he trusted the wrong people. The main point here is not that they "failed" or "made mistakes." The point is that *anyone can fall out of frame*, and when they do, they're likely to struggle relative to when they're in frame.

As we move through the lives of the people in this book, you'll see multiple cases of people struggling to get into—or back into—frame. In some cases, they wandered through the fog of youth before discovering a set of encodings. In other cases, a cliff knocked them completely out of frame, and they struggled through the post-cliff fog. In still other cases, they took themselves out of frame with a project, foray, direction, venture, or misadventure that just didn't fit their encodings. Discovering what you are *not* encoded for can be just as important as discovering what you *are* encoded for.

I find it comforting that even the people in this study, with all of their accomplishments, had episodes when they made missteps that temporarily knocked them out of frame. I came to see that errant turns can be helpful for getting *into* frame. The process of discovery does not allow for a perfect record. You cannot plan or think your way into a life lived perfectly in line with your encodings. Discovering encodings requires trial and error, experimentation, missteps, happy accidents, and disappointment. The key is to begin to recognize when you feel yourself clicking into frame, and equally, to recognize when you've fallen out of frame. The imperative to "Know Thyself" means a continuous process of discovering what is in your constellation of encodings.

Third, to be fully in frame requires a suitable hedgehog home.

Both Glenn and Cooper flourished in the culture of elite military pilots and NASA astronauts, wherein they could count on the people around them to be reliable, trustworthy, and highly capable. And while their work came with extreme danger, they operated within a system of competence, chock-full of checks and counterchecks, with scientists and specialists and engineers and support crews all working together to accomplish a clear mission and decrease risk to the pilot or astronaut in the cockpit. By and large, they could trust those around them, both their motives and their capabilities. Glenn and Cooper had the encoding to trust others with their lives, routinely, repeatedly, for decades. The ethos of fighter pilots, test pilots, and astronauts suited them exceptionally well.

Fortunately, John Glenn eventually found a second hedgehog home, in the U.S. Senate. Not only did his encodings fit with the activities of being a grunt work legislator, but he also found the environment of the Senate—its culture, its rules, its procedures—lined up with his temperament. With Gordon Cooper, while he did engage in a lot of *activities* that aligned with his technology and explorer encodings, I see less evidence that he found a second hedgehog home after NASA that fit him as well as the Senate fit Glenn. The closest might have been at Disney, but he stayed there for only about five years.

Multiple people in this study struggled, at least for a period of time, when their environment didn't align well with their encodings. Barbara McClintock's encodings for solving genetics puzzles remained in frame once she discovered them, but her time at the University of Missouri proved to be a terrible home for her. She simply did not fit with the culture of traditional academia, nor what that culture expected of her as a woman faculty member in her era. When she landed her spot at Cold Spring Harbor research institute, she found a much better home, and she stayed there for the rest of her life. Alan Page didn't have the encodings for the client development and sales process of drawing in big lucrative clients. So, when he went to work at a traditional law firm that relied on its partners to excel at client development, he found himself partly out of frame. Then, when Page joined the Minnesota Supreme Court, he found a perfect home; his encodings came fully in frame with both the activity of legal thinking *and* the environment of the supreme court. Some people in our study, whom you will meet in future chapters, took a more entrepreneurial or loner approach, creating and/or shaping their own environment to fit with their own encodings. Whatever the path, the people in this study flourished when *both* their activities *and* their environment fit with their encodings. A happy hedgehog needs a happy hedgehog home.

Discovering Encodings: From Self-Awareness to Encoded Operating Modes

So, how do you discover and deploy encodings? The essential answer, as I came to understand it through the lives in this study, lies in a highly attuned *self-awareness* of how you instinctively and *specifically* operate in different situations. When life spun them into a situation that activated a set of encodings, they noticed. Even more, they built upon what they noticed, translating their encodings into specific, practical operating modes (ways of living and working) that suited them exceptionally well.

To illustrate, let's turn to two people who did not come fully into frame until midlife, the writers Toni Morrison and Barbara Tuchman.

TONI MORRISON DISCOVERS AND DEPLOYS HER ENCODINGS

Young Toni Morrison did not aspire to be a writer. She loved literature, she loved reading, she loved teaching about books. But she had no idea that she carried within her a constellation of encodings that, when snapped into frame, would make her one of the most significant novelists of the 20th century. She majored in English literature, earned a graduate degree in English, did some university-level teaching, got married, got divorced, and woke up to find herself the primary at-home parent responsible for raising her two boys. At age 34, she took an editing job with a subsidiary of Random House and dedicated herself to her sons. She didn't do much socializing or going out. When not at the office, she was mainly at home.

She'd put the kids to bed at seven and then face empty hours. What to do with herself, awake and alone while her children slept? Morrison picked up a pad of yellow lined paper and a No. 2 soft pencil. And she began to write. Not for an audience, but to create a book for herself. Black girls had never been central characters anywhere across the vast panoply of books Morrison had read. "No one had ever written about them except as props," she related. "Since I couldn't find a book that did that, I thought, 'Well, I'll write it and then I'll read it.'"

She couldn't read the book until she'd finished writing the book, so with two kids and a full-time job, she grabbed every opportunity to fit in some writing. She began getting up before dawn, making a cup of coffee, fitting in a few hours of writing before the boys got up. She discovered that she was encoded for writing best starting at 4 a.m., working into the netherworld transition from dark to dawn, her creative brain like a glow light coming alive with the gradual awakening of the morning.

For Morrison, writing became a compulsion. While she loved her predawn solitude, she also discovered that she had a rare, encoded ability to write in little eddies of time—a sentence here, a phrase or fragment there. And she could do it despite the cacophony of noise and the demands of mothering and work, amid the jumbled chaos of fitting all the little jagged pieces of life together. While she was writing at home one day, one of her young children spit up on her writing pad. Morrison had a really good sentence coming out of her pencil at that very moment, and so she just kept writing; she figured she could wipe the puke away later, but the sentence could not wait. When commuting by car, she'd use the steering wheel as a makeshift desk to pencil out little snippets of text when stuck in traffic. Given a moment of time, she'd fill it with writing a sentence; given an hour after the kids had gone to bed, she'd spin some paragraphs; given a few hours of morning solitude, she'd punch out some pages; given a clear weekend or holiday, she'd add hundreds or even thousands of words. When she was not actually writing, she was *thinking* about writing—when doing dishes, when mowing the lawn, when driving, whenever. "The writing could never take precedence over [my children]," reflected Morrison. "Which is why I had to write under duress, and in a state of siege and with a lot of compulsion."

The more she wrote, the more she discovered she was made to write, that she couldn't live without writing, that she needed no external pressure to write. She just could not help herself. She marched on with writing and rewriting, burning through stacks of lined yellow pads and handfuls of No. 2 soft pencils, all while continuing to commute to her full-time job editing other people's books. She had no career aim in mind that she might become a professional writer, but being home with the kids knocked her life to the side and brought into frame a magnificent constellation of encodings. Once she felt the power of those encodings pulsating through her fingers and onto the page, she never wanted to stop. "If all the publishers had disappeared in one night, I would have written anyway," said Morrison. "Writing was a thing I could not *not* do."

It took her almost five years to complete the book she wanted to read. She accumulated a nice little stack of form rejection cards from publishers before one finally bit and published her book, *The Bluest Eye*, with a modest initial print run. And so, at age 39, Morrison had become a published writer—a relatively unknown writer with a small readership, but a published writer nonetheless. While her first book didn't fall into oblivion, it didn't sell enough for her to become a full-time writer. Morrison thought that maybe the market for her writings might be about 400 people. So, she kept up her editing job at Random House while writing her second novel, *Sula*, which garnered a nomination for the National Book Award, then a third (*Song of Solomon*, published in her mid-40s). Her readership grew, as did her reputation.

After *Song of Solomon*, she made a psychologically significant decision: Filling out her annual tax return, she got to the blank space asking for the filer's occupation. Morrison then did something she'd never before had the temerity to do. She listed her occupation as a writer. Well, there it was, right there on her tax return, a sort of personal declaration of independence: *I'm no longer an editor who writes, or a working professional who writes, or a daily commuter who writes, or a working mom who writes; I am a writer!* She also quit her full-time editing job (though she did part-time editing work for several years). By her early 50s, Morrison found herself fully in frame. She would publish a new novel around every five years on average, never missing a cycle, well into her 80s. Morrison didn't publish *Beloved* (perhaps her most famous book) until age 56, and she believed some of her best writing came *after* that seminal work.

Whenever I hear someone say that the best work of creative people necessarily comes early in life, that after 30 or 40 or 50 the best creative juices have already begun to run dry, I think to myself, "*Really?* So then how do we explain Toni Morrison?" At age 66, she said that her writing would only get better and that she'd only done her best work "so far." At age 72, one journalist marveled that Morrison still got up at 4 a.m. to write, Morrison continuing with her encoded mode of igniting her brain in the netherworld transition of dark to dawn. At age 87, not long before her death, she replied to a question of whether she would keep writing with an emphatic "Oh yeah."

One of the advantages of studying authors is that writers tend to like to talk and write about the craft and process of their writing—how and why they do what they do—which illuminates their encodings and how they translate those encodings into specific ways of working. This is certainly true of Toni Morrison. Then you can read the actual work itself, to fully experience the creative result. In Morrison's case, I read every one of her 11 novels in sequence, feeling the full effect of her encodings permanently on display in the text.

> Toni Morrison at work illustrates a primary observation from the research: When in full hedgehog mode, the people in our study displayed an instinctive awareness of how best to tap their encodings by translating them into ways of living and working that suited the individual exceptionally well. They each cultivated a set of practices—and a self-styled set of operating modes—that simply worked *for them*. Morrison didn't ask, "What practices work best for writing novels?" She discovered what encoded modes worked *specifically for her.*

To illustrate, I've constructed the nearby set of specific examples, "Toni Morrison—Encoded Operating Modes."

Toni Morrison—Encoded Operating Modes

OPERATING MODES	REPRESENTATIVE QUOTATIONS
4 A.M. PATTERN: Gets up before dawn to write, her brain activating as the dark turns to light.	"Writers all devise ways to approach that place where they expect to make the contact, where they become the conduit, or where they engage in this mysterious process. For me, light is the signal in the transition. It's not being in the light, it's being there before it arrives. It enables me, in some sense." "I'm very, very smart in the morning."
GOING "UNDERWATER": Gets so deep in a writing project that it is like losing herself underwater.	"Writing is always a displacement. It's like walking underwater. And everything else looks a little dim and a little far away. . . . You miss things, and friends who don't understand get mad at you." "I'm working hard on a new book. And I am getting deeper and deeper into the book. . . . [S]oon I will be like someone looking through water—everybody will look to me as if I'm in a tank somewhere."
COMPULSIVE ABOUT WRITING: Compulsion better describes her work ethic than does self-discipline.	"I'm a little more compulsive about [writing] . . . and less disciplined. I operate on compulsion." "I've tried to overcome not having orderly spaces by substituting compulsion for discipline, so that when something is urgently there, urgently seen or understood, or the metaphor was powerful enough, then I would move everything aside and write for sustained periods of time."
WRITING IN CHAOS: Able to write amid the chaos of a busy and fragmented daily life, multitasking as necessary.	"Sometimes something that I was having some trouble with falls into place, a word sequence, say, so I've written on scraps of paper, in hotels on hotel stationery, in automobiles. *If* it arrives you *know*. If you know it *really* has come, then you *have* to put it down." "And you learn how to use time. You don't have to learn how to wash the dishes every time you do that. You already know how to do that. So, while you're doing that, you're thinking. . . . Or just on the subway. I would solve a lot of literary problems just thinking about a character in that packed train. . . . There was no blank time."

Continued

WRITES FOR HERSELF FIRST: Morrison sees herself as reader No. 1.	"When I said I wrote my first novel because I wanted to read it, I meant it literally. I had to finish it so that I could read it." "I wrote *Sula* and *The Bluest Eye* because they were books I had wanted to read. No one had written them yet, so I wrote them. My audience is always the people in the book I'm writing at the time. I don't think of an external audience."
QUESTION-DRIVEN: The seed of a novel generally comes as a question she seeks to answer for herself; writing a book is her method of exploring the question.	"Every now and then some incredibly compelling idea comes up and poses itself as a question. Then I find myself formulating characters who can work out answers to the questions." For example, *Song of Solomon*: "How do [men] learn about the heroic possibilities for men?" *Tar Baby*: "How do people from entirely different cultures know love?"
AURAL TO TEXT MODE: Hears the words in her head the way they should be spoken, then writes them.	"[I] make aural literature . . . I do hear it. . . . Even though I don't speak it when I'm writing it, I have this interior piece, I guess, in my head that reads, so that the way I hear it is the way I write it."
WRITING IS REWRITING: Holds a dispassionate objectivity that enables her to rewrite until she gets the words right.	"I don't mind writing badly for a couple of days because I know I can fix it—and fix it again and again and again, and it will be better. . . . [T]he best part of it all, the absolutely most delicious part, is finishing it and then doing it over. That's the thrill of a lifetime for me: if I can just get done with that first phase and then have infinite time to fix it and change it." "As a writer, a failure is just information. . . . I recognize failure . . . and fix it, because it is data, it is information, knowledge of what does not work. . . . It's as though you're in a laboratory and you're working on an experiment with chemicals or with rats, and it doesn't work. It doesn't mix. You don't throw up your hands and run out of the lab. What you do is you identify the procedure and what went wrong and then correct it."

WRITE THE END EARLY: Starts with knowing how a book will end, then figures out how to get there.	"I always know the endings. . . . What I don't know when I begin is how the character is going to get there." "It is like a detective story in a sense. You know who is dead and you want to find out who did it."
NO. 2 SOFT PENCIL AND YELLOW LEGAL PADS: Writes the first draft in longhand, with No. 2 soft pencil.	"I write with a pencil on yellow lined paper. . . . [W]ith a pencil because ink sounded a little arrogant and pencil shows you knew what you are doing but are willing to erase!"
HOMEBODY MODE: Prefers to stay at or close to home, avoids a lot of travel or socializing, so she can write.	"But I myself don't ever go anywhere for stimulation. . . . If I could just sit in one spot I would be happy." "Writing is what I do, for me that is where it is—where the vacation is, the fun is, the danger, the excitement—all of that is in my work."

Note: Operating mode descriptions are in present tense to capture the feel of them fully active during her life.

BARBARA TUCHMAN: A WRITER WITH DIFFERENT ENCODINGS

One of the advantages of having pairs to study is that we can see how two people engaged in similar activities can differ radically in how they operate. This shows that their successful practices are only partly a function of the type of work they do, and largely a reflection of how the individual is encoded. To illustrate, let's look at the other writer in our study, Barbara Tuchman.

Barbara Tuchman didn't discover and fully commit to her writing hedgehog until after the midpoint of her life. Like Toni Morrison, she started working on her first book in the wake of having children (three daughters), her life changed dramatically by becoming the primary at-home parent. Bursting with a natural level of "extra energy" that she attributed to her genetic makeup, she decided to assign herself a project to engage her brain and feed her voracious curiosity. She'd always had an interest in history, from about age six, so she started taking steps toward becoming a writer of history. To do so, she would need a topic, something big and worthy to research, understand, and write about. She chose the relationship between Britain and Palestine, tracing its roots to the Bronze Age.

"I just sat down and started all by myself," said Tuchman of her start. "I didn't have any advice. I had studied history very hard in college but I had not taken a Ph.D. But you know it never occurred to me that I couldn't do it as well as anyone else." Tuchman had more financial resources than Toni Morrison to support her effort, coming from a wealthy family and married to a successful doctor, but she didn't receive much encouragement for her writing. Her family, she later said, "never took me seriously until I was famous."

It took her "six or seven years of very interrupted effort" to produce *Bible and Sword*. Like Morrison, Tuchman accumulated a stack of rejection slips before finding a publisher, a university press that mainly produced niche books. At age 44, Tuchman had finally become a published writer of history—a relatively unknown writer with a small readership, but a published writer nonetheless. And like Morrison, she'd become compulsive about her work, unable to stop herself, one question leading to another, project after project, book after book. In her second two books, *The Zimmermann Telegram* and *The Guns of August*, she unleashed her curiosity on the origins of World War I. At age 51, in 1963, she received the Pulitzer Prize for General Nonfiction for *The Guns of August*. Her readership grew, as did her reputation.

By her early 50s, Tuchman had come fully in frame, an independent historian dedicated to researching the facts, then lighting up the reader's mind with vivid, accessible narrative. She would publish a major book every four years on average, never missing a cycle, right until the year before she died at age 77. Like Morrison, she did some of her best work late, receiving a second Pulitzer Prize at age 60 (the first writer to ever receive a second Pulitzer Prize in the category of General Nonfiction) and a National Book Award at age 68. Both Morrison and Tuchman faced a "success cliff"; this is the type of cliff where a person achieves a level of success and recognition that could impede further creative work. By their early 60s, each of these writers could have coasted to the end. Yet both sustained the cycle of creative work, Morrison pumping out five major books after receiving the Nobel Prize in Literature (at age 62) and Tuchman producing four major books after the second Pulitzer Prize. Both writers produced more than 40% of their major books after the age of 60.

Toni Morrison and Barbara Tuchman
Coming into Frame at Midlife

TONI MORRISON		**BARBARA TUCHMAN**	
Mid-30s	Began work on her first book.	Mid-30s	Began work on her first book.
Ages 39–46	First three books published, *The Bluest Eye*, *Sula*, and *Song of Solomon*.	Ages 44–50	First three books published, *Bible and Sword*, *The Zimmermann Telegram*, and *The Guns of August*.
Ages 46–50	*Song of Solomon* achieved breakout success and acclaim; won National Book Critics Circle Award. Enabled full commitment to a writing career.	Ages 50–51	*The Guns of August* achieved breakout success and acclaim; won Pulitzer Prize. Enabled full commitment to a writing career.
Ages 50–61	Next three books published: *Tar Baby*, *Beloved*, and *Jazz*. Won Pulitzer Prize for *Beloved*.	Ages 52–59	Next two books published: *The Proud Tower* and *Stilwell and the American Experience in China, 1911–45*.
Age 62	Received Nobel Prize in Literature, with specific acknowledgement for *Song of Solomon*, *Beloved*, and *Jazz*.	Age 60	Received Pulitzer Prize for *Stilwell and the American Experience in China, 1911–45*.

Continued

Ages 63–84	Sustained creative work, publishing five more major books: *Paradise, Love, A Mercy, Home*, and *God Help the Child*. Also published nine children's books in collaboration with her son.	Ages 61–76	Sustained creative work, publishing four more major books: *A Distant Mirror, Practicing History, The March of Folly*, and *The First Salute*. National Book Award for *A Distant Mirror*.
Age 88	Died due to complications from pneumonia.	Age 77	Died due to complications from a stroke.

Note: Due to ambiguity in the sources as to some of the precise dates (month and day) relative to birthdays, cited ages in these chronologies may vary by +/-1 year.

Like Toni Morrison, Barbara Tuchman talked and wrote extensively about her specific practices; she even wrote a whole book on her methods, *Practicing History*. They had some striking similarities in approach, despite working in different genres. Like Morrison, Tuchman didn't seek anyone's approval or encouragement to start her writing career. "That more experienced scholars might hesitate to take on a stretch of time that, as it developed, reached from the Bronze Age to Balfour did not occur to me," wrote Tuchman of her beginnings. "I simply plunged in with the fearlessness, as a critic was later to remark, of the autodidact." Like Morrison, Tuchman had very particular preferences for her working tools; Morrison scribbled sentences with Ticonderoga No. 2 soft pencils on yellow legal pads, while Tuchman had an attachment to using four-by-six-inch index cards for taking notes that she carried with her everywhere. Like Morrison, Tuchman wrote, then rewrote, then rewrote again, and again, until she got the words right. One journalist described Tuchman "writing first in longhand, then typing, then 'cutting and pasting' the bits and pieces. Her manuscripts become ponderous affairs, hen-tracked with scribbled notes, penciled insertions, deletions, corrections, flagged with color-coded bits of paper." Like Morrison, Tuchman was so compulsive about doing her work that she didn't need painful self-discipline; once infected with a book project, she simply couldn't stop herself from working on it. Like Morrison, Tuchman would forgo stimulating social opportunities to focus on her work. When the famous film stars Jane Fonda and Barbra Streisand sought Tuchman to write a movie script, she demurred. One of Tuchman's daughters asked, exasperated, "But, Ma, don't you even want to meet Jane Fonda?" Tuchman responded, "Oh, no, I don't have time. I'm working."

Yet there were also some *substantial differences* in their ways of working, differences that reflected their own idiosyncratic encodings. Whereas Morrison wrote first and foremost for herself, creating books that she wanted to read and deliberately *not* thinking of an external audience, Tuchman wrote first and foremost for readers other than herself. Tuchman wrote alone but kept in mind a question that loomed over her, almost like a permanent thought bubble posted above her writing desk: *Will the reader turn the page?*

Whereas Morrison could work brilliantly amid the cacophonous chaos of her life (writing "under duress and in a state of siege"), Tuchman *needed* pockets of quietude to do her best work. While Morrison became adept at grabbing little bits of time to sneak in little bits of writing, Tuchman craved big blocks of time, preferring to go four to five hours without interruption. By her third book, she'd taken to writing in a dairy barn separated from her summerhouse. Later she worked in a kind of hillside retreat on her family's property in Cos Cob, Connecticut. Her private writing cottage sat isolated from the main house by a forest of trees, high on a hill and approachable only by a steep, rocky path. She'd traverse the woods and climb up to her perched writing space, step inside her cozy sanctuary, and go to work. She could look down from windows on three sides, able to see if anyone might be approaching (though everyone knew to not invade her writing space unless invited). When cloistered, she cut herself off from the outside world, no telephone, no connections of any kind, just Barbara and her index cards and her writing tools.

Like Morrison, Tuchman wrote and spoke about her craft and process of writing, illuminating her encodings and how she translated those encodings into specific ways of working. To illustrate, I've constructed the nearby set of specific examples, "Barbara Tuchman—Encoded Operating Modes."

Barbara Tuchman—Encoded Operating Modes

OPERATING MODE	REPRESENTATIVE QUOTATIONS
CURIOSITY-DRIVEN: Unlike authors who write to display their expertise, Tuchman writes to learn new things.	"Living as we do under the shadow of disaster, I thought it would be interesting to see what happened in the 14th century, after the experience of the Black Death and all the other catastrophes." "When you start something about which you know nothing and you have to begin from scratch; it's very exciting."
COMPULSIVE ABOUT WRITING: Compulsion better describes her work ethic than does self-discipline.	"In order to write a book, you must spend five to eight hours a day working on it. I'm compulsive about working." "I can't put my mind to cooking or growing flowers when I'm working. . . . This was such a powerful subject I couldn't leave it alone for five minutes."
WRITING FOR READERS, *not just herself:* Keeps the reader in mind, asking herself, "Will the reader turn the page?"	"I have a desperate need to communicate with readers. I can't *think* of a book without readers. To me, that would be like the tree falling in the forest with no one to hear it." "I never feel my writing is born or has an independent existence until it is read. It is like a cake whose only raison d'être is to be eaten. Ergo, first catch your reader."
PUT THE READER IN A TIME MACHINE: Endeavors to write of the time without foreknowledge of what is to come.	"Though it may seem absurd, I even cut any references to the ultimate defeat of Germany. I wrote as if I did not know who would win. . . . I used to become tense with anxiety myself, as the moments of crisis approached." "No mention of that crisis appears in the following pages for the reason that, as it had not yet happened, it was not a part of the experience of the people of this book. I have tried to stay within the terms of what was known at the time."
THE HISTORIAN AS AN ARTIST: Aims to have her writing stand with literature and poetry.	"I have always *felt* like an artist when I work on a book. . . . I see no reason why the word should always be confined to writers of fiction and poetry while the rest of us are lumped together under that despicable term 'Nonfiction'—as if we were some sort of remainder. I do not feel like a Non-something; I feel quite specific." "When it comes to language, nothing is more satisfying than to write a good sentence. . . . It requires skill, hard work, a good ear, and continued practice, as much as it takes Heifetz to play the violin."

A Constellation of Encodings

HARNESS THE POWER OF NARRATIVE: Writes history not as a litany of facts but as compelling human drama.	"I tend to think of history as drama, as a play with a plot unfolding. . . . I see myself as being like the village storyteller in India who comes to the villagers who stand around a flickering fire. If the villagers get bored, they won't fill his beggar's bowl." "As a form, narrative has an inherent validity because it is the key to the problem of causation. Events do not happen in categories—economic, intellectual, military— they happen in sequence."
SELECT PROTAGONISTS: Uses historical people, almost like characters in a novel, to drive the narrative forward.	"As a prism of history, biography attracts and holds the reader's interest in the larger subject. People are interested in other people, in the fortunes of the individual. . . . [Biography] encompasses the universal in the particular."
IMMUNE TO SUNK COST EFFECT: Able to abandon a research nugget or a piece of writing, even if it costs a lot of time.	"I had suddenly walked over the line into contemporary history; I had become involved, and it showed. Although the publisher wanted the narrative brought up to date, I knew my final chapter as written would destroy the credibility of all the preceding. . . . I tore it up, discarded six months' work, and brought the book to a close."
THE COURAGE TO SELECT: Believes the best historical writing is not just about what to put in but also what to leave out.	"I had read that the Kaiser's birthday gift to his wife was the same every year: twelve hats selected by himself, which she was obliged to wear. There you see the value of corroborative detail in revealing personality. . . . It represents, however, a minor tragedy of *The Guns*, for I never succeeded in working it in at all. . . . [I]t emerged to a final resting place in a packet marked 'Unused.'" "What it requires is simply the courage and self-confidence to make choices and, above all, to leave things out."
FOUR-BY-SIX-INCH INDEX CARDS: Writes research notes on index cards, enables sifting and sorting for insight and writing.	"Use of the cards, the smaller the better, forces one to extract the strictly relevant, to distill from the very beginning, to pass the material through the grinder of one's own mind." "Eventually, as the cards fall into groups according to subject or person or chronological sequence, the pattern of my story will emerge. Besides, they are convenient, as they can be filed in a shoebox and carried around in a pocketbook. When ready to write I need only take along a packet of them, representing a chapter, and I am equipped to work anywhere."

Continued

NEED FOR POCKETS OF QUIETUDE TO WORK: Cloisters herself out of necessity and temperament.	Daughter: "She set up a card table and a chair in an old dairy attached to the stables—a room that was cold even in summer. She would go to work at 7:30 A.M. My job was to bring her lunch on a tray at 12:30 P.M.—a sandwich, V-8 juice, a piece of fruit. Every day, approaching silently on the pine needles that surrounded the stables, I'd find her in the same position, always engrossed. At 5 P.M. or so she stopped."

Note: Operating mode descriptions are in present tense to capture the feel of them fully active during her life.

As with Toni Morrison, we can see how Barbara Tuchman not only brought a big bright set of encodings into frame; she displayed an instinctive *awareness* of how best to tap her encodings by *translating* them into ways of living and working that suited her exceptionally well. She didn't ask the more generic question, "What practices work best for writing history?" She discovered what practices worked *specifically for her*.

More generally, we see the following basic pattern:

> Encoding → Awareness of encoding (implicit or explicit) → Translation into operating modes tailored specifically (and often quite uniquely) to the person → Effect

As with Morrison and Tuchman, some of the operating modes of two people in the same arena of work might overlap. But the key point is that they displayed a package of operating modes that, in aggregate, were specific to that individual. Some of their practices were quite peculiar, idiosyncratic, even quirky, but highly functional for actualizing each specific individual's hedgehog. And they adhered to their encoded operating modes even when they might strike others as odd or irritating. They didn't let what others might think stop them from trusting their self-discovered modes.

Trust the Encodings
Wherever They May Lead

Did you know that you and I might not even be alive right now were it not for Barbara Tuchman?

After Tuchman published *The Guns of August*, a copy of the book ended up in the hands of President John F. Kennedy, who happened to read it shortly before the Cuban missile crisis. Kennedy took a huge lesson from the book. Tuchman concluded that statesmen didn't plan or expect that August 1914 would turn into four years of world war, but once the actors began taking decisive action, irreversible moves and countermoves, even the most powerful people on earth could not easily stop the calamity. As Tuchman herself wrote in the final paragraph of *The Guns of August*, "The Battle of the Marne was one of the decisive battles of the world not because it determined that Germany would ultimately lose or the Allies ultimately win the war but because it determined that the war would go on. . . . Afterward there was no turning back. The nations were caught in a trap, a trap made during the first thirty days out of battles that failed to be decisive, a trap from which there was, and has been, no exit."

President Kennedy kept returning to the lessons of Tuchman's book as he navigated the missile crisis. His brother Robert Kennedy later wrote in *Thirteen Days*, "Barbara Tuchman's *The Guns of August* had made a great impression on the President. 'I am not going to follow a course which will allow anyone to write a comparable book about this time, *The Missiles of October*,' he said to me that Saturday night, October 26. 'If anybody is around to write after this, they are going to understand that we made every effort to find peace and every effort to give our adversary room to move.'" Kennedy went for a naval blockade rather than an all-out invasion of Cuba. He chose to respond to a more conciliatory message from the Soviet premier, Khrushchev, at the height of the crisis (rather than reacting to a more belligerent message from the Kremlin that arrived shortly thereafter). He offered to remove U.S. Jupiter missiles from Turkey to make it easier for Khrushchev to agree to removing missiles from Cuba. And the crisis came to an end without the world coming to an end.

So, here we have the story of a mom at home who decides to become a writer of history. She writes a book that the president reads. The president applies the lessons of the book to help avert a nuclear war. And we're all alive today.

Barbara Tuchman didn't set out to save the world when she wrote her books. She was just following her encodings. Once she discovered her encodings, she simply trusted them and focused the inner fire on writing her books. She didn't stop herself with questions like "Is this a worthy use of myself?" or "What will my parents think?" or "Does my husband approve?" or "Is this going to make me famous?" or "Will it generate huge social good in the eyes of my peers?" or any of that. Like many of us, she might have had moments of self-doubt and self-questioning, but in the end she trusted and followed her encodings and focused the inner fire on fully actualizing them. That doing so might play a role in something as significant to the future of humanity as the Cuban missile crisis was nowhere on her mind when writing *The Guns of August*. Operating with her encodings fully in frame and a great topic in hand, she simply could not stop herself from bringing into the world the best book she possibly could. That was all, and that was enough.

After systematically culling through the lives in this study, I've become deeply skeptical of the whole idea of a "worthiness scale" that weighs those who set out to change the world, do social good, serve humanity, or martyr themselves for a cause as inherently more "worthy" than those who channel their energies without such explicit nobility of purpose. I've also become skeptical of the idea of a life model that says, "First go out and be successful; then go out and do good in the world"—as if "doing good" in the second half of life were a sort of penance for being successful in the first half of life.

> To be clear, I'm not suggesting no one should have a nobility of purpose or seek to better the world. Rather, the research leads me to conclude that *the path to being useful is more of an inside-out approach* of discovering and deploying your encodings. You might get swept up in a larger cause or you might not, but even if you do, the key is to contribute to that cause by deploying your specific encodings.

Recall how Toni Morrison began writing her first books not with a huge external audience in mind but so that she herself could read them. That her work eventually had a huge impact, both artistically and socially, flowed principally from keeping herself in frame, focused (alongside raising her children) on One Big Thing: *books*. When an interviewer asked how she saw her public/social responsibility, how she knew she was "doing the right thing" with herself, Morrison responded, "You make it sound complicated, but it is really just about books. I edit books, I teach books, I write books." Morrison believed that a great book can *both* be true to its historical/political context *and* be an imaginative creation, connected to what's happening in the world while also being timeless, universal, and stunningly beautiful. In another interview, when asked whether she might take on a more political or public role if she didn't write books, Morrison responded, "All I can do is read books and write books and edit books and critique books. . . . There are people who can organize other people and I cannot. I'd just get bored." Morrison felt a strong sense of responsibility to give back, but she did not let that knock her out of frame. Toni Morrison *did* give back, absolutely and in the most profoundly powerful way: *She gave of her encodings.*

You never know where following your encodings will lead. Consider this: In what field did Barbara McClintock win the Nobel

Prize? She received the Nobel Prize in Physiology or Medicine. The announcement for the Nobel Committee's decision read, "In recent years, evidence has accumulated that transposition of genes or incomplete genes are involved in the transformation of normal cells into tumour cells. Thus, genes controlling cell growth have been found to undergo translocation from [one] chromosome to another during cancerogenesis." In a word: cancer. Barbara McClintock didn't set out to advance cancer medicine, and she didn't set forth to "help cure cancer" as her youthful, idealistic career goal. She did not know that her love of solving genetics puzzles would one day result in foundational contributions to medicine and even contribute to the recombinant DNA revolution that would usher in the era of biotechnology. She simply found something she was deeply encoded for and that she wanted to focus all her inner fire into doing, and that's how she spent her life. And yet there it was, for all to see in the Nobel announcement: "The initial discovery of mobile genetic elements by Barbara McClintock is of great medical and biological significance." She'd discovered, trusted, and deployed her encodings, and she would have done so with or without the possibility of a Nobel Prize for her contributions to medicine.

One view of the world argues for a two-phase approach to life: success to significance. First achieve success, then do something significant and meaningful. This study leads me to a very different approach: First discover a set of encodings, then trust that full commitment to a hedgehog built around those encodings is *in itself* a meaning-filled answer to the question of what to make of a life. It might lead to curing cancer or protecting freedom or reducing human suffering or advancing social justice, *or it might not*. It might be about a noble cause and changing the lives of others, *or it might not*. It might lead to doing something big and visible in the world, *or it might not*. Again, the famous nature of the people in this study reflects that I needed people with a lot of material I could access to study their lives, but that does not mean that a fulfilling and meaningful life requires fame and visibility. Coming into frame can be very private and personal.

All the people in our study gained self-knowledge, either implicitly or explicitly, about their own idiosyncratic constellation of encodings. Even if they didn't have the language for it, they sensed when those encodings clicked into frame, and when they were out of frame. Even if they experienced lack of support from others or bouts of self-doubt, they eventually came to *trust* their encodings and follow them, wherever they might lead.

4

Flipping the Arrow of Money

Would you accept offers for many tens of millions of dollars for just two years of work, traveling the world, reuniting with your former bandmates, playing through the catalog of your previous hits, singing the lead vocals in stadiums filled with tens of thousands of screaming fans, and cashing in on what could quite possibly become the first billion-dollar concert tour in history? For Robert Plant at age 59, still bursting with vocal energy and creative verve, this was not a hypothetical question.

Before getting to Plant's answer, let's rewind the tape to the start of Robert Plant's grand life of musical adventure.

At age 13, Robert Plant became utterly entranced with American blues, using money he'd saved from delivering newspapers to buy recordings of James Brown, stuffing a radio under his pillow and hearing Smokey Robinson, and feeling the raw power of blues singers filling every breath with soulful sound. He knew he had to be part of it. And lucky for young Plant, he lived in England, which had some of the best blues clubs that would inspire future icons of 1960s British rock such as the Rolling Stones, Eric Clapton, and—down the road near London—a budding guitarist named Jimmy Page.

Plant threw himself into the club scene, not just grooving in the audience, but also looking for chances to get up onstage and sing. At age

15, he'd already begun singing in a blues band at the Seven Stars Blues Club a few miles from his family's home, just outside Birmingham. By age 16, he'd become the front-man vocalist in a band named the Crawling King Snakes, which led to a seminal moment in Plant's life when the drummer John Bonham (known as Bonzo) joined the band. The Crawling King Snakes disbanded, but Plant and Bonham's friendship endured, the two of them committed to music above everything else in their lives. Sometimes they worked separately, and sometimes together.

Meanwhile, Plant's parents wanted him to finish school, study business, and become an accountant. His father helped Plant land a job as an accountant trainee, which lasted just weeks. "It was a rocky journey, really, with my parents," Plant later reflected. "They just didn't understand it at all. Any of it. In the beginning they thought that it would pass." Finally, when Plant was about 17, he chose music over home: "When I was in Band of Joy with Bonzo, they said, 'You take your choice'—and I didn't go back."

For the next couple of years, Plant cobbled together just enough life sustenance to keep going. He worked labor, laying tarmac, to bring in a bit of money to supplement the drip drops from music gigs and selling fewer than 800 copies of a solo single. He sometimes lived with his girlfriend's parents, he sometimes imposed on friends for a place to crash, he sometimes took a room in a house with other young people rotating in and out of a low-rent communal space. His girlfriend (and future wife) pitched in working at a department store. Plant found ways to fuel himself with calories wherever he could find them. Later, he would reminisce about him and Bonzo snatching milk from doorsteps and siphoning fuel from cars to keep themselves going. "We didn't always have enough money for food, drink and fuel, so we had to get by somehow," said Plant later in life, adding with a twinkle, "But you can rest assured I haven't done any petrol siphoning for a few years." The biography *Robert Plant: A Life* gives a telling title to the chapter about his early years of struggle to make a life for himself in music: "The Real Desperation Scene."

Then, the month before his 20th birthday, after five years of striving without significant success, Plant caught a break when a guitarist from Surrey, near London, needed a new vocalist for his reconstituted band, the Yardbirds. Someone recommended the guitarist check out Robert Plant up in the Midlands. The guitarist, and two other representatives from the Yardbirds, arranged to see Plant do a gig at the West Midlands College of Education in Walsall. Yes, that's where Robert Plant and Jimmy Page, one of the greatest duos in the history of rock, first met.

Shortly thereafter, Plant received a telegram from a manager of the Yardbirds: "Priority—Robert Plant. Tried phoning you several times. Please call if you are interested in joining the Yardbirds. Peter Grant." Plant journeyed to Page's boathouse, where over the course of a week they discovered a shared love for many of the same records and songs. The band also needed a drummer, and Plant recommended his friend John Bonham. Page meanwhile brought in the bassist John Paul Jones. And then, almost like an experimental accident in a chemistry lab, these four forces of music melded instantly together to create a great big thunderous boom that rocked them all.

In a cramped rehearsal room tucked into a basement on Gerrard Street in Soho, the four assembled for the first time. "We set the amps up," described John Paul Jones, "and Jimmy said, 'Do you know "Train Kept A-Rollin" by the Yardbirds?' I said 'no,' so he said, 'Well, it's a 12-bar with a riff on G.' That was the first thing we ever played." The effect stunned them all, the power, the mix, the sound, the chemistry. Plant later described the overwhelming magic of "that great moment in a basement in Gerrard Street when John and Jimmy and John-Paul and I all stood together scratching our heads, and lightning crackled above us, and the gods roared, and William Blake wrote a new poem from beneath the ground, and all Britain was reunited."

Not long after Plant's 20th birthday, the new Yardbirds played their first concert together just outside Copenhagen, Denmark, fulfilling an old Yardbirds obligation. Within two months, they'd jettisoned the Yardbirds name and begun recording their first album together, which would carry the same title as the new band: Led Zeppelin.

Over the next 12 years, Led Zeppelin would become one of the most successful bands in history, with nine studio albums of stunningly good music, including the songs "Stairway to Heaven," "Whole Lotta Love," "Good Times Bad Times," "Immigrant Song," "When the Levee Breaks," "Ramble On," "Black Dog," "Dazed and Confused," "Rock and Roll," and "Kashmir." Plant later summed up the pride he felt in this work: "Now, when I look back, I don't get any sense of great achievement out of the fact that people still like it a lot. I get achievement out of the fact that it was good." One notable aspect of the original band stood out, what Jimmy Page called the "fifth element": the chemistry of four exceptionally talented musicians dedicated to melding their individual talents into a collective whole. As John Paul Jones described the ethos of Led Zeppelin, "Everyone was serving the Zeppelin music. . . . The entire point of being in Zeppelin was to make the band sound good. Whatever we did, the band was the most important thing. . . . Everything was geared toward that." This collective dynamic was the superpower of the band, not any single superstar person.

Then, when Robert Plant was just 32 years old, John Bonham died in his sleep, likely related to an overconsumption of alcohol. Plant and Bonham had been best friends—beloved brothers really—for more than half their lives. Bonzo, the hulking, shaggy powerhouse drummer, drove the backbeat of Led Zeppelin behind the prettyfaced Plant, with his long curls of golden hair, hitting the high notes out front. Whenever Plant would begin to act too much like a star, Bonzo would cut him back to earth in the way only a true best friend can: *You might be the Golden God, Robert, but you're hopeless out there without me!* Once during a five-night series of Led Zeppelin performances in Madison Square Garden, Plant complained that his voice was shot. "Nobody cares about that," growled Bonham. "Just go out and look good." Plant later related stories like these as showing the deep, trusting affection they had for each other. When Plant's five-year-old son, Karac, died from a viral infection, Bonham stood closest by Plant of anyone connected with Led Zeppelin. Bonham attended Karac's funeral and nurtured Plant as he wove the torn fabric of his emotions back together. For Plant, the idea of Led Zeppelin without his brother in musical adventure was utterly unimaginable.

With the end of Led Zeppelin, Plant faced the daunting question of what to make of the rest of his life: "I thought I was all washed up." As he began taking small steps to reconstitute his life, he had one homing beacon guiding him through the fog: music. Zeppelin might be over, but an unquenchable fire for music still raged within him.

Plant never defined himself as just a blues rock singer, much less just the former lead singer of Led Zeppelin. He was an expansive *musical adventurer*. He delighted in doing gigs in exotic, far-off lands. A music executive who'd been trying to reach Plant recounted, "I'd leave messages with his office and eventually he'd call back. He'd say things like, 'I'm north of the Arctic Circle on a boat, playing gigs for the Inuit fishermen. They call me,' and he then said some unpronounceable, twelve-syllable word. When I asked him what it meant he told me, 'Man who looks like an old woman.'"

When asked (at age 62) for the favorite gig of his life to date, Plant said, "Timbuktu," referencing the Festival in the Desert to which he journeyed in his mid-50s. The festival actually took place about 40 miles north of Timbuktu in the midst of the Sahara Desert. Getting to the event involved renting a ride on a tiny airplane and then being ferried overland by drivers who navigated the roadless journey by their memory of sporadic trees they recognized along the way. The festival, for and by Tuareg nomads, brought together North African musicians—some having traveled 50 days to reach the venue—to a rolling sandscape dotted with goatskin tents with people on camels meandering about. "The whole idea of paying your own way to the Sahara to sing . . . it's insane," said Plant. "But isn't that great? If you want to play for the Tuareg you've got to get there. You've got to do it in order to have the experience." Capturing the spectacular remoteness of the festival, with no light pollution from anywhere, Plant described the stars as so bright and thick in the sky that they "dropped like a beautiful cape" to the edge of the earth in all directions.

One of my favorite images from this entire study comes from a video of Plant in a tent sitting amid a group of musicians and Tuareg people, the sound of bongo-like drums melding with hypnotic guitar rhythms in a version of "Whole Lotta Love." It's an image of Robert Plant in sheer bliss. "It's amazing to play out into the sand," enthused Plant. "There are no doors, no gates and no money. It reminded me of why I sang in the first place."

With that image fixed in your mind, let's return to the question of a Led Zeppelin reunion tour.

In the three decades after John Bonham's death, the remaining three players would very occasionally get together for a one-off gig, usually for some sort of charity or special event, pulling in someone to play drums. And Plant would sometimes team up with Jimmy Page to create music, such as with *No Quarter: Jimmy Page and Robert Plant Unledded*. This album fused Arabic music (backed by an Egyptian orchestra) into blues rock, including some refreshing re-imagining of old Led Zeppelin songs. As part of the preparation for *No Quarter*, Plant took Page on one of his grand musical adventures, a trip to Marrakesh, Morocco, to play with Gnawa trance musicians. They also did a street performance of "Yallah" (also known as "The Truth Explodes") in the hubbub of a Marrakesh market square. While they'd planned the street performance ahead of time, the video shows them looking for all the world like just two musical buddies who set up an amp and a drum synthesizer to play a street gig for passersby, and loving every minute of it. Plant and Page (a matched pair in this study) weaved in and out of each other's creative lives for more than 40 years.

Robert Plant and Jimmy Page Together Over the Decades

ROBERT PLANT	JIMMY PAGE	
Age 20	Age 24	Plant and Page created Led Zeppelin, along with bassist John Paul Jones and drummer John Bonham.
Ages 20–32	Ages 24–36	Led Zeppelin era.
Age 32	Age 36	Death of drummer John Bonham and end of Led Zeppelin.
Age 35	Age 40	Page joined Plant to play guitar for two tracks on Plant's album *The Honeydrippers: Volume One*.
Age 36	Age 41	One-off Led Zeppelin performance at Live Aid with John Paul Jones (Phil Collins and Tony Thompson played drums).
Age 39	Age 44	One-off Led Zeppelin performance at Atlantic Records 40th Anniversary Concert. John Bonham's son, Jason, played drums.
Age 45	Age 50	Plant took Page to Morocco to play with Gnawa trance musicians, as part of a joint project that resulted in the album *No Quarter: Jimmy Page and Robert Plant Unledded*.
Age 46	Age 51	Plant and Page joined John Paul Jones for the induction of Led Zeppelin into the Rock & Roll Hall of Fame.
Ages 49–50	Ages 53–55	Plant and Page collaborated to create the album *Walking into Clarksdale*. They toured together and received a Grammy Award for the Best Hard Rock Performance for the song "Most High."
Age 59	Age 63	One-off Led Zeppelin performance at The O2 in London to raise money for the Ahmet Ertegun Education Fund. John Bonham's son, Jason, played drums. Spectacularly successful, which fueled fan and music industry hopes for a full-blown Led Zeppelin reunion tour.

| Ages 64–65 | Ages 68–70 | Released *Celebration Day*, a live album and film of the performance at The O2. *Celebration Day* won a Grammy Award for Best Rock Album. |

Note: Due to ambiguity in the sources as to some of the precise dates (month and day) relative to birthdays, cited ages in these chronologies may vary by +/-1 year. Given that Plant and Page were born at different times of year, the difference in age between them can appear as either four or five years, depending on when the shared event fell relative to their birthdays.

Note: Plant and Page did a lot of other music during this time; these chronologies capture only significant points of overlap.

All this overlap generated excited hopes among millions of fans that Led Zeppelin might reunite to roam the earth once again, like some giant revived dinosaur. The apex of hope came when the three band members joined up with John Bonham's son, Jason, playing drums for a one-off tribute performance in honor of the late Ahmet Ertegun. (Ertegun had championed Led Zeppelin and Robert Plant at Atlantic Records.) The frenzy of anticipation generated an estimated *20 million* requests for 18,000 tickets at The O2 arena in London. The four players blew the place apart. The resulting concert album, *Celebration Day* (also available as a film), would go on to win a Grammy Award for Best Rock Album and a Grammy nomination for Best Rock Performance for the song "Kashmir." Surely, this would be the perfect moment to capture lightning in a bottle, to do the epic reunion tour, and the promoters made huge offers.

Plant went up on a mountain in Wales, having "a meeting with myself," and came down clear in his mind to decline the tour, once and for all. For one thing, he was having a lovely time doing some of the best music of his life with the bluegrass singer Alison Krauss, touring together in support of their joint album, *Raising Sand*. (*Raising Sand* would garner five Grammy Awards—not bad for a 60-year-old rocker who'd been in the music business for more than four decades.) For another, the whole idea of a Led Zeppelin reunion tour sounded like the antithesis of an adventure. No amount of money could knock Plant off the central driving force: his relentless quest to keep extending out, feeding his fire for music adventure, never letting it become a boring repeat zone. Quite simply, he loved singing too much to get confused by money. Plant tried to help an interviewer understand: "You know that Monty Python film where the king is with his son in a castle and he's pointing out the window saying, 'One day lad, all this will be yours'? And the son says, 'But I don't want it, all I want to do is sing!' I think that's my deal."

Of course, the earlier success of Led Zeppelin gave Plant the kingdom anyway, and you might be thinking, "Sure, but it's easy to turn away hundreds of millions of dollars if you're already rich." Perhaps, but that misses the main point. Recall that he endured years of privation in his youth to pursue his music. Robert Plant didn't sing as a means to make money. Rather, he needed enough money to be able to sing. Yes, later in life, his economic circumstances changed dramatically, but the *fundamental reasons for doing his work did not*. It was always about the music, the adventure, and the sheer rapturous bliss of blending his voice with other artists.

"If I don't have a gig, I'd be playing birthday parties, weddings and bar mitzvahs. I've got to do this. I feel the beat," said Plant upon releasing his 15th "collection of songs" after the end of Led Zeppelin. "I can't give up this stuff because I love what I do." As a longtime Plant associate put it, "Success sidetracks people in a lot of different ways, not all of them bad. It's not just that they get greedy and have to support their six mansions and their private planes, running off with groupies and getting divorced. People also get pulled from music by doing charity work, making movies, writing books and collecting art. You very, very rarely meet someone like Plant, who is still just as fanatical about music after forty years at the top. That's almost unprecedented."

Making the Flip

Stop and think for a moment. What is the relationship between work and money? Is the purpose of work to make money? Or is the purpose of money to be able to do one's work? Well, that depends on how we define and think about "work."

> The people in our study flipped the arrow of money. Instead of work being a means to money, money became a means to work. And they made this shift because they embodied an unusual definition of work. For the people in this study, their true "work" could best be defined as *pursuit of excellence in a hedgehog.*

Think back to the people we've discussed so far in this book. None of them defined success primarily in terms of money. Some of them made a lot of money; some of them did not. But the amount of money they made across a lifetime bore little relation to how they thought about the meaning of their lives.

Recall Barbara McClintock simply wanting to do her work solving genetics puzzles; so long as she had the basics of her life covered and full access to her research materials, she felt quite satisfied. Recall also McClintock's matched-pair companion, Grace Hopper, the computer science pioneer who advanced the cause of standard languages, much of that work through her long service in the U.S. Navy. She never showed any interest in doing a hot start-up that could multiply her wealth by hundreds or thousands of times. And while she posthumously ended up with a naval destroyer named after her, she remains much less well known than famous entrepreneurs who made billions. As Hopper's biographer Kurt Beyer put it, "[Hopper] had a sense of duty, to self and country as well, which I think is not typical sometimes for Silicon Valley. . . . That's probably one of the reasons why maybe a lot of people have never heard of her, because she actually didn't make much money during these years."

Think back to Alan Page after his NFL career. Page could have made substantially more money as a partner in a major law firm using his NFL fame to bring in lucrative clients; instead, he served 23 years on the Minnesota Supreme Court. Page's matched-pair companion, Carl Eller, dedicated his post-NFL life to being a community leader, working on drug addiction prevention and rehabilitation, hardly the most financially lucrative choice he could have made.

John Glenn and Gordon Cooper made do on military pay to pursue their love of flying. Can you imagine John Glenn saying, "Well, I'll be happy to go fly combat missions, but only if you give me a bundle of stock options with the upside potential to cash out and retire." Try to picture Gordon Cooper, after his epic save when his spacecraft *Faith 7* conked out with a total power failure, saying in response to President Kennedy's congratulations, "Thank you, sir. I did it for the bonus in my paycheck."

Robert Plant had no idea during his early privation years that he would eventually make so much money that the idea of making more money would make about as much sense as bringing sand to the beach. He just wanted to do his music. Later in life, Plant quietly put his money to use behind the scenes. A friend of his discovered that Plant had generously funded cancer research without ever drawing attention to himself; his friend only found out when his doctor mentioned it in passing. Plant also took pains to never let his money impede his sense of musical adventure. When he launched on an exploration of American bluegrass and country, he generally rode the tour bus rather than jetting in on his own, making sure that his money didn't insulate him from the full adventure or isolate him from other musicians. And no amount of money could ever entice Plant to retire from musical adventuring; he wanted to keep going. "I'm here for the journey, for the whole adventure," he said while doing some of the best music of his life in his seventh decade, "right through to the end."

Jimmy Page and Robert Plant differed from each other somewhat in their encodings, with Plant being a vocalist who sought ever expanding musical adventure with a wide range of people, and Page being a guitarist who came most alive in the magical chemistry of one of the greatest rock bands in history. Yet they both flipped the arrow of money, a crucial element in becoming two of the most exceptional blues rock musicians of all time. Jimmy Page had an unquenchable fire for doing the music of Led Zeppelin, and he loved doing music with Robert Plant. When I watch the film *Celebration Day*, of the concert at The O2 in London, I don't see an aged Jimmy Page looking back to his youthful glory days, or a money-driven Jimmy Page looking ahead to maybe a billion-dollar tour. I see a very young man of 63 years fully on fire, enraptured and lost in the moment. For Jimmy Page, it was always about one thing above all: doing the music. And none more so than doing the music of Led Zeppelin.

Jimmy Page and Robert Plant were fortunate that Led Zeppelin generated a lot of economic fuel to do their music. Without question, most of the people in our study made a lot less money over their lives than the Zeppelin guys. Yet the basic pattern is essentially the same: Once people clicked into frame with something they were encoded for, it lit a fire that burned so hot that they flipped the arrow of money in service to doing it. Even if they made more money than they knew what to do with, like Robert Plant and Jimmy Page, their fire for the work continued to burn within.

A Wide Range of Economic Circumstances

Let's acknowledge an undeniable fact of life: People come from a wide range of economic starting points. Quite simply, the practical challenges of focusing all your inner fire into doing something you are encoded for can be more daunting if you come from economic scarcity than if you come from wealth.

Which raises the question: Could it be that most of the people in this study came from substantial family wealth?

Fortunately, the answer is definitively no.

The people in the study came from a wide range of starting points and economic circumstances, sometimes even within the same pair. To illustrate, let's meet the first two women in history to win an Olympic gold medal in figure skating for the United States.

Carol Heiss's encodings for competitive figure skating came brightly into frame quite young. By age 16, she'd won the U.S. Championships novice division, placed second in both the U.S. Championships and the World Championships. The next year, she became the first woman to land a double axel in competition. Her athleticism and dedication inspired her coach, the Olympic gold medalist Pierre Brunet, to invest heavily in her development and to predict that she would eventually win a world and Olympic title. "This is partly because she wants so much to win it that all the work of practice sessions still seems like a privilege to her," explained Brunet. "You can't defeat an attitude like that." Carol Heiss had, in short, an abundance of encodings that could make her one of the most competitively successful figure skaters in the world.

But one thing Carol Heiss did not have in abundance: money.

Heiss's parents emigrated from Germany, and Heiss grew up in a working-class family. "My father is a baker, the most wonderful father any girl ever had, but he never made much money," said Heiss. "Whatever he made went for his children." To become a champion, Heiss needed consistent access to a skating rink. She needed competitive skates. She needed outfits. She needed ballet lessons (to hone her dance skills for her routines). She needed to travel to competitions. Her mother took on extra work as a textile designer. Her parents did without a car to fund ballet lessons. Her neighbors in

Queens, New York, rallied together to help buy skates. Her godmother traveled with her to her second national championship when Carol's mother could not afford to go. A family friend stepped in to lend help at home.

Then, just as everything seemed to be coming together with Heiss's competitive success, her mother fell ill with terminal cancer. Heiss's mother lived long enough to see Heiss (just turned 16) win the World Championships and a silver medal at the 1956 Olympic Games. The World Championship and Olympic silver medal attracted offers for Heiss to turn professional—not just for a little money, but for a lot of money. Shortly before Heiss's mother passed away, the organizer of a professional skating program pulled up to the Heiss home in a limousine to offer a life-changing sum for Heiss to turn professional. Olympic rules at the time forbade making money off the sport, and accepting the money would kill her gold medal dream. Heiss's mother did not want her daughter to wonder for the rest of her life whether she could have been Olympic champion. Heiss recalled sitting on the stairs out of view, listening as her mother said, "My daughter's dream is to be an Olympic champion, and that would be my wish for her, to make her happy, to at least try. . . . Can you, with all your money, can you give me my good health back and make me better?" When the promoter said, "No, of course not," Heiss's mother continued, "Well, then, my daughter's dream, I want her to have that. We'll find a way."

The cancer took Heiss's mother later that year. Heiss had to take on some quasi-parental responsibilities as the oldest child, rising early to make breakfast for her younger sister and brother and get them off to school while her father worked the early shift in the bakery. Yet the dream remained. "We'll find a way," her mother had said. *We'll find a way.*

Her coach, Pierre Brunet, and his wife sacrificed to help make the economics work, coaching Heiss *without pay* for the years leading to the next Olympics. Not only did Brunet forgo coaching fees, but he also turned away a number of wealthy clients to focus on Heiss. Heiss reciprocated by training six days a week, several hours a day, while also finishing high school and then commuting to and from NYU, where she'd received a scholarship. Yet even with all this strain, Heiss's encodings for competitive skating continued to shine brightly in frame as she delivered an exquisite series of performances: four consecutive national championships and three additional world titles, all leading to a chance to compete for the gold once again at the Olympic Games.

When Heiss traveled to compete in the 1960 Winter Olympics near Lake Tahoe, California, her father had to work and could not make the trip. After Heiss nailed her compulsory figures, securing her an almost certain gold medal (barring a catastrophe in the final free-skating segment), she came off the ice and said, "I wish my father could be here." The next day, less than four years after losing her mother to cancer, Carol Heiss became an Olympic champion. Perhaps her father caught some of the televised coverage from Queens, New York, but the demands of his working life meant that both father and daughter missed out on the chance to share the moment together.

After winning the Olympic gold medal followed by her fifth World Championship title (becoming the first American woman to win five World Championships in figure skating), Heiss retired from competitive skating. Yet she took one more step to close the circle: She accepted a lucrative movie contract, which enabled her to contribute to her family by paying for her siblings' education. "This way I can repay my father for all he has done for me," she said at the time. "He would never accept the money directly, but if I help my brother and sister it will relieve him of some of the expenses." She also paid Pierre Brunet back for the years of coaching he invested in Heiss for free.

Now let's turn to Carol Heiss's matched-pair companion, Tenley Albright. Like Heiss, Albright faced early adversity, though of a very different sort. At age 11, Albright was hospitalized in isolation for treatment of polio, her doctors unsure if she would ever walk again. Albright, later describing herself as fortunate and lucky for the trajectory of her case, did recover. She used ice skating as a form of rehabilitation, starting with tiny tentative steps as she hung on to the railing at the end of the rink, learning afresh how to appreciate her muscles. More skating led to increased strength, which led to more skating, which led to ever increasing strength. She became so adept at skating that she began entering competitions and then *winning* competitions.

Like Heiss, Albright won the Olympic silver medal at age 16, then the Olympic gold medal at age 20. Like Heiss, Albright won the U.S. Championships and the World Championships multiple times. Albright, a few years older than Heiss, became a competitive inspiration. "I was lucky to have such a good opponent," reflected Heiss. "If Tenley hadn't been tops, I couldn't have learned so much trying to beat her." They stood on the 1956 Olympic podium together, Albright winning gold and Heiss winning silver.

Carol Heiss and Tenley Albright
Side by Side to Olympic Gold

CAROL HEISS		**TENLEY ALBRIGHT**	
Early Life	Grew up in Queens, New York. Parents first-generation working-class immigrants. Father worked as a baker.	Early Life	Grew up in Newton, Massachusetts. Father, a graduate of Harvard Medical School, worked as a prominent surgeon.
Ages 10–15	Began competitive figure skating. Won U.S. Championships, novice division. Placed 2nd in U.S. National Championships, 2nd in World Championships.	Ages 10–15	Contracted polio, hospitalized, and recovered. Began competitive figure skating. Won U.S. Championships, novice division. Placed 2nd in U.S. National Championships.

Continued

Age 16	Won silver medal, Olympic Games (1956). Won World Championships. First woman to land a double axel in competition. Mother died of cancer.	Age 16	Won silver medal, Olympic Games (1952). Won U.S. Championships.
Ages 17–19	Won U.S. Championships three times. Won World Championships three times. Earned scholarship to NYU.	Ages 17–19	Won U.S. Championships three times. Won World Championships two times. Entered Radcliffe College.
Age 20	Won gold medal, Olympic Games (1960). First American woman to win five World Figure Skating Championships. Won her fourth U.S. Championship.	Age 20	Won gold medal, Olympic Games (1956). First American woman to win Olympic Figure Skating gold medal. Won her fifth U.S. Championship.
Age 21	Retired from skating career and shifted fully to the next phase of life.	Age 21	Retired from skating career and shifted fully to the next phase of life.

Note: Due to ambiguity in the sources as to some of the precise dates (month and day) relative to birthdays, cited ages in these chronologies may vary by +/-1 year.

Note: Carol Heiss married Hayes Alan Jenkins a few months after the 1960 Olympics, at which point she carried the name Carol Heiss Jenkins. For the purposes of these chronologies and the text in the chapter, which focuses on her competitive skating years before her marriage, I have chosen to use the name Carol Heiss.

While Albright and Heiss both fully committed to their skating, and did so with remarkably similar results, they differed dramatically in their starting economic circumstances. Whereas Heiss grew up in a working-class neighborhood of Queens, Albright lived in the upscale Oak Hill neighborhood of Newton, Massachusetts. While Heiss's father worked as a baker, Albright's father worked as a prominent surgeon who'd graduated from Harvard Medical School. Albright attended a private prep school (Manter Hall School in Cambridge). For her undergraduate studies, she attended Radcliffe, a private women's college that would subsequently become part of Harvard College, and then, like her father before her, attended Harvard Medical School.

In sum, the evidence we have on Albright suggests that her family wealth, quite unlike Heiss's situation, enabled her to focus on skating with little (if any) worry about money.

> Through an economic lens, Tenley Albright had a very lucky start in life. Yet coming from a well-off family did not make her an Olympic gold medal champion. Carol Heiss came from a much more challenging economic circumstance, and Heiss *also* became an Olympic gold medal champion.

Both Heiss and Albright got luck of circumstance, just very different luck. Heiss had the good luck that her parents loved skating and got her onto the ice at a young age, and she had the unusual benefit of a world-class coach who would coach her without pay. Albright was born into tremendous advantage, economically and socially. The key is that each *made the most* of the lucky cards she got.

Making the Economics Work: Drawing from 12 Economic Streams

For some people in the study, making the economics work proved relatively easy, whereas for others it proved much more difficult. Family wealth served as a significant means to pursue a hedgehog in only six of the 34 lives we studied, whereas in ten of 34 cases people endured at least one significant phase of scarcity while in pursuit of a hedgehog. Yet whether easy or difficult (or somewhere in between), they committed to focus their inner fire in line with their encodings *and* they figured out how to make the economics work.

So, how did they do it?

When I first began discussing the emerging findings from this research in our team meetings, I would talk about the idea of doing something that ignites the inner fire and that flows directly from your encodings. Then I would quickly dispense with the economics by saying something like "And you can get paid to do it." Then, one day, in a particularly spirited dialogue and debate, a group of my best researchers revolted: "That's way too simplistic!" They challenged me to use the research data to develop a much deeper and more nuanced understanding of how the people in our study solved the economic equation.

My team and I conducted a systematic analysis of the personal economics across the lives in the study. The evidence showed that my team members were right: It is *not* so simple as "What you can get paid for." It turned out that only about half of the people in our study earned a traditional paycheck as the primary economic mechanism in doing a hedgehog.

> We discovered a wide range of methods people in the study used to make their economics work, categorized into 12 economic streams. Over the course of their lives, the people in the study used some combination of between three and eight of these streams, with a median of four streams per person. This analysis showed that there are many ways to make the economics work, and you might need to draw from multiple methods simultaneously and/or across phases of your life.

In the list below, I've briefly described each economic stream and indicated the percentages of the people in our study who employed that method as it related to at least one hedgehog in life. If you're interested in delving deeper into the specifics of each stream, I've included more detail in appendix 4.1.

Mastering Scarcity: The person went through a phase of scarcity of economic resources while in pursuit of a hedgehog. The phase required some combination of sacrifice, creativity, resourcefulness, living lean, and/or sheer work ethic to meet basic material needs while simultaneously being fully committed to pursuit of a hedgehog. Twenty-nine percent of people in the study used this method for at least one hedgehog in life.

Family Wealth: The person came from a family with substantial economic wealth that directly enabled full commitment to a hedgehog with little (if any) worry about personal economics. Eighteen percent of people in the study used this method for at least one hedgehog in life.

Spousal Economics: The person's spouse provided substantial economics (in the form of income that the spouse generated or by inheriting assets from a deceased spouse) that partly or fully supported pursuit of a hedgehog. Eighteen percent of people in the study used this method for at least one hedgehog in life.

Funding for Education/Training: The person received financial or material support for education that proved directly beneficial to the pursuit of a hedgehog. "Education/Training" has a wide definition here, from traditional schooling to direct training for skills and craft. Seventy-nine percent of people in the study used this method for at least one hedgehog in life.

Cross Funding: The person did non-hedgehog work for a period of time to bring in money while simultaneously pursuing a hedgehog. Thirty-five percent of people in the study used this method for at least one hedgehog in life.

Salaried Hedgehog: The person pursued a hedgehog that came in the form of a salaried position, a "job" that the person was encoded for, that fed the inner fire, and that came with a paycheck. Fifty-three percent of people in the study used this method for at least one hedgehog in life.

Creative Flywheel:* The person created a self-reinforcing positive loop of creative work, wherein doing successful and financially

---

* The flywheel principle comes from my prior work, first discovered in the research for the book *Good to Great*, and then further explored in *Turning the Flywheel*. The essence of the flywheel is that success happens as a cumulative process, like pushing a giant, heavy flywheel, turn upon turn, building cumulative momentum. All flywheels take the form of a reinforcing loop, wherein each turn adds to the momentum and generates economic fuel to turn the flywheel again.

viable creative work (such as acting, writing, music, architecture, design) then generated more opportunities for financially viable creative work. Fifty percent of people in the study used this method for at least one hedgehog in life.

Business Flywheel:* The person created, co-created, and/or controlled a business entity that generated profits and cash flow that could go back into fueling the business and where the activities of the business were directly in line with the person's hedgehog. Thirty-five percent of people in the study used this method for at least one hedgehog in life.

Social Cause Flywheel:* The person created or co-created a social cause organization (directly in line with the person's encodings) that attracted and/or generated funding to be deployed into creating impact, which then attracted/generated more funding to create even more impact, in a continuous reinforcing loop of funding and impact. Twenty-four percent of people in the study used this method for at least one hedgehog in life.

Earned Earlier: The person generated and saved substantial economics earlier in life and then drew upon those assets to further pursue an existing hedgehog or to start a new one. Forty-one percent of people in the study used this method for at least one hedgehog in life.

Direct Personal Support: The person drew support from people in the immediate community (such as friends, family, acquaintances, mentors, neighbors, or other community members) while in pursuit of a hedgehog; this support came in the form of money or donation of goods and services that would otherwise cost money. Twenty-one percent of people in the study used this method for at least one hedgehog in life.

Special Sources: The person drew upon some other economic resource that does not fit neatly into one of the other 11 categories; this includes such resources as government housing, financial settlements from lawsuits, prize money from scientific and literary awards. Thirty-five percent of people in the study used this method for at least one hedgehog in life.

The Greatest Reward

One of the great traps of life is the Curse of Competence Doom Loop. It goes like this: Become reasonably competent at something that doesn't capture your encodings or ignite the inner fire, but it pays well. Work hard at it, become better at it, achieve a modicum of success with it. This then leads to increased opportunities to do even more of what does not fit your encodings or ignite the inner fire, and you are getting paid even more to do it. You gain more valuable experience doing what you're not encoded for, which generates more opportunities and even better pay doing what doesn't feed the fire. And one day, you wake up to discover that years or decades have passed. You're well paid and out of frame. The inner fire is still there but gradually going dormant.

I have great compassion for people who get caught in the Curse of Competence Doom Loop. It happens for understandable, even noble reasons, such as providing for people they love. Yet it can inhibit them from coming fully into frame. Fortunately, in one of the most uplifting findings in this research, people can (and often do) find a hedgehog in midlife or later. We will explore this finding more fully in chapter 9, but for now the key point is that so long as the clock of life continues to run, it is never too late to discover and deploy encodings. It might not be in a traditional "career" or be highly visible to the world (though it might). What matters is whether it fits with your encodings, whether it feeds the inner fire, and whether you can flip the arrow of money to pursue it.

> You might be able to make the economics work with just one of the 12 economic streams, or you might need to creatively draw upon multiple streams. It might prove easy to make the economics work, if you are fortunate with circumstances, or it might be much more difficult than for those with more fortunate circumstances. Life does not deal all of us the same cards out of the deck.

Yet whether easy or difficult, early or late, the people in the study didn't let economics stop them from taking steps in line with their encodings, once they felt themselves clicking into frame. Without question, they had a realistic understanding that *they had to make the economics work*. But they didn't stop themselves by saying, "I can't step forward until I've figured out the money."

Recall Toni Morrison, a middle-aged single mom with a deep sense of responsibility to provide for her two sons, working as an editor while she wrote her first novels. Once she'd discovered her encodings and felt the fire for writing, she committed herself to stepping into writing, at four in the morning and in little bits of time on trains, in cars, whenever she could find a minute. We found zero evidence that once Morrison made the commitment to write, she would let the economics stop her from writing. One way or another, she would write!

When the people in this study put themselves in full hedgehog mode, there is nothing else they would rather be doing, even if they could make a lot more money doing something else. When work is defined as the pursuit of excellence in a hedgehog, then doing one's work becomes not just a means to an end but *an end in itself*. For this is a simple truth gleaned from these lives: When you find something you are deeply encoded for and that ignites a raging fire within, the greatest reward for doing your work is the opportunity to continue doing it.

5

Focus the Fire

In an outdoor stadium in Cortina d'Ampezzo, Italy, surrounded by the jagged edges of the Dolomites towering above the Olympic cauldron, Tenley Albright skated through her final program. Completely absorbed in executing each turn and jump and spin merged with the music, she'd lost herself in what some athletes call the zone. She sensed every wrinkle and divot of the ice as she soared and glided through the crisp alpine air.

But then something unexpected began to seep into her consciousness, a sound coming from outside the boundary of the ice, growing slowly louder, swelling all around her. The audience! They'd joined the performance, not clapping and cheering, but *humming*. She'd choreographed part of her routine to the "Barcarolle" from the opera *The Tales of Hoffmann*, and people began to hum the music in unison—a few people, then more, then Albright found herself skating to the enveloping embrace of humming voices flowing from all directions. "I thought it was in my head," said Albright, "but I suddenly realized that the audience was humming the music. I was close to the boards and I could hear them. That was the most uplifting thing. It was such an amazing feeling of connection."

I still get chills when I think of that story. Now consider a question: How much of Albright's skating career did these gold medal minutes add up to? I ran a conservative calculation and estimated that the last two minutes of Albright's Olympic routine added up to less than

0.001% of the total time she invested in all the years of training getting to those moments.

So, what fed the fire for the other 99.999% of the time? "It's important that it be motivation from within," said Albright. "I would bet you that most people who have succeeded, even though they had an idea of what they wanted to do, didn't just say, 'I want to be . . .' and then name a title or say 'happy' or something like that. I bet it's because they loved what they were doing. It certainly was for me. . . . You do it because you love what you are doing." Albright reveled in the very process of training and improving, step by step, hour after hour, day after day, week after week, month after month, year after year. She loved the experience of being so bad at a new jump that she'd find herself face down on the hard ice with her arms and legs splayed, sliding, then getting up and trying it again. Then again, and again, and again—getting a little bit better each time—until she gained that feeling of "Wow!" (her word) when she hit the move without crashing. She practiced until she could nail it in competition. Then she'd repeat the process on another new skill, going through the stepwise journey again. She also fed the fire by exercising her creativity, extending out to experiment with new routines and moves. She'd invent something new—a jump or spin or swirl or sequence—that would give her the chance to rise from flailing all over the ice to eventually nail it. Then she'd invent another, then yet another.

Those minutes in Cortina d'Ampezzo were an exceptional moment in Albright's life, a highlight that could never be precisely replicated ever again. But it was only a moment. And it was a moment not at all guaranteed.

In fact, she almost didn't make it onto the ice. Less than two weeks before her Olympic performance, she'd crashed on the ice, the sharp point on the back end of the left skate blade burying itself into her right ankle. Her father (a surgeon) rushed to Italy and tended the wound. Even so, Albright didn't even get to participate in the parade of athletes in the opening ceremony, relegated to watching it from her room. Imagine if she'd worked all those years, only to be denied at the last minute by a freak injury. But imagine how much worse it would have been if she'd not derived so much daily satisfaction across all the years of training up to that moment. The preparation was the cake, the Olympics only the icing.

Albright's ankle healed just enough that she could attempt to compete. She made some adjustments to her planned program to compensate for the wound and willed herself onto the ice.

The ankle held. And the people hummed.

Love of the Doing

Let's pause the Albright story to extract a lesson about the inner fire: A big source of fire lay in the fact that when in full hedgehog mode the people in our study quite simply loved what they were doing.

The key word here is "doing."

It's not about being entranced by a romantic vision to, say, become a writer, but about *being in love with the daily act of writing*. Or skating, or playing guitar, or leading a team, or flying, or solving genetics puzzles, or doing ceramic art, or crafting legislative language. It is not about being able to say, "I'm a prominent surgeon" or "I'm a professional athlete," but about being able to say, "I love *doing* surgery" or "I love *doing* my sport."

> There is a big difference between being in love with the *idea* of one's work and being in love with *doing* the work itself. It means not just the love in the 0.001% highlight moments; it means love in the other 99.999%.

Tenley Albright's love of the actual act of skating never abated, and she continued to go to the rink decades after her gold medal. "I become exhilarated when skating," said Albright 12 years after the

Olympics. "When you're used to skating, the feeling of freedom and exhilaration, you hate to think of stopping. It's almost frightening how I can forget what's going on, even time, when I'm on the ice. It's a different world. . . . I love skating." In her eighth decade of life, Albright still skated for personal pleasure. Even in sleep, she dreamed about skating and the glorious feeling of soaring in the air and gliding across the ice.

Even more than winning, Albright wanted to experience "the exhilaration when you know you've done your best," emphasizing that *only you know* if you have done your absolute best on any given day. It's an entirely internal standard of performance, leading Albright to feel disappointed when she won but knew she could have performed better. Albright's genuine delight in the step-by-step process of learning or creating something new and then perfecting it, combined with the internal measuring stick of knowing she did her best, became a perpetual motivation machine. Not just in skating, but equally in her second hedgehog: medical surgery.

"It's hard for athletes to think they could find anything that consumes their interest as much as the sport they love," said Albright. "Medicine is that for me. I'm fascinated by the miracle of the human body." Itching to get on with the next phase of life after skating, she uncovered an interesting fact: The admissions requirements for Harvard Medical School did not seem to specify a college diploma. Premedical classes, yes, but there was nothing in writing that said she needed to graduate from college. Albright bypassed finishing her undergraduate degree and applied directly to medical school. She got in (one of only five women in her entering class, in an era when some faculty openly abhorred the idea of women in medicine) and found herself exhilarated by the prospect of learning a vast array of new skills, step by step by step by step, in an endless, repeating loop of learning. "So once again, I felt like a real beginner," said Albright, adding that while the new regimen was "quite a shock," it was also *exciting*!

She discovered that she loved doing surgery at least as much as she loved skating. The operating room became like the ice rink, a place where she could lose herself in her craft. At age 36, a decade after graduating from medical school, Albright reflected that she'd found many similarities between skating and surgery: "You get the same exhilaration from a good operation that you do from a good performance." She described the feelings in surgery as comparable to how she felt skating: "When you're there in this magical world of the operating room, with a patient and with a team . . . it's sort of like that multidimensional thinking that I was aware of on the ice, where everything comes into your head at once. You have to be focused, but you also have to be conscious of all sorts of things. . . . And then there is that wonderful feeling of completing it, as you put in the last stitch, knowing that you did it the way you wanted to." Though in surgery the stakes were higher. If she fell in a skating competition, no one else got hurt; in surgery, the patient's well-being depended directly on Albright's landing the operation.

Albright felt a deep commitment to practice medicine with "surgical conscience," doing her very best for every single human being under her care. Her personal dedication to the ethos of surgical conscience had roots in her own experience with polio. When 11-year-old Tenley went to the hospital with polio, doctors showed her a long needle they planned to insert into her spine. As they were about to proceed, a terrified little Tenley said, "Could someone please hold my hand?" The half a dozen people in white lab coats didn't move, just looking at each other, frozen by uncertainty and fear, not knowing in that era whether polio could be transmitted by touch. Finally, one of the health professionals took her hand while Tenley squeezed hard with the pain. Albright returned to that story when talking about her life as a surgeon dedicated to the "care" part of health care. As a practicing surgeon, she made a habit of ensuring that someone held the patient's hand when she did a procedure.

Albright's fire did not dim with the end of her skating career. She refocused the fire into her medical work—in love with the doing, excited always by expanding her knowledge, and passionately dedicated to surgical conscience. The gold medal moments in Cortina would stay with her throughout, but with each passing year they became an ever-tinier fraction of her life.

Three Big Sources of Fire

So far in this chapter, I've highlighted love of the doing, but love is not the only big source of the inner fire for the people in this study. Which raises a question: Other than love of the doing, *what fuels the fire within?* Ambition? Fury? Fear? Insecurity? Creativity? Curiosity? Cause? Spirituality? Adventure? People? Passion? Justice? Duty? Honor? Purpose? Values? Vision? Or . . . what? Aspects of each of these showed up in different people across the study, but not all. Some people were fired up by a cause or noble purpose, while others simply wanted to solve puzzles or make music. Some felt a burning ambition to achieve visible success or climb the highest peaks of power, while others sought mainly to be left alone to do their own thing. Some people simply wanted to create something exquisitely beautiful for its own sake, while others felt more fired up by making a social impact. Again, every person in the study differed from every other person in the study in how they were encoded and in what drove them.

That said, there *are three prevalent sources of fuel for the inner fire* across the vastly different lives in the study. In addition to *love of the doing*, the two others are:

Extend Out/Circle Back: This is a continuous dynamic process of extending yourself—growing, learning, experimenting, expanding capabilities, discovering new encodings—while simultaneously drawing upon encodings discovered and capabilities developed earlier in life. Notice how Albright continually extended out in her skating, experimenting and inventing new skills. She extended out in going to medical school, feeling *excited* about being a beginner again. Notice also how she circled back to skating across her life, still going to the ice and applying her encodings for precision and practice, so well deployed in skating, to her surgical practice. This dynamic of extending out and circling back proved to be a powerful source of sustainable fuel for the people in the study.

Choosing Responsibilities: This means making *deep commitments* to *freely chosen* responsibilities. These responsibilities might be visible and public, or they might be personal and private. What matters is that you feel fired up by taking on responsibilities you believe to be important, regardless of whether you will ever get credit or applause for doing so. For Albright, the ethos of surgical conscience lived within her not merely as an abstract idea that she learned in medical school but as a sacred responsibility she felt deep within. She never forgot her own experience as a scared little girl with polio.

I'm going to dedicate two entire chapters to Extend Out/Circle Back and choosing responsibilities in Part III, because they play vital roles in continuous self-renewal over the long arc of a life. But I'd like you to have them in mind as we finish out the story of Tenley Albright as she headed into her fire-filled later decades.

After a multi-decade career focused on doing surgery, Albright extended out and chose a big new responsibility. She founded the MIT Collaborative Initiatives, tapping her natural encodings for creative collaboration, reveling in bringing together people across disparate arenas to stimulate breakthroughs in thinking. She'd mix architects with military officers with business CEOs with leaders of national health systems to work together on problems like childhood obesity, stroke, and PTSD. She sparkled with enthusiasm when talking about her efforts. "I never would have thought of putting karate with cancer patients," she enthused to a gathering of students at MIT about learning the value of bringing martial arts into children's hospitals to give them a feeling of strength.

Watching a video of her engagement with the students, Albright sporting a flower in her hair (a frequent practice) and wearing a bold colorful outfit to match, one cannot help but sense her inner fire still glowing bright in her late 70s. When asked by an attendee what she'd learned from Olympic skating, Albright chose not to dwell on the gold medal phase of her life, graciously turning the conversation to surgical conscience, the practice of medicine, and the power of collaboration. Her presence conveyed a lesson gleaned across the lives in our study: There is absolutely no point in dwelling on what's past; there's just too much energizing stuff yet to do.

And perhaps that explains a fascinating statistic from Tenley Albright's life. When I first began studying Albright, before I delved into all the historical materials we'd collected, I read her full bio document posted on the MIT Collaborative Initiatives website. I read the first paragraph—and found no mention of the gold medal. Then the second paragraph, and no mention of the gold medal. Then on down the page, three paragraphs, four, five, six, and still no mention of the gold medal. Finally, after an account of her medical achievements and honors, the bio ended with a sentence that reads almost as an afterthought: "Earlier, she was a Gold Medal Olympic Figure Skater." Here we have the first American woman in history to win an Olympic gold medal in figure skating and she dedicated less than two percent of her bio to that achievement.

In her 80s, Albright still exuded fire. She convened. She collaborated. She taught young people. She learned about new technologies. She even spent time on the ice. She showed no interest in stopping the process of extending out and circling back, of choosing responsibilities, of continuing to feed and focus the inner fire. After all, if you still feel the inner fire for what you do, and you can still do it, why would you stop? She continued to exemplify a lesson she endeavored to teach her own children: "Do all things not for glory, but for joy."

The Stress and Drudgery Tax

Of course, not *all* of the 99.999% moments count as joyful bliss.

Welcome to the Stress and Drudgery Tax.

Even when right in the middle of the best hedgehog years of their lives, the people in this study paid what I came to call the Stress and Drudgery Tax. To be clear, the tax is not about stress and drudgery *outside* doing a hedgehog but about stress and drudgery *in doing the actual hedgehog*.

Recall Grace Hopper's exquisite encodings for advancing computer software and the adoption of standard languages, and how she never lost the fire. Yet she found herself paying a tax: the frustration of getting people in bureaucracies to change and embrace new technologies. "I find in general that human beings are allergic to change," lamented Hopper. "They do not like change. They've learned something, they're perfectly satisfied doing it, and you come along and say, you're going to do it this way. People push it away. . . . The job of changing people's minds is one of the biggest challenges we have." For more than four decades, spanning the entire second half of her life, Hopper evangelized her beloved computer gadgets and the power of standard software. Yet all along the way, she faced the dreary, frustrating task of battling the entrenched forces of bureaucratic resistance.

Jimmy Page loved playing the guitar, but to perform, he had to pay a tax. Page was naturally introverted, his guitar almost a shield he could hide behind, and even after performing hundreds of shows on multiple continents, he still got quite stressed. "I get terribly nervous before I go on stage," Page shared about his preshow feelings of stress. "I get wound up into a knot. I have to psych myself up to go on stage." But then, once the show started, "the tension explodes and I'm fine. I'm in another world—in a trance almost, doing what I love best, expressing myself through guitar."

There is no level of success or reputation or money that fully buys you out of the tax; even at the zenith of a long and fruitful career, the tax remains. Heading into his late 60s, I. M. Pei had established himself as one of the most successful modern architects of his era. He'd won such high-visibility projects as the John F. Kennedy Presidential Library and Museum in Boston, a seminal modern addition to the National Gallery of Art in Washington, D.C., the Bank of China Tower in Hong Kong, and the Morton H. Meyerson Symphony Center in Dallas. He'd also won multiple awards, including the American Institute of Architects' Gold Medal ("the highest accolade awarded by his peers") and the Pritzker Prize ("the architectural equivalent of a Pulitzer"). You would think that, finally, after more than 40 years of ever-increasing success and stature, I. M. Pei would be able to escape the tax.

Well, think again.

When Pei went to work on what would become one of his most famous achievements, a renovation of the Louvre Museum in Paris, his inspired design of a glass pyramid hit a buzz saw of fierce criticism. "One after another, they got up and denounced the project," said Pei of presenting his pyramid to the Committee on Historical Monuments. "My translator was so unnerved that she started to tremble." The committee's former chief architect labeled it a "gigantic, ruinous gadget." Cultural elites and French media attacked Pei's design, calling it "soulless, cold, and absurd," comparable to "an airport or drugstore," and any number of other condescending insults. As what became known as the Battle of the Pyramid raged, Pei became the target of vitriol. Michael Cannell related in his biography, *I. M. Pei: Mandarin of Modernism*, that people even spit at his feet as he walked through Paris. "My jaw just dropped open," said his shocked daughter, "but he was very poised. His attitude was, Well, grin and bear it."

Throughout his career, Pei could never get rid of the tax. He accepted it as part of the price he had to pay to do the work he loved. Even in the core work itself, the creative process, Pei could never rid himself of the tax. "I get into a great inner turmoil when I have to find the right design for a building," Pei lamented. "It absorbs me completely and I can't think of anything else. This may be a matter of hours or it may take as long as a month of sleeping badly, being irritable, sketching ideas and rejecting them. I am useless to everyone else. It is traumatic for my wife."

> We did not find a single person in the study who remained intensely engaged without paying some level of the Stress and Drudgery Tax. Not one. Perhaps there is someone out there in the world who fully realized a hedgehog without paying the Stress and Drudgery Tax. But I've never met one, and we did not find one in this study. It didn't matter the walk of life; they all paid the tax.

The crucial question is, Does the inner fire for what you're doing far exceed the tax you have to pay to be able to do it? If not, can you change some aspect of it to lower the tax rate? Recall Barbara McClintock leaving the University of Missouri to find a more suitable home at Cold Spring Harbor, thereby lowering her tax rate to a more sustainable level. There might be a point when the tax rate becomes too large to pay, and you decide it is time to leave behind the activity that you love to do. Though the dominant pattern in our study is that so long as they were in frame with their encodings and full of fire for what they were doing, our subjects largely made changes and adjustments to be able to stay in hedgehog mode.

Just because something has stress and drudgery does not mean it fails the test of being in frame. In fact, *quite the opposite*. You know you are in a hedgehog when you feel so compelled by what you are doing, so compelled to focus the fire on it, that you are willing to pay a lot of Stress and Drudgery Tax to be able to do it.

Does Focused Mean Monomaniacal?

To enter full hedgehog mode means not just feeling a lot of fire but choosing to *focus* the fire on One Big Thing. Which raises a series of questions. Does this level of focus require sacrificing everything else in life? Can you have other life priorities or do you need to pursue the One Big Thing with monomaniacal zeal? Just how much focus do you need to have to qualify as being, well, *focused*?

To address these questions, let's look at the matched pair of Alice Paul and Lucy Burns, who lived out some of the most fire-focused episodes in our study. These two women led in the fight to win the 19th Amendment, enshrining women's right to vote in the United States. Paul and Burns began their work as activists for suffrage while studying in England, inspired by the Pankhurst-led suffragettes. In fact, Paul and Burns met for the first time in a London police station, having been captured in a mass arrest of protesters for suffrage. They returned to the United States fired up by the cause, and they chose the responsibility to become leaders in the U.S. suffrage movement. Together, they co-founded the organization principally dedicated to achieving a constitutional amendment.

Both Paul and Burns demonstrated an extreme level of commitment, not just marching in the streets and getting arrested, but also subjecting themselves to hunger strikes and enduring force-feeding while incarcerated.

During force-feeding in Britain, three wardresses held Alice Paul down while another held her head in place. A fifth person then pushed a thick tube up her nose, snaking the slimy hose to her throat to force globs of milky eggs into her stomach. When she returned to the United States, her fire only sharpened. Again she subjected herself to a hunger strike in jail, where she also endured isolation, having been separated into her own cell with windows boarded up and only a sliver of air seeping through. She was subjected to psychological intimidation, her captors sending her to a psychiatric ward where Paul worried that they were trying to prove that she might be insane. She suffered through sleep deprivation, bright lights blasted into her eyes every hour through the night. The very embodiment of Shakespeare's line "And though she be but little, she is fierce" (from *A Midsummer Night's Dream*), Paul sent an implicit message to her nemesis and chief adversary in the suffrage fight, President Woodrow Wilson: *I might die, Mr. President, but I will not quit.*

Lucy Burns also focused her furious fire and deployed her encodings into the cause. She was a spectacular field general with a charismatic voice. She had a flair for spectacle, rallying women in the western United States with a tour by train dubbed the Suffrage Special and dropping leaflets from an airplane (back when airplanes were still quite a novelty in people's lives). Burns led the creation of flash-point banners that called out the president's hypocrisy in championing the fight for democracy abroad in World War I while women at home could not vote; the banners, carried at the east gate of the White House, labeled the president "Kaiser Wilson." She wrote powerful speeches and edited *The Suffragist* newspaper. Like Alice Paul, she held firm under extreme duress. During one incarceration, Burns's jailers handcuffed her hands above her head and manacled her to the steel bars of her jail cage, part of a failed attempt to stifle Burns's defiant leadership that inspired other jailed suffragists.

To get a quick overview of Alice Paul and Lucy Burns marching side by side for suffrage, see the nearby chronologies.

Alice Paul and Lucy Burns
Side by Side for Suffrage

ALICE PAUL		**LUCY BURNS**	
Early Life	Raised in a wealthy New Jersey family; her father a successful banker.	Early Life	Raised in a wealthy New York family; her father a successful banker.
Ages 20–24	Graduated from Swarthmore, did graduate work at the University of Pennsylvania, studied in England. While in England, became involved in the U.K. suffrage movement.	Ages 22–29	Graduated from Vassar College, did graduate work at Yale, then studied in Germany and England. While in England, became involved in the U.K. suffrage movement.
Age 24	Met Lucy Burns in a London police station when they were both arrested in a suffrage protest. Jailed multiple times in the U.K., participated in hunger strikes. Was force-fed.	Ages 29–30	Met Alice Paul in a London police station when they were both arrested in a suffrage protest. Jailed multiple times in the U.K., participated in hunger strikes.
Ages 25–26	Made increasing commitment to suffrage movement. Returned to the United States. Spoke at the National American Woman Suffrage Association convention.	Ages 30–32	Made increasing commitment to suffrage movement. Remained in the U.K. working with Pankhurst-led suffragettes before returning to the United States.
Age 27	Joined the National American Woman Suffrage Association, became chair of its Congressional Committee.	Age 33	Joined the National American Woman Suffrage Association, became vice-chair of its Congressional Committee.

Ages 28–29	Co-founded the Congressional Union for Woman Suffrage to focus on passing a federal amendment to the Constitution. Split from National American Woman Suffrage Association.	Ages 33–34	Co-founded the Congressional Union for Woman Suffrage to focus on passing a federal amendment to the Constitution. Split from National American Woman Suffrage Association.
Ages 30–32	Engaged in a whirlwind of activism, including protests, marches, and political campaigns.	Ages 35–38	Engaged in a whirlwind of activism, including protests, marches, and political campaigns. Arrested multiple times.
Age 32	Jailed and participated in hunger strike. Endured force-feeding and other brutal tactics.	Age 38	Jailed and participated in hunger strike. Endured force-feeding and other brutal tactics.
Ages 32–35	Engaged in the final fight for the suffrage amendment, which eventually won the required two-thirds majority in Congress, then achieved ratification in three-quarters of the individual states.	Ages 38–40	Engaged in the final fight for the suffrage amendment, which eventually won the required two-thirds majority in Congress, then achieved ratification in three-quarters of the individual states.
Age 35	The 19th Amendment is signed into law.	Age 41	The 19th Amendment is signed into law.

Note: Due to ambiguity in the sources as to some of the precise dates (month and day) relative to birthdays, cited ages in these chronologies may vary by +/-1 year.

Yet for all their similarities and fierce commitment, these two women showed strikingly *different* patterns on having life priorities outside the cause.

Let's start with Alice Paul. During the crux years of the fight for the 19th Amendment, Alice Paul's monomaniacal focus stood out. She showed little understanding of the need for life priorities outside the cause. Doris Stevens, who fought alongside Paul, never forgot their first meeting: "I had come to Washington to take part in the demonstration on the Senate . . . en route to a much-needed, as I thought, holiday in the Adirondacks. 'Can't you stay on and help us with a hearing next week?' said Miss Paul. 'I'm sorry,' said I, 'but I have promised to join a party of friends in the mountains for a summer holiday and . . .' 'Holiday?' said she, looking straight at me. Instantly ashamed at having mentioned such a legitimate excuse, I murmured something about not having had one since before entering college. 'But can't you stay?' she said. I was lost. I knew I would stay. . . . And it was years before I ever mentioned a holiday again."

In *Alice Paul: Claiming Power*, J. D. Zahniser and Amelia R. Fry provide a comprehensive account of Paul's leadership, vividly capturing her utter relentlessness. She paused rarely, even to celebrate interim successes. On January 10, 1918, the U.S. House of Representatives took up the question of a constitutional amendment for women's suffrage. After four decades of struggle since first being introduced to Congress, the amendment appeared poised to finally receive the two-thirds majority required to move it to the Senate. The suffragists watched from the gallery as the vote proceeded—the yeas and nays accumulating. It would be close, with no room for losing even a single vote. Finally, well into the evening, the vote concluded at 274 to 136, hitting precisely the two-thirds margin required for victory in the House. The gallery roared with clapping, stomping, cheering, singing, crying, hugging. Forty years—*40 years*—we did it!

But Alice Paul had already left the building, walking briskly back to the National Woman's Party headquarters, knowing that an epic battle loomed to win the required two-thirds majority in the Senate. When the giddy suffragists finally made it back to headquarters, they found Paul already hunkered down at her desk, working on a strategy. Paul welcomed them by pausing briefly from her concentrated efforts, saying simply of the work ahead to convert senators, "Eleven to win before we can pass the Senate."

It would take more than a year to win the Senate, followed by another year to achieve approval in three-quarters of the states to secure the amendment. On August 26, 1920, the secretary of state signed the 19th Amendment to the U.S. Constitution into law: "The right of citizens of the United States to vote shall not be denied or abridged by the United States or by any State on account of sex." And with that, it was done.

By age 35, Alice Paul—as a primary strategic architect of the suffragist victory—could theoretically rest easy, secure in the knowledge that no matter what she did with the rest of her life, she'd already made a monumental contribution to the cause of women's rights.

And what did Alice Paul do with herself?

She went right back to work.

By late the following year, she'd already begun the fight for a new amendment that she herself authored, what would become known as the Equal Rights Amendment. She would work on women's rights for the rest of her life, worldwide and at home. Even as she entered her 90s, Paul kept her fire focused on the cause, tracking closely the state-by-state progress of the Equal Rights Amendment.

Before doing this study, I might have held up Alice Paul as an idealized example of discipline and dedication. I might have written something like "Sure, she was an obsessed monomaniac, but that's just what it takes." And I might have invoked Alice Paul as vindication of my own somewhat obsessive nature, falling prey to confirmation bias. But now, after this study, my thinking has evolved.

When you look at Alice Paul and Lucy Burns side by side, you can see how Burns also played a pivotal and heroic leadership role in the fight for suffrage. Yet, unlike Paul, *Burns did integrate other priorities into her life*, both during and after the suffrage fight. Burns allowed herself recovery breaks during the most intense years of the fight for the 19th Amendment, making time for visits to her close-knit family in Brooklyn—somewhat to the consternation of Paul, who simply didn't understand the idea of other priorities. According to the professor of history Sidney R. Bland, Alice Paul told him that Burns was "never quite as committed as we'd like"—an astounding statement that says more about Paul than it does about Burns, given that Burns also endured hunger strikes and torturous force-feedings. According to Professor Bland, "Lucy Burns was the first of the 'silent sentinels' to be incarcerated; she spent more time in jail than any American suffragist."

Lucy Burns never wanted to live a purely monomaniacal life like Alice Paul's, but that does not mean she lacked fire or focus. Alice Paul didn't appear to have much of anything else in her life than her work for women's rights because, the evidence leads me to conclude, she didn't feel the need for much of anything else in her life. Lucy Burns, in contrast, *did* feel the need for other aspects of her life. That Paul focused nearly 100% of her fire on the fight for suffrage and women's rights doesn't make her a more worthy template to follow. Lucy Burns *also* focused her fire during the fight for suffrage, just not in the purely monomaniacal manner of Alice Paul.

In the decades after winning suffrage, Lucy Burns reoriented her life in a direction quite different from Alice Paul. Burns's sister died in childbirth, and Lucy chose a huge personal responsibility on which she repurposed her inner fire: raising her late sister's daughter. For the rest of her life, Burns focused on family and church, largely unseen by the outside world.

Again, one of the things I most want you to take from this book is a deep skepticism about any judgmental "worthiness hierarchy" that favors a singular measure of what to make of a life. There is absolutely no legitimate way to judge Alice Paul's life as better than Lucy Burns's life, or vice versa. They are *different*. Different people, different encodings, different priorities, different temperaments, different choices, but both lived out fire-filled lives.

Side Passions and Relationships: Data Across the Study

The suffrage pair raises a question about being in hedgehog mode: What does the data show across the entire study—were people more like Alice Paul or more like Lucy Burns? We examined two categories in which people expended fire outside their primary hedgehog:

1. Invigorating side passions.
2. Family and relationships.

INVIGORATING SIDE PASSIONS

While the people in our study focused intently on the primary activities that I write about in this book, most also allowed themselves some form of invigorating side passions. Robert Plant, for instance, had a side interest of tremendous passion: his beloved boyhood favorite Wolverhampton Wanderers Football Club. Not only did Plant follow the ups and downs of the team, but he also became a vice president and an ambassador of the club. One friend relayed that Plant "calls me at home to talk about every game. I can get through a full bowl of spaghetti while he's ranting on; I just put the phone to one side on the table and let him get on with it."

Or consider Alan Page, who cultivated multiple side passions, including being a car fanatic. "He is a car freak, and he has always been a car freak, and he will always be a car freak," said Page's wife, Diane. When Alan and Diane first dated, Page would arrive to pick her up in a drag-racing Dodge Charger painted purple with the word FREEDOM emblazoned in gold block letters across the side. He'd won multiple races at a Minnesota drag-racing venue, making me wonder what the Minnesota Vikings' front office thought about one of its star players roaring down a drag strip. Page also cultivated a passion for long-distance running. While still playing in the NFL, he subjected his defensive lineman's frame (which reached 245 pounds during his playing career) to the rigors of training for a marathon, becoming the first active NFL player in history to complete a full 26.2-mile race. Page continued to invest in his running, in the later years of his NFL career and after. He completed multiple marathons (hitting a personal best of 3:27:50, a pace faster than eight minutes a mile). He even extended the distance to complete at least one 62-mile ultramarathon. After his NFL career, Page had largely replaced football with running as his primary physical activity. No matter the weather, Page would get up at 5:19 a.m. (yes, exactly 5:19 a.m. every single day) and head out for his morning run. "I've been out after it snowed nine inches overnight and they haven't plowed. And the coldest it's been is 34 below," said Page, who allowed that he might reconsider at 40 degrees below zero. One of Page's friends quipped, "If you were in Minneapolis and you didn't know what time it was, and if you could find your way to Lake of the Isles and saw Alan running, you'd know it was 6:00 in the morning."

In sum across the study, we found evidence that 30 of 34 people (88%) engaged in invigorating side passions while in hedgehog mode. The side passions across the study covered quite a wide range, including gardening, knitting, painting, composing poetry, woodworking, running, bicycling, doing aerobics, skiing, golfing, playing tennis, mountain climbing, fly-fishing, reading, visiting art galleries, hosting dinner parties, playing poker, studying the occult, engaging in a deep meditation practice, teaching Sunday school, and disco dancing.

FAMILY AND RELATIONSHIPS

We were unable to confidently discern the extent of personal/family relationships across all the lives in our study; sometimes the private side of their lives remained, well, *private*. Nonetheless, we did find evidence that about half of the people in our study—18 of 34 (53%)—placed a high priority on family responsibilities in the form of building an enduring close spousal relationship and/or parenting attentively while in a hedgehog. And these 18 people split evenly between men and women. The remaining people in our study (also split evenly between men and women) either clearly did not, or the evidence is lacking or mixed. If we had the full evidence inside their private lives, I believe the percentage would be higher than 53%.

My point here is not that some of the people in our study figured out how to "have it all." They didn't. They made choices. Recall the story of Toni Morrison and how she integrated writing with raising her two sons as a single mother, even as she held down a full-time job to economically support her family while launching into her writing career. "There were only two things without which I couldn't live: mother my children and write books," said Morrison. "Then I cut out everything that didn't have to do with those two things." As Morrison clicked into frame as a writer, she became ever more focused. Morrison felt that life offered a lot of time to get things done because, as she said, "there are a lot of things I don't do. I don't talk on the telephone, I don't ski, I don't go on vacation, I don't have a social life, it's close, intimate friends, and I'm not giving dinner parties."

If we widened the lens beyond family, we found substantial evidence that the people in our study formed and nurtured relationships across their lives. These came in many possible forms, such as friends, colleagues, mentors, mentees, partners, allies, teachers, coaches, teammates, creative collaborators, and others. Alice Paul might have been obsessed with the pursuit of women's rights to the exclusion of other priorities, but she didn't work alone. She had a web of relationships, likely quite like the types of deep connections that get forged in battle. She had a band of sisters with whom she marched, and fought, and suffered, and risked, *together.*

I'm reminded of the book *Adaptation to Life* by George E. Vaillant, based on a seminal study (known as the Grant Study) that followed the lives of a cohort of men in real time across decades of their lives. The theme of lasting relationships runs through Vaillant's book, a key correlative factor in those who adapted well to the challenges of life. The lives of the people in this book would underscore that point. It's not just about filling your life with *activities* that you love doing, but about doing them alongside and with people you love and who, in turn, love you.

Sustained Focus

We've reached the end of the first part of the book, and we're about to turn the page to the question of what happens when a cliff upends life as you've known it and throws you into the fog. But first, before we move into the center section of the book, let's step back for a brief recap. In chapters 2 through 5, we built out a foundational perspective on how the people in our study answered the question of what to make of a life. They all found a hedgehog and spent a significant portion of their lives in hedgehog mode, which consisted of three elements: discover and deploy encodings, flip the arrow of money, and focus the inner fire on One Big Thing.

> Think back to the people you've met so far in these pages and notice the almost overwhelming level of fire they showed: Barbara McClintock, Grace Hopper, Alan Page, Carl Eller, John Glenn, Gordon Cooper, Toni Morrison, Barbara Tuchman, Robert Plant, Jimmy Page, Tenley Albright, Carol Heiss, I. M. Pei, Alice Paul, and Lucy Burns. They didn't just have a momentary burst of fire; they sustained and focused the fire for extended periods of time.

One of the most uplifting findings from this research is how nearly all the people sustained the fire well past the midpoint of life and many did some of their best work years to decades after age 50. One of the questions I most wanted to understand is what enables some people to feed the inner fire well into later decades (so long as they had the luck of good health). The third section of this book will address that question in rich detail, but for now keep in mind that the compounding effect of focused fire for decades utterly dwarfed any short-term spikes of energy along the way. They persisted before success. They persisted beyond success. And they persisted through the seismic cliffs that altered or shattered their lives along the way.

The point here is not about superhuman endurance, endless self-inflicted suffering, awe-inspiring work ethic, or even self-discipline. I've come to see that for individual lives it is more about feeling intrinsically compelled than about being fanatically disciplined. I used to think of myself as a disciplined person, but the more I studied these lives, the more I came to see that I never really needed discipline to keep going. If you so love what you're doing, and you feel so well encoded for it that you simply cannot stop yourself from doing it, then how is that discipline? I love the time of bliss in the hours of transition from night to dawn, and there is nothing in the world I would rather be doing than creative work as the light changes. I still hit nearly every single day excited by the work at hand, checking my watch in the middle of the night hoping that it is far enough into the morning to justify getting up, thinking to myself, "Please, oh please, let it be at least 4 a.m., so I can get going!" That's not discipline; that's love.

The question of sustained motivation largely melts away when people get into frame with a set of their encodings, doing something they just want to keep doing because it feeds the fire within. And one of the most powerful and sustainable forms of fuel to the fire, if you are lucky enough to find it, is doing something you derive so much pleasure from that you can't imagine not doing it. Of all the sources of fire, I've concluded that perhaps the biggest is sheer unadulterated love of the doing. It's like a personal flywheel within: If you discover something you're encoded for and you love *doing* it, then you can't help but want to do more of it, which means you can't help but get better at it, which means you can't help but move toward the intrinsic satisfaction of excellence in what you do, which further reinforces doing what you are encoded for and love to do.

Love, I came to understand, is greater than discipline. Love is greater than ambition. Love is greater than ego. Love is greater than fear. Love is greater than achievement. Love is greater than determination. Love is greater than passion. Love is greater than purpose. *Love is greater than.*

Part II

Navigating Cliffs and Fog

6

Cliffs

I can pinpoint the precise moment when the idea of looking at life through the lens of cliffs planted itself in my brain, 25 years before I started this project. It happened when my wife, Joanne, faced a cliff that ended her identity as an elite professional athlete.

Joanne won the Ironman World Championship in Hawaii at age 26. She became a primary female athlete in Nike's first rendition of its famous "Just Do It" campaign. She had invitations to compete all over the world. Joanne loved the sheer bliss of day-in, day-out training, losing herself for hours cycling up and down the steep wooded hills around Palo Alto, running trails feeling the lithe and speed of supreme fitness, and reveling in the camaraderie of swimming endless intervals with Los Altos Masters swim club. And she was deeply encoded to *compete*. There are athletes who *want* to win, and there are athletes who *need* to win. This encoding cannot be coached into existence, it cannot be learned, it cannot be manufactured, it cannot be created by motivational tools or speeches or books or podcasts. It's an encoding that bound Joanne to the founding ethos of Nike, captured in its very name: Nike is the Greek goddess of victory. And it's an encoding that pulled her through an epic moment of personal will in the final hour of a ten-hour battle on a stark lava-scape.

Competitors at the Hawaii Ironman face two adversaries: fellow competitors and the course itself. When we arrived for Joanne's first Ironman, she peered out the window as the 757 glided toward the

Kona airport, which just happened to sit right alongside the run course. "My God," she said, "it looks like a giant pan of overcooked brownies out there." Unlike the lush, tropical rainforests you might find in other parts of the Hawaiian Islands, all you see on the Kona coast of the Big Island—for miles—is black-and-brown-crusted lava from volcanic eruptions. Looking closer, we could see a ribbon of road cutting right through the black lava, the Queen Kaʻahumanu Highway, where the bike race and marathon would be fought. When the flight attendant opened the cabin door, it felt as if someone opened a giant furnace, the heat hit us like some sort of invisible shock wave. Ninety-degree temperatures, 80% humidity, black unsheltered asphalt surrounded on both sides by black-crusted lava—perfect conditions for heatstroke and hallucinations. It's one thing to endure the Hawaii Ironman: a 2.4-mile ocean swim followed immediately by a 112-mile bicycle race and capped off with a full 26.2-mile marathon run. It's another to *race* the Hawaii Ironman, to *compete* for a win.

In her championship race, Joanne exited the bike-to-run transition, after more than six hours of swimming and cycling, feeling strong. She pounded up the first hill of the marathon, looking determined, focused, in control. Yet within, she carried great anxiety about what her body would do as the miles unfolded. A marathon runner should log at least 30 miles per week in training (and many marathoners log 50 or more miles per week). Joanne's running had fallen that season to a mere 16 miles per week, due to a persistent hamstring injury. She could run strong to maybe 20 miles . . . but then what?

At 16 miles into the marathon—after more than eight hours of swimming, cycling, and running—Joanne had built a sizable gap on her competitors. Then the hamstring-limited training began to catch up, her thighs and calves starting to cramp. With seven miles to go, she still had a ten-minute lead, but she'd begun to lose time on those chasing her. Her stride began to disintegrate. Her lead kept dropping as she willed herself toward the Kailua Pier, the finish line, and rest.

Her lead shrank to nine minutes. Then an eight-minute lead. Then seven . . . and six . . . and five . . . and four . . .

Along the way she stopped, right in the middle of the road. She looked down at her legs. She looked up, as if pleading for someone or something to help her, but of course no one could help her. Entirely on her own, her body crumbling, she curled her hands into fists. She stood there for a long moment, eyes closed, face etched with pain. Then she bent down and began gripping and massaging her quadriceps. *Please! . . . Let me run.*

Then her faced changed, the contortions smoothed out, and her eyes seemed to fix on something distant. She took a breath. Her lips pressed together. And then, somehow, she found the strength to move forward. One stride, then two, and she began . . . to run.

Three miles to go . . . two miles to go . . . the lead kept shrinking.

With a mile to go, she rounded the corner off the highway and into town, heading toward the pier. A quarter mile to go—people lining the street yelling and screaming—she slowed for a moment, looked over her shoulder, and urged herself with a last little pleading, barely audible "c'mon." She summoned the last bit of energy to propel her legs forward, crossing the finish line after more than ten hours of racing, with only a minute and a half to spare.

It was a peak moment in life. She'd not only won a world championship, she'd also won something even more important: the self-respect that comes from knowing deep down that she could not have run one step faster. When the moment came, out there on those lava fields, with her body falling apart, her mind and spirit had not broken.

Now consider what it must be like to be so perfectly built for athletic competition, to have the ability to endure extreme tests and emerge victorious, to get up every day with a love of training and a clear and simple goal. Imagine what it must feel like to have found something for which you are exquisitely constructed, that brings you joy in the daily ardor of your effort, and that you can earn a living at.

And now imagine what it must feel like to have it all ripped away from you.

That chronic hamstring injury only worsened. Surgery failed. Physical therapy failed. Strength training failed. Acupuncture failed. Yoga failed. Massage failed. Rest failed. Everything failed. Finally, Joanne had to confront the brutal fact that the hamstring injury would end her career.

Then, one day, sitting at our kitchen table, she gasped in despair, "I feel like I'm dying."

I feel like I'm dying.

The words sliced right through me. If no longer a world-class competitive athlete, then what? The most important person in my life felt as if she were dying, right in front of me, and I had no answer, no useful reply.

I did not know it at the time, but that desperate moment planted the seed for what would become the idea of studying how people move through the cliffs of life. It would sit in my brain gestating for 25 years before I turned my attention to doing the study that led to this book.

Joanne did eventually get past the cliff and reconstitute her life in a stunningly beautiful way, creating personal meaning that far exceeded winning the Ironman. But as with many of the people in this study, she had to first endure a painful period of feeling lost in the fog, only to emerge in a place that she'd never planned or expected.

Life Through the Lens of Cliffs

Joanne's story leads us into the next part of what to make of a life: *navigating cliffs and fog*. Recall the core construct of the study: My research team and I identified matched pairs of people rising through life on a similar path. Then they both hit a similar or near-identical cliff. A "cliff" is a significant event that alters the trajectory of a life and forces choices about what's next. The big cliffs can radically change a life and throw people into a befuddling fog as they seek to reconstitute their lives and reenvision the years to come. We then studied their lives up to the cliff, through the cliff, and after the cliff.

> Again, the Big Question is not about cliffs per se but about what to make of a life. Cliffs became a powerful way to shed light on the Big Question, because life-altering cliffs force people to reconsider the question anew. Looking at two people going through the same or similar cliffs proved to be a powerful tool for uncovering common and divergent elements of how to construct—and reconstruct—a life over the long arc.

Across the entire study we have a range of cliffs. Some cliffs came out of the blue, unexpectedly breaking life into jagged pieces that needed to be put back together. Some cliffs were inevitable and foreseeable, giving people the opportunity to prepare somewhat ahead of time. Some people had cliffs that came entirely from forces outside their control, while other people played a role in creating their own cliffs. While some cliffs come as terrible, even tragic events, there can also be positive or success cliffs.

Whatever form the cliff took, each cleared a threshold of magnitude to be included in the study. To calibrate the magnitude of cliffs, my research team and I developed a set of calibration criteria, taking into account three factors: (1) the extent of life change brought about by the cliff; (2) the extent to which the cliff was beyond the person's control; and (3) the extent to which the cliff was unforeseen and/or uncertain before it happened. Using these criteria, we categorized cliffs into minor cliffs, major cliffs, and mega cliffs. To qualify for the study, a cliff had to clear a minimum threshold of being at least a major cliff. (In appendix 6.1, I've included the definitions and scoring methodology for these components.)

I've listed nearby the complete set of matched pairs in the study and the specific cliff we used for the match. (See "Matched Pairs Across the Study.") To be clear, these are not the *only* cliffs these people experienced in their lives; every life we studied had *multiple* cliffs, albeit some much bigger than others. This list delineates just the cliffs we used to construct our matched pairs.

Matched Pairs Across the Study
(Alphabetical by Last Name of the First Person in the Pair)

MATCHED PAIR	CLIFF MATCH
Tenley Albright Carol Heiss	End of competitive figure skating career; cliff marked at official retirement.
Maryon Pittman Allen Cardiss Collins	Death of husband coupled with immense pressure/responsibility to step into his seat in Congress; cliff marked at husband's death.
Lucy Burns Alice Paul	Winning ratification of the 19th Amendment, end of role as key leader of U.S. suffrage movement; cliff marked at ratification.
Jimmy Carter Gerald R. Ford	Getting fired by the American people; cliff marked at losing presidential election while seeking a second term.
Charles Colson John Ehrlichman	Prison sentence related to activities and scandals during the Nixon White House; cliff marked at sentencing to prison.
Gordon Cooper John Glenn	End of military career and life-defining role as pioneering astronaut/pilot; cliff marked at resignation from NASA and military.
Carl Eller Alan Page	End of football career; cliff marked at official retirement from the NFL.
Michael J. Fox Maurice White	Onset of Parkinson's disease; cliff marked at firm diagnosis.
Benjamin Franklin Roger Sherman	The American Revolution and formation of a new nation; cliff marked at the year 1776, when the revolution became inevitable, then irreversible.
Georgia Frontiere Katharine Graham	Death of husband coupled with inheriting ownership of and responsibility for family company; cliff marked at husband's death.

Grace Hopper Barbara McClintock	Hitting the wall of limited opportunities for women in science in traditional academia pre-1950; cliff marked at leaving university role and platform.
Toni Morrison Barbara Tuchman	Becoming the primary at-home parent; cliff marked at redefining and reorienting life around parenting responsibility.
Jimmy Page Robert Plant	End of Led Zeppelin, triggered by death of John Bonham; cliff marked at formal dissolution of the band.
Meryl Streep Debra Winger	Turning 40 as a leading female actor in films, perception and reality of decline in role options; cliff marked at age 40.

Two Lives Torn Asunder

To illustrate the cliff-match method at work, let's turn to two people whose lives were redefined by a tragic, devastating mega cliff: Cardiss Collins and Maryon Pittman Allen.

Cardiss Collins's life split in two at 2:28 p.m. central standard time on Friday, December 8, 1972. That's the moment when United Flight 553 crashed in subfreezing drizzle on approach to Chicago Midway Airport. Among the 40 passengers who lost their lives in the crash was the U.S. Representative George Collins, Cardiss's husband.

Not only did Cardiss Collins lose George and the life they shared together, she also faced a monumental decision. Congress has a long-standing practice known as the widow's mandate or widow's succession whereby the spouse of a deceased member of Congress assumes the vacant seat, by special election or direct appointment. About a week after the funeral, Chicago's mayor, Richard Daley, asked Collins if she would consider taking her late husband's seat in Congress. There would be a special election, which she would almost certainly win if she ran.

At age 41, at what would turn out to be the midpoint of her life, Cardiss Collins had never shown interest in serving in Congress.

She'd grown up with a single mom who cleaned other people's houses. After graduating from a vocational technical high school in Detroit, she moved to Chicago to find work, eventually landing a job at the Illinois Department of Labor (as a stenographer) and then the Illinois Department of Revenue. She worked full time, got married, had a son, and attended night school at Northwestern University. After 12 years of persistently chipping away at Northwestern's course requirements, she earned a degree from the business school and began climbing the civil service ladder, becoming an accountant and revenue auditor. Cardiss and George had been each other's primary confidants and partners, with Cardiss running George's campaigns backstage. They'd assembled the pieces of a solid life structure; with George serving in Congress and Cardiss working as a civil servant, they'd built security and a family together. Now that entire structure had collapsed.

Collins was not at all sure she wanted to leave the Illinois Department of Revenue for a radically different role in the remote world of Congress. For one thing, she was shy and reserved, comfortable in the numbers, tallies, and balance sheets; the blood sport of congressional politics didn't strike her as the best game for an introvert. Not only would she herself need to move to Washington, D.C., she'd also face a personally wrenching choice: to either pull her teenage son out of his Chicago school or leave him in the care of his grandmother. She found herself encouraged by friends and pressured by local party members to take the seat. As a person of faith ("I don't answer to anyone but Jesus," she would say of her ultimate decision), she sought spiritual guidance, and a local alliance of ministers swarmed her with urgings to fill the seat.

Reeling, confused, disoriented, uncertain, Collins had to make one of the most significant decisions of her life under time pressure while only just starting the long personal process of grieving. What if the most consequential time in your life, when you most need to talk with your life partner, comes about precisely because you've lost that person? That's what happened to Cardiss Collins, except that in her case she had to make a huge decision with all sorts of people—some well meaning, some self-interested—offering their advice. I imagine Cardiss desperately wishing she could talk it all through with George, but now she was alone.

Now let's turn to Maryon Pittman Allen, who faced a cliff remarkably similar to Cardiss Collins's. Pittman Allen and her husband, the Alabama Senator James Browning "Jim" Allen, took a vacation to their beach condominium. Getting ready for dinner, Jim stepped out of the bath and fell to the floor, hit with a heart attack. In the final moments before losing consciousness, he said to Maryon, "I'm going . . . I love you and don't ever forget that." They were the last words Maryon ever heard from the love of her life.

Like Cardiss Collins, Maryon Pittman Allen had been married for approximately 14 years when hit with the sudden, shattering cliff of losing her life partner. Like Collins, Pittman Allen had a lot of life left to figure out; in fact, Collins and Pittman Allen would each live almost exactly the same number of days after their tragic loss (14,667 days for Collins and 14,662 days for Pittman Allen). Like Collins, Pittman Allen had to decide whether to take Jim's seat in Congress amid a cacophony of voices—some well meaning and some self-serving—and she had to do so under time pressure.

"If I could have done just exactly as I pleased at that sad, sad time," reflected Pittman Allen later, "I would have gone quietly back to Washington, closed out my husband's office . . . and moved back home to Alabama. . . . I would have let the world pass me by without even a sidelong glance for at least a year. But no one ever thought to ask me what I would have liked to do." Pittman Allen found herself reeling, torn, uncertain, and desperately missing the one person she most needed to talk to, but could not. She described her pained confusion: "I went, like a thief in the night, into a big walk-in closet in our bedroom, turned on the light, closed and locked the door, buried my face in one of Jim's suits and screamed soundlessly and desperately inside me . . . 'Jim Allen, what have you done to me? You've gone off and left me with the whole damned State of Alabama going wild crazy with grief over you, and I don't know what in the hell to do about it.'"

Cardiss Collins and Maryon Pittman Allen faced a strikingly similar tragic cliff. Each needed time to grieve in her own personal way, yet each faced pressure to decide on taking her late husband's seat in Congress. Both would need to answer anew the question of what to make of their lives. Each of them would eventually reconstruct their lives, though in strikingly different ways.

Two Lives Reconstructed

Reeling from her husband's death and besieged by people pressuring her to take his seat in Congress, Cardiss Collins decided *not* to decide about the rest of her life right then. Instead, she decided to simply take one step forward. She would seek to finish George's term, just that one partial term. "It's what [George] would have wanted," she said. Collins became a member of Congress, representing the Seventh Congressional District on the West Side of Chicago. With little time to adjust, her feelings remained raw. One day, on her way into a congressional office building, she realized that she was wearing the same dress she'd worn to George's swearing in. A staffer noticed that her eyes glistened with tears.

Collins began her congressional tenure by watching and learning. "My biggest roadblock has been my shyness," she said of settling into congressional work. "I was basically an introvert, and I didn't think it was wise to make noise [around] Congress until I knew what I was doing." Step by step, she came out of her shell, tiptoeing into voicing her views. "Once people learned I had something to say," said Collins of her gradual emergence as a legislative leader, "I gained confidence." Collins earned a reputation as someone to listen to, not because she spoke a lot, but because she spoke so little, reserving her comments for the right moment of insight and impact.

Along the way, something quite unexpected happened. She found herself falling in love with the job. She decided to run outright for a second term and won nearly 90% of the vote. She stepped into sponsoring and introducing legislation, accreting credibility layer upon layer, like laying down bricks. She drew upon her accounting skills to bring disciplined financial thinking to the conversation, which led to her becoming treasurer of the Congressional Black Caucus at the start of her third term, which then led to her becoming chair of the entire Congressional Black Caucus.

The more she gained confidence, the more she came out of her shell, to the point where *The Washington Post* ran a feature story titled "The Coming Out of Cardiss Collins" that extolled her forceful leadership. She might have been reserved by nature, "quietly determined" as one colleague put it, but she also had a fighter's instinct. She reveled in a good political fight when she felt passionate about the topic. When she stepped into leadership within the Congressional Black Caucus, she went after President Carter, whom she saw as a disappointment in living up to his promises. "We will no longer befriend those who have abused our friendship," she said in a contentious speech. "We will no longer wait for political power to be shared with us. We will TAKE it!" Cardiss Collins had certainly come out of her shell!

Recall the image of a constellation of encodings that comes into frame only when the frame shifts. That's exactly what happened for Cardiss Collins. Prior to the life-splitting moment when she lost her husband, she had no inkling whatsoever that she carried within her a set of encodings that would make her an exceptionally effective member of the U.S. House of Representatives. Life had dealt her a painful blow, dropping her by tragic chance into a slot incredibly well suited to her encodings. Cardiss Collins served 12 consecutive terms in Congress, nearly a quarter century.

> Cliffs, as terrible as they can be to live through, can also reveal encodings you never knew you had. When a cliff wrenches you out of one frame and throws you into another, you might discover entirely unforeseen capabilities. The big cliffs of life force you to confront yet again the question of what to make of a life, and you might well answer the question very differently than you ever envisioned before the cliff.

And what of Maryon Pittman Allen? Pittman Allen stepped into Jim's congressional seat, and she did so for partly the same reason Collins stepped into George's: because that's what he would have wanted. Jim had asked Maryon to promise that if anything happened to him, she'd seek his seat, urging her to at least give it a chance. Like Collins, she had to enter the world of Congress without having had time to work through her personal grief. "I'm trying to do this thing with taste and dignity, I'm not sure I can do it," she said. "I feel like I'm an open, bleeding, raw, walking wound. I have to cover it all up during the day here in the Senate with a front."

However, unlike Cardiss Collins, who found that Congress lined up with a newly exposed set of encodings, Maryon Pittman Allen found herself out of frame. She hated dealing with what she called the "lusting bats" of politics who circled around looking for ways to ply her vulnerability to their own advantage. She lacked Cardiss Collins's instinct to learn and observe until she'd figured out how to be effective in the byzantine machinations of congressional work. "I have a penchant for being irreverent," she said several weeks after being sworn in. "I guess I'll have to start being dignified now. . . . The hardest thing to do is to keep your mouth shut. I never have before. Sometimes I just want to scream at some of these people and say 'you goddam idiot.' . . . [Before taking Jim's seat] I just spoke for me. Now I'm going to have to think about what I have to say." And though she knew she had to learn to be more senatorial to succeed, Pittman Allen, who had been a sharp-penned newspaper columnist, simply was not encoded for circumspection. In one memorable turn of phrase, she publicly described a political ally whom she disliked as having the persona of "a sidewalk drill."

Unlike Cardiss Collins, Maryon Pittman Allen found that she just didn't love *doing* the actual daily work, later saying she would leave politics "for those whose stomachs are lined with lead." Finally, unlike Cardiss Collins, who thrived for 283 months as a member of Congress, Pittman Allen served only about six months. After having been appointed to the seat by Alabama's governor after Jim's death, she lost a special primary election that she'd expected to win. "I had this terrible guilt about Jim's death," reflected Pittman Allen. "He died and I lived . . . so I felt compelled to play senator even though it wasn't my real calling. . . . I suppose it was some sort of punishment I had to put myself through because Jim was . . . dead."

Pittman Allen would eventually find herself beautifully in frame after the cliff, though it would take time. Initially, she returned to journalism, when Katharine Graham of *The Washington Post* asked her to write a weekly feature column, "Maryon Allen's Washington," covering politics, fashion, and society in Washington, D.C. She seemed quite well suited to the work, many of her columns landing a prominent placement in the newspaper. But as much as she loved doing the column, she never loved living in Washington, D.C. So, after nearly two years covering the D.C. scene, she decided to return to her home state of Alabama.

That's when she clicked into frame with a new hedgehog late in life, one that would tap her creativity for more than a quarter century. She had deep encodings for restoring beauty back into old things. She applied these encodings across a range of projects, from buildings to artifacts, and she developed a rare expertise in reinvigorating exquisite bridal gowns that dated back tens or even hundreds of years. "Maryon Pittman Allen can take one look at a wedding gown and know immediately the time period in which that dress was made," said one article about her work. Show her a dress from the 1800s, and she could pinpoint a date; show her a dress from the 1700s or the 1930s, and she could immediately envision its original beauty. She found her work deeply satisfying, especially when someone chose to be wed in a stunning heirloom that had been worn 50 or even 150 years before. Doing the work of restoring old things to their prior beauty fed her inner fire, and she continued doing it into her ninth decade of life.

Whereas Cardiss Collins's cliff threw her unexpectedly into frame, revealing encodings and a fire for legislating that she didn't know she had, Maryon Pittman Allen's cliff initially threw her into a world that didn't fit her encodings, and it took her longer to get back in frame.

> My compassion for people going through a cliff has increased and deepened by doing this study. To harshly judge people for "not getting their act together" quickly in the shadow of a cliff reflects a profound ignorance of the often long and arduous process of getting to the other side of a significant cliff. If your life is knocked sideways or torn asunder by a cliff, and especially if that cliff comes with mourning a loss and/or feeling the deep pain of grief, you can find yourself lost in thick, murky fog for a very long time.

Cardiss Collins and Maryon Pittman Allen emerged from the fog on the other side of the cliff in very different places because they were very different people with different encodings. They both lived through the cliff, made it through the fog, found a new hedgehog, and kept the inner fire burning for decades. Both found a way to reconstruct their lives after one of the most devastating cliffs imaginable. Each answered the question of what to make of a life after the cliff in her own way.

The Fruitless Search for a Cliffless Life

As we got deeper into the research studying pairs of people matched at a cliff, a question gnawed at me: What about people who do not have a significant cliff? Would cliffless lives show a substantially different pattern from lives with cliffs? To answer this question, my research team set out to find "non-cliff" lives to study. We conducted basic analyses on 141 candidates and culled the possibilities to 24 prime-target "non-cliff" lives. We launched headlong into constructing rigorous life timelines and analyses of the supposedly "non-cliff" lives, beginning with the first six prime candidates: labor activist Dolores Huerta, military leader George C. Marshall, Supreme Court Justice Sandra Day O'Connor, architect I. M. Pei, guitarist Carlos Santana, and fashion magnate Vera Wang.

But then the research veered to a surprising place. The more we burrowed into these lives, the more we found that *they also had cliffs!* After we culled back through the larger set of candidates, it became increasingly clear that our search for cliffless lives would fail, yielding not even a single case. Yet the effort proved valuable nonetheless. For one thing, these first six all became rich life cases that further validated and deepened our primary research findings, and I decided to retain them as an adjunct set to add even more robustness to our findings. But of even greater value: *Sometimes a non-finding is itself a finding.* That we could not find a set of cliffless lives to study, despite our extensive efforts, indicates the possibility that there is *no such thing as a life without cliffs.*

Cliffs are perhaps the most universal element in this book. Your life might not yet have taken twists and turns that brought your greatest encodings into frame. Your circumstances might make it more difficult for you to flip the arrow of money than for some other people. You might not have yet found something that you love doing so much that you'd never want to stop doing it. You might not yet have found One Big Thing on which to focus most of your inner fire. You might struggle to find meaningful ways to keep the inner fire growing ever brighter and hotter as the decades of life pass by.

> Not everyone who reads this book will get all the elements across all the chapters to click into place (though I hope they do for you), but of this I am nearly certain: You're going to have cliffs; I'm going to have cliffs; the people we love are going to have cliffs. It is very likely that some of those cliffs will force a rethink or rediscovery of what to make of a life. Perhaps you will be so lucky as to get through life without a major cliff, but I wouldn't bet on it.

The cliffs of life can take many forms, in the lives we studied and in our own lives. Here is a short list of possible cliffs that can hit a life: mourning the end of a significant relationship, experiencing a dramatic change in personal finances, dealing with a health event or diagnosis, feeling upended by a natural disaster, getting fired or laid off, seeing demand for your work/job/profession dry up, discovering that someone important is untrustworthy, reeling from a business or professional setback, losing an incredibly important person in your life, leaving behind a life-defining role or impossible-to-replicate experience, or any other version of waking up to the fact that one phase of life has come to an end.

The positive or success cliffs of life can also take many forms. Here is a short list of possible positive cliffs: crossing a major education milestone without clarity about what comes next, experiencing a spiritual or faith awakening that recasts the entire lens of life, accomplishing a life-defining goal only to wake up lost with no clear direction, achieving success only to discover that success doesn't make you happy, being showered with a life-altering financial windfall and discovering that doesn't make you happy either, successfully raising children to adulthood and sending them off into the world, getting a huge unexpected opportunity or promotion that requires a big life change, feeling an irrepressible call to service, making the decision to retire, or any other version of a "positive" event that ends one phase of life and calls for significant consideration about what comes next.

When I began doing this research project through the lens of cliff matches, I did not fully appreciate the pervasiveness of cliff events in people's lives. But the more I discussed the study with a wide range of people, the more I came to realize that cliffs appear to be a universal part of the human condition. The long arc of a life is never perfectly smooth. Look closely enough, and life is fractured, diverted, kinked, disrupted, severed, and transformed along the way. Look closer still, and people can find themselves reeling from cliffs and wandering in the fog, only to emerge in places they'd never imagined. Which brings us right to the cusp of another prevalent element of our human experience, the subject to which we now turn: *fog*.

7

Fog

The news rocked the world of entertainment: Michael J. Fox, the beloved actor who'd made millions of people laugh in television series such as *Family Ties* and movies like *Back to the Future*, had Parkinson's disease. Still exuding a youthful buoyance at age 37, he did two major interviews to make his condition public, including an extensive television conversation with Barbara Walters discussing his condition openly. He told the story of waking up in Florida, where he'd been filming the movie *Doc Hollywood*, to feel his left pinkie finger uncontrollably tapping. When the twitching simply would not go away, Fox consulted multiple doctors and eventually found his way to a neurologist, which led to his diagnosis.

With the announcement, Fox's public identity changed from Michael J. Fox the actor to Michael J. Fox the actor with Parkinson's. Fox would become a highly visible and effective spokesperson for the Parkinson's community. In the first few years after going public, he founded The Michael J. Fox Foundation for Parkinson's Research and wrote the influential memoir *Lucky Man*, making Parkinson's central to his life's story alongside his famous acting career. Over the subsequent two decades, Fox's public identity as a leading advocate continued to grow, as did the work of his foundation, which raised and funded more than $1 billion for Parkinson's research.

A cursory overview of Fox's story might look like a straight-ahead three-act play. Act 1: Fox finds a hedgehog (acting). Act 2: Fox gets hammered by a *cliff* (Parkinson's). Act 3: Fox finds a second hedgehog (founder and guiding light of The Michael J. Fox Foundation for Parkinson's Research) that gives him a new purpose. But as I worked systematically through the mountain of research materials we'd gathered on Fox (which included more than 600 articles, multiple books, video footage from a slew of interviews, and his extensive filmography), I came to see the experience of his unfolding journey as quite different from a simple one-two-three-step model. It was decidedly less clear and anything but linear. Pause and consider: How much time passed from when Fox knew he had Parkinson's to when he got clear in his mind to go public? Seven years.

Seven years.

Fox entered the fog the moment he first heard the neurologist say, "You have Parkinson's." The shock force of the words rendered everything else the neurologist said incomprehensible. Fox quipped that after the word "Parkinson's," the doctor could have said "You are a three-toed Martian and you eat squirrels" and it would have made just as much sense. He reeled in disbelief and sought a second opinion, then a third. Same result. Michael J. Fox absolutely had Parkinson's. For the next seven years, Fox wrestled in private with the implications of his disease, for his work, for his family, for how he should approach the question of what to make of the rest of his life. At one point a couple of years after his diagnosis, Fox stayed up in the middle of the night assembling pages of scribbled notes into a long, rambling personal manifesto, trying to make sense of his life. Yet he was so disoriented in the fog that he didn't even mention having Parkinson's in his self-accounting.

What is fog? Fog is when you go through a phase of immense uncertainty and lack of clarity about the best path forward, perhaps even having no clear idea where you want to go. When in the fog, you can feel confused or disoriented or unsteady or reeling—or maybe all of these. You might be expending a lot of energy in the fog, but it can feel more like wandering and stumbling than purposeful strides toward a clear destination. In the thickest fog, you can feel truly lost.

Fox moved through the fog in steps. First, deal with the drinking. In his memoir *Lucky Man*, Fox wrote openly about struggling with a drinking problem and how it became more ominous after his diagnosis. (*Lucky Man* is a beautiful book, strikingly personal and revealing, and a poignant portrait of life in the fog in the wake of a mega cliff.) In one pivotal section, he described waking up after having passed out on the couch with an open can of beer on the floor beside him, his wife fixing him with eyes that had seen versions of this reel too many times. I will leave it to Fox's memoir to own the full vivid specifics of that deeply personal moment in his life, but to me it read like a shot ringing straight through the fog to strike Fox dead center in the heart. That very day, Fox decided to stop drinking, and he sought guidance from people who could help him do that.

Parkinson's had thrown Fox into the fog, but it also sharpened the distinctions between control and non-control, between choice and acceptance, between action and equanimity. Fox could not change the fact of Parkinson's. Sure, he could mitigate symptoms and perhaps slow its advance, but he could no more control the fact that he had Parkinson's than you or I can control the fact that one day we will die. In response, Fox began to parse life into two buckets: what he could change or influence, and what he could not. He could not stop Parkinson's, but he could stop drinking. And he did.

Fox's acting career veered through "wilted salad days" of feature film disappointments and wrong turns during the first few years after his diagnosis. U.S. box office receipts for Fox's films in the first six years after his Parkinson's diagnosis fell to less than half that of the films he made in the six years prior. It was a period that Fox called "hugely frustrating."

Yet the combination of the disease and the disappointments helped Fox gain a couple of key points of clarity amid the fog. First, he began stepping away from feature films and back toward an activity that he was deeply encoded for and loved to do, comedic television series. He had a studio contract to do several films geared to capitalize on his name, but he found himself uninspired. "I'm slogging through another one of these things," he said to himself while working on one of the films. Once he'd met his obligations, he decided not to re-up his contract and to stop chasing hits. Second, he realized that he didn't want to live a life with so much time away from his family, with young children and his rock-solid life partner, Tracy Pollan. About five years after his diagnosis, Fox found himself far away from home in New Zealand working on a film and had a piercing moment of clarity: He didn't love what he was doing. "What am I doing here?" he asked himself. "I used to have this nice 9-to-5 job doing a TV series [*Family Ties*]. I loved it. I was getting paid a lot of money, and I could be home every night. I must be stupid." Fox didn't want to wake up halfway across the world in a nice hotel room; he wanted to be at home, present for the daily melee of children growing up.

Fox then made a huge step through the fog: He went full force back into a sitcom shot within walking distance of his Manhattan home, *Spin City*. It didn't matter that some people saw a return to television as a backward slide, a step down for an A-list movie actor. Fox had made a shift profoundly helpful to reducing the fog of life, a shift captured in a line in his memoir: *Whatever anyone else thinks about me is none of my business.*

Yet even with his happy turn back to television and the fog beginning to lift, Parkinson's continued to assert itself ever more. Fox compensated by timing his medications to coincide with his time on set. But tremors on his left side escalated to the point where he underwent brain surgery to calm them down. People began to whisper, rumors began to swirl, and Fox began to realize that he had no control over whether he'd lose his secret. One way or another, the fact of his disease would become public. But he could potentially control when and how, and he stepped out of the fog of secrecy.

Even then, Fox still had to work through layers of fog. He'd gone public, but *now what*? Even in the Barbara Walters broadcast and in a *People* magazine story, he didn't describe himself as being on the edge of launching an entirely new second career advocating for the Parkinson's community. He shared no grand vision about becoming a catalytic leader of a cause and igniting a national conversation about Parkinson's. The evidence leads me to conclude that any thoughts he had about becoming the founding leader of a foundation for Parkinson's research were quite nascent, if they were there at all. He hoped to extend his *Spin City* gig from five years to seven years, and he planned to just keep on acting for years to come. He told Walters he expected that a cure would be found within about a decade. After that, he planned to live the rest of his life without the disease.

Parkinson's, of course, had other ideas.

While Fox would not find himself cured within a decade (or even by the time I'm writing these words), he found something else: a community. It began to dawn on him that he could choose to play a very special role giving voice to the Parkinson's community. Fox found himself beginning to emerge from the fog in a very different place than he'd planned. He joined a Parkinson's chat room anonymously, reading comments from members of the community as they shared what his coming-out meant to them and the powerful impact of his visibility. Fox later recalled one impactful vignette from a person who shared the experience of going through a checkout line: "I went to the market this morning and the cashier asked me why my hand was shaking. I told her it was Parkinson's, and she was really interested. 'Oh, just like Michael J. Fox.' For the first time in years, I didn't feel embarrassed." Stories like these started to change Fox's entire ethos, and he began taking steps from simply "going public" to becoming an active spokesperson for the community. Then he began to use his name, humor, infectious personality, and irrepressible optimism to raise money to fund research toward better treatments and ultimately a cure. In short, he was finding himself drawn into a new frame as his entire life shifted sideways and exposed big bright encodings that might have otherwise remained undiscovered had it not been for the disease.

Within two years of going public, he'd retired from *Spin City*, making it through four seasons rather than the seven he'd voiced hope for in the Barbara Walters interview. He founded The Michael J. Fox Foundation, and he began to write *Lucky Man*. Only remnants of fog remained, which was more about *how* to best serve the community through the foundation than about whether it would be a significant focus of his life. He would continue to do some television acting, often in guest roles. "I can play anyone," said Fox, "as long as they have Parkinson's." But he'd found a new big thing that fit his encodings and he refocused his inner fire, dedicating a huge portion of himself to his role in the Parkinson's community.

Not only did Fox contribute mightily to the community, but being part of the community contributed to Fox, feeding his inner fire even as he struggled with the daily pain of living with the disease. He even called Parkinson's a gift (though he added a huge qualifier: It's a gift that keeps on taking). "If I walked into a room with God or Buddha or Bill Gates or Sergey Brin or whoever could figure out a way to fix it for me," reflected Fox in an interview more than two decades after his diagnosis, "I don't think I'd do it."

I don't mean to suggest here that I came to see getting Parkinson's as somehow a "good thing" for people; I would not wish Parkinson's on anyone. The point here is that fog tends to follow cliffs, and that it can take a long time to work through the fog to reframe and reconstruct life after a cliff. Fox's clarity and acceptance did not happen in one big step. It didn't follow a linear path. It didn't flow from a well-formulated plan. It happened in years of zigzag steps and dawning realizations and organic evolution. "I couldn't say, 'Yeah, I went here and I went here and I went there. I climbed the mountain and I saw the wise man and he told me the answer and now I know it and now

I'll share it with you,'" explained Fox. "It was much more of a wandering journey."

Maurice White: Exiting the Fog in a Different Place

Let's now turn to Fox's matched-pair companion in the study, a spectacular performing artist who also hit the terrible cliff of Parkinson's disease, tumbled into the fog, and then emerged from the fog beautifully in frame and generously giving of his encodings—but in a very different place.

Like Michael J. Fox, Maurice White had enjoyed a hugely successful performing career before early-onset Parkinson's. The band he founded and led, Earth, Wind & Fire, sold more than 90 million albums, garnered 18 Grammy nominations (winning six), and earned a spot in the Rock & Roll Hall of Fame. As I watched a video of the song "September," I couldn't help but wonder what it must have been like to be able to perform like Maurice White, his rhythm, his movements, his stage presence, his voice, his blending with the band, his rapturous joy at moving thousands upon thousands of people to swing and sway and dance and snap their fingers and tap their feet together. When the video ended, I could not help but feel a shot of pain thinking about Parkinson's etching away White's performing capabilities.

White would also lose the experience of delivering exquisite concert moments with his bandmates, holding center stage as 12 musicians blended together into one single harmonious instrument of rhythm and sound. White gave his blessing to the band going on without him, honoring the enduring vitality of the music that could continue to inspire long after he left the stage. Still, I wonder what it must have felt like to be left at home while the band toured, never again to feel those magic moments. "To stand backstage with your comrades-in-arms as the houselights go down and 20,000-plus ear-deafening screaming people stand up—now, that's a huge rush and a strong bonding element," White wrote late in his life. "I miss that feeling to this day."

Maurice White and Michael J. Fox found out they had Parkinson's within months of each other, in 1991. Like Fox, White found himself reeling in stunned disbelief when he heard the words "You have Parkinson's," especially because he'd assiduously lived in strict adherence to a healthy lifestyle. He didn't drink. He didn't take drugs. He didn't smoke. He practiced yoga. He exercised consistently. He practiced meditation. He took vitamins. He ate meticulously. He dined on tofu, snacked on fresh fruit, drank carrot juice, and became a connoisseur of vegetables. He preferred to get a good night's sleep while on tour, rather than going out to enjoy the hedonistic pleasures offered on the after-gig party circuit. He centered himself in the sanctuary of his mountaintop retreat in Carmel Valley, where he could work in reclusive tranquility. And throughout, he'd dedicated himself to the pursuit of a spiritual life anchored in the belief that he and his life's work owed to trusting a higher power that he referred to as the Creator. So, after decades of healthy living infused with a deeply spiritual practice, White found himself "blindsided" to discover that a disease completely out of his control would shape much of the rest of his life.

Like Michael J. Fox, Maurice White did not go public about his disease for more than seven years. And like Fox, White found himself in the fog, what he later described as entering a wilderness of his mind. At first, he continued to tour with the band, determined to keep Parkinson's locked away in a box. But the disease continued its relentless progression. White's performances began to suffer, and he wrestled with questions. Should he leave the band? Should he shut down the band altogether? Should he give his blessing for the band to flourish without him? Earth, Wind & Fire, after all, was his creation and had been his central identity for nearly a quarter century. In fact, the very name of the band derived from White's personal astrological chart, on which a reading showed White to have only three of the four primary elements—earth, air, and fire, but no water. Could Earth, Wind & Fire thrive without Maurice White? Could Maurice White thrive (to the extent Parkinson's would allow) without Earth, Wind & Fire?

Finally, after fraught conversations with members of the band, the fog cleared enough for White to see that the band could go on without him, and that it was time to step away. People all over the world still loved the music, and they would continue to love the music—not just the recordings, but in live performance. Amazingly, as I sit here three decades after White confronted the brutal fact that Parkinson's had eroded his ability to tour, Earth, Wind & Fire continues to tour. And of sheer delight to me, I discovered that young people on my team who'd not even been born when White stepped away know and love songs like "September" and "Shining Star."

Still, the fog of secrecy shrouded White's life. When the Rock & Roll Hall of Fame elected to induct Earth, Wind & Fire, White wasn't sure he wanted to attend the ceremony. Think about that for a moment. Imagine that the band you created is being inducted into an iconic pantheon, but you're unsure if you even want to go. If he went, he felt he could not perform the way people expected, and if he didn't perform, he'd have to give a reason, and that reason was Parkinson's. His brother (also in the band) helped him get clear on the decision: White had to attend the ceremony. It was time to go public.

In his hotel room, White perused a newspaper account of the hall of fame ceremonial evening. A few paragraphs into the article, he hit a sentence that began, "Maurice White, who recently disclosed his battle with Parkinson's disease." He recognized it as a moment of crossover, after which his life would never be the same. In his memoir, White gave a powerful description of that precise instant, a vivid image of what it can feel like to be standing at a cliff-induced fracture point: "Seeing those words in print was like looking into two mirrors that face each other and reflect into infinity, leaving me nowhere to hide."

Maurice White emerged from the fog in a very different place from Michael J. Fox. He initially considered getting involved as a public figure to raise funds for Parkinson's research and to increase awareness of the disease. Instead, he chose to remain focused on music. For White, he always viewed *the music itself* as a form of healing and growth. Long before Parkinson's asserted itself in his life, White said, "I see our music as medicine." Not as medicine in the traditional sense, but as medicine for the soul, an antidote to living in a negative and cynical society increasingly devoid of spiritual meaning.

White had always sought to build Earth, Wind & Fire into more than just a successful band. He wanted to build a visionary band with a higher purpose. "I wanted our music to convey messages of universal love and harmony without force-feeding listeners spiritual content," said White of his guiding philosophy. "I wanted to create a library of music that would stand the test of time. . . . Expanding awareness and uplifting spirits is so important in this day." Whereas Fox moved into a new life largely defined by his commitment to the Parkinson's community, White reembraced his life defined by music and how music could be used to *elevate* people in a dispiriting age—to "Keep Your Head to the Sky" as captured in a seminal Earth, Wind & Fire title.

Even though White could no longer tour and perform, he could work in the studio, writing songs and arranging music for the band and for others. He could also serve as an executive and creative producer. He built a recording studio and invested in his own record label, Kalimba Productions. He worked on reinterpretations and extensions of Earth, Wind & Fire music with cover artists and a Broadway musical. He worked with young creatives, feeding his energy into the ever evolving mosaic of jazz- and R&B-infused music. White had committed himself to music by his early 20s, and he remained committed to music as a central focus of his life for more than five decades, while adjusting as best he could to age and Parkinson's.

Michael J. Fox and Maurice White emerged on the other side of the fog in very different places because they were very different people with different encodings and different answers to the question of what fed the inner fire. White would have likely been both unhappy and ineffective if he'd tried to do what Fox did, just as Fox would have been unhappy and ineffective trying to do what White did. On the last day of his life, not long after his 74th birthday, White and the writer Herb Powell talked, as they did often while collaborating on White's compelling and revealing memoir, *My Life with Earth, Wind & Fire*. In the last conversation they ever had together, they talked about what remained the animating force and primary ethos of White's life: *music*. Right to the end, there was always the music.

Fog Is Not a Defect

Let's step back to cull out one of the most important lessons from this study: Fog can descend on anyone, even those who attain piercing clarity in other phases of life.

Michael J. Fox showed remarkable clarity and dedication to One Big Thing (acting) from quite early in his life. He began to discover his love and encodings for acting even before age 16. In drama class and theater, he displayed a remarkable propensity to immerse himself in a character, memorize lines with ease, and make people laugh. At age 16, he landed his first television role, in the Canadian Broadcasting Corporation series *Leo and Me*. At age 17, he persuaded his parents to let him drop out of high school to pursue an acting career. In a stunningly supportive parental step, his father drove young Michael from Vancouver to Hollywood, under the theory that if you're going to be a lumberjack, you'd better go to the forest. Fox spent about three years as a struggling actor in Hollywood, cobbling together a series of small roles. He lived in a tiny apartment. The phone company cut off his service. He even began selling off his furniture, at one point selling off chunks of his sectional sofa, piece by piece, just to keep going. Yet he persisted until, finally, he landed the role as Alex P. Keaton in the television series *Family Ties*. With his creative flywheel beginning to spin, Fox had no doubt that acting would remain the central vocation of his life.

Similarly, Maurice White began to discover his love and encodings for One Big Thing before age 20, and by his early 20s he unequivocally committed himself to music. When White made the commitment to go all in on creating a life in music, he struggled just to eat. He later reflected in his memoir, "No money, many days hungry, I was dropping weight. . . . Every day I would go down to this Greek restaurant. . . . They had this great deal: pita bread, some veggies, and a piece of meat, all for $1. I ate that way for a few months, one meal a day, one dollar a day." White worked his way out of scarcity within a couple of years (ages 21 to 22), getting ever more steady work as a drummer. Even so, it would take another six years before he would create the band Earth, Wind & Fire (at age 28) and another few years with three marginally successful albums to finally release a first hit album (at age 31). Yet throughout, he had unwavering dedication to a life in music. After he founded Earth, Wind & Fire—almost like creating a perfect instrument for himself—White enjoyed years of absolute clarity that leading the band would be the primary activity of his life.

How many people do you know who'd become so clear before even turning 18 that they could persuade their parents to support dropping out of high school to pursue something with incredibly low odds of success, as Michael J. Fox did? How many people do you know who'd remain so resolutely dedicated to a path that they'd persist through years of struggle and rejection to eventually succeed at it? How many people do you know who became so clear about their life choice that they'd be willing to survive on one meal a day until they got the flywheel turning in order to pursue it? How many people do you know who throw themselves so fully into a hedgehog that they're willing to pay such a high level of Stress and Drudgery Tax? How many people do you know who not only made an unwavering commitment to a hedgehog by age 21 but also developed an entire life philosophy to infuse into their work before age 30, as Maurice White did?

The point here is that both Fox and White demonstrated a capability for resolute clarity and commitment that showed up early in their lives. Yet even with this ability, they later found themselves wandering in the fog when reeling from a cliff.

Here in this study, we have a bevy of impressive and accomplished people, and they also had episodes of fog. Some went through relatively brief and wispy episodes, but others spent years wandering through thick layers of fog. Sometimes they knew the next mountain they wanted to climb but felt uncertain of the route; others had no idea what the next mountain should be, or even whether they wanted to be in the mountains at all.

> *Fog is not a defect.* Fog is not a character flaw. Fog is not rare. Fog is normal, natural, common, and highly prevalent. Fog can descend in youth, in midlife, in later years. And in the wake of a cliff, the fog can envelop us in murk so thick that we can see only one or two steps ahead. Even the most successful, capable, energetic, ambitious, and otherwise clearheaded and self-directed people can find themselves in a major fog funk.

Have you ever felt lost in the fog? Have you ever gone through a time of life when you're unclear or confused or befuddled or disoriented or uncertain or reeling? Have you ever felt as if you were wandering and stumbling? Have you ever felt pressure or impatience (from yourself or others) to "figure it out and get on with it" and where that pressure only increases the anxiety because you know you're in the fog without a sharply drawn map or definitive plan for how to get beyond it? I've been in the fog more than once in my life, quite thick fog, and I imagine I might one day be in the fog again. Perhaps you or someone you love is in the fog right now.

I've noted how this research profoundly changed me and what I think about how life works. And one of the most significant transformations is my appreciation for the inevitable fog of life. Fog, I came to understand, is a common human experience, even for people who otherwise seem to have great clarity about what to make of their lives. And if episodes of fog enveloped *even people in this study*, none of us should judge ourselves harshly when we wake up one day to find ourselves befuddled and confused in the fog.

The Many Forms of Fog

While fog almost inevitably follows major cliffs, it can also roll in with smaller cliffs and at other points in life. Here are four forms of fog that can roll in:

- Fog of youth
- Fog of disappointment
- Fog of success
- Fog of retirement

FOG OF YOUTH

While some of the people in our study found a clear path quite early, others had a somewhat foggy phase in their teens and 20s. Even someone as clear and resolute as Alice Paul (once she found herself committed to the fight for suffrage) had a somewhat fog-filled wandering phase in her youth. In college at Swarthmore, she majored in biological sciences, a field she never seriously pursued after graduation. After college, she went to New York to do social work related to labor issues and study at the New York School of Philanthropy. After living in New

York for a year or so, she entered graduate school at the University of Pennsylvania, thinking she might pursue an academic/teaching career. She then completed a master's degree. There is some discrepancy in the sources as to whether her master's was in sociology or political inquiry, but either way she embarked on a vector quite divergent from biology! She then traveled abroad, first in Germany, then on to England, where she studied at the London School of Economics. Biology, social work, economics . . . where was young Alice Paul going? What was all this wandering exploration adding up to?

Paul took her first steps toward fighting for suffrage in England, when she joined protests organized by the militant suffragist Emmeline Pankhurst, which led to her meeting Lucy Burns in jail, joining a hunger strike, and being force-fed. But even then, Alice Paul had not fully emerged from the fog of youth. Upon her return to the United States, she pinged back to an academic path, completing a PhD in economics. Was she going to become a professor of economics or a teacher or a practicing economist or a social worker or a writer, or . . . what exactly?

Yet while intently exploring in the fog of youth, Alice Paul kept taking steps that led her toward activism for suffrage. She spoke at a suffrage convention about her experiences in England. She joined the Congressional Committee of the National American Woman Suffrage Association. At age 28, she took a big step when she helped architect a suffrage parade the day before Woodrow Wilson's first presidential inauguration, a seminal moment that revealed her encodings for quiet, fearless leadership and a penchant for crafting spectacles of protest. She also began to show what would be one of her most distinctive leadership encodings: strategic insight. Paul had an impressive ability to see with piercing clarity the grand strategies that would lead to victory. In particular, she saw that the best strategy lay in pursuit of a constitutional amendment, rather than seeking suffrage state by state, and she co-founded with Lucy Burns the Congressional Union for Woman Suffrage dedicated to that strategy. Finally, after years of iterative steps, Alice Paul emerged on the other side of the fog with an absolute commitment of her entire being to the cause of suffrage.

Now consider: How long did Alice Paul take to emerge from the fog of youth? If we take entering college as the starting point, the wandering journey to her first direct work on suffrage took about six years, then another three years before she fully committed to suffrage as the all-consuming primary focus in her life.

> Alice Paul shows that the fog of youth can swirl around for years, even for those who later become utterly obsessed with and committed to One Big Thing. If you're young and feel lost in the fog (or if you're the parent of youth lost in the fog), I urge keeping in mind the case of Alice Paul. Yes, some people find a clear, resolute path very early in life and spend little time in the fog of youth. But many others wander in the fog of youth for years before they find themselves clicking into frame with something they are encoded for and that draws the full focus of their inner fire.

I've frequently been asked what role parents played in our study subjects getting through the fog of youth and finding a hedgehog. Were their parents helpful and supportive? Did they give guidance or direction? How did they respond when our study subjects discovered encodings that veered toward a path that diverged from parental hopes and expectations? The evidence is mixed, though more than half tilted toward support and encouragement. On the supportive side, Toni Morrison's parents encouraged her love of books from a young age; later, her father worked two jobs and her mother worked as a washroom attendant to help pay for Morrison to attend college to get a degree in English literature. Yet we also observed cases when well-meaning parents did not support the pursuit of a path that veered away from their hopes and expectations. Recall Robert Plant's parents' exasperation with him running around the Midlands with John Bonham in pursuit of music gigs and how they tried to get him to become something they deemed more respectable, like an accountant. Similarly with John Glenn's parents' lack of enthusiasm for his passionate desire to be an aviator, preferring instead that he join the family business.

My conclusion, based on the evidence we do have, is that parents encouraging young people to follow their encodings might be helpful. But the evidence also shows that parental support and encouragement are not absolute requirements. In fact, well-meaning parents and mentors can actually increase the fog of youth if they encourage or drive young people away from their encodings. Far more important than parental support is trusting one's encodings when they pop into frame, regardless of what your parents (or other well-meaning adults) might encourage, support, demand, hope, expect, or impose.

The heir to a family business empire once asked me to help him think about building it into an enduring great company. At the time, he was in his early 30s, having assumed active leadership only a few years earlier.

One day we had a conversation that went something like this:

"At what age did you know you would inherit leadership of your family empire?" I asked out of curiosity.

"By age four or five," he replied. "I'm like a prince who was destined to become king."

"That's really different from my life experience," I said, reflecting on how my own father neglected me and never had any expectations for me of any kind. Oddly, this made me feel *fortunate*, not deprived. I might have lacked the family heir's wealth and resources, but I had complete *freedom* to paint on a blank canvas and to shape my life without burdensome family expectations. He did not. We each drew very different family cards at the start of life, and it was not at all clear to me that he got the better draw.

> What if your parents have expectations for what you are supposed to do and become from early in your life, but their expectations do not fit with your encodings? What if following the expectations of your family knocks your life out of frame, and sends you into the fog? What if those expectations prolong the fog so that it lasts not just years but maybe decades? Or maybe even your entire life? Your encodings are your encodings, regardless of what your parents or anyone else thinks they or you should be. And the task, first and foremost, is to trust your own encodings.

I always had the sense that my friend the business prince would have loved to have been a philosopher, maybe even a professor of philosophy. He'd studied classics in college and philosophy at grad school, and he could lose himself for hours in reading, studying, thinking. He once dedicated a year of his free time to systematically reading James Joyce's *Ulysses*, toggling between the text and the underlying references to philosophy and literature Joyce layered into the work. Plato's *Republic* held more sway in his thinking about management than the books assigned in business school. The Aristotle-inspired ideal of human flourishing struck him as a more meaningful aspiration than maximizing business profits. He was a very smart and effective businessman, but perhaps he could have become a truly great professor of philosophy. Yet he did not feel entirely free to dedicate his life to philosophy. I remember thinking that while he had been given the keys to the kingdom, they could just as much be keys to a gilded prison.

But there is a beautiful coda to this story. Decades later, as we corresponded about the findings in this book, he circled back to that earlier conversation to remind me that much of our work together had been about how to lead the company as an expression of his encodings (even though we didn't have the language for it at the time). When we first met, he was somewhat in the fog of youth, trying to reconcile his family's expectations around the business with his love and encodings for philosophy. He was searching for a way to meld them together. He emerged from the fog clear in his mind to define the core purpose of the company in terms of ideals he learned studying Plato and other philosophers. He rejected conventional business school dogma that the purpose of a company is to maximize shareholder wealth, replacing it with the purpose *to provide a place for people to flourish and to enhance the community*. To be clear, the company would also seek to grow profits and generate robust cash flow, but mainly as a necessary *means* to fuel the core purpose. In the subsequent three decades, he did indeed blend the two elements together, philosophical purpose and business success reinforcing each other. His mother even gave him a business card with "Philosopher King" as his internal title.

"I managed to REFRAME the situation, recognize my activities and environment such that my encodings came into frame," he commented in linking the findings in this book to his own journey through a fog that lasted for years when he first took over the company. The result, he concluded, was a hedgehog that has lasted now more than three decades. If he'd never wrestled with the fundamental tension between his encodings and family expectations, he might never have exited the fog. But he did wrestle. He did reframe. He did fall in love with building the company. He did exit the fog. And the fire within only grew as the decades passed.

FOG OF DISAPPOINTMENT

Every person in our study, no matter how successful, experienced disappointments. They made mistakes and missteps. They endured setbacks. They went down dead-ends. Sometimes the zeitgeist flowed in their favor, and sometimes the zeitgeist veered in another direction. Sometimes they experienced public disappointments, and sometimes they lived through deeply painful personal ones. Sometimes these disappointments came early, adding to the fog of youth, and sometimes they came later. And sometimes disappointment came not in the form of outright failure but as befuddling disappointment *relative* to expectations.

Let's return to Maurice White. Before his Parkinson's cliff, White traversed a particularly foggy patch triggered by the whipsaw of the success-disappointment cycle.

In his 30s, White enjoyed the upward climb of Earth, Wind & Fire as it grew into one of the most popular bands of the 1970s, selling out concerts and cranking out a string of hugely successful albums. White invested heavily in making spectacularly memorable stage performances and expensive stage illusions. In one stage sequence, humanoid creatures in what appear to be helmeted space suits replaced band members one by one, sending the band members away into a giant pyramid onstage, as the band rocked out the lyrics "we've got to get away" until only the rhythm players remained. Then the pyramid lifted off the stage, while these strange creatures watched and waved goodbye, the pyramid floating upward. Then—bang!—the pyramid exploded. The humanoids then removed their helmets, revealing that they'd transformed into the departed band members. The crowd went wild. White just kept upping the ante of each spectacle, even hiring a world-renowned magician to create more effects. My favorite image is of a guitarist levitating above the stage in the middle of a performance. White had built a powerful creative and business flywheel, each tour creating cash to reinvest into the next album and the next spectacular tour, then the next, and the next.

But then the music landscape changed. In the early 1980s, Earth, Wind & Fire's brand of music, which had fit perfectly with the zeitgeist of the 1970s, fell out of favor with the rise of rap and hip-hop. Despite putting out what White saw as some of the band's best work, the flywheel slowed. Earth, Wind & Fire's album *Faces* achieved gold status, but not platinum. White took it as a huge commercial disappointment. "I was shell-shocked. Stunned," he reflected.

White began rushing out new music, only to experience another spate of disappointment. Reeling and disoriented, he made an impulsive decision to end the band and go solo. But then his first solo album proved to be a commercial disappointment. Earth, Wind & Fire then came back together. White had made clear and disciplined decisions guided by his spiritual philosophy during the band's ascent, but the streak of disappointments enveloped him in fog. White described in his memoir that these "so-called failures" threw him out of whack, creating a feeling that he had to prove himself all over again. For a time, before he re-centered himself, he even lost trust in the higher power that he'd always seen as a guiding force in his work.

> White's case highlights the danger of becoming addicted to the success cycle. If your identity and ego become wrapped up in the success that comes from what you do, you can set yourself up for quite a foggy period when disappointment breaks the success cycle. And, unless you are a statistical outlier, a singular case of one that I have yet to see either in my research or in life, you will absolutely experience disappointments, no matter how successful you become.

I use the phrase "fog of disappointment" rather than "fog of failure" to capture the idea that fog flows from the *mismatch* between hopeful expectations and how life *actually* unfolds. And as it turns out, this mismatch can work in the other direction as well, when success outcomes vastly exceed expectations and hopes, which can throw people right into the fog of success.

FOG OF SUCCESS

This study crystallized another form of fog, a surprising one: the fog of success. What do you do after succeeding with the 19th Amendment? What do you do after you've already won a championship, or risen to the top of the great aviator ziggurat, or built one of the most successful bands, or won an Oscar or Emmy or Grammy? What do you do after a Nobel Prize? There is even a term, "the Nobel Curse," that (in various renditions) refers to the disorienting life change of winning the prize. Even though Toni Morrison had started writing a new novel before she learned of her Nobel Prize (and therefore had a distinct project to return to), she nonetheless described struggling to get clear in her post-prize writing: "After the Nobel Prize I had to struggle—that was a mighty battle for me . . . you've won this money, and you've won this prize, and that word will never leave my name. It will always be Toni Morrison Nobel, forever, forever." Success need not be at the epic levels achieved by the people in this study to be disorienting. Any career-defining accomplishment or significant achievement that breaks life into "before and after" is a cliff. It's a good cliff, but a cliff nonetheless. And with a cliff comes fog.

> If you're so focused on getting to the top of the mountain that you've been unable to seriously consider what comes after, then you can reach the top of the mountain, only to find it shrouded in fog. If your answer to the question of what to make of a life has been about a specific goal—and then you actually achieve that goal—you might face an existential conundrum: *So now what, now what's the point?*

This can be particularly disorienting if you thought success would make you eternally happy or fill your life with meaning, only to discover that it does neither. Achieving success or accomplishing a huge goal (whether personal or public) does not answer the question of what to make of a life. In fact, it can have the exact *opposite* effect, forcing the question back to the center of your existence, to be addressed anew.

In my previous research into the question of what makes great companies tick, my colleagues and I observed a prevalent precursor to corporate decline: the post-BHAG stall. BHAG (pronounced "bee-hag") stands for "Big Hairy Audacious Goal." In *Built to Last*, Jerry Porras and I discovered the power of having a BHAG to galvanize an organization, acting as a powerful mechanism to stimulate progress. But we *also* discovered that companies can become adrift and on the verge of decline after achieving the BHAG. To avoid this trap, a company needs to have an enduring reason for being (its core purpose) that acts like a star on the horizon, forever chased but never reached no matter how many goals the company achieves. When it comes to individual lives rather than companies, a similar idea applies. Only in this research, I would replace the concept of organizational purpose with being in a personal hedgehog, being so fully in frame and full of fire that even success can't stop you from desperately wanting to continue doing it *for its own sake*.

When I look at the people in this study, I'm struck by how many of them became less purely success- and goal-driven as their lives evolved, yet their inner fire seemed only to grow and expand. Think back to Robert Plant going off to the Festival in the Desert and later forgoing the billion-dollar Led Zeppelin reunion tour. Think back to Barbara McClintock feeling that it is almost unfair to receive a Nobel Prize for doing something that gave her so much joy in the daily doing. Think back to Tenley Albright dedicating less than two percent of her bio to winning a gold medal. Think back to Michael J. Fox letting go of superstar feature film status to be closer to his family and returning to his love of doing sitcom (*whatever anyone else thinks about me is none of my business*). Think back to Maurice White re-centering his life to what would always be his encoded reason for being: doing music that elevates the human spirit.

Just because you've achieved success doesn't mean your encodings have expired. If part of the answer to the question of what to make of a life is to continually discover and deploy encodings in a direction that feeds the inner fire, then success (in whatever form and level) is simply more of a by-product that happens along the way. When we forget that, success itself can be a catalyst for fog.

FOG OF RETIREMENT

While working on this chapter, I had a chance conversation with someone who'd retired a few years earlier. As I described the study and some of the findings, he suddenly realized, "Oh my, that's where I've been for the last few years. I retired, and ever since I've been in the fog! Now I have a name for what I've been feeling." He expressed relief to know that the people in our study also had episodes of fog, that fog is not something to be embarrassed about. Then he wondered if it was too late for him (in his mid-60s) to get out of the fog. To which, based on the findings of this study, I replied, "Mid-60s? Oh, you're still young!"

We found scant evidence that the people in our study had an explicit goal of working until a target retirement age to be followed by a life dominated by leisure. The vast majority of people in this study remained engaged in some permutation of a hedgehog well past the age of 60, in some cases into their 70s, 80s, even 90s. That said, nearly half the people in our study had a "retirement" from one hedgehog partway through their lives and faced the challenge of transitioning to the next one. Sometimes these were relatively smooth transitions, such as Tenley Albright's shift from skating to surgery. In other cases, such as John Glenn's decade-long, iterative journey from astronaut to senator, the transitions proved bumpier and more fog filled.

> My point here is not to judge the wisdom of retirement but to point out that retirement can be a cliff. For some, it can be a welcome cliff, for others an unwelcome cliff, for some a voluntary cliff, for others an involuntary cliff, for some a smooth and planned cliff, for others a shockingly unexpected cliff. But whatever form it takes, retirement for many is a huge life cliff. And as we have learned in this chapter, thick fog often follows big cliffs.

While working on this chapter, I received an email from a friend with the subject header: "I'm retired. . . . Now what??" This friend had been immersed as a heralded CEO for more than a decade, having led a spectacularly successful turnaround of a famous American company. He'd been so deeply immersed in his CEO role that he'd not had a chance to prepare for the moment. Suddenly he faced a foggy landscape, made all the more confusing by people urging him to join boards, to take another CEO role, to teach, to write a memoir, and so forth. Upon reading his email, I called him right away and shared the fog finding. "Be careful," I offered. "You're in the fog." When he asked what I thought he should do, I replied that he should be wary of directive advice from anyone, including me. However, I did offer one key lesson from the research: *When you're lost in the fog, avoid big irreversible decisions.*

Imagine being lost in the fog and deciding to run full tilt in some direction because, well, you just so badly want to be out of the fog. "I hate this feeling of being in the fog, and I've just got to get out of it," you say to yourself. "So, I'm just going to do a big leap to get out of it as fast as possible." But there's a problem: *When you're in the fog, you can't see clearly!* You might simply end up running in circles, crashing headlong into trees, tripping over boulders, maybe even hurtling yourself off another cliff and ending up even deeper in the fog.

The Bug Book

Before we leave this chapter, I'd like to share with you a tool I created to navigate through the fog of youth and that I still draw upon today as I navigate through the foggy terrain of life. It's called the bug book.

When I was in my mid-20s, I'd taken a job at the Hewlett-Packard Company (HP) and, though I didn't have the language for it at the time, sensed that I was out of frame. I'd made the mistake of listening to well-intentioned advice from my professors, who suggested that getting practical experience at a great company would be a wise step. I loved the values that Bill Hewlett and David Packard stood for, but

I felt miscast inside a large company working on software for personal computers. I knew early that while I respected HP and felt grateful for the opportunity, I'd never flourish there. So, at the suggestion of Rochelle Myers, who'd co-created the creativity course at the Stanford Graduate School of Business, I decided to use working at HP as a personal laboratory to study myself, or more precisely, to study myself like a bug.

I bought one of those lab notebooks commonly used in high school and college science classes, the ones with both horizontal and vertical lines dividing up each page. I wrote "Jim" on the front of the lab notebook, not to designate that the book is owned by Jim but that the *subject* under study is Jim. And I began making notes about "the bug called Jim." I made dispassionate clinical notes, like a scientist making precise observations about a bug moving about in a lab container. I would note things like my utter incapacity to endure with enthusiasm meetings that could have been half as long and twice as productive. I noted that I lacked the political instinct to be more discreet in pointing out people's logical inconsistencies; it simply didn't occur to me that being right doesn't matter if you offend people by asking a series of questions that trap them in a corner. I'd note that I was much more curious about the grand history of how Hewlett and Packard started and built a company than I was about how to work within the immediate confines of HP. I found myself interested in observing how Bruce Woolpert, a great division manager, got people to want to do their very best work (so interested, in fact, that I would later partner with one of my best students to create a case study on Woolpert to use in my Stanford course).

Yet I found myself utterly uninterested in how the career ladder at HP worked. I simply never gave a thought to the idea of moving up the hierarchy, especially because bigger jobs meant even more political acumen that I so clearly lacked. I'd note my natural capacity for creative thought in the morning hours (and my chafing at those creative hours being consumed by interruptions, meetings, and chitchat).

I noticed my natural capacity for refreshing midday naps that would give me a highly productive "second morning" in the late afternoon, along with the observation that daily corporate life didn't lend itself to my "first morning, followed by midday nap, followed by second morning" mode of work. I also started tracking the quality of my days relative to the activities in those days, making notes about what makes a really good day (the types of days I'd like to fill my life with) and what makes for bad days.

> The key to the bug book lies in trying to be like a scientist of the self. A scientist studying a bug doesn't judge the bug—the scientist doesn't say "good little bug" or "bad little bug" or "hey, bug, I don't like the way you look" or "bug, you should have eight legs, not six" or any other harsh or adulatory judgment. The scientist simply records, "Interesting, the bug has six legs, four long legs and two short legs at 90-degree angles," or other details.

I carried my bug book with me all the time, making notes when I'd notice things about the bug named Jim. Then, one day, I had a turning point in discovering my encodings. I was asked to research, learn, and teach the team about networked personal computing and its strategic implications for HP. I became enthralled with researching and trying to understand something big and new. And even more, I found myself entranced with the challenge of how to convert my understanding into digestible concepts. I'd started to discover an encoding that would animate me for the rest of my life: the ability to take a mass of information and make sense of it, to go from "chaos to concept." Then came the day of epiphany, when I got to share my learnings with our internal team. I discovered that I had a peculiar capability for packaging and teaching the concepts to other people in ways that would stick. I made copious notes in the bug book about the experience, and I discovered something essential: The bug named

Jim was made to research, learn, make sense of things, wrap concepts, build frameworks of understanding, and then teach for impact. I didn't have the language for it at the time, but that experience brought some of my own encodings into frame.

Shortly thereafter, my life changed when Joanne won the Ironman World Championship, and I quit my job to spend three years focused almost entirely on supporting her athletic career and negotiating her sponsor relationships with Nike and other companies. Yet throughout, I kept making notes in the bug book, and the more I observed, the more I knew with certainty that I was encoded to research, think, write, and teach. And I kept making small steps in that direction, writing some articles. I also began reading and thinking a lot about the question of how great companies get started and how they operate. Then, at age 30, I got the opportunity to teach at the Stanford Graduate School of Business, which then led to doing the research for the book *Built to Last* with Jerry Porras, and I was on my way, never to look back. I'd navigated to a life in frame, and I attribute much of that to the bug book.

To this day, I continue to use a permutation of a bug book, though it has evolved into a systematic spreadsheet that I update daily. Each evening, before I fall asleep, I open a spreadsheet and insert three sets of information. First, I detail the ingredients of the day, how I spent my time. Second, I note how many "creative hours" I got into the day, which I track to ensure that they're kept above 1,000 per every 365-day cycle (to sustain my rhythm of creative work). Third, I note the quality of the day, a score of how the day felt, on a plus-two, plus-one, zero, minus-one, minus-two scale. I also make notes when I get a plus-two day or a minus-two day about *why* the day proved exceptionally positive or exceptionally negative. Over time, I'm able to do sorts and correlations. What makes for plus-two days (super-positive days)? What makes for minus-two days (super-negative days)? What is the pattern? What changes can I make to get more plus-two and plus-one days and fewer minus-one and minus-two days? Forty years after

I started the bug book, I remain a "scientist of the self" and continue to make dispassionate observations about the bug named Jim.

To be clear, I'm not suggesting that you should necessarily adopt the bug book. It worked for me, and it might not work for you. I share it to show a bit of my own wandering journey through the foggy terrain of life, and how I built my own idiosyncratic mechanism of self-knowledge. I leave it to you to develop your own mechanisms for navigating the fog.

A Compass in the Fog

I'd like you to conjure the image of a compass that you're carrying with you as you move through the fog. Only instead of the normal north-east-south-west directions on the compass, you have a lens framed by the hedgehog elements. The fundamental answer to "What's on the other side of the fog?" is essentially the same answer from the first half of this book: discover and deploy encodings, flip the arrow of money, and focus the inner fire. As you're wandering in the fog, you use the compass as you take a series of *iterative steps* toward having all three elements come together into One Big Thing.

And that is a key phrase: "iterative steps."

The people in this study surprised me with the extent to which their lives were so often *un*planned. Their lives were organic, unfolding, iterative, adaptive. They were like explorers adventuring into a vast unmapped territory, making discoveries and adapting to whatever they hit along the way. Culling through tens of thousands of documents on the people in this study, I was continually struck by how their lives went down paths and ended up in places that they never expected. The path out of the fog lies in a series of small steps, a highly iterative, often unplanned approach that I think of as *simplex stepping through life*. And it is to this idea of simplex stepping that we now turn.

8

Simplex Stepping

How did people in this study get through the fog when they could not see clearly? A big part of the answer lies in simplex stepping, taking an iterative series of "next best steps" until the fog lifted.

The term "simplex stepping" is inspired by a concept from a professor on my college campus named George Dantzig. It made a big impression on me when I first learned about it in a mathematical sciences course. It wasn't the math mechanics that caught my attention, but the sheer elegant beauty of Dantzig's seminal insight and what struck me as its philosophical implications.

Consider the following challenge: You want to find an optimal outcome to a huge complex problem that has many variables; furthermore, each variable has many possible values. One approach might be to calculate every possible permutation of the mix of values and then select the best result. But suppose there are too many possibilities for even the most powerful computer to process them all. How could you find an optimal result? Dantzig showed that it is possible to move in an iterative series of small steps that will lead you to an optimal outcome *without* ever needing to calculate the total set of possibilities. His approach proved reliable, and it revolutionized optimization. He called it the "simplex algorithm."

I kept thinking about the simplex algorithm while studying the lives in this research, noticing a repeating pattern of people iterating in a series of small steps when lost in the fog. They couldn't get above the fog to see the entire terrain of possibilities and map the most direct path to the best destination. They essentially had to simplex step their way through the fog.

Imagine you're trying to find your way to a destination, but you don't know what that destination is. Imagine all you can see is a small 360-degree circle around you, and you cannot see possible steps beyond that circle. So, you simply take what looks like the next best step within that small circle. Then you reset and look around the little 360-degree circle of visibility from the vantage point of your new location, and ask, "Okay, now standing here, what looks like the next best step?" You take that next step. Then you reset and take the next step. Even if a step doesn't prove particularly helpful, or even feels like a small mistake you need to reverse, you simply readjust and ask, "Okay, so now what looks like the best next step?" You just keep next-stepping, one step after another, until you reach a destination. Now suppose, without ever knowing where all the other untaken steps could have taken you, you feel confident that you've reached a great destination. This is the essence of simplex stepping through the fog of life.

To vividly illustrate simplex stepping, let's turn to the story of Katharine Graham.

Katharine Graham: Simplex Stepping into Leadership

Katharine Graham had never planned or expected to be a CEO. Her father had entrusted leadership of The Washington Post Company to her husband, Philip Graham, while she invested herself in the role of supportive spouse. But when she lost her husband to the illness of manic depression, which culminated in his taking his own life, Katharine Graham's life fractured apart. Looking back in one direction lay her first 46 years of life largely focused on being a dutiful daughter, wife, and mother. Looking the other direction lay decades of life to be defined by . . . well, what exactly?

Over the cliff and into the fog Katharine Graham did go.

I cannot possibly describe the contours of her grief as well as she did in her own memoir, *Personal History* (hands down, the best CEO memoir I've ever read), but one vivid detail sticks with me: For a time, she couldn't bring herself to even look at anything in Phil's handwriting. And mixed in with the fog of grief, Graham also struggled in the fog of uncertainty of what to do with the company and how to go about doing it. As Phil's illness worsened in the last year of his life, Graham had begun to worry about what would happen if she lost Phil, whether that be to another woman, divorce, institutionalization, or worse. Not just what would happen to her, but also what would happen to her family's company. When a close friend told her that she (Graham) could run the company if it came to that, Graham responded, "Me? That's impossible. I couldn't possibly do it. You don't know how hard and complicated it is. There's no way I could do it."

But then the worst *did* happen, and Graham faced the very real question: What should she do?

Standing at the fracture point, she saw three options: (1) sell the company, (2) find a professional manager to run it, or (3) begin learning about the company without doing anything dramatic. She emphatically rejected the idea of selling the company; no need to make such a big and irreversible decision right out of the gate. She also rejected the idea of hiring someone else to run the company, sidestepping yet another potentially huge decision that, while not irreversible, could be costly if she made the wrong choice. So, she chose the third, small-step option: "I thought, well, the only intelligent thing is to try to learn what things are about so that if I had to make an ultimate decision I will at least know what's going on."

In interviews and her own writings, Graham consistently disabused people of the notion that she'd made some giant bounding leap into leadership, like Superwoman tossing off a jacket to expose a superhero outfit underneath emblazoned with "CEO" in big letters. Rather, the image that comes to mind is more like closing her eyes and stepping off a curb. Then finding herself still standing, somewhat to her own astonishment, Graham took another step. Feeling a little more solid, she took another step, then another, then one after another, unsure of where she was going, but taking little steps the best she could. Writing about this period in her memoir, Graham peppered her text with phrases like "put one foot in front of another," "the only sensible step," "gradually I put things into place," "nothing to do but feel my way," "a process of nibbling around the edges," and so on. In taking those first simplex steps, Graham hoped to hold the company together well enough (and stave off any catastrophes) until one or more of her children might be ready for leadership.

But then something quite wonderful and unexpected began to happen. She found herself falling in love with the job. "To my surprise, I found I really loved it," said Graham. "I love the problems of management and business and they fascinated me." She began to gradually transition from hesitant trepidation to exuding more joyful energy for doing the work, to the point that she came to see her work nearly as essential to her being as food and water. And her sheer love of the role inspired those around her. "What made me really fall for Katharine Graham was her excitement and enthusiasm," reflected her longtime editor Ben Bradlee. "She loved it all. Once she got over feeling nervous, stopped thinking she would bring the *Post* and *Newsweek* to the brink of failure, she had this wonderful enthusiasm that was very contagious."

She also began to discover she could be good at it, *really* good at it. The tragic cliff had knocked everything sideways, and a big bright set of encodings came into frame. Katharine Graham didn't know it at the time, but when she took that first little step off the curb, she'd started a journey to become not just a placeholder but one of the great corporate leaders of the 20th century.

It happened in steps. Many of her first steps were not about *what* but about *who*. Suppose you're tossed into a leadership role for which you feel unprepared, and in which you find yourself lost in the fog without a clearly articulated vision for what to do or where to take the company. What steps should you take? Graham did what many great leaders do; she practiced the "First Who" principle: First get the right people on the bus, then figure out where to drive the bus. If you don't know what's coming down the road, your best bet is to have people with you who can adapt to and perform brilliantly no matter what challenges and opportunities come along the way. Step by step, person by person, hire by hire, seat by seat, Graham gradually assembled a busload of the right people around her.

One step involved bringing Ben Bradlee over from *Newsweek* (which the company also owned) to *The Washington Post*. Graham and Bradlee formed a working partnership of mutual trust and respect that would prove indispensable in the monumental (and monumentally scary) journalistic episodes like the Pentagon Papers and Watergate. Of course, Graham had no idea those episodes lay in her future. It's not as if she said, "I'd better get Ben Bradlee in here; I'm going to need him when the Watergate story happens." She just took what appeared to her to be the right next step, getting Bradlee into the role of deputy managing editor at *The Washington Post*.

Graham gradually increased her involvement in business decisions. She hadn't yet fully cleared the fog to see herself as the true CEO of the company with a strong vision for its future. Yet step by step, she was learning to lead and making the company stronger for when the big decisions came.

And the big decisions *did* come.

Seven years into her leadership journey, Graham faced a step more akin to jumping out of an airplane than stepping off a curb. Her editorial team got a copy of the Pentagon Papers, a revealing set of documents about the U.S. involvement in Southeast Asia, including the Vietnam War. The question: Should *The Washington Post* publish the Pentagon Papers?

Inside the company a fierce debate raged. On the one hand, prudent legal advisers argued that publishing the papers risked retaliation in the courts. *The New York Times* had been enjoined from publishing the Pentagon Papers, so *The Washington Post* could be seen as publishing in defiance of the law and the court. And that, in turn, could endanger the company's pending public stock offering. On the other hand, Graham's reporters and editors pushed hard for publishing, one pointedly arguing that "the only way to assert the right to publish is to publish." The editorial staff would "consider it a disaster" if *The Washington Post* didn't publish.

But in a larger sense, Graham in this moment faced an even bigger question: What is our vision for this paper, what do we want to be? Do we want to be a successful local paper, or do we want to be one of the great journalistic enterprises in the world that is routinely mentioned in the same breath with *The New York Times*? For seven years, Graham had simplex stepped through the fog and gradually reached a point of piercing clarity that all came together in that blinding moment of decision.

It truly was a dramatic moment. With editors and her board chair assembling for an evening conference call, Graham joined in from her home. She heard both sides of the argument. Finally, she asked her board chair, whom she greatly respected, for his advice. "I guess I wouldn't [publish]," he finally said. Graham noticed that he didn't outright say *No!* Nor did he amplify the risks. "I guess I wouldn't" left a little bit of space for a final decision and Graham paused to consider. Then, in a burst of words at the culminating go/no-go moment, Graham said, "Go ahead, go ahead, go ahead. Let's go. Let's publish."

And with that, as I read it, Katharine Graham emerged from the fog with absolute clarity that *The Washington Post* would not settle for being a good regional paper, but would become a truly great national paper. The decision also marked a major step in Graham becoming one of the greatest CEOs of all time. She showed that even as she had a deep core of personal humility, and even though she lived with fear and anxiety, she could lead with utterly fierce resolve.

Then just the following year, after the Supreme Court had ruled in favor of *The Washington Post* on the Pentagon Papers, Watergate began. "Watergate" is a broad wraparound word connoting a series of scandals related to break-ins orchestrated by people in or connected with the Nixon White House. The word "Watergate" stemmed from the most famous break-in, at the Democratic National Committee headquarters, which resided in the Watergate complex of offices in Washington, D.C. Watergate culminated in the resignation of President Nixon.

Interestingly, Graham later described the unfolding Watergate episode not as taking a plunge but like wading into a stream, getting deeper and deeper with each step. One story led to another story, led to yet another story, as her reporters Bob Woodward and Carl Bernstein peeled the onion layer by layer, moving ever closer to the Oval Office. (The book and subsequent movie *All the President's Men* tell the story from the reporters' point of view.) And even though this Watergate episode lacked the single dramatic moment of decision like the Pentagon Papers, Graham nonetheless faced the question of backing her journalistic team through a harrowing odyssey.

By this point, Graham had found herself fully in frame as leader of The Washington Post Company, guided by her unwavering commitment to elevating *The Washington Post* to the highest levels of journalistic success. A 29-year-old Bob Woodward experienced a catalytic moment when Graham asked him to join her for lunch about seven months into pursuing the Watergate story. She peppered Woodward with questions, clearly worried. *The Washington Post* was out in front, a good thing, but no one else seemed to be on the scent, which made her pointedly wonder aloud to her editors, "If this is such a great story, where the hell are the other newspapers?" At the lunch with Woodward, she pressed him on whether, in the end, he and Carl Bernstein would get to the publishable truth about Watergate. Woodward hedged. The Nixon culture of fierce secrecy made the job of getting to the bottom of Watergate exceptionally difficult. Woodward admitted that he wasn't confident that they'd ever be able to get the full story.

"Never?" Graham reacted. "Don't tell me never."

Woodward later described this moment as like a shot of Adrenalin, showing her full support and resolve, but also making clear her standards: "Never" was unacceptable. "At that moment she achieved the perfect managerial pitch," recalled Woodward. "She wasn't going to meddle, try to edit or second-guess, but she did, after all, want a better performance. Her skill was to raise the bar, gently but relentlessly." Raising the bar, gently but relentlessly—now *that* is a powerful leadership encoding.

Graham also raised the bar gently but relentlessly for herself. As I got to know Katharine Graham through her own words and the words of those around her, I was struck by her continuous leadership growth. No matter how successful she became, she maintained a learning mindset: *First learn; then lead.* She continued stepping forward by getting great people around her, learning from them, and then applying what she learned to make better decisions. The Washington Post Company and its journalistic reputation gained momentum, which attracted even more great people, which produced even greater success, which then attracted even more great people, compounding flywheel momentum turn upon turn in a giant reinforcing loop of business and journalistic success.

All this caught the attention of a (then) relatively unknown investor from Omaha named Warren Buffett who began buying up stock in The Washington Post Company. Business advisers raised concerns (*Be careful, he might be hostile!*), but Graham read up on Buffett, met him, and drew her own conclusions. As Graham got to know Buffett, she realized that he posed no threat, but a huge opportunity. Recognizing his intellectual genius, and thriving on Buffett's love of teaching, she availed herself of the chance to make Warren Buffett a mentor. She essentially went to business school with Warren Buffett as her personal professor.

She learned from Buffett in steps, cumulatively building a foundation of managerial and financial capability. Buffett would show up at board meetings with stacks of annual reports from a wide range of companies, giving Graham homework assignments to read them and build her business acumen. Graham dutifully did her homework, and then she and Buffett would sit down to discuss and glean insights about the ingredients of business performance. Then, at the next board meeting, Buffett would drop another stack of annual reports in Graham's lap, and they'd repeat the process. Step by step, Graham built a foundation of financial competence and managerial excellence under the tutelage of her mentor. Keep in mind, she did this long before Buffett had become well known to the world as the Oracle of Omaha. She simply followed her encoded operating mode of getting the right people around her, learning from them, and then deploying that learning to great effect.

Then, in her 13th year after stepping off the curb, Graham led the company through one of its most difficult episodes, when a pressmen strike stopped the presses. Not just by turning off the power, but by vandalizing the printing operations, damaging all 72 printing press units to the point where *The Washington Post* could not even produce a paper on-site. To get the paper published during the strike, she green-lighted a plan to land helicopters on top of the building to ferry printing plates to other regional newspapers that agreed to print. *The Washington Post* missed only one single day of a printed paper.

Graham had resolute clarity that she carried the responsibility to ensure the *long-term* viability of the company, not just for the shareholders, but also for the myriad people whose livelihoods derived from working at the company and for the cause of journalism. Graham supported union rights, including the right to strike, and she reached agreements with the other unions that were striking alongside the pressmen. "But," she wrote later, "I do not believe in the right to vandalize, frighten, destroy, and assault." The more militant strikers intimidated businesses who advertised in *The Washington Post*, not just by picketing outside storefronts, but also by invading to intimidate inside stores, even going so far, according to Graham, as killing fish in a store's fish tank by pouring oil in the water. In one personally painful moment, Graham looked out the window one day to see a sign with large letters blaring the message "Phil shot the wrong Graham," hurtfully invoking her late husband's suicide.

Graham described the anxiety she carried around during these months as like being pregnant with a rock. But no matter how much she wanted to get rid of the anxiety, and even though some close advisers encouraged her to capitulate, Graham would not fail what she saw as her responsibility. Negotiations reached an impasse, Graham holding firm that she would not agree to demands that would undermine the long-term viability of the company and the pressmen believing Graham would crumble in the end (as the company had done in the past). When the pressmen rejected a final offer, the paper began hiring replacements. After 139 days—what Ben Bradlee described as "the longest five months of all our lives"—the strike was over and printing returned to full capacity. Katharine Graham had led the company through the storm.

Courage, the saying goes, is not the absence of fear but the ability to act in the presence of fear. Katharine Graham lived and led with fear and anxiety that would never fully abate, no matter how successful, or powerful, or famous, or wealthy she might be or become. Warren Buffett described her as marching forward with knocking knees. Ben Bradlee related that she talked about worrying awake at night, "picking the wool off the blankets." She paid a hefty Stress and Drudgery Tax, not just in leading through dramatic episodes, but also in shouldering the more routine duties of effective leadership such as giving speeches. Even the prospect of making remarks at the staff holiday party would loom for days or weeks ahead of time, filling her with dread. Graham herself copiously conveyed her inner turmoil; a quick count across her memoir yielded some permutation of words of fear or anxiety (for example, "dread," "terrified," "anxious," "worried," "fretted," "frightened," "nervous," "anguish") 289 times in reference to herself. Even so, despite her trepidatious nature, Graham showed unwavering will and firmness of purpose when making decisions that would determine not only whether the enterprise would survive but also whether it would become a great company.

Notice that she built her courage step by step, decision upon decision, action upon action, result upon result. "I made endless unnecessary mistakes and died over them," Graham related about her early days in leadership. We don't know what would have happened if Graham had faced the Pentagon Papers decision or Watergate in her first couple of years, when in the thickest fog of grief and self-doubt. But by the time she faced those decisions, she'd already been simplex stepping through the fog for more than seven years, building her decision-making muscle and surrounding herself with the right people. Her exceptional leadership encodings had been there all along, yet it took time for those encodings to lock clearly in frame. While the cliff event happened in one shattering moment, Graham's evolution into a truly great and decisive CEO happened on a more gradual gradient.

In the end, Katharine Graham achieved a spectacular result. Warren Buffett later summed up Graham's CEO performance: "The Pentagon Papers and Watergate are milestones in journalistic history that will be recalled and studied for centuries. But these heralded journalistic successes were matched as well by quiet business success. On June 15, 1971, The Washington Post Company went public at $6.50 per share (adjusted for a subsequent 4-for-1 split). When Kay stepped down as CEO on May 9, 1991, the price was $222, a gain of 3,315 percent. During the same period the Dow advanced from 907 to 2,971, an increase of 227 percent." Now that I have studied Graham's life and leadership, my own assessment is that she stands as one of the absolute best examples of a leader who took a company from good to great, with some of the gutsiest business leadership decisions of all time.

Toward the end of her tenure as CEO, Graham faced a mini cliff: her impending retirement and leaving behind the leadership role that had dominated the second half of her life. She met that cliff with a stunningly beautiful coda, writing her memoir.

Interestingly, she got started in the transition from CEO to writer in small increments, again stepping off a curb and putting one foot in front of the other. She took the first simplex step (of what would turn out to be a 14-year project) at about age 66, nearly eight years before stepping away from the CEO role. Evelyn Small, who helped Graham with research for the book, recalled that Graham invited her to her office for a chat about a special assignment. Graham began talking about the idea of a memoir, yet dwelled on her lack of clarity about whether she really should do it, along the lines of: I'm not a writer. I don't have diaries. I don't have perfect memory of details and events. I don't know where or how to start. She went on talking about her uncertainties, verbally wandering around in the fog that can surround writers in the early inception of creating a book.

Graham started through the fog by taking a single small step. She asked Small to go to her house and look through some boxes of letters and papers just to see what might be there. "She asked me to go have a look," wrote Small later of how Graham ended that foggy meeting, "then come back and advise her." Small found "a treasure trove of history" in those boxes, and she persuaded Graham to take more steps. They began interviewing people across Graham's life, then transcribing the interviews and culling through the transcripts looking for nuggets. When Graham came across a particularly good one, she'd write "nugget" alongside the golden find. They did this for years, until they'd accumulated a great big pile of gleaming nuggets. Only then—after six years of culling documents, doing interviews, making transcriptions, and sifting for nuggets—did Graham make the definitive decision to write the book, which would take her another eight years to finish and publish. Graham would receive a Pulitzer Prize for her book at age 80.

A Simplex Method for Life

Looking backward from the end of the story, Katharine Graham's life adds up to an impressive overall result, almost intimidating in the scope and magnitude of what she accomplished. But looking forward from the cliff and peering into the fog, it looks and feels quite different. At the start of her post-cliff life, Graham didn't know what lay on the other side of the fog. She had no distinct destination, no overwhelming sense of destiny, no instantaneous epiphany. If someone would have asked her, "Where do you want to be in five years?" I suspect she would have had no clear answer at the start, other than just not wanting to mess things up and tank the company. She had no idea not only that she would become one of the greatest corporate CEOs of all time but that she would also make some of the most courageous decisions in business history and then top it all off with likely the best CEO memoir ever written. All this lay in the future, and the future lay completely obscured by a thick fog of grief, self-doubt, and outright fear. She worked her way out of the fog and into the clear by *simplex stepping*.

Across the study, we can extract a more general pattern: When lost in the fog, simply take what looks like the next best step. Not a big step, but a small step. Then reassess and take another small step. Then reassess, and step again. Then reassess, step again, reassess, step again, reassess, step again. Keep moving in steps. And one day, the fog will begin to lift and the cumulative effect of all those steps will become clear.

> The lives in our study show the great utility of moving in small steps when otherwise befuddled and uncertain. You don't need a plan. You don't need a goal. You don't need to have the answers for what to do with the rest of your life. You just need to begin simplex stepping. You might get a long way down the road before you even know where you are going.

Simplex stepping works in part because it allows you to take small steps, *to get moving*. And movement creates energy that fuels more movement, a feeling of momentum even if you don't yet know where that momentum is taking you. If you just sit in the fog doing nothing and hoping the fog will clear on its own, you might never get to the other side. As Richard P. Carlton, former CEO of 3M, once put it: You so often get where you are going by stumbling, but you can only stumble if you're moving.

Katharine Graham illustrates a contrasting pattern in the study: While cliffs can happen in a single dramatic episode or single shocking moment, gaining hedgehog clarity generally happens as a more gradual awakening. On the one hand, Graham could easily identify the point at which her life sheared in two; she even considered titling her memoir *Two Separate Lives*, seeing her own life as two lives separated at the cliff. On the other hand, the evidence shows no discernible blinding flash of epiphany when Graham found her hedgehog. Yes, the Pentagon Papers gives us a defining moment, but the evidence indicates that Graham had emerged out of the fog of uncertainty about her role at some point before that decisive moment.

The cliff can be like being jolted out of a deep slumber by a screeching fire alarm. Gaining clarity and coming into frame can be more like waking up without an alarm clock; at some point, you are aware that you've shifted from sleep to wake, but you only recognize that fact after the shift from sleep to wake already happened. Or think of it as being out on a long walk that starts in the fog. As you ramble, the fog gradually lifts. There comes a moment when you realize that you're already standing in bright sunshine with a long clear view. You know it happened ("I'm standing in the sun!") but might not be able to pinpoint the precise instant that it happened.

Katharine Graham showed a strong instinct to *not* make big irreversible decisions early after the cliff, with the fog thick and dark. She didn't sell the company (which would have been a catastrophically bad and irreversible decision). She didn't hire someone else to run it. She just started learning and moving in simplex steps. By the time she had to make the Pentagon Papers decision, she'd emerged with clarity that *she* held leadership responsibility as the full and true chief executive of the company, no one else but her. Katharine Graham instinctively grasped that when deep in the fog, it's best to take an iterative series of small simplex steps, if conditions allow. She also understood that life sometimes calls for momentous decisions and bold commitments, though it's best to avoid big irreversible decisions until the thickest fog has lifted.

> This study shows that *there are fog phases of life and there are clarity phases of life*. In the fog phases, we see simplex stepping as a highly functional method of navigation. In the clarity phases, we continue to see simplex stepping at work, but we also see more big decisions and life commitments. In both phases, we have *action and movement*, not just sitting in a room contemplating.

Simplex stepping through the fog can lead to a point of breakthrough clarity—clarity of hedgehog, clarity of purpose, clarity of direction, and ultimately, the courageous clarity to make huge decisions. And as with Katharine Graham, the wise course likely lies in taking small simplex steps until the fog clears. Katharine Graham never fully quieted the inner turmoil of anxiety and self-questioning, but once she'd emerged from the fog, she found herself quite capable of momentous choices no matter how loud her knees might be knocking.

Georgia Frontiere: Preclearing Fog *Before* the Cliff

Let's now turn to Katharine Graham's matched-pair companion in the study, Georgia Frontiere, whose case gives clues about how it might be possible to accelerate getting through the fog after a cliff.

When Georgia Frontiere's husband, Carroll Rosenbloom, drowned while swimming in the ocean, Frontiere inherited controlling ownership of a major business enterprise, the Los Angeles Rams NFL franchise. Like Katharine Graham, Frontiere stepped into a significant business leadership role for the first time in her life. Like Graham, she elected to keep the company rather than sell it, and she rejected the idea of hiring someone else to lead it. "I plan to be active 24 hours a day [running the Rams]," she said before her first season. Like Graham, she chose to move forward while still in grief. "I can't sleep more than four hours a night," she lamented. "My brain keeps flashing back to that beach in Florida where he drowned." Like Graham, she fell in love with the job and became absorbed in her work, noting, "I can't go anywhere without thinking about the team." Like Graham, she felt inspired by the larger goal of the enterprise beyond just being a business. In Graham's case, the company's higher goal related to the role of journalism; in Frontiere's case, the company's higher goal was all about winning, and Georgia Frontiere absolutely wanted to *win*. "I don't care about criticism," she said. "All I care about is winning." And Frontiere, like Graham, had a fierce resolve to do whatever must be done for the enterprise to succeed. "I try to be kind to everyone I deal with," she said, "but kindness should not be mistaken for weakness."

However, Frontiere's situation at the cliff *differed* from Graham's situation in one significant way. While Katharine Graham had never assumed she'd eventually run the company, Georgia Frontiere had a quite different pre-cliff experience. In Frontiere's case, her husband had prepared her for running the Rams years before the cliff. He taught her about the business. He taught her about football. He taught her about leadership. He taught her that it's okay to be fiercely competitive and obsessed with winning. She traveled with him to games. She visited the team offices to see how the business worked. And she fell in love with football. "I know what Carroll thought and did for the last 20 years, and why he did it," she explained. With Georgia being two decades younger than Carroll, they both knew that she would likely outlive him to become the primary owner of the Rams. "I always knew that someday I'd own the team," said Frontiere. "He drummed football into me to such an extent, gave me so many instructions, that I was completely prepared to become an owner. I just wasn't prepared for the way he died."

In the basic outline of the pair, Graham and Frontiere are similar, both inheriting ownership and assuming leadership responsibility for high-profile business enterprises at a time when almost no women held similar roles. But Frontiere, unlike Graham, had years to adjust to the idea of owning and leading the Rams. When Frontiere woke up on a Tuesday morning at age 51, alone without Carroll, *she'd already been simplex stepping under Carroll's tutelage for years before the cliff.*

> Setting Graham and Frontiere side by side crystallized an observation about cliffs and fog: In some situations, it might be possible to "preclear" some of the fog by *simplex stepping before a cliff, if you can see the cliff coming.* And that, in turn, can allow you to accelerate through the post-cliff fog.

Looking across the entire study, we can see a range of awareness of an impending cliff. At one end of the continuum, such as Michael J. Fox and Maurice White getting a Parkinson's diagnosis, the cliff came as a shocking surprise. In other cases, the person can see an increasing likelihood of the cliff before it actually happens, but there remains considerable uncertainty as to whether the cliff will actually happen. For example, Alice Paul and Lucy Burns could sense an increasing likelihood that the success cliff of winning the 19th Amendment would happen, but they did not know for certain that it would happen until Tennessee voted to ratify. There are also cases where the person knows for certain that the cliff will eventually happen, but there is considerable uncertainty as to the precise timing and/or form of the cliff, such as the end of an athletic career.

Some of the people in our study who could see a cliff coming used what I think of as a "point reallocation" strategy. In this approach, you gradually shift the focus of life from 100 points in one direction to put more points in finding another direction. Recall how Alan Page's journey from football player to supreme court justice happened as an iterative series of steps with organic overlap from one to another. During the beginning of Page's NFL career, 100 of 100 points of his professional energy went into football and related activities. Then, when he began taking a few law classes, the points went to something like 90 to football and ten to law. Then, as he fell in love with law school, graduated, and passed the bar, the point split might have gone to something like 75 to football and 25 to law. Then, when he began practicing law toward the end of his NFL career, the point allocation shifted further, maybe something like 50 to football and 50 to law. Finally, when he retired from football, and went to work full time as a practicing attorney and joined the Minnesota Supreme Court, he'd shifted to zero to football and 100 to law.

Just because you can see the cliff coming doesn't necessarily make the cliff itself less painful or difficult when it finally arrives. Nor does it mean that you will avoid fog. Yet simplex stepping in anticipation of a cliff might shorten the time from cliff to clarity. For a number of people in our study with foreseeable cliffs, they precleared some of the fog before the cliff. Sensing that Led Zeppelin would eventually come to an end, Robert Plant had already begun to think about life after the band a few years before John Bonham died. He even applied for a spot at a teacher-training college. In the end, Plant didn't pursue a teaching career, but it shows he'd already begun wandering through the fog of a post-Zeppelin life while still gyrating around the stage as the Golden God lead singer in Led Zeppelin.

Georgia Frontiere's pre-cliff simplex stepping helped her emerge from the fog much more quickly and with greater initial confidence than Graham. "I understand football. I understand business," she said without equivocation before her first NFL season as owner, going on to describe herself as "the person to whom all major decisions involving the Rams or their image filters through." Before her regular season began, she'd already written a position paper to establish her leadership direction for the enterprise. Not long after, she jettisoned the vice president of operations off the bus, a controversial decision given the VP's popularity with the sports media and the players . . . and the fact that he was Frontiere's stepson. It was "the toughest decision in my life," said Frontiere, adding that it "had to be made."

Frontiere also gained clarity about what *not* to change, including most of her late husband's team strategies that led to the Rams accumulating six consecutive years in the playoffs. Less than a year into her tenure, the Los Angeles Rams made it to the Super Bowl for the first time in the team's history (where the Rams lost to the Pittsburgh Steelers), followed by earning playoff spots in seven of the next ten seasons. She also built a seven-person advisory board that included former President Gerald R. Ford and other seasoned leaders, though she remained clear that *she*, not the board, ran the business. A writer for *The New York Times* described, "She is a woman with the mental toughness to make things happen in the real world. She is in charge."

Then, about ten years into her leadership, in the early 1990s, the Rams began to struggle, not just on the field, but also as a business. Frontiere concluded that staying in their stadium in Anaheim (where the Rams then shared their home field with the California Angels baseball team) would exacerbate the Rams' decline. Dwindling attendance and declining revenues added to a sense of team malaise, which made it even harder to build winning seasons, further accelerating a downward spiral. The media began to speculate that Frontiere might simply sell the Rams, take a capital profit, and be done with the whole thing. But even though she'd received an offer in the range of hundreds of millions of dollars, Frontiere had no interest in selling the team. "It's too much a part of my life," she explained. "What would I do on Sunday?" She loved being in business, she loved the Rams, and she loved competing to win. So, instead of selling, she decided on a bold plan to move the team to another city that would more robustly support the Rams. "I want to win football games," said Frontiere, "and I have to find the environment or make the environment that's conducive to winning."

Frontiere engineered a deal to move the team to her childhood hometown of St. Louis, garnering a commitment for a sparkling new stadium. There, Frontiere's Rams would become known as the "Greatest Show on Turf." The tagline fit perfectly, reflecting Frontiere's distinctive ethos (for an NFL owner) of entertainment and show business. Prior to marrying Carroll Rosenbloom, Frontiere had pursued a career in show business. She'd sung and performed in theater productions. She'd sung and danced as a chorus girl in Las Vegas. She'd played a lead role in a touring rendition of the stage musical *Oklahoma!* She'd hosted a Miami talk show for entertainers. In short, she'd cobbled together a career in show business, an entertainer to the core. Articles about Frontiere often derided her earlier life in show business, but those articles missed a fundamental point: Frontiere's entertainer encodings proved well suited to one of the biggest show business stages in the world, the NFL and the Super Bowl.

And Frontiere's Rams would get to the Super Bowl for a second and third time, including the Rams' first-ever Super Bowl Championship in 2000. Gliding along on a convertible in the celebratory parade after winning the Super Bowl, she heard fans all up and down the route cheering, "We love you, Georgia." "I've never felt so much love," said Frontiere, shining at age 72, "and I've never loved so much."

Spectacular Potential: Always There, Often Hidden

Both Katharine Graham and Georgia Frontiere were incredibly underestimated in their early lives. There is no evidence that anyone around Graham imagined that she would one day become one of the greatest

CEOs in business history (other than perhaps Graham's friend mentioned earlier). There is no evidence that there was anyone (other than perhaps Carroll Rosenbloom) who imagined that Frontiere—a former Las Vegas chorus girl and lounge singer who'd been married five times by her early 30s—would one day become known as Madame Ram, appear in an American Express commercial as a savvy business icon, oversee the "Greatest Show on Turf," and win a Super Bowl ring. Neither Graham nor Frontiere fully clicked into frame as business leaders until after age 50, and they flourished in line with their encodings well into their 60s and 70s.

To be clear, I'm not suggesting that highly visible success like that achieved by Graham and Frontiere need be the primary measuring stick of a life well lived. (Again, this study tilts toward such public visibility because that's where the data is.) That said, their stories do lead me to a lesson that hit me repeatedly while doing this research: *Beware the urge to judge people under the arrogant and ignorant assumption that you can see them and their lives in their entirety.*

> People can be in a phase of life where they are simply out of frame, with exquisite encodings hidden from view. Or they might be deploying their encodings into something private and personal, largely invisible to all but those who know them well. Or they might be in the fog, simplex stepping in small unseen steps toward something spectacularly unexpected. Life's not done until it's done, and there remains always the potential to discover encodings that had previously been unseen and to summon the full force of inner fire into a stunning result.

By this point in the book, we've seen case after case of people flourishing when they click into frame with their encodings and focus their energies on a big thing that feeds their inner fire, whether that be early in life, midstream, or later in life. When they do, it benefits not just themselves but those around them. Which brings me to one of the most fundamental ways doing this study transformed me and my relationships with people.

I used to spend a lot of emotional energy feeling frustrated with what people are not. This caused me and the people around me a lot of unnecessary pain, especially the dedicated members of my teams at my research and teaching lab, The Good to Great Project, in Boulder, Colorado. Over the years, I made the mistake of trying to mold or shape or cajole or inspire or transform people into the way I felt I needed them to be. Or even worse, to try to make them more like me. I also made the mistake of putting people in roles that did not fit with their encodings. Being the great people that they are, they tried valiantly for excellence in their responsibilities. They suffered, and I suffered.

But as I got deeper into this research, observing the vast differences across the people in this study and how they flourished at their best when life lined up with their encodings and what fed their inner fire, I gradually began to change. Subtly at first, I began to shift away from trying to change people into what I wanted them to be. Simultaneously, I shifted toward finding or creating the best possible match between their encodings and their responsibilities. It didn't happen overnight, it was more of a managerial form of simplex stepping. I'd sense something about a person's encodings, and then I'd make a shift in their responsibilities to fit those encodings. Then I might observe something else about their encodings, discovering something wonderful about them when they thrived in a task, and I'd make another shift in responsibilities. Together, we essentially simplex stepped toward them coming into frame in a seat on the bus.

In one episode, I'd miscast a member of my team into a role utterly out of frame with his encodings. He'd worked with me as a summer intern and impressed me to the point that I'd offered him a three-year full-time position after graduation, but in a public-facing role very different from what he'd done in his summer internship. He worked incredibly hard and desperately wanted to do a great job, yet the disappointments piled up. Sometimes, made ill by the stress of the mismatch, he'd go into the restroom to throw up. My attempts to mold him failed, and I felt increasingly frustrated. He thought I'd fire him. Fortunately, for him and me, I began to grasp that he had not failed me; rather, *I had failed him* by putting him in a role out of frame with his encodings. Furthermore, I felt somewhat responsible for his future; I did not want to see this wonderful young man start his professional life getting fired. So, I began making a series of iterative steps, testing him with different tasks that drew upon what I sensed to be his intellectual gifts, and he showed signs of flourishing. Finally, after a few more simplex tests, I moved him out of the public-facing role and into a vitally important role on this research project. In the final year of his three-year position with me, he delivered exceptionally high-quality work that made a huge contribution to the research behind this book. He closed out his time on my team with a significant success he can carry with him for the rest of his life. And I carry a deep gratitude for him and for all that he contributed to this project.

When people's responsibilities largely fit a big bright set of their encodings and fed their inner fire, they lit up like lightning bolts. I felt increasingly calm and confident in them, in their choices, in their work, in their self-management. The more their work aligned with their encodings, the more I trusted them. The more I trusted them, the more they trusted themselves. And the more they trusted themselves, the better their work became. I found myself thanking them for their work more often, spontaneously and genuinely. I began to appreciate them even more precisely *because* they are encoded differently than me.

I puzzled on how this shift happened, and concluded that it came directly from getting to know the lives of the people in this study. Each life, and each pair of lives, flowed into my brain as I moved the mountain of research day after day, week after week, month after month, for years. And like a flow of water that gradually smooths the sharp edges of a stone, their lives began to shape and smooth not just my thoughts but also my emotions and my relationships. By studying some of the most beautiful examples of people whose latent potential popped into view when they came into frame, I became increasingly attuned to seeing and sensing the encodings and fire of those around me.

Then, one day, I woke up to realize that my entire emotional state had changed, not just in my work, but across my entire life. *Instead of feeling frustrated with what people are not, I'd made a monumental shift to feeling grateful for what they are.* I wish I'd made this shift decades earlier, but as the Supreme Court Justice Felix Frankfurter pointed out, "Wisdom too often never comes, and so one ought not to reject it merely because it comes late."

9

The Roulette Wheel of Life

When Jimmy Page's parents moved the family to 34 Miles Road in the Surrey suburb of Epsom, young Jimmy Page discovered a guitar that by some strange quirk of fate had been left in their new home. "It was just there, like a sculpture," recalled Page of the guitar's mysterious appearance in his life. "It was just in the house." At first, Page didn't do anything with it; the guitar sat there silently waiting while Jimmy approached his teen years.

Then rock and roll began to infiltrate the airwaves. When songs like Elvis Presley's rendition of "Baby Let's Play House" seeped into Page's auditory cortex and animated his body with its raw rhythmic energy, he felt an urge to see if he could replicate the chords. He picked up the guitar that had silently waited and began to learn. And something clicked. "So there was this immediate connection between this guitar and what I was listening to on the radio," recalled Page. "I was obsessed with it. But I don't know how that guitar got there, and I don't know where it went. . . . But that guitar was like an intervention."

By age 14, Page had his own band, the James Page Skiffle Group, with a contract to play a gig on the BBC television show *All Your Own*. He then played in a number of bands around his hometown of Epsom, which led to the opportunity to do "session work" (playing guitar on other people's songs and albums) while still living at home.

At age 18, he played on the No. 1 U.K. hit "Diamonds," which led to working with some of the great bands and players of the time, including Donovan, Joe Cocker, the Rolling Stones, and The Who. He played a small segment on The Beatles' movie *A Hard Day's Night*. All this session work—three sessions a day, six days a week—led to joining the Yardbirds, which at various points featured two other future great guitarists, Eric Clapton and Jeff Beck, who'd grown up at the same time in the same county as Page. And when Page went searching for a new vocalist for the Yardbirds, he found Robert Plant, which led to finding the drummer John Bonham, which led to bringing them together with the bassist John Paul Jones, which led straight to creating Led Zeppelin. And all of it happened before he'd even turned 25.

In reading through the hundreds of source documents we collected on Jimmy Page, along with the voluminous books (such as Chris Salewicz's *Jimmy Page: The Definitive Biography*, Martin Power's *No Quarter: The Three Lives of Jimmy Page*, and Page's beautifully curated book *Jimmy Page: The Anthology*), I was continually struck by the confluence of circumstances. The discovery of the guitar. The same county as Eric Clapton and Jeff Beck. The blues-influenced rock music tsunami sweeping across England in the 1960s. The epicenter of the recording scene within 20 miles of Page's teenage home. The desperate demand for good session guitarists. The supportive parents who let Jimmy take over the living room to practice. The glorious coming together of four talents who somehow found each other—Page, Plant, Bonham, Jones—to create Led Zeppelin.

Without all these fortuitous events, would Jimmy Page have become, well, *Jimmy Page* the guitar Mozart and a founding leader of Led Zeppelin? What would have become of Jimmy Page if he'd come of age in a different decade or in a different location, say, the wheat fields of Kansas or the snow-laden outskirts of Helsinki or the colorful streets of Delhi? Would Jimmy Page have discovered his encodings for guitar? Would he have focused his inner fire early and obsessively on pursuing a life in music, leading to the formation of Led Zeppelin?

Jimmy Page is not the only person for whom spins of the roulette wheel played a role in finding a path that so perfectly fit his encodings. Think back to some of the lives we've discussed in earlier chapters.

Suppose the U.S. Navy had not assigned Grace Hopper to the Mark I computer project, which placed her at the big bang of the birth of the computer revolution and recast her life. Would Grace Hopper have found her life as a pioneering computer scientist, playing such a significant role in the advancement of software?

Suppose a Cornell professor had not invited Barbara McClintock to take a graduate genetics class, the only such course on campus and one that she likely would not have otherwise taken. Would Barbara McClintock have become a Nobel Prize–winning cytogeneticist who discovered mobile genetic elements?

Suppose John Glenn had not seen the announcement posted on the physics department bulletin board about the Civilian Pilot Training Program that made possible his pilot's license. Would John Glenn have become an aviator and astronaut?

Suppose Katharine Graham's father had never bought The Washington Post Company and made it the family business. Would Katharine Graham have discovered the leadership encodings that made her one of the greatest corporate leaders of all time?

Suppose Alice Paul had been born in a different era, after suffrage had already been achieved. Would Alice Paul have found her activist encodings and focused the full force of her inner fire on the struggle for women's rights?

Suppose, suppose, suppose, suppose, suppose.

For *every* person in the study, some element of luck—spins on the roulette wheel of life—played a role in finding a hedgehog. (To review: To find a hedgehog means that you've found an arena of activity that meets three tests: You're encoded for it, you flip the arrow of money in doing it, and it focuses the inner fire. To be in hedgehog mode means you've made a full commitment to organize your life and channel a huge chunk of your energy toward the pursuit of this One Big Thing.) Sometimes the spin played a relatively minor role, just altering the vector of life slightly at a key moment. Sometimes the spin played an essential role in opening or closing a vital opportunity or life path. And sometimes the spin hurtled a person headlong into an enormously fulfilling hedgehog mode for decades.

One Life, Many Potentialities

By this point, you might be feeling a gnawing unease from questions lurking in the background throughout the first half of the book. If finding a hedgehog plays such a central role in what to make of a life, then when and how did the people in our study find it? What if you've not yet found the One Big Thing that you're encoded for and captures the full intensity of your inner fire? Or what if someone important in your life—a child, a spouse, a friend, a sibling—hasn't yet found it? Or what if you once had it, but then lost it due to a cliff event; can you replace it with one equally fulfilling and meaningful? In this chapter, we come to the point where spins of the roulette wheel played a huge role in people's trajectories, their paths altered by seemingly random luck events largely out of their control. On the surface, this can seem a little dispiriting. Is it ever too late? Is there always hope?

To get into this, let's look at some data. I tabulated across the study when people found and fully committed themselves to a particular hedgehog. About two-thirds (68%) of our study cases found and committed to a first hedgehog before the age of 30, while nearly one-third (32%) didn't do so until their 30s or 40s. For me, the data gets particularly interesting when you look at the second and third hedgehogs (for those who were serial hedgehogs). Of the 17 second hedgehogs, nearly half (47%) came in their 50s or 60s. And the third hedgehogs arrived decidedly late, with four out of five (80%) coming in their 60s or 70s.

Hedgehogs Found and Committed to by Decade of Life
Summary Data Across the Study

TOTALS	Pre-20	20s	30s	40s	50s	60s	70s	Total Count
First Hedgehog	8	15	6	5	0	0	0	34
Second Hedgehog	0	2	3	4	6	2	0	17
Third Hedgehog	0	0	0	1	0	2	2	5
All Hedgehogs	8	17	9	10	6	4	2	56

PERCENTAGES	Pre-20	20s	30s	40s	50s	60s	70s
First Hedgehog	23.5%	44.1%	17.6%	14.7%	0.0%	0.0%	0.0%
Second Hedgehog	0.0%	11.8%	17.6%	23.5%	35.3%	11.8%	0.0%
Third Hedgehog	0.0%	0.0%	0.0%	20.0%	0.0%	40.0%	40.0%
All Hedgehogs	14.3%	30.4%	16.1%	17.9%	10.7%	7.1%	3.6%

I do not conclude from the data any ironclad law that a person must find a first hedgehog before age 50. If we were able to study a large representative sample of the entire general population, I hypothesize that some people do indeed find a first true hedgehog well after age 50. This study is a carefully selected set of life cases using matched pairs, not a large random sample, so I'm unable to make any definitive statements about the general population. That said, I can think of people in my own life who came into frame quite late. They might have gotten waylaid by responsibilities or social expectations or hard knocks in the first half of life; then something big changed (retirement, death of a loved one, getting fired, divorce, disease, accident, financial windfall, a call to service, a faith conversion, or any number of other redefining life events), and they came fully into frame for the first time. I cannot say with certainty from this study what the percentages are across the general population or make any systematic statements about how very late first hedgehogs happen. It would be a fascinating follow-up study, but it is not this study.

Yet within the data of this study, I'm struck by the fact the second and third hedgehogs were sometimes so dramatically different from the first that they could potentially have been a first hedgehog. This suggests that had the study cases not found their first hedgehog early, they could still have one later. I'm also struck by dramatic cases, such as Katharine Graham, Cardiss Collins, and Michael J. Fox, where a cliff forced the discovery of a path that diverged so radically from what came before that their later lives became almost unrecognizable relative to their earlier lives. This gives well-founded hope that whatever has (or has not) happened in life up to any given point, there remains potential to discover previously unseen encodings that form the foundation of a spectacularly new vector.

> *All of which brings us to one of the most important points in this entire book: the difference between finding "the" hedgehog and finding "a" hedgehog.* If we hold to the idea that each of us has only one hedgehog and much of life depends on whether we find *it*, then this would be a very depressing study. But if we embrace the view that each of us has many possibilities to potentially discover—that the constellation of encodings within each of us is vast and largely undiscovered—then the challenge changes dramatically from the low odds of finding that one elusive unicorn hedgehog to finding just one of many possibilities.

I like to think of it this way: There is a giant roulette wheel of life wherein each slot in the wheel represents a potential path. Sometimes the ball might drop into a slot that brings a big bright set of encodings into frame and ignites the inner fire, and sometimes not. There is an element of luck in which path life takes, but the crucial point is that there are multiple possibilities on the wheel.

If Jimmy Page had grown up in the wheat fields of Kansas or the snow-laden outskirts of Helsinki or the colorful streets of Delhi, would he have found his hedgehog? It's a little bit of a trick question. Would he have the *particular* role as lead guitarist in Led Zeppelin? Unlikely. But would he have found a *different* path that had all three elements working together (encodings, economics, and fire) in One Big Thing? Quite possibly. For Jimmy Page, guitar might have been slot No. 7 in the roulette wheel of life. But if the roulette ball had dropped instead into a different slot, say No. 26 or No. 12 or No. 11 or No. 33, Jimmy Page could have discovered perhaps a very different path that fit his encodings, maybe as a graphic designer, or a chef, or a photographer, or a curator of ancient artifacts.

If Barbara McClintock had not discovered genetics, perhaps the ball would have dropped into being a geologist, or a farmer, or a park ranger, or an espionage code breaker. If John Glenn had not discovered flying, perhaps the ball would have dropped into being a firefighter, or a Formula 1 race car driver, or a heart-lung machine operator, or a mountain guide. If Tenley Albright hadn't found medical surgery, maybe the ball would have dropped into being an architect, or a carpenter, or a fashion designer, or a hostage negotiator.

There is no guarantee that the ball will drop into a slot that perfectly aligns with a set of encodings and that ignites the inner fire, but equally, life can give us many spins of the roulette wheel before it is done. I don't know if some people have more potential slots on the roulette wheel than others, but I'm confident that people carry within themselves the encodings for multiple possible paths. There is no one single purpose to find, no one single thing you are beautifully made for.

And what is my evidence for this? *The entire structure of the study, built around the cliff-match method.*

> As you've already seen multiple times in this book, the cliffs of life sometimes bring one hedgehog to an end, but people in our study found a second or third one to replace the first one, sometimes one radically different from what came before. That they did so provides empirical validation that there is not just one to discover.

The challenge—met by every person in this study—is to find a path in line with a set of encodings, a path that feeds the inner fire, a path on which to flip the arrow of money and make the economics work. It might have come early. It might have come midstream. It might have come in the wake of a life-shattering cliff. It might have come late as a beautiful coda to life. And for half the people in our study, *it happened more than once.*

What Is the Role of Luck?

The roulette wheel discussion brings me to an even larger question: How should we think about the role of luck in the overall arc of a life—not just in relation to the hedgehog, but as a more general factor in the lives we studied?

The answer comes in two parts: (1) understanding the pervasive reality of luck, and (2) grasping the essential distinction between luck and the concept of return on luck.

To get into both parts of this topic, let's look at the unfolding lives of Gerald R. Ford and Jimmy Carter. To be clear, my point in the following narrative sequences is not that Ford and Carter, or all the other people in the study, were merely lives of luck. My point is to illustrate the role of luck, which will then lead us to the vital distinction between "luck" and "return on luck."

GERALD R. FORD'S LUCK, GOOD AND BAD

Let's start with the fact that Gerald R. Ford was almost not even Gerald R. Ford. Seeking escape from her husband, his mother left Omaha with her infant son, Leslie King, to stay with her parents in Grand Rapids. After securing a divorce, she began building a safe new life for herself and her son, and within a few years she'd remarried. In one of the most significant events in his life, Leslie King got a caring stepfather, a man of granite-rock integrity and vast reservoirs of instinctive parenting skills. Leslie King so abhorred his birth father ("a bad man," he would later say) and so loved his stepfather (whom he called "one of the truly outstanding people I ever knew in my life") that as a young man he fully embraced an official name change to mirror his stepfather's, becoming Gerald R. Ford Jr.

Imagine the sheer good luck that the one person Ford had as perhaps his most important role model just happened to be the man his mother married in the wake of a disastrous and dangerous marriage. If Leslie King's mother had stayed in her first marriage, or if she'd divorced, only to marry a less admirable man, or if she'd never married again, or if she'd moved instead to some other city, or any number of other ifs that could have happened, then the odds drop precipitously that Gerald R. Ford would have been the 38th president of the United States of America.

Yet while Ford's stepfather proved to be a spectacularly good parent, he had the bad luck to start his own business less than a month before the 1929 stock market crash. The family business teetered right on the edge of bankruptcy in the depths of the Great Depression. For future President Ford, that meant no money to pay for college.

Fortunately, he had a supportive and resourceful high school principal who took it upon himself to arrange a scholarship for Ford. The principal also wrote (unbeknownst to the Fords) to the University of

Michigan football coach, opening the door for Ford to join the Michigan football team. And while Michigan did not offer a football scholarship, the coach did arrange a job for Ford to wait tables at the university hospital. With an additional few dollars a week from his step-aunt, periodically selling his blood to the university hospital, and borrowing money along the way, Ford jiggered together enough support to graduate from the University of Michigan with a degree in economics. He later described the confluence of events and support that enabled him to go to college as "the luckiest break I could have had."

The Green Bay Packers and the Detroit Lions recruited Ford to play professional football after graduation, but he'd set his ambitions on law school, so he turned them down. Yet there remained a familiar problem: He had not the money to attend law school. In a perfect coincidence of timing, it just so happened that the Yale football team needed an assistant line coach at this precise moment. Had Ford graduated a year earlier or a year later, the Yale spot would likely have been held by someone else. Ford's lucky timing gave him the chance to get paid to plant himself at Yale, where he took classes at Yale Law School as a part-time student, gained full admission after initial rejection, and eventually graduated in the top third of his class at age 27.

Ford returned to Grand Rapids to practice law and nurture a nascent interest in politics that emerged when he'd volunteered to work on the Wendell Willkie presidential campaign during one of his Yale summers. But within just 11 months, as luck would have it, Ford's life took a radical detour when the attack on Pearl Harbor brought the United States into World War II.

As it would turn out, Ford almost didn't make it home, saved only by a stroke of good luck in a near-death moment. He was serving as an assistant navigator on the aircraft carrier USS *Monterey* when a typhoon engulfed the ship. As the carrier rolled about in the ocean swells, some of the parked aircraft ripped away from their attachments and began crashing into each other, sparking a gasoline fire and sending smoke into the air intakes. Ford, as officer of the deck, sped up a series of ladders to his post. Suddenly the entire aircraft carrier rolled hard enough to throw Ford off his feet and hurtling toward the edge of the deck. "I went sliding just like a toboggan," Ford later said. "Couldn't have lasted more than two or three seconds, 'cause it was only one hundred and some feet wide. But anyhow, I spread out as much as I could. There was nothing to grab on to. But fortunately around a flight deck there's a little raised metal rim so that tools won't roll over the side. And I hit that with my feet, and it spun me around, and I dropped, half in and half out of the catwalk that goes all the way around just below a flight deck. . . . If I'd gone another foot, I'd have gone over the side. We lost about five men overboard. For me, it was just one of those quirks. Pure happenstance. If I'd had a different angle, different speed . . ." If indeed. A few degrees of angle and the United States would have had a different 38th president.

A couple of years after returning from the war, Ford decided to run for the U.S. Congress as representative from Grand Rapids. Right out of the gate, he got a huge luck event. President Truman called Congress into special session right in the heat of the election campaign. Ford's primary opponent, an entrenched four-term incumbent, sat trapped in Washington. Meanwhile, Ford campaigned furiously at home in Grand Rapids, even making a campaign promise to milk the cows of one potential voter if he won. (Ford *did* return to milk the cows.) This fortuitous opening helped propel Ford to victory with more than 60% of the vote.

From the moment of his swearing in to the U.S. House of Representatives, at age 35, Ford said, "I knew I wanted the House to be my career." He loved the doing of his work in the House, and he had a particularly useful encoding for a practical politician: He made friends across both sides of the aisle. Donald Rumsfeld, Ford's future secretary of defense, later recounted in his book *When the Center Held* that Ford described himself as having "a good many adversaries" in Congress, but no enemies. Gerald R. Ford came fully into frame serving in Congress, rising to minority leader at the relatively young age of 51.

But then, nine years later, events far beyond Ford's control radically changed his options. When Vice President Spiro Agnew resigned, President Nixon faced the question of selecting an ideologically compatible Republican replacement that a Democratic-controlled Congress would accept. The one best choice: Gerald R. Ford, the man with many friends and no enemies.

Ford had never expressed any interest whatsoever in becoming vice president or president, yet he found himself being propelled into the vice presidency. "I couldn't help but notice the irony," he reflected. "Here I'd spent twenty-five years trying to become Speaker of the House. Suddenly, I was a candidate for president of the Senate [a position held by the vice president], where I could hardly ever vote and where I'd never get a chance to speak." A Congress controlled by Democrats overwhelmingly confirmed the Republican Gerald R. Ford with more than 90% support.

By the time Ford stepped into the vice presidency, the Watergate scandal (in which Ford played no part) had grown into a raging political firestorm closing in on the Nixon White House. Ford began to realize that he would likely become the 38th president of the United States, due entirely to forces outside his control.

In *Write It When I'm Gone*, the journalist Thomas M. DeFrank (who covered Ford closely and with whom Ford developed a warm relationship) told the story of a conversation he had with Vice President Ford. Ford expressed irritation that some journalists derided him as a mere "plodder," and he gave a revealing self-description of how his rise flowed from a combination of preparation and luck. "I never planned on moving from one spot to another, but I always felt that what I was doing would prepare me for the next opportunity," Ford said. "You have to have the confidence that you're available and competent if lightning strikes, and if that's plodding, it seems to have worked."

The conversation turned to a newspaper column accusing Ford of being a Brutus in waiting. "Why do they [the media] do this?" Ford implored.

"They're angry and they're bitter because they know Nixon is finished," replied DeFrank. "It's over. He can't survive, and you're gonna be president."

"You're right," said Ford. "But when the pages of history are written, nobody can say I contributed to it."

Less than four months later, Gerald R. Ford became president, despite having never aspired to the role. There are a number of well-written biographies of Ford, including James Cannon's *Gerald R. Ford* and Scott Kaufman's *Ambition, Pragmatism, and Party*. Having devoured every book I could find on Ford, I came to see him as truly the accidental president.

As with any president, Ford's time in the White House inevitably came with a series of luck events. That's the nature of the presidency. All sorts of big, unexpected things entirely out of the president's control happen—some good, some bad—and those events can define a presidency as much as the president's own agenda. Ford also had lucky near misses that kept him alive.

On a sunny Friday morning, President Ford walked out of the Senator Hotel in Sacramento, California. The day would break 100 degrees late that September afternoon, but at 10 a.m. the temperature was a quite pleasant 70ish and Ford decided to walk. Partway to the Capitol (where he had a planned meeting with the governor of California), Ford encountered a woman in the crowd wearing a long, flowing red gown. She began to raise a .45-caliber gun. In the ensuing commotion her weapon somehow didn't fire. A Secret Service agent wrestled the gun out of her hand. The woman who'd had the gun just kept repeating, "It didn't go off. It didn't go off." She'd loaded bullets but had somehow neglected to load one into the firing chamber. When Ford walked into the governor's office a few minutes later, he didn't mention the assassination attempt and just went straight into talking about policy. The governor didn't even know of the incident until about 30 minutes into the meeting, when the president received a brief report on the assassination attempt.

Just 17 days later, Ford dodged another bullet, this time from a gun that did go off. Coming out the north entrance of the St. Francis Hotel in downtown San Francisco, Ford waved to a cheering crowd. At that very moment, a former Marine named Oliver Sipple just happened to be in the right place at the right time to save the president. A flash of chrome caught Sipple's eye as a woman near him raised and pointed a revolver directly at the president. Sipple reacted instinctively, knocking the gun off angle with his hands at the precise instant the woman pulled the trigger. The bullet veered slightly to hit the hotel wall behind Ford. If not for the luck of Sipple being right there at the exact right moment, the United States might well have had Nelson Rockefeller (Ford's vice president) as its 39th president.

The great irony of Ford's life is that becoming president knocked him out of his truest element, that of doing his work in the U.S. House of Representatives. Ford lost the 1976 presidential election against his matched-pair companion, Jimmy Carter. Immediately after Carter's inauguration, Ford and his wife, Betty, boarded a helicopter waiting to ferry them to Andrews Air Force Base. Ford had just spent 895 days holding the highest office in the land, but he had no interest in taking a reminiscent look over the White House. Instead, he asked the pilot to take a long slow circle over the building where he'd happily toiled in the halls of Congress for nearly a quarter century. As Ford looked down upon the giant dome of the Capitol, he said, "That's my real home."

JIMMY CARTER'S LUCK, GOOD AND BAD

Let's begin Jimmy Carter's luck story with a lifesaving event eerily similar to Ford's rolling aircraft carrier moment. After graduating from the U.S. Naval Academy at Annapolis, a path he chose in part because his family could not otherwise afford a full college education, Carter served active duty in the Navy for seven years. One January night, at age 24, Carter stood watch on the bridge of the surfaced USS *Pomfret* submarine. At about 2 a.m., in the midst of increasing storm swells, he saw a huge wave coming straight at the front of the *Pomfret*, just seconds before it hit. The water slammed down, thrashing Carter about like a small toy tossed into a gigantic washing machine. Carter tried to keep a grip on the railing, but the water tore him away. Disoriented, tumbling about, struggling to find his way up amid the swirling chaos, he fought to survive. Finally, when the wave receded it miraculously dropped him right on the deck. Carter related in his memoir *A Full Life* that even just a slight difference in the angle of the ship would have resulted in his being lost to the vast ocean.

What are the odds that two people who would later run for the presidency against each other barely survived, by inches of angle, eerily similar near-death experiences at sea?

You might be wondering why I included near-death misses for Ford and Carter, when these incidents don't seem to offer any actionable lessons for living. I do so as vivid illustrations of the first main point of these narratives: to establish the sheer fact of luck that affected the lives of the people in this study. Also, sometimes near-death experiences can stimulate people to make more of their lives: *I could have so easily died, so I'd better make the most of the time I have.* Carter's realization of "how fragile was my existence" after nearly being swept away to his death on the USS *Pomfret* further fueled his inner fire to build a meaningful life, however long or short that life might be.

While in the Navy, Carter got one stroke of luck in the form of a person, when he crossed life paths with a man who would become an important mentor, Captain (later Admiral) Hyman Rickover. Carter wrote in his memoir about interviewing with Rickover for a position in the Nuclear Navy. As Carter sat in a chair with the front legs cut slightly shorter than the rear so that the occupant never felt comfortable, Rickover grilled him with increasingly difficult questions. Finally, Rickover came to the final series of questions: "How did you stand in your class at the Naval Academy?" Carter responded that he'd been 59 of 820. Rickover's eyes remained fixed straight into Carter's; then he asked, "Did you always do your best?" Carter almost said yes, but then stopped himself, recognizing that he'd not done his absolute best with absolutely every single opportunity at the Naval Academy. "No, sir, I didn't always do my best." Rickover said nothing. He just kept the laser focus of his eyes boring straight into Carter for what seemed like a very long time. Finally, he asked, "Why not?" Rickover then abruptly ended the interview by turning around to a desk behind him.

To Carter's surprise, Rickover chose him to join his team of officers and became a great mentor, whom Carter called upon even when he was president. But even if Carter had not joined Rickover's team, the end of that interview altered Carter's entire life ethos. Rickover's question stayed with him: *Why not the best?* Why *not?* Why not? The question "Why not the best?" even became the title of Carter's first book, written to coincide with his first presidential campaign, his way of introducing himself to the American people. The luck of crossing paths with a great teacher or mentor can change your life in 30 seconds.

When Carter was 28, his father succumbed to pancreatic cancer. Carter resigned from the Navy to help with his family's cash-strapped warehouse and peanut-farming business in Plains, Georgia. It would turn out over the course of Carter's long life that he was very fortunate to have escaped pancreatic cancer himself. Not only did his father die of it (at age 59), but so did his sister Ruth (at age 54), his brother, Billy (at age 51), and his other sister, Gloria (at age 63). "There was no record of another American family having lost four members to this disease," Carter later wrote. Unlike for four of his direct relatives, the roulette wheel of health spun mightily in his favor, for what would turn out to be a 100-year life.

Carter took over running the family business. He liked it well enough, but he found himself increasingly drawn to community leadership, and he began to contemplate somewhere in the recesses of his mind the idea of elected politics.

But for Carter to make a big move into state-level elected politics, he needed a luck event out of his control to break his way. And he got one. The Supreme Court of the United States issued a decision in a Tennessee case, *Baker v. Carr*, which rendered Georgia's longstanding "county unit" system unconstitutional. Prior to the ruling, Georgia state elections gave votes in small rural counties disproportional weight per person over big urban counties. According to Carter's math, "some rural votes equaled one hundred votes in urban areas." This practice rendered it essentially impossible for a new moderate like Carter (who would not have the support of the entrenched political machines) to win election via direct appeal to individual voters. With the Supreme Court ruling, Carter could draw enough equal-weighted votes from individual voters to potentially win a state-level election, and at age 38 he decided to run for the Georgia State Senate. Without the Supreme Court decision, Carter likely would not have run for a state-level office, would likely never have become governor of Georgia, and would likely never have been president of the United States.

In elected politics, Carter began to develop a distinctive political brand that stemmed directly from a deep encoding that showed up across his life, that of being an *outsider*. This wasn't a cynical poll-driven political strategy; it was simply part of his encoded makeup, the core essence of his political ethos. Carter came fully in frame as a politician when he self-positioned as the righteous, incorruptible reformer standing outside the corrupt incompetence of the incumbent government. It just so happened that his outsider chic lined up perfectly to catch the zeitgeist of a sour nation in the mid-1970s. After what David Halberstam called "the best and the brightest" insiders led the United States into the disaster of the Vietnam War, followed by the national trauma of Watergate and the resignation of President Nixon, Americans—particularly young Americans—wanted an authentic outsider with reformist zeal to ride into town.

Carter's outsider brand got an unexpected lucky boost when the journalist Hunter S. Thompson became one of Carter's biggest fans by a quirk of sheer happenstance. Paul Scanlon, Thompson's longtime editor at *Rolling Stone* magazine, wrote that Thompson's writing became required reading for any "progressively minded college student in the 1960s." Thompson's 1971 book, *Fear and Loathing in Las Vegas: A Savage Journey to the Heart of the American Dream*, became almost a tone poem of disillusionment in the early 1970s, the two main characters taking drugs and driving to Las Vegas in search of the lost American Dream. The book opens with, "We were somewhere around Barstow on the edge of the desert when the drugs began to take hold." From there, the book takes the reader on a journey so strange that I wondered if the only way to have any real hope of understanding it would be to mix some concoction of chemicals like those the characters take, something along the lines of mescaline and LSD washed down with tequila, before wrestling with the text. (I did not test this theory.) Even if one could not fully understand just what the heck Thompson was writing about, one thing was absolutely clear: He personified the rising zeitgeist of cynicism about the established order combined with idealistic hope. The cynicism fully flourished in writings like *Fear and Loathing*, but the hope came in finding Jimmy Carter.

It happened quite by accident. Thompson had traveled to cover Senator Ted Kennedy making a political visit to Georgia, which included a Law Day luncheon at the University of Georgia Law School. "The only thing I remember about the first hour or so of that luncheon was a powerful sense of depression with the life I was drifting into," wrote Thompson, who blunted his darkening mood by sneaking Wild Turkey bourbon into his iced tea glass. Thompson thought of escaping, but he had to stay until the end for Senator Kennedy's perfunctory remarks. More Wild Turkey, more bored depression. One more speaker to go before Kennedy, some remarks by Georgia's 49-year-old governor, Jimmy Carter.

Carter didn't bring a script, instead riffing off some handwritten scrawls on a legal notepad. At first, it all seemed pretty standard boring stuff and Thompson expected nothing more. But as Carter got deeper into his remarks, Thompson noticed that people in the room had quieted, not in rapturous awe, but in befuddled irritation. Instead of ingratiating himself to the establishment crowd, Carter struck an angry defiant tone that conveyed a message along the lines of, *I'm not here to make friends. I'm standing out here pointing in, not joining your little insider club, and I'm going to fire a torpedo right into this insular little luncheon and talk about how injustice must be reformed into justice, whether you like it or not.* Carter became a lot more interesting to Thompson than his glass of Wild Turkey when he said, "One of the sources for my understanding about the proper application of criminal justice and the system of equities is from Reinhold Niebuhr. The other source of my understanding about what's right and wrong in this society is from a friend of mine, a poet named Bob Dylan." What? Reinhold Niebuhr and Bob Dylan? Thompson grabbed his tape recorder and clicked the record button.

Thompson called Carter's speech the "most eloquent thing I have ever heard from the mouth of a politician," further describing it as "the voice of an angry agrarian populist, extremely precise in its judgments and laced with some of the most original, brilliant, and occasionally bizarre political metaphors anybody in that room will ever be likely to hear." Carter himself later said it was "probably the best speech I ever made."

If Thompson had not been there with his tape recorder, the speech would have been lost to history. And Hunter S. Thompson—the gonzo journalist, the pied piper of antiestablishment idealists, the unhinged voice of the edgy counterculture—became Jimmy Carter's enthusiastic ally, playing his recording of the speech to any and every one he could get to listen. When the 1976 presidential election came along, Thompson wrote a seminal *Rolling Stone* feature that further cemented Carter's credibility as a genuine outside reformer, which is a big part of how Jimmy Carter surfed into the White House atop the gigantic zeitgeist wave of disillusionment sweeping the country in the mid-1970s.

Once in office, Carter's luck changed, from largely good to largely bad. He dealt with energy price shocks, double-digit inflation, the Soviet invasion of Afghanistan, and most of all, the Iran hostage crisis. The crisis began when Iranian students stormed the U.S. embassy in Tehran on November 4, 1979, taking Americans hostage. Carter worked with ceaseless energy to try to get the hostages released, but the days clicked by without a resolution. Ten days . . . 20 days . . . 50 days . . . 100 days . . . on and on it went, day after day after day after day. News programs began to intone the number of days or weeks or months since the start of the crisis, continually reminding the public that the hostages remained in captivity.

At day 173 of the crisis, Carter sent a Delta Force special operation to rescue the hostages, which went tragically awry. The mission required six helicopters to work, and Carter approved eight helicopters to give a buffer against uncertainties. One of the helicopters developed a rotor blade problem. Down to seven helicopters. Then a second helicopter hit a freak sandstorm that one officer described as "like a rolling fog bank" that swirled thousands of feet in the air and extended miles across the desert; navigation instruments began to fail and the helicopter returned to the USS *Nimitz* aircraft carrier. Down to six helicopters. The remaining helicopters landed at the assembly point, code-named Desert One, on a dry lake bed. A final check showed that a hydraulic pump on one of the helicopters had turned bright-glowing red, imperiling its hydraulic system. Down to five helicopters. After consulting with the Delta Force commander on the ground, Carter canceled the mission.

C-130 refueling aircraft had also landed on the lake bed, parked next to the helicopters. As one of the helicopters lifted above the desert floor to depart, the swirling sand rising up in the rotor wash caused a "brownout," rendering the pilot unable to see that the helicopter was flying not away from the nearby C-130 but straight into it. In the ensuing fireball, eight servicemen lost their lives. (The video documentary *Desert One* gives a superb and riveting accounting of the entire episode.) The catastrophe, for which Carter was widely criticized, further undermined people's confidence in him and his administration.

In a particularly bad twist for Carter, it would turn out that the one-year anniversary of when Iranian students stormed the U.S. embassy in Tehran fell on the precise day of the presidential election in 1980. So, just as people went to the polls, the other big story of the day would be marking one full year with the crisis unresolved, with endless replays of captured Americans being paraded around blindfolded. Carter eventually got the hostages freed at day 444 of the crisis, working feverishly for their release even after losing the election, right until the last minutes of his presidency. The Iranians held the aircraft with the freed hostages on the Tehran airport runway until the minutes just after Carter had officially left office.

Carter later reflected, "I have often been asked if there was one substantive action or decision I made as president that I would have changed. Somewhat facetiously, I have answered, 'I would have sent one more helicopter to ensure the success of the hostage rescue effort. . . .' But I truly believe that if I had done so, I would have been reelected."

It's Not About Luck: It's About Return on Luck

The series of luck events in the lives of Gerald R. Ford and Jimmy Carter bring us to a bit of a paradox. On the one hand, the evidence clearly shows that luck plays a significant role in the long arc of their lives. On the other hand, the evidence simply does not support the idea that luck alone is the primary explanation for the trajectory of their lives.

How then do we put these two facts together and resolve the paradox? The answer lies in grasping the difference between luck and return on luck. I realize that some people find the whole topic of luck uncomfortable because, well, it just seems so out of your control. But what *is* in your control is how you *respond* to luck.

> Luck is something that happens to you, largely out of your control. *Return* on luck is what you make of your luck (good or bad) when it comes. The question is not whether you will get luck, both good luck and bad, but what you do with the luck that you get.

My colleague Morten Hansen and I first articulated this distinction in our nine-year research project for the book *Great by Choice*. In that work, we studied some of the most successful entrepreneurs and company builders from the second half of the 20th century. As part of our analysis, we studied the variable of luck. We defined a "luck event" as one that meets three tests: (1) You didn't cause it; (2) it has a significant potential consequence, good or bad; and (3) it has an element of surprise—some aspect of the event is unpredictable before it happens.

Using this definition, we discovered that the most successful companies in our research did get a lot of luck, but they did *not* generally get *more* good luck, less bad luck, bigger spikes of luck, or better-timed luck than our control set of direct comparisons from the same industries. What the more successful companies achieved, instead, was a higher *return* on luck; *they made more of the luck they got.* By separating "luck" from "return on luck," we were able to account for the undeniable fact that luck happens (a lot) yet capture the truth that luck alone cannot explain the success of the great companies and entrepreneurs we studied.

I fully recognize that studying companies does not directly translate to studying individual lives, and we should be careful about carrying ideas from my prior research on what makes great companies tick to what makes people tick. That said, I found that the construct of distinguishing "luck" from "return on luck" was helpful in looking at the lives we studied.

Luck in this study fell into three broad buckets: "what luck," "who luck," and "zeit-luck."

What luck: This is luck that comes in the form of a specific consequential event or sequence of events, such as the opening or closing of an opportunity by factors outside the person's control, contracting or avoiding a disease in the genetic health lottery, personal tragedy that upends the person's world, a lifesaving close call, a sequence of small events that compound into one big luck event, or any number of other possibilities. Ford and Carter surviving near death by inches of angle were extreme versions of "what luck." That the incumbent for Ford's first congressional run got called back to Washington and could not campaign at home was "what luck" for Ford. Others in the study include the mysterious appearance of the guitar for Jimmy Page and the terrible bad luck of the onset of Parkinson's disease for Maurice White and Michael J. Fox.

Who luck: This is luck that comes in the form of crossing paths with a person who then significantly affects one's life, such as a friend, a spouse, a teacher, a school administrator, a mentor, a coach, a parent, a teammate, a partner, or some other life-altering relationship that came about by the random bumping of life. Gerald R. Ford's stepfather and his high school principal were "who luck" for Ford; Admiral Rickover and Hunter S. Thompson were "who luck" for Jimmy Carter. Others in the study include Warren Buffett, who mentored Katharine Graham; Alan Page's parents, who valued and sacrificed for his education; and Carol Heiss's skating coach, who trained her without pay in the years leading to her Olympic gold medal.

Zeit-luck: This is luck that relates to the zeitgeist of the times, wherein big social, cultural, political, technological, economic, and/or global events play a gigantic role in people's lives. Zeit-luck came in the swirl of Watergate that led Ford to becoming president, a role that he never sought or particularly wanted. Zeit-luck for Carter came in the shifting mood of the country that favored populist outsiders, which propelled him to the presidency. Other zeit-luck examples in the study include the historically ripe moment to achieve suffrage in the case of Alice Paul and Lucy Burns, the popular rise of fusion music in the 1970s in the case of Maurice White, the birth of computers plus World War II in the case of Grace Hopper, the perfect timing of the golden age of test piloting and the start of the U.S. space program in the lives of Gordon Cooper and John Glenn.

> Luck plays a role in survival. Luck plays a role in opening and closing opportunities. Luck plays a role in the peculiar twists and turns that can define a life. Luck plays a role in uncovering encodings. And luck sometimes plays a significant role in when and how one phase of life comes to an end and another begins. That said, for the people in this study, we can see that while luck spun through their lives, the other part of the story is what they *did* with their luck. They are not merely lives of luck; they are also lives of *return* on luck.

Yes, Gerald R. Ford got a lucky intervention when his high school principal took it upon himself to help Ford get to the University of Michigan. But Ford got a huge *return* on luck by working hard at both football and academics, chosen as most valuable player in his senior year (a quite unusual accomplishment for an offensive lineman in football) while simultaneously achieving the course requirements for a degree in economics. Yes, Gerald R. Ford got a lucky break during his first campaign when his incumbent opponent got trapped in Washington, but Ford got a huge *return* on luck by campaigning with ferocious vigor. Gerald R. Ford might have gotten hit with luck throughout his life, but his story makes more sense through the lens of return on luck.

Similarly with Jimmy Carter. Yes, Jimmy Carter got a hit of "who luck" in meeting Admiral Rickover, but he got a huge *return* on luck by making the most of every opportunity to learn and lead in Rickover's Nuclear Navy. Yes, Jimmy Carter got lucky when the Supreme Court ruled in *Baker v. Carr* and later when his antiestablishment ethos melded perfectly with the zeitgeist of disgust with the inside establishment, but he got a huge *return* on luck by running smart, intense campaigns that landed him in the Governor's Mansion and the White House.

I could go through every single person in the study with the same message. Yes, they got hit with luck events along the way (both good and bad), and some of these luck events came in the form of huge life-altering cliffs. But *return* on luck better explains their lives than mere luck alone.

Seizing NATILIE Moments

One of the key ways that people get a high return on luck is in seizing what Morten Hansen and I described as NATILIE moments. NATILIE (pronounced like the name Natalie) stands for "Not All Time In Life Is Equal." NATILIE moments are episodes of outsized opportunity or peril that call for summoning a level of energy and focus far beyond the person's normal set point. Life serves up NATILIE moments, which often come as luck events, that count much more than other moments.

Consider the NATILIE moment of Michael J. Fox and the lucky opportunity to play Marty McFly in *Back to the Future*. The movie had already been in filming for a few months, *without Fox in the role*, but the producer Steven Spielberg and the director Robert Zemeckis decided they needed to change out the lead actor. They wanted Fox. But Fox, then age 23, already had a full-time gig playing a lead role as Alex P. Keaton in the television series *Family Ties*. The movie studio couldn't wait until the end of the *Family Ties* season, especially with all the Marty McFly scenes that had to be reshot. At the same time, *Family Ties* ran on a rigorous schedule, rehearsing and delivering a live performance every single week. The producer of *Family Ties* supported Fox doing *Back to the Future*, but he also made clear that neither the script nor the schedule of the television series would bend to the demands of filming the movie.

So, Fox summoned the energy to do *both*. He wrote in his memoir that he lived the following schedule: At 9:30 a.m., he'd get driven to the *Family Ties* studio in Hollywood, then work on the show all day. At around 5 p.m., the *Family Ties* cast would do a run-through. After that, at 6 p.m., Fox would get picked up and driven over the Cahuenga Pass to Universal Studios or to a remote filming location. He'd then work on *Back to the Future* until sometime between 2 a.m. and 5 a.m. Then a teamster would drive Fox home, where he would crash asleep for a few hours. Then, at 9:30 a.m., the whole cycle would start again. Then again, and again, and again, and again. To be clear, Fox did not (and likely could not) sustain this schedule indefinitely, but he held the intensity for the three and a half months needed to complete the film. Yes, Michael J. Fox was lucky that *Back to the Future* needed a new lead actor, but that is only part of the story; the other part is what Fox *did* with the NATILIE moment when it came, summoning unequal intensity to meet an unequal moment of opportunity. Luck *and* return on luck.

> Not all time in life is equal. Some moments count more than other moments, when what you do in that moment has an outsized impact on the trajectory of a life. Luck events can serve up NATILIE moments. The question is not whether you will get NATILIE moments in life, but whether you meet those unequal moments with unequal intensity, summoning the best you have to give when the moment comes.

Bad Luck, Adversity, and "Fortunate Enough"

When people think of luck, they mainly think of good luck. But life also gives us bad luck.

Cardiss Collins got hit with unimaginable bad luck in the loss of her husband on Flight 553. I would not wish on anyone the grief she endured, and I certainly do not mean to imply that bad luck is somehow good luck (*bad luck is bad luck, period*) or that Collins's tragedy was "in the end a good thing." It was a terrible thing, and to trivialize her loss would be the height of disrespect. Still, even in the fog of grief, she chose the responsibility to complete George's unfinished congressional term and carry forth the work for his constituents the best she could. The hand of tragedy spun the roulette wheel of her life, and when the ball dropped into a slot where she would discover her encodings and fire for serving in Congress, she made a steady, relentless climb out of the abyss and into a multi-decade career as a highly effective congressional leader. That climb is not luck; it is return on luck.

The people in this study all had bad luck and/or faced adversity of one type or another in their lives. Recall the wide range of economic circumstances we uncovered in the chapter on flipping the arrow of money, and how some of them lived through episodes of significant economic scarcity. Recall also how the women in our study often ran into hurdles not faced by their male counterparts, such as challenges for women in academic science (McClintock and Hopper) and preconceptions about women in leadership (Graham and Frontiere). Similarly, people of color in our study confronted realities that I would not have faced. Maurice White titled a chapter "Black Tax" in his memoir, wherein he wrote about the barriers within the music industry he had to overcome to make Earth, Wind & Fire successful, invoking the expression "making a way out of no way."

There could be a set of circumstances a person faces that would render it nearly impossible to do what the people in this study did. A devastating traumatic event or a crushing health condition, for instance, could be so huge as to significantly impair the potential to find a hedgehog and thrive beyond cliffs and fog. Or a person could face a combination of circumstances and/or string of bad luck events that, in total, make it very difficult to build a life that works, perhaps even difficult to survive. I've had people in my own life who faced a confluence of circumstances that overwhelmed them, and in some cases even contributed to their lives ending long before they should have.

So, while it is true that all the people in our study overcame bad luck and/or adversity, it is also true that they all benefited from having circumstances *solid enough* to come fully into frame at least once, to get past the cliffs, and to feed the inner fire. None of the people in our study faced a confluence of adversities so severe as to make it essentially impossible to build a fulfilling life. And in this, they were fortunate.

The End of the Beginning

With the end of this chapter, we transition to the final section of the book, about feeding the inner fire long beyond the energy of youth. To set us up for that, let's complete the story of Ford and Carter and what became of their lives *after* the presidency.

In our research, we matched Ford and Carter at the cliff event of losing their incumbency elections as the 38th and 39th presidents of the United States. It's one thing to get fired from a job, but it's entirely another level to get fired by tens of millions of your fellow citizens. Now, *that* is a cliff! At first, reeling from the initial shock and embarrassment of such an epic and public repudiation, they were lost in the fog. Carter later reflected upon his "involuntary retirement" that he "awoke to an altogether new, unwanted, and potentially empty life. . . . It was deeply discouraging for me to contemplate the unpredictable years ahead."

The great irony of Jimmy Carter's life is that losing the presidential election at such a young age knocked him sideways and reframed his life into a spectacular four-decade run. Carter had penciled into his diary the idea of retirement at age 60, presuming he got a second term. But tossed out of office at age 56, Carter felt he was "too young to consider retirement." Compounding the cliff effect, Carter would discover upon losing the presidency that he and his wife, Rosalynn, were in substantial debt and in danger of losing the family business. To avoid any conflicts of interest, Carter had built a wall of separation between himself and the business for his presidential years, handing its management to others and receiving no updates. So, the financial loss on top of the election cliff came as a shock.

Still full of energy, Carter gave himself a couple of projects to work on, his way of simplex stepping out of the fog. After returning to their home in Plains, he and Rosalynn began refurbishing their house with their own hands, laying down a new floor in the attic. He also began writing his presidential memoir, a good simplex step to begin digging out of the financial hole they'd fallen into. He also began simplex stepping through the arduous task of raising money for a presidential library. The library project felt more like an obligation than an inspiration. "As a defeated Democratic candidate with no prospect of returning to public office and few wealthy friends or supporters," he later wrote, "I found this task difficult and time-consuming."

Then, one night, Carter shot wide awake with an idea for how to turn the library from an obligation into a freely chosen responsibility that would feed his inner fire. Carter conceived of a mini Camp David for achieving peace agreements. "I know what we can do at the library," he said to Rosalynn. "We can develop a place to help people who want to resolve disputes. There is no place like that now. If two countries really want to work something out, they don't want to go to the United Nations and get one hundred fifty other countries involved in the argument." In that moment, as Rosalynn conveyed in *Everything to Gain*, Jimmy felt fired up with a possible vision for what next to make of his life. Instead of a staid presidential library and museum, the Carters threw themselves into creating something entirely new and distinct, the Carter Center.

The post-cliff fog lifted and Carter stepped into a new way to deploy his encodings and feed his inner fire, as an independent statesman and sage. Jonathan Alter, author of the Carter biography *His Very Best*, aptly described Carter in his post-presidency as a "freelance secretary of state"—a role perfectly suited to Carter's outsider encodings. Carter always had an encoded operating mode of caring more about achieving what he believed to be the right outcomes than what other people thought or felt about him. Carter touched on this theme in a strikingly self-reflective after-action review of his own presidency in *White House Diary*: "I believe I developed good relationships with almost all members of Congress, but sometimes I was not adequately concerned with how my proposals affected the views of the voters on whom they relied for reelection. . . . A somewhat less rigid approach to these sensitive issues could have paid rich dividends." He also eschewed the Washington social scene, further hewing to his reformist outsider mode but with the consequence of alienating some influential people. Yet his outsider encodings and his lack of desire to be well liked by those in power made him quite effective in staring down dictators about human rights, fighting for free and fair elections, and addressing the chronic health needs of impoverished peoples. Unintimidated and unimpressed by strongmen, he could convey a clarion message along the lines of, *I'm not here to get you to like me. I'm here to get you to make things better for your people. So, let's go to work.*

Jimmy Carter did not know it when the American people fired him, but he would have some of the most meaningful decades of his life after the presidency. In addition to conflict resolution, he worked on global health (eradication of diseases), democracy (improving elections), and a range of human rights issues around the world. He helped build houses with Habitat for Humanity, swinging a hammer on construction sites creating housing for the poor. He also published more than two dozen books, some autobiographical, some spiritual, some artsy, some with global gravitas. One might think that being president of the United States would be the most fulfilling years of a person's life. But in Carter's case, the evidence leads me to conclude that he came more fully in frame *after* his presidency. Carter captured his love for his postpresidential life by invoking a cartoon that he particularly enjoyed, in which a child says, "When I grow up, I want to be a former president."

And what of Gerald R. Ford? Like Carter, Ford experienced a period of fog after the presidency. He kept open the option of running again for the White House, though more passively by not closing the door than actively campaigning for himself. Then, in a truly befuddled fog moment, he considered the idea of being Reagan's vice presidential partner in 1980. It's hard to envision a former president in the White House serving as vice president. In the end, Ford turned Reagan down, marking the moment that the fog had cleared enough to accept that his life as an elected politician had truly come to an end.

In his mid-60s, Ford finally settled into a second hedgehog analogous to Carter's, as an independent statesman and sage. He became a counselor to the Republican Party. He served as a geopolitical sage on corporate boards. He served as an energetic ambassador and fundraiser for the Betty Ford Center for the treatment of addiction, which his wife, Betty, formed.

In a beautiful and unexpected turn, Ford and Carter became "who luck" in each other's lives, as they transformed from political adversaries into deep personal friends. They led together on more than 25 initiatives, on issues ranging from the Middle East and nuclear disarmament to the national deficit and toxic divisiveness in American politics, and they co-chaired multiple conferences at the Carter Center.

Carter had initiated their circle of friendship with the very first sentence he ever said as president. Upon taking the oath of office,

Carter began his inaugural address by thanking Ford for all he had done in service to a nation in need of healing: He turned to Ford, sitting to Carter's right on the inaugural platform, and extended his hand. Ford, visibly stunned by the moment, stood up to shake Carter's hand, sat down, then stood again as thousands of people gave the outgoing president a standing ovation. Carter did not rush the moment, instead giving an extended pause to center the energy of the crowd on the former president and allow waves of appreciation to wash over Ford.

Ford and Carter, one conservative and the other liberal, brought the circle toward a close with a personal agreement that feels almost unimaginable in an era of fiercely partisan, deeply divisive politics: Whichever one of us dies first, the other promises to give the eulogy. Ford passed first, and at the funeral Carter spoke explicitly of the love he felt for his former political adversary. He then closed his eulogy with the same words with which their friendship began nearly 30 years earlier: "For myself and for our Nation, I want to thank my predecessor for all he has done to heal our land."

In rendering this one final joint service to the nation, Ford and Carter showed the renewing power of choosing responsibilities so long as the mind allows. Their presidencies might have ended prematurely, but not the inner fire. Right until the end, together and apart, the fire burned bright.

Part III

Feeding the Inner Fire Long and Late

10

Extend Out/ Circle Back

When Meryl Streep faced turning 40, she feared that perhaps the best phase of her career had ended, a feeling reinforced when she received three separate offers to play a witch. "Everybody has troughs and dismal times—every single person," she later reflected. "I remember as I was hovering around 40, I thought each movie would be my last, really. And all the evidence of other 40-year-old women at that time . . . would lead you to believe it was over."

Well, not quite.

It turned out that when Streep hit 40, she had more than two-thirds of her life's work *ahead* of her. Not only did she triple the number of starring roles in feature films, but she also sustained her creative excellence. Consider this simple statistic: Streep earned more Oscar nominations *after* age 40 than any other actor in history (male or female) had achieved across the *entirety* of their careers.

In fact, Streep earned just as many Oscar nominations in her 60s as she did during her hyperproductive 30s. As of 2024, she'd earned 21 nominations, 75% more than any other actor in history, and I would not be surprised to see her land another one in her late 70s or even her 80s.

How did she work through the "witch offer" phase of her 40s, regain full stride in her 50s, and then *accelerate*? How did she keep the fire fully fed long and late?

Streep found and fully committed to her hedgehog in her 20s, earning a scholarship and working side jobs to pay for Yale School of Drama, where she played 12 to 15 acting roles a year. "It was terribly intense," she reflected. Yet while the schedule was stressful, she began to discover the depth of her encodings for the craft of acting and to deploy them with intensely focused fire. In one of her most memorable lead roles at Yale, Streep played Constance Garnett, a somewhat crazed 80-year-old translator of Russian literature who romped and rolled around the stage in a wheelchair, in the comedic musical *The Idiots Karamazov*. One of the playwrights said of Streep's performance, "She invented the part . . . marvelously transforming herself into that 80-year-old littérateuse."

She began her post-Yale career in New York City, where she fed her voracious appetite for acting, taking on eight stage roles in two years. She had no plan or grand ambition to become a film star. She simply began expanding out of Yale, deploying her encodings. One of her stage performances captured the attention of the director of *The Deer Hunter*, and she landed the part of Linda, whom Streep later described as "a small-town girl from a working class background, a lovely, quiet, hapless girl, who waited for the boy she loved to come back from the war in Vietnam." With Linda, Streep received her first Oscar nomination, at age 29.

Streep's early films earned her a reputation as one who could brilliantly play complex, often unhappy or even tragic characters. Her first Oscar win (at age 30) came for the role of Joanna Kramer in *Kramer vs. Kramer*, wherein she played a conflicted mother who leaves her son and husband and then returns for a custody battle. For her second Oscar win (at age 33), she played Sophie in *Sophie's Choice*, an Auschwitz survivor carrying the guilt of an unimaginable choice. Streep said that she could read the crux scene in *Sophie's Choice* only once: "When we shot it, I didn't want to do it again. I didn't want to be there." Other Oscar nominations in her 30s included tragic roles in *Silkwood* (in which she plays a historically based character whose hero's journey comes to a premature and mysterious end), *A Cry in the Dark* (about a mother fighting to prove her innocence when accused of killing her own child), and *Ironweed* (set in the Depression era, a heart-cracking film of sadness and despair, wherein Streep plays a singer with dashed dreams). She played other roles, but the core of her acting reputation lay in roles like these.

Then, facing the turning-40-in-Hollywood cliff, worried that her prime years as a top-star actor might be over, Streep made an unexpected shift: She turned toward comedy. From age 40 to 43, she did four comedic films in a row, *She-Devil*, *Postcards from the Edge*, *Defending Your Life*, and *Death Becomes Her*. In the quite campy *Death Becomes Her*, she played opposite Goldie Hawn as immortal rivals (having taken an anti-aging elixir) battling for the same man, including a sort of sword fight with shovels. The film ends with their two disconnected heads talking to each other after bouncing down a flight of stairs.

Her transition to comedy created confusion, consternation, even criticism among some in the business. These were not what many thought of as Meryl Streep roles. *Where's Linda? Where's Joanna Kramer? Where's Sophie?* One director said, "The one thing Meryl couldn't do was the one thing she desperately wanted to do. . . . She had to prove she's a great comedienne." You didn't go to a Meryl Streep movie for pure entertainment, to laugh, to enjoy lighter fare, to come away happy; you went to *feel intense human drama*. Or at least that is how many viewed her at the time. Of course, had any of those critics seen her at age 25 wheeling around the stage as Constance Garnett in *The Idiots Karamazov*, they might have seen the encodings for comedy that she'd always had. In reading about Streep extending her film acting into comedy, and the critical skepticism she endured, I kept thinking about a line from the writer James A. Michener: "Critics are invaluable in advising me how to spend my money. They are not qualified to tell me how to spend my talent."

Then Streep took another surprising step outward by becoming an action hero in *The River Wild*, wherein she played a mom and former river guide who takes her family on a Idaho river trip, only to be hijacked on the river by a couple of armed criminals on the run. Training for the role, Streep developed her arm muscles, though she said, "I worked out because I knew this river rafting would be tougher than the rowing machine at my gym, which, incidentally, I never use because I'm not really big on working out." At one point in the filming, Streep's boat overturned, throwing her underwater in a cold, raging current dragging her under. A rescue kayaker frantically chased her until she finally emerged about 500 yards downriver. "When I got to the shore," Streep recalled, "my legs actually went out from under me." Streep's fiercely protective supermom character outsmarts the bad guys in the end.

Before you get the idea that Streep went through some sort of radical reinvention, we need to temper the story with what came next: *The Bridges of Madison County*. Only one year after *The River Wild*, she circled back to deliver a classic Streepian performance as Francesca Johnson—a nuanced character torn between family duty and a once-in-a-lifetime love. The entire film flows inexorably toward a tear-jerking moment of decision, made powerful by the minimal dialogue and the pounding sound of rain. With Francesca, she'd returned to home base, and she would continue to circle back there over the next quarter century.

Yet Streep also kept extending out, playing a ruthless senator in *The Manchurian Candidate*, an endearing catastrophist in *A Series of Unfortunate Events*, and fusing drama and comedy in the character Miranda Priestly in *The Devil Wears Prada*. When the elevator doors open and Miranda Priestly walks out, terrifying her staff with a quiet imperiousness and lines like "The tales of your incompetence do not interest me," there's not a shred of Linda, or Sophie, or Joanna, or Francesca anywhere to be seen. About two years after Miranda, Streep extended out even further, singing ABBA songs and dancing all over a Greek island in the musical comedy *Mamma Mia!* Yet *in the same year* as *Mamma Mia!*, Streep (aged 59) also circled back to play a conflicted character as Sister Aloysius Beauvier in *Doubt*, whose last lines end in tears of despair, "I have doubts, I have such doubts."

From there, Streep accelerated into her 60s, doing some of the best work of her life, garnering six Oscar nominations over the next nine years (including a win for *The Iron Lady*). In her 60s, Streep circled back to play dramatic characters and comedic characters, but she also continued to extend out in playing major historical figures like Margaret Thatcher. The inner fire for acting seemed only to grow and her range only continued to expand.

Extend Out/Circle Back and Feeding the Inner Fire

We've now moved into the third part of the book, about what it takes to feed the inner fire across the long arc of a life. Meryl Streep exemplifies one of the key elements uncovered in the research: Extend Out/Circle Back. The basic idea of Extend Out/Circle Back is a looping process of, on the one hand, pushing out the edges and doing new things and, on the other hand, returning to the wellspring of encodings tapped before.

> Extending out feeds the inner fire by animating the human yearning for growth, learning, discovery, and challenge; it activates the joy of self-development, capturing the youthful energy that comes from starting anew. Extending out can reveal previously hidden encodings, a continuous process of discovery that feeds the inner fire. (*Wow, that's exciting—I never knew I had that inside me!*) Circle back *also* acts as a source of reinvigoration, but in a different way. Circling back reframes big bright encodings discovered long ago, which also feeds the inner fire. To circle back by tapping encodings discovered earlier in life is like *refueling* for the next phase of extending out.

One of the prime benefits of studying the long arc of lives lies in seeing how the dual dynamics of continuity and change play off each other. You can see clearly what remains relatively constant and what changes as the decades click by. You can see how our study subjects held true to some core elements as anchors amid the swirling tumult and raging storms of life. You can also see how they sought continuous growth, learning, evolution, exploration, adventure, new challenges, and creative expression.

Meryl Streep embodied the Extend Out/Circle Back dynamic across six decades. Streep extended out in moving from classic theater to feature films. She extended out in moving from her early serious and tragic roles into comedy and action. She extended out in moving to musical films and playing major historical figures. Streep skirted the trap of becoming imprisoned by what she'd done before, refusing to let other people's expectations of what makes a "Meryl Streep film" constrain her exploration and expansion. By the continuous process of Extend Out/Circle Back, she gradually expanded the definition of a Streepian role to cover a vast range of genres while also retaining her foundations as a nuanced dramatic actor.

Meryl Streep Films
A Continuous Journey of Extend Out/Circle Back

AGE	FILMS	OSCAR NOMINATIONS	OSCAR WINS
28	Julia		
29	The Deer Hunter	Nomination No. 1	
29	Manhattan		
30	The Seduction of Joe Tynan		
30	Kramer vs. Kramer	Nomination No. 2	Win No. 1
32	The French Lieutenant's Woman	Nomination No. 3	
33	Still of the Night		
33	Sophie's Choice	Nomination No. 4	Win No. 2
34	Silkwood	Nomination No. 5	
35	Falling in Love		

AGE	FILMS	OSCAR NOMINATIONS	OSCAR WINS
36	Plenty		
36	Out of Africa	Nomination No. 6	
37	Heartburn		
38	Ironweed	Nomination No. 7	
39	A Cry in the Dark	Nomination No. 8	
40	She-Devil		
41	Postcards from the Edge	Nomination No. 9	
41	Defending Your Life		
43	Death Becomes Her		
44	The House of the Spirits		
45	The River Wild		
45	The Bridges of Madison County	Nomination No. 10	
46	Before and After		
47	Marvin's Room		
49	Dancing at Lughnasa		
49	One True Thing	Nomination No. 11	
50	Music of the Heart	Nomination No. 12	
53	Adaptation.	Nomination No. 13	
53	The Hours		
55	The Manchurian Candidate		
55	A Series of Unfortunate Events		
56	Prime		
56	A Prairie Home Companion		
57	The Devil Wears Prada	Nomination No. 14	
57	Dark Matter		
58	Evening		
58	Rendition		
58	Lions for Lambs		
59	Mamma Mia!		
59	Doubt	Nomination No. 15	
60	Julie & Julia	Nomination No. 16	
60	It's Complicated		
62	The Iron Lady	Nomination No. 17	Win No. 3
63	Hope Springs		
64	August: Osage County	Nomination No. 18	

Continued

AGE	FILMS	OSCAR NOMINATIONS	OSCAR WINS
65	The Homesman		
65	The Giver		
65	Into the Woods	Nomination No. 19	
66	Ricki and the Flash		
66	Suffragette		
67	Florence Foster Jenkins	Nomination No. 20	
68	The Post	Nomination No. 21	
69	Mamma Mia! Here We Go Again		
69	Mary Poppins Returns		
70	The Laundromat		
70	Little Women		
71	The Prom		
71	Let Them All Talk		
72	Don't Look Up		

Note: Due to ambiguity in the sources as to some of the precise dates (month and day) relative to birthdays, cited ages in this chronology may vary by +/-1 year.

Part of Streep's encodings lay in an unquenchable curiosity about what it would be like to be a specific individual within a particular story and then internalizing that character. "Acting is my way of investigating human nature," she explained. It's an ethos she carried across the decades, as Streep succinctly put it, "I've always been curious to know what it's like to be you." As she continued to extend out into her 60s, Streep kept the curiosity motor running full bore, describing it as the key ingredient in the secret sauce that "most animates my work," adding, "I'm really interested." Streep's approach reminded me of a lesson I learned from the late John W. Gardner, author of the book *Self-Renewal*: Don't try to be "interesting"; be *interested*.

Throughout, Streep returned to the wellspring of her encoded operating modes that served her acting well, no matter what type of new role she'd be exploring. One of her encodings lay in her ability to get those acting with her to feel that they were in a scene *not* with Meryl Streep playing the character. She could get them to believe they were in the scene *with the actual character*. She deployed this encoded mode no matter whether drama or comedy, history or musical, action hero or unlikable antihero, 20-something character or 70-something character.

In *Kramer vs. Kramer*, Streep rewrote Joanna Kramer's courtroom speech (wherein she makes her own case for custody) to better capture what she felt the real Joanna would say. "It appears in the movie, word-for-word, exactly as she wrote it," said the director. "It's some of the best writing in the picture—and it's hers." The director of *Sophie's Choice* described the first read through of the script: "Before we began to read, we were sitting around for an hour, doing the usual kibitzing. . . . She said the first line of dialogue, and it had nothing to do with the actress I'd been talking to. My reaction was shock. Somewhere along the line, she had created this woman inside of herself."

Nearly a quarter century later, Streep drew on this same encoded mode with a radically different character, Miranda Priestly. A fellow actor described a read through of *The Devil Wears Prada*, the moment when Streep flipped a switch from being Meryl one moment and Miranda the next: "I think we all had an idea of what Miranda would sound like. . . . It was a strident, bossy, barking voice. So when Meryl opened her mouth and basically whispered, everybody in the room drew a collective gasp. It was so unexpected and so brilliant." Streep wanted to convey the sheer power wielded by Miranda Priestly, and she perceived that the most powerful people command by being the quietest. If you truly have power, like a monarch, then you don't need to raise your voice to command attention; by speaking softly, you cause everyone else to quiet down and listen. Later, in discussing how she prepared for the very far extend out in the musical comedy *Mamma Mia!*, Streep said, "I approach my comic work as if it was very serious drama. . . . There's no difference in how I make a character."

I was not surprised to find some element of extending out in the study—that the pursuit of growth and learning would correlate strongly with ageless zeal. (It was another lesson I'd been taught by

John W. Gardner.) What did surprise me, however, is the equally important element of circling back and the revitalizing power of the two elements together, each reinforcing the other in a powerful interplay that feeds the fire.

When I described Streep's Extend Out/Circle Back evolution to a friend of mine who worked for NASA as a rocket scientist, he lit up and drew me a picture. "It's like a rocket using the gravity of a planet as a source of acceleration!" Now, I'm not a rocket scientist or astrophysicist, so I'm a bit out of my depth here. But the essence of what he drew is a rocket moving outward in expanding ellipses, extending out away from the planet, then circling back close to the planet and harnessing the planet's gravity to accelerate the rocket out on to an even wider ellipse, then back again to gain more acceleration to go out even farther. "That's what it sounds like Streep did," he said excitedly. "She'd circle back not as a form of retreat or deceleration, but as a source of *acceleration* to go further outward." Yes! That's a very good metaphor for exactly what we observed.

Debra Winger: Extending Out in a Different Direction

Now let's turn to Meryl Streep's matched-pair companion in the study, Debra Winger.

Winger became an actor in the wake of a near-death experience at age 17. She'd been working over the holiday break as a costumed troll at an amusement park. While being ferried across property in the back of a truck, she noticed her troll outfit (which she'd taken off) sliding backward. She left her seat to grab it at the exact moment that the truck swerved, throwing her off the truck. She hit the asphalt. Hard.

Winger ended up in the hospital with a cerebral hemorrhage, partially paralyzed and blind. She nearly died. At one point, struggling with her condition, she formulated a plan to find her way to the hospital balcony and tumble off. When she tried to feel her way to the jumping-off point, her outstretched hand landed on an unsuspecting nurse. The nurse screamed. Winger screamed, then began to laugh. In her wonderfully poetic memoir, *Undiscovered*, Winger later wrote of her thwarted attempt as a turning point that filled her with life. "And as my sight eventually returned," she continued, "I came to see it as a message from the universe. This is not your decision to make, darling."

Winger had dabbled in acting, but coming out of the hospital, she'd gained a piercing clarity. "I wanted to act before, but I was still under the pull of my parents and sort of under the middle-class work ethic. It was a hobby, you know. You don't actually do that for a living," she said years after the accident. "But when somebody experiences death, near death, you realize you're all alone at the end. And I said I can't do something another day that I won't be completely fulfilled in."

Winger made a full commitment to focus her fire on acting. She took three years of acting classes. After a few years of landing small parts, including a stint as Wonder Girl in the show *Wonder Woman*, Winger got a NATILIE moment. The original female lead in *Urban Cowboy* had not jelled for the role, and the director began searching for a replacement. Winger, still largely unknown, didn't garner a slot to read for the role, so she talked her way into the studio lot and sat herself on the steps outside where the readings would take place. The director walked by, then stopped, curious if she was there to read for the part. Winger went right to how she envisioned the feisty character who frequented a South Texas tavern. As she later described the moment, "I squinted up at the kind face, and in my best Texas, I replied, 'Who wants to know?'"

She got the reading, which led to landing the part, which led to her first breakout movie. Winger seized the NATILIE opportunity and threw herself into the role, even spending an entire night in a cemetery to get herself into the right emotional state for a funeral scene. Winger followed *Urban Cowboy* with an enormously fruitful run of films in her late 20s and 30s, including three Oscar nominations (for *An Officer and a Gentleman*, *Terms of Endearment*, and *Shadowlands*). Winger and Streep stood side by side as two of the most productive and successful female actors. Winger did 15 films from ages 25 through 40, and Streep did 16 from ages 28 through 40 (see nearby side-by-side listing of early films for Streep and Winger). Both earned tremendous respect for their performances, the *Los Angeles Times* noting at one point that Winger's "only real competition" was Meryl Streep.

Meryl Streep and Debra Winger
Early Film Careers Side by Side

MERYL STREEP, FEATURE FILMS AGES 28–40, 1977–89	DEBRA WINGER, FEATURE FILMS AGES 25–40, 1980–95
Julia	Urban Cowboy
The Deer Hunter*	Cannery Row
Manhattan	An Officer and a Gentleman*
The Seduction of Joe Tynan	Terms of Endearment*
Kramer vs. Kramer**	Mike's Murder
The French Lieutenant's Woman*	Legal Eagles
Still of the Night	Black Widow
Sophie's Choice**	Betrayed
Silkwood*	Everybody Wins
Falling in Love	The Sheltering Sky
Plenty	Leap of Faith
Out of Africa*	A Dangerous Woman
Heartburn	Shadowlands*
Ironweed*	Wilder Napalm
A Cry in the Dark*	Forget Paris
She-Devil	

*Oscar Nomination, **Oscar Win

Winger loved the core work of acting, and she could not help but completely drain everything out of herself in doing a role. "For me, a day on a set is like a month, it's that intense," she said at 33. "My only interest—and sometimes my self-flagellation—is about 'Did I work hard enough?' 'Did I go deep enough?' 'Did I understand enough?'" For Winger, it was about going so deep into a character that she would learn something, often about herself. "Always in a role something is revealed to me," she said of the payoff for her draining full-immersion process. "That's why I do it, that's why I act." Each film had a three-part cycle: months preparing, then months filming, then months *recovering*. Winger poured so much of herself into a role that she'd need to disengage to rest and repair, often to someplace where she could be anonymous, such as to her getaway cabin near a remote mountain village in southern New Mexico. Winger had always followed her natural instincts about when to take a break, saying, "There's just not a flight plan. When I run out of gas, I land for a while." She exemplified an important distinction in life: *Don't confuse the need for a break with the need to quit.*

To do the work she loved, Winger paid a hefty Stress and Drudgery Tax of being famous. The idea that someone would *want* to be famously recognizable would likely strike her as utterly incomprehensible. She found the business and press at times "horrifying" in how it made her feel: "I always felt like, 'Why can't it be about the work? Why does it have to be about me, and why do I have to feel like a thing?' I never asked for that; I really just wanted to do parts and do them well." She didn't relish being in the epicenter of the see-and-be-seen Hollywood machine. She enjoyed driving long distances far from Los Angeles, unnoticed. "If I'm around Beverly Hills for very long," she said as her fame star burned brightest, "I start longing for a Greyhound bus station in the Midwest." Even when invoking her celebrity might help her, she'd prefer to remain anonymous. Once, when she was trying to get a table for one at an elite restaurant in New York, the maître d' didn't know who she was and wouldn't find a seat for her. Even though hungry and feeling stung by the condescending, disinterested tone of the maître d'—"I am sor-ree, mademoiselle, but we have no room"— Winger didn't drop a hint of her star status. Instead, she walked alone, nearly half a mile, back to her hotel and ate room service.

Coming upon age 40, Winger noticed a change in the mix of opportunities, and she responded by changing the mix of how she allocated her own life. She received scripts, but the proportion of opportunities that interested her began to decline: "It was like 1 to 7 interesting things. Then it was 1 to 10. And I thought, 'I've got some things I want to do in life.'" She moved to upstate New York, far away from the Hollywood movie mill. She married for a second time. (Winger had been married for about three and a half years in her early 30s.) She eventually decided to step away from feature film acting and focus her fire elsewhere.

She chose the responsibility to nurse her mother through the final months of life. She wanted to have another child (she'd had one child in her first marriage) and to invest herself in parenting well. Along the way, she allowed herself more time for one of her enduring loves, gardening, relishing the Zen-like process of working the earth with her own hands. She also became a farmer, tending an apple and feed-corn farm that she'd acquired. She taught at Harvard, in a class titled The Literature of Social Reflection. She explored various strains of spirituality and religious traditions, including the deeper elements of Judaism that connected her back to having been raised in a Jewish family.

Winger didn't quit acting so much as she quit Hollywood. "I didn't feel that I was walking away," she later reflected. "I just was following my life and it wasn't there in Hollywood." She continued to deploy her encodings for acting by doing some stage performances at the American Repertory Theater and working with her husband (a director, screenwriter, actor) on various productions. In reading through the materials on Winger through these years, I'm struck by how she simplex stepped through this phase of her life, reallocating her energy from a more public life to a much more private life. A few years into her private segue, she could finally shop unnoticed. "I can't even get help," she said, but not as a complaint. "That's when I knew I was successful in my bid for obscurity."

Then a very odd thing happened: Winger became a symbol, not of her own making, with the release of a documentary titled *Searching for Debra Winger*. The film focused on the challenges facing women as they move beyond their younger years in the film industry, invoking Winger as an emblematic example. Winger had been interviewed for the film but had no idea her name would be in the title.

Winger had a different take on her own evolution, seeing it not as abandoning her acting life but as *living life in a different direction*. She didn't frame her transition as saying no to feature film acting so much as saying yes to the other elements of life she wanted to nurture at that time: "I didn't differentiate between 'That's it' and 'That's it for now.' . . . I did a lot of interesting stuff . . . and I didn't feel like any of it was 'instead of.'" Yet even with Winger's clarity, she felt a sense of loss and fog as she worked through this time of transition. "The first couple years were really hard," she said in an interview for the film. "I felt half dead, I felt really scared at my choice, and I felt really unsure that I would ever feel vital again." She did learn to feel vital again, largely by focusing her inner fire on activities less visible to the world than leading roles in big-hit Hollywood films.

Winger later used the analogy of fading out and fading in to describe how the whole process felt to her. She faded out of feature film acting for a while, and faded into other parts of her life. Then, in her late 40s and early 50s, she began to fade back into more acting. At age 53, she delivered a stunning performance as a complicated mother in the movie *Rachel Getting Married*. Her performance generated a *Winger's back!* buzz, to which Winger replied, "I don't know what people mean by me being 'back.' . . . I've been acting all along. I understand that I haven't been in people's viewers, but acting has never not been a part of my life, just more time in between and less high-profile." Winger continued her fade in, doing television shows, a Netflix series, and films.

The fire had never gone out inside her; she'd simply channeled it in different directions. Winger never lost her love of acting itself, and she returned to reanimate her encodings and fire for acting later in life, though with more perspective. "I'd never claim to be evolved," she said of her journey, "but I've certainly re-volved several times."

Winger's "fade out" and "fade in" pattern links back to the iterative stepwise method of transition we discussed in the "Simplex Stepping" chapter. From the outside, the transition might look like flipping a light switch from on to off. From the inside perspective, however, it can feel more like a dimmer knob that can fade the lights up and down. Transitions between life phases were often more like turning a dimmer switch than flipping an on-off light switch. The dynamic of Extend Out/Circle Back married to simplex stepping captures this organic evolutionary process.

In the case of Debra Winger, it looked to the outside world as if she simply woke up one day, threw her hands in the air, and said, "That's it! I'm done! Goodbye!" But if you look closely, she'd begun her transition before she passed age 40. She'd already moved to upstate New York. She'd already been well practiced at saying no to films that didn't interest her. She'd already begun working on her farm. By Winger's own account, she'd been thinking about and organically evolving toward her fade-out for five years before she stopped reading scripts.

One false caricature of Winger would be a story along the lines of this: Hollywood star burns out and then "retires" to a life of leisure. I came to see Winger's story as one of the most wonderful in this study, showing us a life full of meaning and fire. That the fire showed less visibly in the world for a time made it no less hot and bright. At age 55, she gave a rare and lengthy interview. In it, the journalist described a picture on her wall of a barn standing strong as a fire expands outward and upward from within the sturdy structure, painted by her friend the poet Ted Kooser. "That," Winger said, referencing the painting, "is what I feel like inside."

Don't Confuse Public Visibility with Inner Fire

I had a little tab in my research notes for what I called Zen Garden elements. I carried in my mind the image of a person fully engaged in making the most exquisitely beautiful Zen Garden that few people ever see. If the person is deeply encoded for doing it, had some way of making the economics work, and absolutely felt full of fire in the daily work of cultivating the garden, then that person would be just as much in a hedgehog as a president or a CEO or a rock star or a gold medal Olympian.

Winger did much of her extending out in a more personal and private direction, including being an *actual* gardener. For Winger, gardening became a means to deep reflection, connecting her to the annual cycle of awakening spring to vibrant summer to fading fall to the stark simplicity of winter. She also made a practice of planting gardens upon important births and when she lost someone in life. "Sundays on the farm mean I'm hands-on in my garden," she related. "I'm planting, watering, working in the dirt. I love it." She also extended herself to teach literature, reveling in the simplicity of riding a bicycle across campus and engaging with students. But notice, she also circled back, both visibly and not. She circled back into acting (visible) and into continuing to cultivate the seeds of her own spiritual path that had been planted years before (less visible), reconnecting with the Torah and learning about other spiritual traditions.

> Extend Out/Circle Back can be a very private journey. You might have a role in the world that is more visible, in your work or profession, yet doing a big part of your Extend Out/Circle Back into activities largely unseen except by people close to you. It doesn't matter whether

> other people see what feeds the inner fire in your life. What matters is *that* you feed the inner fire. You might have a Zen Garden personal hedgehog or a private side of your life that is even more fire filled than anything highly visible in the world.

Like Debra Winger, Meryl Streep also integrated a less visible realm into her life, one that captured a significant portion of Streep's inner fire: being a mom. For three decades, from age 30 to 60, she would have at least one child under the age of 18. The evidence indicates that she made significant choices to prioritize parenting while also continuing her public-facing work as an actor. Streep began acting on the stage, developing her craft at the Yale School of Drama and spending a portion of her early career on the live stages in New York City, and I believe she would have loved doing live theater in mid-career. But Broadway performances ran in the evenings and weekends, a direct conflict with family time: "I have a committee at home, aged 12, nine, six and one, and they're the reason I never returned to the stage. They don't care what I do all day as long as I'm home at night." She didn't get drawn into the consuming role of directing. She became increasingly selective in considering film projects that might take her away from home for big chunks of time. "Motherhood has a very humanizing effect," she explained. "Everything gets reduced to essentials."

Streep's films made her an internationally recognizable icon, at a level she never envisioned when starting out. Yet acting was only the most visible part of her life achievements, and not necessarily the most difficult or important. "When you have your hand on the dike, you know how much water you're holding back," said Streep while discussing a role wherein she played a mom. Then she added, "If you're a mom, you know how much you're doing, but you're not going to get a lot of credit for it. Mothering is an invisible achievement."

Extend Out/Circle Back
Across the Study

When I began this research, I wanted to understand how and why some people remain continuously self-renewed—exuding ageless zeal, expanding their capabilities, and sustaining meaningful engagement—as the years and decades of life accumulate. Part of the answer lies in the continuous process of Extend Out/Circle Back in whatever walks of life the study subjects chose.

Robert Plant embodied Extend Out/Circle Back across his entire musical adventure. In his early 50s, Plant was driving country roads in the middle of the night when he heard the voice of the bluegrass artist Alison Krauss come through his car radio. According to Plant's friend, "Robert told me that he pulled the car over. He was in the middle of the countryside on a beautiful summer's night. He said he turned up the radio, got out of the car and stood there under the stars listening to Alison sing. Robert described it to me as like hearing a voice from another planet." Plant called Krauss, the first step toward a collaboration that would come to full fruition in the album *Raising Sand*. Not only did Plant extend out into the musical genre of bluegrass, but he also had to do something he'd never done before: to merge his voice with another. Plant mused, "Can an old dog ever learn a new trick?" Could the former Golden God front singer of Led Zeppelin learn to blend his voice with someone who, in his words, could "sing like an angel"? "She kind of nurtured me through this thing because she liked the idea of my voice and hers," said Plant of working with Krauss. "The two voices really did blend great, but I got a lot to learn." Then Plant summed it up when he gave himself over to being a duo: "Hey, presto, I was born again!"

Even with this beautiful act of extending out, Plant also circled back by bringing Led Zeppelin songs into the mix of their work together. A perfect, vivid example is Plant and Krauss performing "Black Dog" on *CMT Crossroads*, a country music show. If you want to get the full effect, first listen to the original Led Zeppelin version of "Black Dog," with 22-year-old Robert Plant hitting the high notes right out of the gate with "Hey, hey, mama, said the way you move, gonna make you sweat, gonna make you groove" followed by the crashing chords of Jimmy Page's guitar, John Paul Jones's underlying bass rhythm, and John Bonham's pounding drums exploding outward with pure rock energy. Then watch the *CMT Crossroads* version, with Plant, on the cusp of turning 60 and full of fire, doing a rich and resonant blend of the same song with Krauss, slow and melodic, seductive and mature.

If you look at Plant's set lists, with Krauss and other bands, he frequently included a few Led Zeppelin songs, though always transformed. In discussing a gig he did with the band Strange Sensation, Plant emphasized that doing an old Zeppelin song is not about nostalgia but about expanding: "We put that Hungarian Yiddish bit in the middle [of "Black Dog"], and I went into that kind of rap moment, then into a Mose Allison type of thing, hit the high note, then dipped it and turned it around and took it somewhere else. It's good for some people to go, 'What was all that about?'"

Extend Out/Circle Back showed up not just in the lives of people in arts or performance; it showed up in other walks of life.

John Glenn did Extend Out/Circle Back in going to the U.S. Senate, moving himself into a new arena yet circling back to a long-held passionate interest in civics. He also did a rather spectacular circle back, when he volunteered himself to go back to space in his 70s!

Barbara Tuchman did Extend Out/Circle Back, branching out from her early work related to World War I to study and write about 20th-century China and 14th-century Europe. She also circled back to the core question that animated all her work: *human nature*. "Well, I leap about because my subject is human conduct and I think that one can learn more about it and tell more about it if one can study it as it is affected under different circumstances," said Tuchman. "That way you find out what is permanent, what is deep in human nature

[and] how it's affected in different times. To me this is more interesting than constantly going back over the same period."

Georgia Frontiere did Extend Out/Circle Back in a huge way, when she became a highly active owner of the Rams NFL franchise (extend out), yet she drew from her lifelong love of show business to create the "Greatest Show on Turf" with her team (circle back). Frontiere had the seeds of interest in show business from childhood, performing in a singing group with her mother and inspired by the image of one day performing in the great entertainment spectacle of European opera. She returned to water the seeds of her early passion for entertainment in making her beloved Rams into a great, big, wonderfully compelling show.

Which brings me to a useful method for reigniting the inner fire, especially in episodes of fog: the value of *watering seeds planted earlier in life*. Across the study set we found evidence of seeds planted early in life. In some cases, those seeds flowered into a first hedgehog. In other cases, those seeds lay largely dormant for years to decades, only to flower later in life. Recall how Alan Page had been enthralled with the courtroom drama series *Perry Mason* way back when he was a kid, which planted some of the seeds for his transition from football to law. Katharine Graham had shown an interest in newspaper work early in life, working in her 20s as a labor reporter in San Francisco for a tabloid and then joining the editorial pages of her father's paper, *The Washington Post*. After marrying Phil Graham, she largely stopped watering those seeds, and they went dormant; in the wake of the cliff, she reactivated them.

> This pattern of circling back to water early seeds led me to some useful questions for figuring out the next phase of life that will feed the inner fire: Do you have dormant seeds from earlier in life that, for whatever reason, you've never watered? These might be interests you've always had, but your life went a different direction. How can

> you use those seeds as clues to figure out what's next? And how can you take steps to water those seeds? The elements of a fire-filled "what's next" might already be inside you, in seeds of interest you buried away long ago.

The Changing Color of Fire

While the fire remained burning hot long and late for the people in our study, the *feel* of that fire sometimes changed in a very interesting way: They gave themselves permission to have more *fun*. By "have more fun" I don't mean that they took more vacations or time off to go have fun. Rather, they evolved to have more fun in doing what they were encoded for, more fun in the pursuit of excellence in a hedgehog. Instead of giving themselves permission to "retire and go have fun," they gave themselves permission to *not* retire (at least in the traditional sense of retiring to a life of pure leisure) *and* to have more fun in hedgehog mode, to be even more in love with the doing than ever before.

Well past the midpoint of her long career, Meryl Streep said, "I still love acting. I love it. Love it. Love it, love it, love it. It still feels like the wind in my hair." Streep never ceased investing herself in delivering an exceptional performance in whatever character she played, in whatever project she committed to, in whatever genre she undertook. But her selection criteria for which characters and projects she undertook put a greater premium on fun. Streep said of playing the lead in *Florence Foster Jenkins*, at age 67, that it was "one of the most fun things I've ever done, without question," adding that choosing the role because it would be fun "seems like a pretty damn good reason."

In finishing up this chapter, I realized something about this entire project and its role in my own life. I've puzzled on the question of why

I seem to have at least as much energy at age 67 as I had at 37, perhaps even more. I need less sleep. I feel on the balls of my feet, tilted forward. I can't wait to get up before 5 a.m. and throw myself into each day. The inner fire burns brighter than ever. There are multiple elements that feed into this, including the sheer good luck of health to this point in my life. But I now see that one huge element has to do with this very project being an invigorating fusion of Extend Out/Circle Back. By taking on an entirely new subject at this stage of life, shifting from studying what makes great companies tick to studying people and what makes their lives tick, I'm clearly extending out. At the same time, I'm also circling back, returning to encoded operating modes I discovered years ago, particularly my penchant for doing big research projects, going from chaos to concept, and then writing and teaching what I learn. I'm incredibly energized by discovering entirely new elements of myself in doing this project, and by how the study itself has changed me in such profound ways. I'm equally energized by circling back to activate and reactivate interests and encodings I'd discovered long ago.

Along the way, something else marvelous has happened: I've given myself permission to have more *fun* in my work. As I head into the final years of my 60s, I'm working harder and enjoying it more than ever before. And a big part of that is the sheer unadulterated *fun* of doing this great big Extend Out/Circle Back.

It's as if the color of the inner fire has changed. When young and scared, desperate to find my way in the world without a father, I used to describe my inner drive as like hot coals burning in my stomach. It's as if I were propelled by sheer fury, a channeled ferocity, to survive and achieve. I worked hard in school, not because I found it fun, but because—one way or another—I had to escape where I came from and prove I was worthy. As I progressed through life, feeling increasingly secure, I found that I no longer needed those searing-hot coals of fury in my stomach, and I hoped they might finally cool down.

But what happened surprised me. The fire did not cool down or disappear. The fire not only remained but *increased*, yet it felt different. Instead of deep angry red and orange, it's as if the colors became more yellow and green. Whereas the earlier fire had almost physically hurt as it burned from within, the fire shifted to more of a sustained warming glow. I'm now at the point where many of my college classmates have retired, whereas I feel that I'm still early in the game. Why would I stop when there is still so much opportunity to revel in Extend Out/Circle Back, and when it is all just so much *fun*?

11

Choosing Responsibilities

Charles Colson heard the first half of his life fracture away when a federal district judge rapped his gavel with a thwack of finality, sentencing Colson to prison for one to three years for obstruction of justice. Only one and a half years earlier, barely 41 years old, Colson stood at the apex of unelected political power, working in the White House as special counsel to the president of the United States. He'd been a primary architect of Richard M. Nixon's 1972 reelection, in which Nixon won 97% of the electoral votes and every state except Massachusetts.

Colson had risen to power using his peculiar encodings for being a political "hatchet man," a title bestowed upon him by an article in *The Wall Street Journal* that Colson did little to dispute. People described him doing Nixon's dirty work with various phrases like "a one-man department of dirty tricks," "viciously loyal," a "cobra," "the most amoral person I ever met in my life," "an engaging rogue," as having "a real knack for organizing, targetting [sic] a man, a group or a cause he wants to defect, discredit, or demolish." Colson's reputation created an almost larger-than-life image as a stealthy political assassin. As one person put it, "He's like the old gunfighter. Killings 250 miles away are charged to him." By Colson's own self-description, he was willing "to be ruthless in getting things done."

Then came Watergate. President Nixon resigned. Multiple people went to prison, including Charles Colson.

Colson entered a federal prison camp in Alabama, which he later described as "a big, old, one-story dormitory building with cots lined up every few feet. Everything in the place was a beige fog. The dirty floors, the blankets, the lockers—everything was beige or a drab brown. When I was assigned my cot, I took the mattress outside, removed the cover, and shook it. Half a pound of dirt blew into the wind." It was also dangerous. Colson learned that another inmate had been talking about wanting to kill him. Colson confronted the inmate who, as it turned out, believed Colson had been part of a politically motivated investigation that had sent him to prison. Colson managed to convince the enraged man that he'd had nothing to do with his case, and they connected by sharing stories of how each of them had refused to lessen their plight by blaming higher-ups.

While incarcerated, Colson began to think about how he could use the rest of his life guided by a faith conversion he'd undergone the summer before his indictment. More than a few people might have been surprised to hear him say, upon leaving the courthouse after his sentencing, "I can work for the Lord in prison or out of prison. That's how I want to spend my life. And what happened today is the Lord's will and the court's will, and I, of course, accept that fully." Upon hearing of Colson's religious conversion, some were quite skeptical, even cynical. A columnist wrote, "I cannot accept the sudden coming to Christ of Charles Colson. If he isn't embarrassed by this sudden excess of piety, then surely the Lord must be." One of his former rivals for power in the Nixon administration quipped that if Charles Colson had become a Christian, then he'd rather take his chances with the lions. But Colson was quite earnest, as the entirety of the second half of his life would show.

When Colson left prison at age 43, he found himself in the fog, still unclear what to do with the remaining years that lay before him (he would live another 37 years as it would turn out). He'd lost his political power. He'd lost friends. He lost access and invitations and much of what else goes with being in the Washington, D.C., power circle.

Like other people in this study, he began simplex stepping through the fog. He worked in steps on a manuscript that would become the influential and introspective book *Born Again*. Meanwhile, he explored and considered other avenues for reentering productive society, perhaps practicing law in a state where he'd not been disbarred or going into business. One businessman said, "Write your own contract, and I'll guarantee you a million dollars after taxes in three years."

But nothing fueled the fire.

Then, one morning, Colson awoke with an image in his mind, almost like a lighthouse beacon in the fog: "I plodded to the bathroom, stared through sleepy-eyed fog into the mirror and reached for the shaving cream. Then suddenly startled, I stared back at my reflection. A series of pictures flashed across my mind. Men in prison gray moving about. Classes. Discussions. Prayers." In that moment, Colson had the glimmer of an idea for something he could choose to be responsible for: bringing faith to prisoners and helping them get their lives back together, within prison and after.

Yet even with this powerful vision, Colson took only small steps, uncertain if he wanted to go all in on this idea. "I couldn't stand to go back into prisons, those rotten, stinking holes," he later said of his uncertainty. "I even threw clothes away because they smelled of that prison." So he began with a simplex step, starting a small program of prison ministry with a member of his prayer group who'd been an influential congressman. Working together, they persuaded the director of the Federal Bureau of Prisons to approve a plan to bring small groups of inmates to Washington, D.C., for two-week discipleship programs.

Colson saw the seminars as just a temporary step, an effort that consumed only a quarter of his time and that he would pass along to others once he figured out what to do with the rest of his life. Yet the more he worked on prison ministry, the more it fed the fire. Here, right in front of him, lay a responsibility he could choose. The other options were lucrative, but boring in comparison. "I really didn't think I wanted to do all this," Colson said in an interview a few years after starting his prison ministry. "All I can say is that over a period of 18 months after my release, it became evident I couldn't do anything else. I didn't feel at peace about anything else I wanted to do." The turning point came when his wife, Patty, weighed in that if he wanted to go all in on doing prison ministry, she'd be right there with him.

Colson broke out of the fog. He channeled his book royalties into a nonprofit he formed called Prison Fellowship. Within seven years, the Prison Fellowship flywheel had grown to a staff of 170 people working with 15,000 volunteers serving 15,000 inmates across 12 countries. Within another seven years, it had more than 270 employees working with more than 30,000 volunteers serving more than 600 prisons, and would eventually expand its reach to more than 100 countries.

Colson visited prisons as part of his work. On one occasion, he went to Attica prison in New York, the site of the deadliest prison revolt in U.S. history, where he gave a talk from a raised platform separated and protected by guards. He'd been instructed to not directly interact with individual prisoners. "Our time was nearly over and I wanted to go down among the inmates and talk and shake hands with them," Colson later wrote. "But the lieutenant was standing at the head of the small flight of steps, blocking the way down to the floor. On an impulse, I moved suddenly. 'Okay, lieutenant, the speech is over,' I shouted and then, not waiting for him to answer, jumped from the platform and headed down the center aisle." A teeming throng of prisoners encircled Colson, Christians and non-Christians seeking connection and encouragement, and Colson engaged as many as he could in spirited discussion.

Over time, Colson expanded his self-chosen responsibilities to include working on overall prison reform. In 1983 he said that "80 percent of American prisons are barbaric—not just brutal, but barbaric." Having come from a conservative political tradition and also having been in prison himself, he had the credibility to challenge both conservatives and liberals to confront the brutal facts about the American way of prisons. "[It is] crucial to expose the widespread illusion about punishment and prisons," Colson wrote in a 1985 article. "Some on the liberal side believe we can create humane facilities that will 'cure' criminals of their errant behavior; many on the conservative side confuse prison and punishment by arguing that we should simply lock everyone up and 'teach them a lesson.' The result is a national policy that stuffs our facilities with humans, half of them nonviolent, gives them nothing meaningful to do, then stands back in amazement when prisoners riot." I do not feel qualified to assess Colson's range of proposed reforms or his advocacy for restorative justice, and I'm not advocating his particular views on the topic. The main point is that Colson saw that he had a particularly effective form of credibility that he'd gained from his experiences, and he chose to spend and reinvest that credibility equity on behalf of prisoners and prison reform.

Like other people in our study, Colson's post-cliff journey happened in organic iterative steps, even his steps toward aligning his life with his Christian faith. "I've discovered that every year you grow a little more than the year before. It isn't like all of a sudden you turn a switch and you go from A to B. You do in one sense, because your whole worldview is very different; you realize you've got to see things the way God sees them, not the way you do. So that part changes fast, but it doesn't immediately reflect itself in how you live. That part takes time."

Colson did more than prison-related work, including authoring or co-authoring more than 20 books, creating a radio program, and launching a center to help people live in line with their Christian faith. But the core of his post-cliff life lay in bringing faith to prisoners and working on prison reform. For Colson, his "ultimate joy and fulfillment" came in fully embracing the responsibilities that called to him. He gave his ministry most of the second half of his life and much of his money.

At age 73, more than three decades after Watergate, Colson (along with the rest of the world) finally learned the identity of "Deep Throat," the secret informant who fed critical information to Bob Woodward and Carl Bernstein that helped crack the Watergate story wide open for *The Washington Post*. An interviewer asked Colson, "You were yourself indicted in the Watergate cover-up. I wonder if this closes a chapter for you in any way with the revelation of Deep Throat." To which Colson replied, "Oh, no, goodness. I've gone beyond that. I don't even—I don't think about Deep Throat except when something like this happens. No, no. I closed that chapter a long time ago. That was a part of my life—I'm grateful for it because out of it came my conversion to Christ and the work that I do in the prisons, and it's the most rewarding thing in my life. I've often said, 'Thank God for Watergate.'"

Colson continued to reinvest himself in his responsibilities, right until the end, when he collapsed in the middle of a speech at age 80. He died three weeks later, succumbing to the effects of an intracerebral hemorrhage. Once he found his second hedgehog and filled it with freely chosen responsibilities, he never lost the fire. He'd been recognized for his work, including a Presidential Citizens Medal, bestowed upon him at the White House. He also received the prestigious Templeton Prize. The prize came with a $1 million award that he funneled back into Prison Fellowship. Yet Colson never confused his spot in the pantheon of annual Templeton recipients (which would include Mother Teresa, Billy Graham, Aleksandr Solzhenitsyn, and, later, the Dalai Lama) with his ongoing work and responsibilities. "I'm standing here," he thought to himself as Prince Philip began asking questions at the ceremony about Colson's work, "because thousands of inmates whose lives Prison Fellowship has been able to touch are counting on me."

When he returned home from the Templeton Prize ceremony, he didn't dwell on the medal. He simply asked that it be put in an appropriate place, then turned to reread a letter that he'd received three years earlier from two prisoners in Siberia, on behalf of 3,000 other prisoners. The letter explained how one of Colson's books had been translated into Russian, shared among them, and discussed in groups. "All I can say is, I'm not even sure where the Templeton medal is hanging at this moment," Colson reflected later. "But I keep the prisoners' letter in my briefcase, and when I'm overly tired, depressed, or discouraged, I take it out and read it again. If I'm allowed a period of reflection before death, I'm sure I'll keep that letter on my bedside table."

The Freedom to Choose . . . Responsibilities

A turning point for me in this study came when I happened across a comment from Toni Morrison buried in a 1985 interview: "You see, the point is that freedom is choosing your responsibility. It's not having no responsibilities; it's choosing the ones you want." Morrison's comment cast a light back over the lives in this study to highlight a crucial ingredient in feeding the inner fire: *Freedom does not mean the absence of responsibilities; freedom means that you get to choose your responsibilities.*

The Colson case illustrates the renewing power of freely choosing responsibilities. Toward the end of his time in the White House as special counsel to the president, Colson felt burned out, depleted, uninspired, drained. He adopted the phrase "exhausted volcano" to describe how he felt standing at the apex of power, having helped to elect a president in one of the largest landslides in American history. "Always in the past it was the drive to climb new heights that gave life meaning," he later wrote. "But what happened when there were no more mountains to scale? I was only 41. Surely there must be other stiff challenges. But what? What could I do next that would ever be as fulfilling as helping elect a president, being one of the small handful of men who each day made decisions that shaped the future of a nation?" Then came the breaking point of the Watergate scandal, disgrace, and prison.

You would think his life was over, and in one sense life as he knew it *was* over. He could not erase the taint of scandal from his life. He could not undo his own guilt. He could not return to climb the mountains he'd climbed before. And yet the best, most fulfilling, most meaningful, most respected, most energizing, most renewed years of his life lay ahead of him, not behind. And a big part of why lies in having made the shift from seeking recognition and prestige and power—from pride-driven ambition—to choosing responsibilities to which he made himself accountable.

One of the most poignant moments for me in doing this research came while watching the Michael J. Fox documentary *Still*, in a scene where Fox is working with his physical trainer. Fox, his shoulders visibly shaking, talks with his trainer about what he needs to do to feel better. But the *reason* he gives for sustaining his effort centers not on lessening his own pain but on what his example means to people in the Parkinson's community. "People express to me that I make them feel better. I make them do things they might not otherwise do. And that's, that's the most powerful thing you could ever feel and that's a huge responsibility and I don't want to f—— it up." In the film, you can see—and it is difficult to watch—how much Parkinson's had etched away the physical being of Michael J. Fox. But you can also see the fire in his eyes, undimmed, burning bright, fueled by a responsibility that he freely chose.

Think back across the lives in this study. Recall Gerald R. Ford and Jimmy Carter choosing the responsibility to render one final joint service to the nation with their mutual pact about one giving the eulogy for the other. Recall Grace Hopper choosing the responsibility to advance standard languages to make computers more useful to the rest of us. Recall Carl Eller choosing the responsibility to tackle the problem of substance abuse in youth and athletics. Recall Barbara Tuchman choosing to write history through the eyes of people who were living it, writing from the perspective of not knowing what was coming next, because this approach (in her view) would be the only responsible way to grasp and convey human nature in historical context. Recall Maurice White honoring his self-chosen responsibility to remain focused on creating music that, in the words of one album title, can keep your head to the sky in a cynical age.

One form of responsibility is doing your work in a way that holds to an inspired standard you choose to live by. Tenley Albright's full embrace of "surgical conscience" is not just a phrase she learned in the medical community but a personal responsibility she held sacred. She'd been inspired by her father's sense of responsibility in his work as a surgeon. "I remember one time I was doing an appendectomy on a seven-year-old girl," Albright related. "[My father] stuck his head in the door, saw what I was up to, and said, 'Make the incision just where you would on Lilla.' Lilla is one of my daughters, who was then six or seven years old. My first reaction was, 'How could he say such a thing?' And then I realized he was telling me that every single case is just that personal, whether it is your daughter or someone else's daughter."

As I worked on this book, I puzzled where core values fit into the research findings. To be clear, there is no single unified set of core values across all the people in the study. That said, each person developed a set of values somewhere along the way, some more explicitly than others. These values might have come from family, or mentors, or teachers, or military service, or the ethics of their field, or the social milieu in which they lived, or their faith traditions, or reading and reflection, or personal experience, or some combination. I came to see that living to a set of core values is a choice, a personal responsibility of the highest order. And *only you know* how well you fulfill that responsibility.

Responsibilities need not be grand "save the world" ambitions or highly visible. They can be deeply personal, private, largely hidden from the world. Recall Debra Winger choosing the responsibility to nurse her mother through the final months of life and Lucy Burns choosing the responsibility to raise her late sister's daughter. Recall Robert Plant choosing the responsibility to support cancer work without ever being known for it.

> Choosing responsibilities is not about seeking public credit for good deeds or doing penance to atone for bad deeds. It's not about fitting into societal expectations. It's not about acting out of guilt. It's not about giving money to good causes (though you might well do so), and it's certainly not about applause for one's philanthropy. It's about responsibility, not recognition. It's about choosing to give of your encodings, fire, and resources toward something you believe must be done and holding yourself to personal account for it.

Your responsibilities need not be what other people see as your obligations, or what societal judgment says your responsibilities "should" be (though you might well choose to adopt responsibilities that other people inspire or that society values). The key idea here—whether public or private, whether in line with what other people think you should do or not—is the combination of two words: "choosing" and "responsibilities." My enduring great friend Tom Tierney puts it this way, "What are you doing that meets the 'but for' test? What are you getting done that would not otherwise happen 'but for you' *even if almost no one ever knows about it?*"

Charles Colson's "exhausted volcano" turned into an inexhaustible flow of hot, molten lava when he chose to make himself responsible for honoring what he heard as God's call. He could have chosen not to do so—it was a call, not a commandment, after all—but instead he turned away from wallowing in the past, pulled forward by his renewed sense of responsibility. And that's part of the magic of choosing responsibilities. It spins you away from self-absorption and looking backward, and toward what's next, outward, and forward. Which brings us right to the edge of a lesson I learned decades ago that came flooding back to me in doing this research. I call it the "Mothershead Mantra."

The Mothershead Mantra

During my freshman year in college, I met the remarkable Professor John L. Mothershead Jr. Day after day at 9 a.m., I sat in the front row of the balcony of Cubberley Auditorium on the Stanford campus, enraptured as Professor Mothershead lectured about the great ideas of philosophy. Already in his late 60s, he taught with vibrancy and verve. Before me stood one of the first of many sages I would meet in my life, and I wanted to learn more. So, I asked if he would join me and a few other classmates for dinner at my dorm, Roble Hall. He agreed.

Sitting at a round table in the dining hall, I began with a question: "Professor Mothershead, you teach us about all these great philosophers and their ideas, but I'm curious about something. When you look back to reflect on your own experience, how do you sum up the overall learnings from your own long life?"

"I reject your question," he said. Not meanly, but with the warmth of a compassionate bodhisattva teaching an earnest, wayward student. "First, I'm not done yet." I made a mental note to myself to always ask people, no matter how many years they've lived, what they've learned in life only *so far*.

Then he continued: "There are two ways to go through life. The first is to ride through life sitting in the saddle looking backward. The other is to ride through life sitting in the saddle pointed forward. I'm the second. I have no interest in looking backward. I reject your question."

> As I worked systematically through the lives in this study, I kept thinking about that seminal teaching moment with Professor Mothershead. The vast majority of the people in our study showed evidence of living to the Mothershead Mantra, pointing forward in the saddle, never backward, right until the point where their bodies finally said, "It's time to get off the horse."

Once Charles Colson emerged from the fog, feeling called to his work with prisoners, and once he fully committed to those responsibilities, he rarely looked back. He could not change the past, he could not erase Watergate and the Nixon years, he could not undo the wrong things he'd done, he could never get everyone who hated him for his role in the Nixon years to love him, to forgive him, to embrace him for what he had become since. He could not change the fact that his obituaries would inevitably cover his time of scandal, disgrace, and prison. He would always be known, at least in part, as Nixon's hatchet man. Once he got out of the fog and chose his post-cliff responsibilities, he focused forward. Watergate receded ever more into the background as his chosen responsibilities pulled him forward, ever forward.

Let's turn now to Charles Colson's matched-pair companion in the study, John Ehrlichman. Ehrlichman led a life remarkably parallel to Colson up through midlife, working as a lawyer and counsel to President Nixon. His office sat directly above the Oval Office, with a spectacular view of the Washington Monument. He served the president on matters of domestic policy, right in the vortex of power between the White House and Congress. Then Ehrlichman was publicly disgraced for his role in Watergate and sentenced to prison. For an overview of Charles Colson and John Ehrlichman as a pair, see the nearby side-by-side life chronologies.

Charles Colson and John Ehrlichman
Parallel, then Divergent, Lives

CHARLES COLSON		JOHN EHRLICHMAN	
Ages 17–28	Attended Brown University. Served in the U.S. Marine Corps. Worked for a U.S. senator. Earned a law degree from George Washington University.	Ages 17–26	Attended UCLA. Served in the U.S. Army Air Corps flying combat missions over Europe in World War II. Earned a law degree from Stanford University.
Ages 29–37	Co-founded a law firm. Began working on Richard M. Nixon's political campaigns, including extensive work on the 1968 presidential campaign.	Ages 27–43	Co-founded a law firm. Began working on Richard M. Nixon's political campaigns, including extensive work on the 1968 presidential campaign.
Ages 38–41	Accepted appointment as special counsel to the president and worked in the White House.	Ages 44–48	Accepted appointment as assistant to the president for domestic affairs and worked in the White House.
Ages 41–43	Scandal, indictment, and prison, related to the events known as Watergate. Served prison sentence at a federal prison camp in Alabama.	Ages 48–53	Scandal, indictment, and prison, related to the events known as Watergate. Served prison sentence at a federal institution in Arizona.
Ages 44–74	Founded and led Prison Fellowship, dedicating himself to bringing faith to prisoners and addressing prison reform. Created *BreakPoint* radio program and founded the Colson Center. Authored or co-authored multiple books.	Ages 53–65	Lived a quiet life in Santa Fe, working mainly as a writer of articles and books. Authored multiple books that drew heavily on his previous experiences in the Nixon White House, including the Watergate era.
Ages 75–80	Retired from chairmanship of Prison Fellowship. Continued to travel, speak, and write. Passed away at age 80.	Ages 66–73	Lived in Atlanta. Worked on a Watergate documentary, *John Ehrlichman: In the Eye of the Storm*. Passed away at age 73.

Note: Due to ambiguity in the sources as to some of the precise dates (month and day) relative to birthdays, cited ages in these chronologies may vary by +/-1 year.

Ehrlichman's life began to tear apart even before he went to prison. As the Watergate scandal deepened, Nixon felt the need to show that he was cleaning house. Ehrlichman later described a meeting with the president wherein it became clear that Ehrlichman would soon be asked to resign. Nixon ended the conversation by noting that members of the White House staff must have the president's confidence—a stinging comment to one of Nixon's most loyal staffers who saw himself as a protector of the president. At home, after he told his family about his impending departure from the White House, one of Ehrlichman's children asked, "If you're not guilty, why is he asking you to leave?"

A few days later, Ehrlichman had an astounding moment of despair. Flying on Air Force One with the president, he ambled to the flight deck, directly behind the pilots. "As I stood there, I was taken with the realization that I could end everyone's troubles by throwing myself against the controls, wedging myself between the pilot's control yoke and the pilot," he wrote in his memoir, *Witness to Power*. "We'd all be gone in about a minute and a half. I stood there chatting with the navigator, measuring my chances for a moment; then turned and went back to my seat."

When Nixon finally fired Ehrlichman, commanding him to resign, Ehrlichman felt the deep wound of abandonment. Choking back tears, he asked for one thing from the president: "Just explain all this to my kids, will you? Tell them why you had to do this?"

When Ehrlichman had been in the inner circle of the White House, he once said of abandoning an agency nominee, "I think we ought to let him hang there. Let him twist slowly in the wind." Now it was Ehrlichman's turn. Around the time of his forced resignation, *Newsweek* featured Ehrlichman and Nixon's White House Chief of Staff H. R. Haldeman on the cover. "[The cover] featured a composite photograph of the two of us wearing dark glasses, scowling like Mafia dons," Ehrlichman described. "We had been cast as the villains of the saga."

Ehrlichman was indicted, convicted on multiple counts, and sentenced to prison. Around the time of his trials and sentencing, he spent two weeks alone in a secluded lodge on the Oregon coastline, where he struggled to come to terms with having lost everything he valued, including his reputation and the warm allegiance of family, friends, and mentors. Finally, he realized that he had to begin to step forward, even though part of stepping would be through prison. "I had to go slowly in some direction, a step at a time," he later wrote. "I wasn't sure that I could take a step and then another, but it was clear to me that I had to try."

He decided to move to Santa Fe, where he would live before entering prison and after. Of Santa Fe, he later said, "There are lots of refugees around, of one kind or another. From that standpoint it's a very good place to be." There, he began to regroup, step by step, and with each little step he'd pause to say to himself, "I did that; it's an accomplishment. Congratulations." He kept taking steps toward life as a writer. In fact, he completed and published his first novel, *The Company*, between his sentencing and his entering a federal correctional institution in Arizona at age 51.

After serving 18 months in prison, he returned to Santa Fe, remarried, had a son, and grew a beard. A somewhat typical day might involve a few hours of writing in a pink adobe house from which he could see town and the surrounding mountains, lunching with his wife, playing with his son, maybe some fishing or other relaxing, and sometimes enjoying dinner at one of the nice restaurants that welcomed him as almost a local celebrity. "I'm certainly a great deal more content than I was about the life that I'm leading," he said about his writing career a few years after leaving prison.

In addition to a slew of articles on a wide range of topics, from the role of China in global affairs to the joys of trout fishing, he worked on his books. Ehrlichman proved himself to be an excellent writer, though he did not extend out beyond using the White House as the stage setting. Rather, he returned repeatedly to revisit the Nixon years (including the Watergate era) in various forms and plotlines, either in disguised fictional form or in his memoir. To illustrate, here is a brief description of his novels, along with a review comment.

The Company: a novel of political intrigue related to keeping a potentially damaging CIA report secret. From *The Washington Post*: "Ehrlichman's novel does give us a strong whiff of the paranoia and isolation of the presidency under Richard Nixon."

The Whole Truth: a novel of political intrigue involving a presidential cover-up of a potential scandal. From the *Chicago Tribune*: "It features a besieged President whose chief transgression is not lying but getting caught at it. The hero is a younger, romanticized version of Ehrlichman—an idealistic, ferociously ambitious West Coast lawyer who, seduced by the power and glamor of White House life, undertakes an illegal act at the bidding of his President and then is expected to take the fall for it."

The China Card: a novel about espionage and rapprochement between the United States and China. From *The New York Times*: "Mr. Ehrlichman, already an expert on White House intrigue . . . skillfully merges fact with fiction, marching the likes of Mr. Nixon, Mr. Kissinger, Alexander Haig and H. R. Haldeman onstage."

Ehrlichman returned once again to the Watergate saga in his final years, collaborating on a documentary about Watergate and his role in it, with the working title *John Ehrlichman: In the Eye of the Storm*. The producer asked Charles Colson to be interviewed, which Colson turned down because he "wanted to leave Watergate in the past." Then Ehrlichman personally called Colson to ask that he participate, and Colson finally agreed. "When we talked, I could hear how much the project meant to him," Colson wrote in *The Good Life*. "He saw the film as a definitive statement about Watergate." The project, which appears to have never been broadcast, was one of the last things Ehrlichman worked on before he succumbed to complications from diabetes at age 73.

The evidence we have on Ehrlichman indicates that he expended a lot of energy looking backward, perhaps trying to correct history to be more congruent with how he saw his role in Watergate. I can understand the urge, especially because Ehrlichman had been one of Nixon's most loyal soldiers. Then Nixon made him resign. Colson later wrote a succinct sentence about Ehrlichman: "Nixon had betrayed him." I found no record that Nixon ever made good on Ehrlichman's plea that Nixon explain to his children why he had to be fired.

In Charles Colson's case, he gave over his life (once the fog cleared from the Watergate-to-prison cliff) to fulfilling what he embraced as his responsibilities. With John Ehrlichman, I had a harder time answering the question from the research materials: What responsibilities did he choose that might have spun him around to point forward in the saddle?

Now, to be clear, I'm not saying that Ehrlichman chose no responsibilities. He chose the responsibility to complete his book projects and launch them into the world. He chose the responsibility to share his insights and experience in his opinion pieces and articles. And to be fair, we found more evidence on Colson than on Ehrlichman. We found and collected more than 200 articles and documents on or by Colson published after 1975, compared with fewer than 80 for Ehrlichman; Colson published more than two dozen books, whereas Ehrlichman authored four. This gave me much greater visibility into Colson's journey than the evidence allowed in Ehrlichman's journey.

There remains the possibility that Ehrlichman chose responsibilities that remain largely hidden to the outside world. Many people in my own life have chosen personal responsibilities, and in some cases sacrificed mightily for them, yet those responsibilities would be seen only by people close in their lives. I have a friend who left a highly visible career to care for a family member being eaten away by a debilitating disease. He never went public with why he abandoned his successful career, choosing to keep private the huge responsibility he chose to fulfill. Parenting well is a huge responsibility, for instance, yet often invisible to the public eye. I'm very open to the possibility that Ehrlichman chose significant private responsibilities that we simply could not see in the evidence. Still, the evidence we do have suggests that Ehrlichman might have had a more difficult time changing direction in the saddle and living the Mothershead Mantra.

For Charles Colson, Watergate would always be there, but growing ever smaller as he rode pointed forward in the saddle. The evidence suggests that Ehrlichman cared a great deal about restoring his reputational legacy, based on the subtextual themes of his first two novels, his memoir, and his final few years working on the Watergate documentary. Yet, ironically, the Nixon era dominated his obituaries far more than Colson's. We analyzed six major obituaries for Colson and Ehrlichman, choosing largely the same publications. For Colson, the average text in his obituaries related to the Nixon-era aspect of his life (including prison) was 42%; for Ehrlichman the average was 72%.

Colson's story shows that *vibrant renewal is possible*, even after scandal and disgrace, but *not* by trying to erase or correct the past.

Many of Colson's obituaries followed a narrative of a man reviled in his earlier life, whose faith conversion had initially been viewed with suspicion and who largely redeemed himself through his nearly four decades of work on behalf of prisoners. I'll share one excerpt, to illustrate, from *The Wall Street Journal*: "Still, for nearly four full post-Watergate decades, Colson, who died this past Saturday at age 80, steadfastly practiced what he preached about prisons, prisoners and penal reform. Where criminal justice was concerned, he was God's good man, not Nixon's bad man."

Responsibilities Beyond Self

When I look across the people in the study, and how they fed the inner fire long and late, I'm struck by how the responsibilities they chose faced outward, beyond themselves. I don't mean that they all did something big and visible in the world but that they chose responsibilities for something or someone beyond their own individual success, comfort, recognition, enjoyment, or achievement. I'm not saying they were divinely motivated saints; they had a mixture of motivations, some more selfish and some more selfless. Yet to feed the inner fire long and late, the evidence leads me to conclude that dedicating a sizable portion of energy to choosing responsibilities pointed outward beyond self is one of the most powerful forms of fuel.

Which brings me back around to complete the cliff story of my wife, Joanne, when injuries ended her world-level competitive athletic career. After her gasp moment, "I feel like I'm dying," Joanne completed an MBA and explored a range of business and nonprofit options. But none of them fed the inner fire. Then, when we moved to Boulder, where I would set up my research and teaching lab after leaving my faculty position at Stanford, the roulette wheel of life spun her into an entirely unexpected second hedgehog. She got a call from her former high school cross-country coach and physics teacher. The high school had unexpectedly lost its head coach for the boys and girls cross-country running teams just before the start of the season. Would Joanne consider taking the head coaching job?

She'd never thought of coaching a team, never seen coaching as part of her encodings. But she loved what running and competition had done for her own development in high school, and she felt an urge to pass on that love. She accepted the job. Only it wasn't just a job. She chose it as a responsibility, not just for the mechanics of the program, but to teach and develop young people, to help them discover the joy of being fit, to give them the experience of being part of a first-class team that can win, to instill in them the importance of running not just for their own accomplishment but also for their teammates, to teach them how to improve step by step, to instill in them the importance of finishing strong, and ultimately to inspire them to make physical fitness an enduring part of their lives. Along the way, the team won four state championships, including one year where they won both the boys' and the girls' titles on the same day. But even more important, the entire team grew, reaching more than 100 kids every year, most of whom would never run varsity but who would still compete in junior varsity races and fall in love with running.

To this day, when she gets a handwritten card from a runner from decades ago, thanking her for the experience of being on a team of such excellence and for the gift of running for a lifetime, well, that means more to her than all of her individual championship trophies collecting dust in boxes in the basement. When Joanne received recognition in the local sports hall of fame, she spoke almost nothing about her Ironman World Championship from years before. She spoke instead about coaching young people, and the joy she felt in having an impact on their lives.

She'd found a second hedgehog, discovering that she had deep encodings for building teams with a powerful combination of being internally supportive *and* externally competitive. When she married these newly discovered encodings with chosen responsibilities that were about the kids, not about her, she lit up with a flame that I'd not seen in more than a decade. Later, she applied these encodings to creating a women's cycling team. She named it CrushPod, perfectly reflecting the ethos of being externally competitive (Crush) and internally supportive (Pod). She'd had a series of impressive individual accomplishments in life, but in choosing responsibilities that tapped her encodings as a coach and team builder, she gained a measure of meaning that individual accomplishments alone could never provide.

One of my critical readers, Alan Khazei, told me after reading an early version of the manuscript that this part of Joanne's story—going from world champion to coaching high schoolers and building teams—inspired him as much as any of the primary cases in the book. "The truth is," he said, "millions of people like Joanne choose to serve as teachers, coaches, firefighters, veterans, volunteers, and a myriad of unfamous paths. They're choosing responsibilities that fit their encodings, choosing responsibilities that feed their inner fire, choosing responsibilities beyond themselves." I agree, and I would broaden the possible realms of responsibility to include very private spaces, like caring for people you love, or quietly living to the ethos of whatever field of endeavor you play in.

By its very nature, this study relies on people with highly visible accomplishments. I worry that some readers might misinterpret this as an implicit worthiness hierarchy that valorizes achieving fame over taking more unseen paths. I also worry that some of the people in the study can feel so unapproachable in what they made of their lives that readers might discount the relevance of learning from them, or be left wondering, "Well, their lives are interesting, but could I ever do what they did?" I share that feeling. Studying Charles Colson made me feel somewhat intimidated by the standard he lived to after prison. Could I ever do what Colson did with the second half of his life? Unlikely. But as it turns out, that is an irrelevant question.

> You and I don't need to try to be exactly like any of the people in this study. The relevant question, as it pertains to this chapter, is not whom do we want to emulate, but what responsibilities do we feel compelled to choose? All of us, no matter what we do in life, and no matter how the roulette wheel spins, can choose responsibilities beyond ourselves. It doesn't matter how many people you touch with the responsibilities you choose; it might be many, or it might be only one or a few. What matters is the very act of honoring a self-chosen responsibility.

As I cast back through the research, I became clear on a fundamental point about feeding the inner fire over the long arc of a life: When a person acquiesces to a life without responsibilities—*freely chosen* responsibilities, to be sure, but responsibilities nonetheless—the fire has already started to go out.

Of course, there is a bit of a chicken-and-egg conundrum here: Do people stop choosing responsibilities because the fire has gone out, or does the fire go out because they stop choosing responsibilities? Which is the cause, and which is the effect? I cannot say with certainty. But whichever way the arrow of causation points, I can offer this hypothesis grounded in these lives: If you simply make the decision that you *will* choose responsibilities in line with your encodings and that you feel compelled (for whatever reason) to undertake, that very act will feed the inner fire. And with that, the fire can continue to burn from within, growing hotter as the years click by.

The Dangerous Lure of "Legacy"

A number of years ago, a few people began to ask me, "What do you want your legacy to be?" and "What do you want to be remembered for?" At first, this question struck me as reasonable, until I asked Joanne what she thought. "It's a waste of time to think about your legacy or how you want to be remembered," Joanne said. "It's self-centric and distracts from doing what's right in front of you. Besides, you won't be here to enjoy it anyway."

This study reinforced Joanne's wisdom. Charles Colson achieved a legacy, but not by trying to achieve or burnish his legacy. He had responsibilities to fulfill, too much work left right in front of him to get sidetracked into the irrelevancy of how he would be remembered. He cared far more about how God would assess *the way he spent his life while alive* than what people would think of him after he was dead. Colson spent his energy principally on responsibilities so far beyond Watergate and Nixon that it was almost as if he'd gone to another solar system. My own read of Colson's story is that he did in fact build a "legacy" that outlived him, but only as a residual side artifact of living to the responsibilities he chose.

> What is so striking in the vast mountain of materials we collected in this study is how little the people spoke or wrote about "legacy" or how they wanted to be remembered after they were gone. Yes, many of them made a lasting impact on the world they touched, but they did so by honoring the responsibilities they chose, by doing the work that lay right in front of them. *Once life is done, the encodings will be gone, so best to make use of them while there's still time on the clock.*

For those wrestling with how to make use of the time they have, this study has given me questions, not answers. Questions like "What responsibilities can you choose, even if you receive no credit?" "What can you help make happen that might not otherwise happen without you choosing that responsibility?" "What responsibilities can you choose that fit your encodings?" Most of all, I've come to see the power of changing the question from "What do you want your legacy to be after you are gone?" to "What responsibilities will you choose right here, right now, with the limited time you have left on this earth?"

12

Feeding the Inner Fire (and Doing Great Work Late)

One of the biggest lessons of this entire work is that our younger selves need not tower over our older selves. This study punctures the debilitating myth that the brightest moments of inspired creativity, energy, and usefulness necessarily come from our younger selves. Throughout, we have seen some of the most groundbreaking, creative, and/or impactful work coming *after* the midpoint in a life, sometimes well into the final third. Here are a few delicious vivid details from our research:

Toni Morrison didn't write *Beloved* and *Jazz*, two of the books highlighted in her selection for the Nobel Prize, until well past the midpoint of her life; she published *Beloved* at age 56 and *Jazz* at age 61.

Robert Plant garnered 86% of his 21 Grammy nominations, and all of his eight wins, after the age of 50. As I write this in 2025, Plant continues his creative work (in his mid-70s), and it is entirely possible that he will bring forth more award-winning music.

Katharine Graham didn't even discover and begin to act on her brilliant encodings for inspired leadership until more than halfway through her life, and she wrote the best-written CEO memoir of all time in her 70s.

John Glenn became not only the first American to orbit Earth but also the oldest American to go to space for NASA just three years shy of entering his 80s.

Cardiss Collins didn't even discover that she had the makings of a great legislator, with leadership encodings that would vault her into becoming chair of the Congressional Black Caucus, until more than halfway through her life.

I. M. Pei completed some of his most well-known works well into the second half of life, including the Louvre Pyramid in his 70s and the Museum of Islamic Art in Doha at age 91.

Barbara McClintock didn't have her "burst of intellectual activity" when the whole theory of transpositional genetic elements came together until after she'd passed the midpoint of a very long life.

Jimmy Carter didn't become a prolific writer until after the presidency, publishing more than two dozen books after age 60.

Meryl Streep earned ten of her 21 Oscar nominations after age 50. As I write this in 2025, Streep (in her 70s) continues to act, making it possible that more than half of her total lifetime nominations will come after age 50.

Or consider the following question: If you count the pages in three major biographies of Benjamin Franklin, how many pages remain on average *after* Franklin hits age 60? The answer: 53%. Imagine coming at life with the idea *that turning 60 means that more than half* of what might be the most interesting, energetic, and creative in a life has yet to be written.

And that brings us to our final matched pair in the study, taking us all the way back to the 18th century.

The Two Oldest Leaders at the Constitutional Convention

Pop quiz: Which Founding Father of the United States meets all the following criteria?

- The only founder to help draft and sign the Articles of Association, the Declaration of Independence, the Articles of Confederation, and the Constitution of the United States.
- One of five members on a committee to draft the Declaration of Independence.
- Served in the Continental Congress during the American Revolution.
- One of the two oldest delegates at the Constitutional Convention.
- One of the most critical figures in creating and gaining acceptance of a compromise between large states and small states that enabled the Constitutional Convention to reach a successful conclusion.
- Played a crucial role in the creation of the Bill of Rights as amendments to the Constitution of the United States.

This person rose up in life from the working class, making himself into a self-taught scholar. He became a successful entrepreneur, and he published popular almanacs. By his early 40s, he'd accumulated substantial wealth, but instead of focusing his energies on gaining more wealth, he turned his attention to public service and civic leadership, including roles in his state's legislature.

As tensions with Great Britain grew, particularly after the Stamp Act of 1765 (when Great Britain levied a tax on all paper goods without consent of the colonies), he became increasingly involved in the colonies' response. With the Declaration of Independence, he joined others in pledging "to each other our Lives, our Fortunes and our sacred Honor." Long before the American Revolution, he adopted the philosophy that "we had better die in a good Cause than live in a bad one," and he fully embraced that philosophy in defying the king with his signature on the Declaration of Independence. He then helped craft the Articles of Confederation.

Through the years of his leadership during the age of revolution and in the formation of the United States, he gained tremendous respect among his fellow founders. Thomas Jefferson said of him that he "never said a foolish thing in his life." Patrick Henry called him "one of the three greatest men at the Constitutional Convention." John Adams described him as "one of the most sensible men in the world" and "as honest as an angel and as firm in the cause of American Independence as Mount Atlas." A biographer described him as having a quality of good sense "so highly developed that it resembled genius."

This leader played a pivotal role in the Constitutional Convention. He brought forth and championed the idea of a compromise between the small states and the large states, creating a bicameral legislature with proportional representation by population in one chamber (what became the House of Representatives) and equal representation by state in the other chamber (what became the Senate). He'd originally been more in favor of a unicameral legislature, but came to the practical conclusion that there must be a compromise between large and small states, and he advanced the bicameral construct. Without this imperfect compromise, it is quite possible (perhaps even highly probable) that the Constitutional Convention would have ended in failure.

So, we return to the pop quiz. Who is this remarkable leader who played such a large role in the formation of the United States?

The answer: Roger Sherman of Connecticut.

Maybe you're so strong in your knowledge of U.S. history that the quiz proved easy. I admit that until I'd done this study, I would have failed the quiz. I love history, and I knew something of other, more famous founders such as Alexander Hamilton, George Washington, John Adams, Thomas Jefferson, Benjamin Franklin, and James Madison. Yet I knew almost nothing of Roger Sherman.

You might be curious, how did we land upon Roger Sherman for this study? I wanted to include Benjamin Franklin, if I could find a matched-pair companion who had a similar early path and whom I could match at the life-altering cliff of the American Revolution and formation of the United States. A member of my research team and I came up with an idea: Let's start with all the people who both signed the Declaration of Independence and served in the Constitutional Convention (as Franklin had), then work backward to see if any of them (a) began life in the working class, (b) became a successful businessperson, (c) retired from business pursuits to pursue other interests, including public service, (d) led a life that was redefined by the zeitgeist of the American Revolution and the formation of the United States. Sifting and sorting, we settled upon Roger Sherman as the matched-pair companion to Benjamin Franklin. Sherman turned out to be a wonderful find, especially because he and Franklin served together as the two oldest leaders at the Constitutional Convention.

Roger Sherman and Benjamin Franklin
Lives Joined at the American Revolution

ROGER SHERMAN		BENJAMIN FRANKLIN	
Early Life	Born in Newton, Massachusetts. Worked alongside his father, a farmer and cobbler. Moved to Connecticut.	Early Life	Born in Boston, Massachusetts. Apprenticed with his brother, a printer and publisher. Moved to Pennsylvania.
Ages 22–30	Became a successful entrepreneur in surveying, co-owning a shop, and publishing almanacs. Engaged in church activities and became involved in community leadership.	Ages 21–30	Became a successful entrepreneur in printing, writing, newspapers, and publishing almanacs. Formed the Junto, wherein Franklin advanced ideas and projects for public service.
Ages 30–41	Continued success arc as an entrepreneur while becoming increasingly active in church work and community leadership; joined the county court, became a justice of the peace, elected to the Connecticut Assembly. Passed the bar as a self-taught lawyer.	Ages 30–42	Continued success arc as an entrepreneur while becoming increasingly active in civic and public leadership; led formation of a firefighting company, became local postmaster, elected clerk of the Pennsylvania Assembly. Became a self-taught scientist.

Ages 41–51	Shifted his attention increasingly to church work and to civic and public leadership. Became a superior court judge, served on a school committee, served as treasurer of Yale University. Served in the Connecticut Assembly. Retired from business affairs.	Ages 42–50	Shifted his attention increasingly to scientific work and to civic and public leadership. Conducted his lightning rod experiments. Founded the University of Pennsylvania and a hospital. Served in the Pennsylvania Assembly. Retired from business affairs.
Ages 51–55	Drawn increasingly into becoming a revolutionary leader. Joined the Continental Congress and helped shape the Articles of Association created in response to "intolerable acts" of Great Britain that fueled revolutionary fervor.	Ages 50–70	Gradual transition from loyalist to revolutionary leader. Spent most of his time in England. Worked to change the Pennsylvania proprietorship and to reconcile the colonies with Great Britain amid rising revolutionary fervor.
Ages 55–72	Dedicated to the cause of independence and the formation of the United States. Served on the committee to draft the Declaration of Independence. Helped draft Articles of Confederation. Continued to serve in the Continental Congress. The second oldest delegate to the Constitutional Convention, where he and Franklin worked to achieve a crucial compromise on House and Senate structure. Served as a member of Congress and played a key role in the Bill of Rights. Passed away at age 72.	Ages 70–84	Dedicated to the cause of independence and the formation of the United States. Served on the committee to draft the Declaration of Independence. Served as diplomat to France; secured alliances and negotiated peace agreements. The oldest delegate to the Constitutional Convention, where he and Sherman worked to achieve a crucial compromise on House and Senate structure. Served as president of the Pennsylvania Society for Promoting the Abolition of Slavery. Passed away at age 84.

Note: Due to ambiguity in the sources as to some of the precise dates (month and day) relative to birthdays, cited ages in these chronologies may vary by +/-1 year.

Sherman didn't have the encodings for poetic erudition, like Jefferson. He didn't have the encodings for intimidating, awe-inspiring command presence, like Washington. He didn't have the encodings for seductive charm combined with incisive wit and memorable turns of phrase, like Franklin. His contemporaries described him as odd, and his biographer wrote that "his manner seems to have been the personification of awkwardness." John Adams wrote, "Sherman's air is the reverse of grace; there cannot be a more striking contrast to beautiful action, than the motions of his hands; generally he stands upright, with his hands before him, the fingers of his left hand clenched into a fist, and the wrist of it grasped with his right. But he has a clear head and sound judgement." Another contemporary wrote, "Mr. Sherman exhibits the oddest shaped character I ever remember to have met with. He is awkward, un-meaning, and unaccountably strange in his manner. But in his train of thinking there is something regular, deep, and comprehensive . . . no Man has a better Heart or a clearer Head. If he cannot embellish he can furnish thoughts that are wise and useful. He is an able politician, and extremely artful in accomplishing any particular object;—it is remarked that he seldom fails."

Sherman altered the vector of U.S. history, yet he remains relatively unknown. Partly, this stems from the fact that his leadership encodings were well suited to the unglamorous grind of committee work behind the scenes. He thrived in the logic of the law (having passed the bar as a self-taught legal scholar) with a gift for crafting legal, legislative, and founding documents that could long endure. In this, he was like a brilliant engineer of towering skyscrapers whose work lay hidden in the skeletal structure of the edifice, vital to the whole but largely unseen.

Sherman influenced events with a rare instinct to wait until precisely the right moment to speak. Historian George Bancroft wrote of Sherman, "In the convention he never made long speeches, but would intuitively seize on the turning point of a question, and present it in terse language, which showed his own opinion and the strength on which it rested." This ability to sense "the turning point of a question" proved to be one of Sherman's most effective leadership encodings.

Sherman's leadership encodings played a crucial role in the Constitution of the United States, not once, but at least twice. The first came in advancing what became known as the Connecticut Compromise (the moniker reflecting the fact that Sherman heralded from Connecticut), which led to the bicameral legislature solution to address the interests of both large states and small states. The second, in what I believe is one of the great unheralded saves in U.S. history, came in his role on the Bill of Rights.

In 1789, the First Congress took up the question of adding a Bill of Rights to the recently ratified U.S. Constitution. James Madison (representing Virginia in Congress) had initially proposed to change the text of the actual Constitution that had been finalized at the convention by altering the preamble and weaving the Bill of Rights into the body of the text. Madison's approach alarmed Sherman, and he made a forceful counterargument: "I believe, Mr. Chairman, this is not the proper mode of amending the Constitution. We ought not to interweave our propositions into the work itself, because it will be destructive of the whole fabric. We might as well endeavor to mix brass, iron and clay. . . . The Constitution is the act of the people, and ought to remain entire. But the amendments will be the act of the State governments. Again, all the authority we possess is derived from that instrument; if we mean to destroy the whole, and establish a new Constitution, we remove the basis on which we mean to build." Sherman had not been a proponent of adding a Bill of Rights into the Constitution in the late 1780s, but he saw clearly that *if* a Bill of Rights were to be included, it must be done *as amendments*.

Part of the genius of the U.S. Constitution is that it blends stability and adaptability, preservation and progress, continuity and change. The fixed text in the Constitution provides a stable foundation, yet the amendment mechanism provides the equally important capacity to change. Had the text of the Constitution itself been revised to add a Bill of Rights, it could have set a precedent for eroding the Constitution through political machinations over the decades, to the point where it could lose its power as an enduring framework. Roger Sherman won the argument: The text of the main Constitution remained intact, and the Bill of Rights was eventually ratified and appended as amendments.

Interestingly, nearly 200 years after the fact, the chief of the manuscript division of the Library of Congress made the first discovery of an original draft of the Bill of Rights constructed as amendments, written in the select committee. It was in the handwriting of . . . Roger Sherman. While this document likely reflects the working consensus of the entire select committee (rather than Sherman's views alone), the document shows Sherman's active presence in shaping *how* the Bill of Rights would be structured into the Constitution. Without Sherman's guiding hand, the path of U.S. history might have taken a quite different turn on one of the most consequential decisions to face the young nation and its Constitution. Yet he remains far less well known than Washington, Hamilton, Franklin, Adams, Jefferson, and Madison. Sherman sought impact, not fame, responsibility, not credit. He chose the responsibility to protect the Constitution, deploying his leadership encodings into the work right in front of him. Sherman might not have gained the famous legacy of his fellow founders, but he is one of the primary reasons the Constitution itself endured.

After the Bill of Rights, Sherman continued to serve in Congress, moving from the House to the Senate for the Second Congress. He retained his Senate seat for the Third Congress, but his health declined precipitously early in the term, and he passed away (still a senator) at age 72. If Roger Sherman had retired to a life of languid leisure in his 50s, living luxuriously off his accumulated wealth, he would not have done the best work of his life. Fortunately, at least through the lens of the founding of the United States, Roger Sherman spent the last third of his life in hedgehog mode, focusing his inner fire on one very, very big thing: establishing the enduring foundations of the United States of America.

(Note: Sherman's life remains relatively undocumented, compared with other prominent founders of the United States. In the source notes for chapter 12, I've included some of the most useful materials we found on Sherman, if you're interested in learning more about this unsung hero of the Constitution.)

Let's turn now to Benjamin Franklin, who, like Roger Sherman, passed the midpoint of his life with the best, most creative, most impactful years of his life *ahead* of him, not behind. As it would turn out, everything to the halfway point for Franklin was almost a warm-up, a nice start to a most remarkable life.

Benjamin Franklin Rekindles the Fire

Like Roger Sherman, Benjamin Franklin rose up from the working class to become a successful entrepreneur in the 18th century. In the first phase of his adult life, he built a print shop and publishing business, including a newspaper and almanacs. Through his publications, he deployed deep encodings for the written word. He could be pithy with memorable Franklinisms like "Fish and visitors stink in three days," "Haste makes waste," "Lost time is never found again," "He that lies down with dogs shall rise up with fleas," and "Wish not so much to live long as to live well." Many of Franklin's phrases were not wholesale creations, but sharply edited versions of common wisdom and proverbs. Franklin shone not just as a creator but also as an editor.

Throughout his long life, Franklin also used his sharp pen for searing commentary and satirizing the idiotic hypocrisies of powerful incompetents. In one piece, he skewered the British Parliament for its practice of shipping convicts to the American colonies and its laughably stupid argument that it was a project designed to help improve the colonies. Franklin wrote a piece that essentially said (using my own language to convey the essence of Franklin's essay),

> Thank you, Mother Britain, for caring so much for us that you are willing to send us your convicts for our benefit, how very thoughtful and kind of you. Following the same logic, we'd like to reciprocate by sending you our newborn rattlesnakes every year for your improvement. You'd be getting the better end of the bargain, because rattlesnakes (unlike criminals) give a loud warning before they strike. Love you very much, B. Franklin.

Franklin proved adept at making money, though (like others in this study) he flipped the arrow of money, seeing it not as a primary goal or a means to leisure or amassing wealth to create a family dynasty but as a foundation for making the most effective use of his one life to give. As Carl Van Doren wrote in his Pulitzer Prize–winning biography of Franklin, "He had wanted wealth only that he might be free, and to be free only that he might be useful." Or, as Franklin wrote to his mother, "I would rather have it said, 'He lived usefully,' than, 'He died rich.'" Later, when the Sons of Liberty raided ships carrying tea from the British East India Company and threw the valuable cargo into Boston Harbor, Franklin offered his own money to pay for all the lost tea, if it would bring the temperature down. Franklin, a prolific inventor, didn't patent his inventions, gifting them freely to the world for the betterment of mankind.

At age 42, Franklin retired from business and moved more fully into his second hedgehog, as a pioneering scientist and experimental inventor. Fueled by an irrepressible curiosity, he could not help but try to figure out how the world around him worked. One of my favorite images is Franklin and the whirlwind. At about age 50, he was riding horses with friends and his son in Maryland, when they noticed a whirlwind beginning in the valley below. His friends observed in idle curiosity, but Franklin (who later wrote "my curiosity being stronger") went tearing after it, riding alongside the rising swirling vortex of dust and debris. He snapped his whip into it to see what would happen, but the whirl kept whirling. When the whirlwind veered into the woods, growing bigger and stronger even as it hit the trees, Franklin kept apace, making mental notes about how this circular, rising, moving windstorm worked. "I accompanied it about three-quarters of a mile, till some limbs of dead trees, broken off by the whirl, flying about and falling near me, made me more apprehensive of danger; and then I stopped, looking at the top of it as it went on, which was visible by means of the leaves contained in it for a very great height above the trees."

Across his life, Franklin displayed an encoded operating mode of active curiosity. Never content to just ponder, he felt compelled to observe directly, to experiment, to test and measure, to invent, to question, to figure out how the world around him worked—to chase the whirlwind. Franklin charted the Gulf Stream, identified the meteorological forces of storms, and became famous for his experiments with lightning and electricity. He established many of the terms we still use today in discussing aspects of electricity, such as "charge," "conductor," "electric shock," and "battery." Not bad for a self-taught scientist.

In his 50s and 60s, Franklin kept himself busy, but without as much traction or success. He expended a huge amount of energy battling to get the Penns (then the proprietors of Pennsylvania, essentially a form of private ownership) to cede power to the Pennsylvania Assembly and to pay a share of taxes. The Pennsylvania Assembly sent Franklin to England to petition for restructuring the proprietorship. Despite Franklin's efforts, the Penns remained proprietors of Pennsylvania for nearly another two decades. In his late 50s, Franklin showed signs of beginning to think about the final years of his life, indicating in a letter penned at age 57 that upon his next trip to England he may never again see America. Then the world began to rip, tear, and disintegrate around him. As the spirit of rebellion grew in the American colonies, Franklin tried to bring about a reconciliation. He desperately hoped that what he called the "fragile, noble vase" of the British Empire would not shatter. In a letter to his son, Franklin wrote, "The Friends of both Countries wish a reconciliation; the Enemies of either endeavor to widen the Breach, God knows how it will end." Franklin spent nearly his entire 60s in England, endeavoring to achieve reconciliation between Great Britain and the American colonies to avoid a rupture or war. He failed.

The breaking point for Franklin came in January 1774, when he appeared twice before the Privy Council. In the first appearance, Franklin aimed to argue for the removal of the Massachusetts governor. Thomas Hutchinson, the governor, favored harsh treatment of his fellow countrymen if they did not bow their necks in subservience to Great Britain, and his continued presence as governor further fueled rebellious fervor. The Privy Council, however, turned its attention to Franklin's own actions related to the Massachusetts governor. Franklin himself had leaked some of Hutchinson's private letters to influential people in Massachusetts, hoping the leaked letters would redirect his countrymen's rebellious fury away from Parliament by making the governor the target of their ire. He miscalculated; the letters had only fueled further passions on both sides of the Atlantic.

Franklin asked for three weeks to prepare a defense of his actions, and he returned to the Privy Council on Saturday, January 29, 1774. Entering the "Cockpit" of the Privy Council, Franklin found himself surrounded in a room packed with not only members of the Privy Council but also members of the House of Lords and even the prime minister. Only days earlier, they'd all heard news of the Boston Tea Party. Some had also been enraged by Franklin's leak of the Hutchinson letters. Instead, the solicitor general, Alexander Wedderburn, launched into a virulent attack on Franklin so cruel, personal, vindictive, sarcastic, and vulgar that parts of it had to be excised when printed. Pounding the table, sneering, pointing an accusing finger at Franklin, Wedderburn snarled away nonstop for an hour, while Franklin stood silent. Summed up the Franklin biographer H. W. Brands: "Franklin walked into the Cockpit an Englishman and walked out of the Cockpit an American."

After the Privy Council breakpoint, having failed to achieve reconciliation, Franklin wrote a letter to his sister: "You and I have almost finished the journey of life; we are now but a little way from home, and have enough in our pocket to pay the post chaises." I came across this fascinating tidbit in the wonderfully readable biography *Benjamin Franklin: An American Life*, by Walter Isaacson. Forty percent of the pages in Isaacson's book come *after* the point where Franklin pens this remarkable nearing-the-end letter, underscoring yet again a theme through this book: *Life's not done until it's done, and you never know what's coming next.*

Franklin could have settled into a glide path of descent, living a life of leisure and secure in the knowledge that he'd already lived a fruitful and useful life. He'd achieved economic wealth in his first hedgehog as a business entrepreneur and publishing magnate. He'd made pioneering scientific contributions. He'd been a civic and community leader, playing a catalytic role in forming a fire department, a hospital, and the University of Pennsylvania. He'd served in the Pennsylvania Assembly, both as a member and as its agent to Great Britain. He'd played a major role in getting the British Parliament to repeal the Stamp Act, which helped forestall the permanent breach with Great Britain. That seems enough for a lifetime! His body had already begun to fail him, and he would endure gout, kidney stones, boils, failing eyesight, and other unpleasant effects of aging in the 18th century.

Still, Franklin's mind remained sharp. He'd built a gigantic storehouse of credibility across his long life of success and service. With the entire world around him at a historical fracture point, Franklin decided to step up, not down, and to reinvest himself fully in the cause of independence. He played an influential role in the development of the Articles of Confederation (the precursor to the Constitution) and served in the Continental Congress. He accepted a dangerous and exhausting mission navigating icy waterways to Quebec, in an unsuccessful bid to bring Canadians into the colonies aligned against

Great Britain. Franklin became ever more of a revolutionary, while his own son remained a loyalist—a familial rupture that would never fully heal.

Then, in 1776, at age 70, he joined the committee to draft the Declaration of Independence, which would initiate the ultimate step of separating not just from Parliament but from allegiance to the king. On the drafting committee, Franklin made an enduring contribution to history. Jefferson had drafted the famous ringing words of the second paragraph as "We hold these truths to be sacred and undeniable." *Say what? Come on, Thomas, you can do better than that!* Franklin suggested a simple edit, to replace "sacred and undeniable" with "self-evident." If you go to the Library of Congress website, you can view one of the original working drafts of the declaration. After the words "We hold these truths to be" you can see a phrase scratched out. Above the scratch out, you can see the phrase "self-evident" from Franklin's edit. Once it was finalized, Franklin, along with Roger Sherman and 54 others, signed the declaration, knowing full well a stark truth: *If we lose, we all die.*

Franklin then took on one of the most important responsibilities of his life, as the U.S. ambassador in France. For nearly the entire decade of his 70s, Franklin brought together a lifetime of experience and drew upon his vast storehouse of credibility (he was likely the most famous American and revered by the French for his scientific accomplishments) to secure an alliance with France against the British. While in France, carrying the huge responsibility and knowing that, if he failed, the entire revolutionary effort might well fail, Franklin found his energy renewed despite his increasing age and health problems. At age 74, he wrote in a letter to a friend, "I do not find that I grow any older. . . . Being arrived at seventy, and considering that by travelling further in the same road I should probably be led to the grave, I stopped short, turned about, and walked back again; which having done these four years, you may now call me sixty-six." Heading into his late 70s, still serving in Paris, Franklin cemented (along with John Adams and John Jay) a peace agreement with Great Britain.

As Franklin prepared to finally return home to Philadelphia, he said, "I am now entering my 78th year. Public business has engrossed 50 of them. I wish now to be, for the little time I have left, my own master. If I live to see this peace concluded, I shall beg leave to remind Congress of their promise, then, to dismiss me."

As it turned out, Franklin had more life ahead of him, more responsibilities to choose. Upon his return, at age 79, Pennsylvania elected him president (what today we would call governor) of the state. Then, at age 81, he served at the Constitutional Convention, carried in daily on a sedan chair, lending his presence to the proceedings. William Pierce of Georgia said of Franklin during the convention, "He is 82 [sic] years old, and possesses an activity of mind equal to a youth 25 years of age." When the Constitutional Convention came near to failing over the competing interests of large and small states, Franklin joined forces with his matched-pair companion, Roger Sherman, to advance Sherman's compromise concept of separating the House and the Senate. In the end, Franklin drew upon his earned respect and facility with language to formally move for adoption of the Constitution in a final speech (read aloud for him by the Pennsylvania delegate James Wilson) to secure enough support of the delegates to send it to the states for ratification. Franklin had come to see the wisdom in human affairs of embracing *the best imperfect result.*

"Mr. President," Franklin's speech began, "I confess that there are several parts of this constitution which I do not at present approve. But I am not sure that I shall never approve them. For, having lived long, I have experienced many instances of being obliged by better information or fuller consideration to change opinions, even on important subjects, which I once thought right but found to be otherwise. It is therefore that the older I grow, the more apt I am to doubt my own judgment and pay more respect to the judgment of others." Franklin went on to express his astonishment that the proposed constitution turned out "so near to perfection as it does," and he closed out with, "Thus, I consent, sir, to this constitution, because I expect no better and because I am not sure it is not the best." After Franklin's motion, delegates stepped forth one by one to sign the document, which garnered 39 signatures with only three delegates in attendance who did not sign.

Even after all that, Franklin looked to the future, and he chose one final responsibility. Franklin came to believe that the United States could not endure, morally or practically, with slavery. In his final year of life, he served as president of the Pennsylvania Society for Promoting the Abolition of Slavery and presented a formal petition to abolish slavery. In the last published piece of writing of his life, under the pen name Historicus, Franklin flayed the hypocrisy of pro-slavery arguments. Right until the end, he applied his encodings to freely chosen responsibilities. He passed away just six weeks after penning perhaps one of the best pieces of writing in his life, at age 84, finally ready to let go.

In learning about Franklin, I felt somewhat overwhelmed by the magnitude of his life, especially because he'd done it all in the 18th century, when even just making the journey from Philadelphia to London took more than 60 times the amount of time it takes today. A conservative estimate shows that Franklin spent nearly an entire year (summed up across his life) just in transit across the oceans to and from the American continent and Europe.

I also take *solace* from Franklin's life, in learning that he endured an extended trough in his 50s and 60s (relative to the rest of his life). If Benjamin Franklin can make mistakes and misjudgments, then I don't feel so bad about my own mistakes and misjudgments. If Benjamin Franklin can spend years on efforts that ultimately ended in failure, then I don't feel so bad about my own efforts on projects that ended up being dead ends or cul-de-sacs. If Benjamin Franklin can feel dispirited and in a fog funk, then I don't feel so bad about my own existential fog funks. If Benjamin Franklin can enter his 60s with half of the most significant pages of his life yet to be written, then I feel quite good about the possibilities for the late decades of life.

In writing about Benjamin Franklin and casting back through all the remarkable people in this investigation, I'm struck by the imperfections in their lives. Their stories led me to a gigantic, calming exhale about my own life imperfections, letting go the anchoring weight of past mistakes and missed opportunities. I take from studying them a reminder that I wrote for myself and that I return to whenever I find myself being pulled around backward in the saddle by past regrets: *You cannot straighten out the road behind you.*

Why Capabilities *Increase* with Age

Why did the people in our study do some of their best work—and make some of their biggest contributions—relatively late in life? The evidence leads me to propose that total capability consists of three sub-capabilities that, when added together, only grow with time.

SUB-CAPABILITY NO. 1: RAW ENCODINGS

We've covered encodings extensively in this book, so I'm not going to dwell on them here, other than to make two observations. First, with the exception of purely physical encodings (like athletic speed or the ability to hit high musical notes), I see little evidence that encodings dim dramatically over time. Second, people can discover previously hidden encodings as the frame of their lives shifts, which serves only to increase one's capabilities. The journey to discover ever more of one's encodings need not end until the clock runs out.

SUB-CAPABILITY NO. 2: CUMULATIVE EXPERIENCE

The people in our study simply got better at doing what they were encoded for, layering experience upon experience over a long period of time. They learned how to recognize patterns, they learned from mistakes, they honed existing skills and added new skills. I was repeatedly struck by the relatively low correlation between the amount of time spent on a project or activity and its ultimate impact, especially in the later phases of life. Franklin's single edit from Jefferson's "We hold these truths to be sacred and undeniable" into "We hold these truths to be self-evident" flowed from years of cumulative experience. By the time he got to the drafting committee of the Declaration of Independence, Franklin had likely edited thousands of pages of newspaper stories, editorials, almanacs, and his own writings. Yet that tiny edit transformed the second paragraph of the Declaration of Independence from a forgettable turgidity into secular scripture that inspires across centuries and around the globe. How long did it take for Franklin to make this seminal contribution? *Seventy years and 70 seconds.*

Similarly, Sherman's decades of working on legal, legislative, and founding documents enabled him to quickly see that Madison's proposal to alter the primary text of the Constitution to insert a Bill of Rights endangered the entire edifice of the Constitution. At the crucial moment of that monumental decision point, Sherman had lived fully three decades longer than Madison. Yes, Madison was a legislative genius, but Sherman's cumulative experience helped him see in a flash the danger in Madison's proposed approach and how to counter it.

SUB-CAPABILITY NO. 3: CREDIBILITY EQUITY

Sherman and Franklin made a huge impact late in life partly by drawing upon storehouses of credibility they'd built over decades. It wasn't just Franklin's words at the end of the Constitutional Convention that held sway, but also that these words came *from Franklin*. It wasn't just that Sherman articulated a strong argument to preserve the actual text of the Constitution and use the amendment mechanism to include the Bill of Rights, but also that the argument came *from Sherman*. Credibility acts as an exponential multiplier, and compounds upon itself. Credibility need not require fame; you might have credibility equity at home, in your community, among your close colleagues. Think again of Sherman, and how he'd built credibility equity behind the scenes, never becoming famous but having tremendous influence.

> When you sum these three capabilities together, you can see that *total* capability *increased* over the decades for the people in our study. Late in life, they still had their encodings (and most kept discovering new ones). Their extensive cumulative experience continued to grow. They'd built credibility equity that they could draw upon as an exponential multiplier. By this logic, our most creative and productive years can happen long after the midpoint of our lives.

There is one other element of effectiveness that expanded as people added years: the ability to *lead*. Which brings me to a surprising twist in this study. I'd not expected to write about "leadership" in this book, but as it turned out, I gained new insights on leadership that I'd never had before.

A New Lens on Leadership

There is a great irony for me as I finish this project: I learned more about effective leadership in doing this study than in all my decades of studying what makes great organizations tick. That's an irony because many people who know my prior work would categorize me as a "leadership expert" based on five books wherein I'd studied and written about some of the greatest corporate leaders of all time. Yet it took *this* project to finally see perhaps the most important ingredient in effective leadership: *leading from your encodings*.

My transformation in understanding the essence of leadership began when I served a two-year appointment as the Class of 1951 Chair for the Study of Leadership at the United States Military Academy at West Point. I finished my second year in the chair at the same time I began this research project, in 2013. Little did I know then that my West Point service would later fuse with this study.

While at West Point, I wanted to define the essence of leadership. By serving in a chair at one of the world's greatest leadership development institutions, one that's been in the business of building leaders of character for more than 200 years, I hoped that I would finally find a satisfying answer to the question, "What is leadership?" The word "leadership" is tossed around a lot, but *what exactly is it*? At West Point, influenced directly by the reflections of General Dwight D. Eisenhower, I finally crystallized a short definition of leadership that best fits with everything I've studied and observed.

That definition is simply this: *Leadership is the art of getting people to want to do what must be done.* Leadership is not personality. Leadership is not charisma. Leadership is not power. Leadership is not giving orders. Leadership has nothing to do with position or rank or title or any of that. True leadership only exists if people follow when they would otherwise have the freedom to *not* follow.

I want you to notice three elements of this definition. First, as a leader, it's your responsibility to see what must be done. You might do this by your own insight or in collaboration with others, but however you do it, you need to get clear. Second, it's not about getting people to do what must be done but about getting them to *want* to do it. Third, it's not a science; it's an art. And it is this third element—the artistry—where leadership intersects with this study. *Each of us is a different "leadership artist" because each of us has different encodings.*

Roger Sherman and Benjamin Franklin differed dramatically from each other in their leadership encodings. Sherman, the awkward figure with a piercingly sharp legal mind, positioned himself for leadership in a way that fit his encodings—serving on influential committees, employing logical argument, restraining himself until the right instant to insert his argument at "the turning point of a question," and shaping durable legal structures. Franklin, the charming, socially graceful personality who became the most famous American in the world during his lifetime, drew upon a quite different set of encodings in his leadership—spinning stories and parables to make a point, writing humorous satire to highlight idiocies and change minds, and ingratiating himself into powerful circles of society. They both exercised the art of getting people to want to do what must be done, but they were very different leadership artists with very different leadership encodings.

Both Benjamin Franklin and Roger Sherman made their greatest leadership contributions without having raw executive power. They could not direct the Constitutional Convention, yet they deftly moved it toward the bicameral Connecticut Compromise. Sherman could not impose his will on Congress, yet he nonetheless won Congress to his argument for the Bill of Rights as amendments appended to the original Constitution, even over the initial opposing arguments of none other than James Madison. Sherman had few of the personality attributes that we often (and wrongly) associate with leadership—charisma, charm, social grace, inspiring oratory, or fame—yet he led brilliantly. He did so because he led from his own encodings, not by trying to emulate any of the other founders.

> Leadership effectiveness flows not from following the leadership recipes of others, or in having something we might call a "leadership personality." There cannot possibly be a universal recipe for leadership, for the simple reason that we are all encoded differently. The key is to trust your own leadership encodings, not to follow someone else's. If someone offers you a leadership recipe based on what worked for them, remember that it worked for them because it reflected *their* encodings, which likely

> differ substantially from *your* own encodings. It's okay to have a recipe for leadership, so long as it is *your* recipe that flows from *your* encodings and *your* inner fire.

I've become incredibly optimistic that people—perhaps even the vast majority of people—can become highly effective leaders. Once you come to see that leadership has nothing to do with position or power or personality or money or title or any of that, you can see that the opportunity for leadership exists in every walk of life, and in almost every situation. Imagine you're walking down the street as an individual citizen, just going about your day, when you come upon someone in trouble who needs help. It could be a car crash, an accident, a health issue, someone under threat, or whatever. *Something must be done!* Further, imagine that you need *other people* to join you in helping this person. In that situation, you don't have a title, or a formal position, or a rank on your lapel, or people who work for you, or a budget to spend, or formal power of any kind. If you can draw upon your encodings to get people to stop what they are doing and join you in doing what must be done, then you are being a leader.

What must be done? What are your leadership encodings that you've discovered about yourself—encodings that you've perhaps not seen in other leaders, but that you've nonetheless found particularly effective in your own leadership? How can you deploy your leadership encodings to accomplish what must be done? How can you feed your own inner fire by stepping forth to lead?

Bogle's Eyes

This chapter has been fundamentally about one overarching point: to dash to bits the pervasive belief that the fire inevitably declines as we age and that we flourish at our creative best when young. That soul-crushing belief is true only if we capitulate to believing it. The fire can burn on, not burn out.

I want to close this chapter with a vivid image seared into me of what the fire looks and feels like, from a life-altering day I spent with a man named Jack Bogle. Bogle likely contributed more to individual investors than any other person in history, championing the promulgation of low-cost mutual funds that favored the individual investor, not the fund managers. Bogle discovered the seeds of his hedgehog early in life, when he wrote his college thesis on the then-emerging field of mutual funds. At age 44, he had his big cliff, when Wellington Management Company fired him, leaving him without a job. At age 45, he founded Vanguard and brought forth into the world the revolutionary investing vehicle of the low-cost index fund.

Bogle and I crossed paths at a gathering in New York, when I was in my late 50s and he was in his late 80s. I saw Bogle a few paces ahead of me, leaning on his cane. I approached, saying, "Mr. Bogle, I don't mean to impose, but I just wanted to let you know how much I admire what you've created and I'm inspired with all of your work."

Bogle's face lit up with a flash of recognition. "Oh, Jim—so nice to meet you. We should talk sometime; we'd have a lot to discuss. Do you ever get near Philadelphia?"

"Well," I responded, "I could certainly get to Philadelphia."

I traveled to Bogle's office at Vanguard, and we spent the better part of a day together, discussing a range of shared questions. Now, I want you to picture us sitting there in animated, nonstop discussion for an entire morning. As the hours melted by, I was increasingly aware of the intensity in his eyes. The body might have been 88, but Bogle's inner fire lighting up those eyes made me feel as if I were sitting across from a 22-year-old Jack Bogle getting lit up by his senior thesis. There are missionaries and mercenaries; Jack Bogle was a missionary, through and through. For him, extracting high expense ratios from individual investors, especially when most fund managers fail to consistently outperform a simple market index, is almost a form of legalized stealing. "It's just wrong," he thundered. Hardly endearing himself to the rest of the fund industry, Bogle earned the nickname, not always said with kindness, Saint Jack.

Bogle never wavered, no matter how much he was criticized. He'd clicked into frame with something he was deeply encoded for and into which he focused his inner fire. He also made a spectacular flip in the arrow of money in the way he did it, deliberately giving up the chance to become a multibillionaire. He set up Vanguard as a mutual structure, where the funds are owned by the individual investors who invest in the funds, which means that profits from operating the funds flow back to the individual investors in the mutual funds rather than to a third party owner or public stock holders. With Vanguard growing from a start-up into one of the largest mutual fund companies in the world, with trillions of dollars of assets under management, Bogle could have easily been a member of the multibillionaire club if he'd set the firm up to channel the profits more to himself. But he did not do that, for the simple reason that the mutual structure better aligned with his self-chosen responsibility to best serve the interests of the individual investor.

As we talked, I realized that Bogle's great work lay not just in the index fund, or even in founding Vanguard, but in a more profound role: He became a *teacher* through his voice and writing. He'd not merely brought forth an investment product but taught his insights to millions of individual investors, empowering them with the knowledge to be able to manage their own financial destiny. Even after he retired from active duty as CEO of Vanguard, his responsibility to advance the cause of the individual investor remained. He had more to teach, more to share, more students to create.

Finally, after hours of stimulating and exhausting conversation, Bogle suggested that we walk over to the cafeteria to get some peanut butter and jelly sandwiches. We walked to another building, across a courtyard close enough that most people could walk to it in about five minutes. It took us more like 20 minutes, Jack taking small steps,

Feeding the Inner Fire (and Doing Great Work Late)

using his cane, still affected at some level by the heart transplant he'd had years before. The fire raged within, but I could see that the vessel would not last much longer. We lost Jack Bogle a little over a year later.

Did Bogle have a great life? I think his answer, right until the end, would have been, "It's not done yet." The image I will carry forever in my mind is the juxtaposition of Bogle's eyes and Bogle's aging body. Bogle's eyes burned with fierce intensity undiminished by the ravages of age, a fire of the hottest blue.

A couple of years after my meeting with Bogle, I began the systematic deep dive into the assembled research materials on each of the lives you've learned about in this book. As I worked through each life, I kept thinking of Bogle's eyes. All the people in our study were lucky enough to live decades beyond 50, more than three decades beyond 50 on average, with some clocking into their 90s and even over 100. For the most part, their lives remained on a decidedly upward arc full of fire, even if that arc became less visible in the world. Indeed, they generally continued to *accelerate* after 50, long after. Even if they languished in the fog at various points, even if they got lost in cul-de-sacs or made costly mistakes, even if they struggled in the wake of huge cliffs—they found fuel to feed the inner fire.

If I could have met the people in this study when they were well beyond 50, I imagine nearly all of them would bore into me with their own version of Bogle's eyes. Barbara McClintock might offer me a jelly bean or a handpicked walnut as she shows me around her maize fields. Grace Hopper might pull out her color-coded nanosecond wires and enthuse about the ever-increasing power of her beloved computer gadgets. John Glenn and Gordon Cooper might joyfully terrify me in a diving, swooping airplane ride. Toni Morrison might give me a piece of difficult literature, then hit me with her big, deep room-filling laugh, while Barbara Tuchman might sparkle in showing me the index cards with wonderful historical details that never made it into her books. Robert Plant might drag me into a vinyl record store in search of lost musical treasure, while Jimmy Page might lead me on a tour of his carefully curated collection of favorite guitars and then grab one to riff on the opening chords of "Whole Lotta Love." Michael J. Fox would certainly make me laugh *and* make me care about the Parkinson's community, while Alice Paul would likely leave me feeling insignificant and awestruck in the presence of her sheer uncompromising commitment. Roger Sherman would likely stun me with his granite-jawed intensity while he waited for precisely the right moment to turn the tide of argument, while Benjamin Franklin might delightedly show me his latest invention or satirical writing.

I don't think of the people in this study as inspirational; I think of them as *inspired*. I don't aim to inspire you to be exactly like any of the specific people in this study. I hope, rather, that you're able to find yourself clicked into frame, inspired by what fits your encodings and ignites your inner fire, and that you commit to pursue it with excellence.

For me, for however much time luck and grace allow, through whatever cliffs and fog I have yet to endure, with whatever responsibilities I choose and creative extensions I pursue, in whatever wonderful adventures of daily life I get to share with Joanne, I hope to come at them with the fire still burning bright. I hope to have my own version of Bogle's eyes.

13

Questions Are Better Than Answers

In the beginning of this book, I noted that multiple seeds ultimately led to this study. The first came with the loss of my father, leaving me with unanswered questions about how to navigate life. The second seed came when Joanne prematurely lost her identity as a professional athlete, which planted the question of how people reconstitute themselves when they hit a life-altering cliff. The third seed came in being inspired by the work and wisdom of the late John W. Gardner and his book *Self-Renewal*.

I crossed paths with Gardner when I taught at Stanford, right on the verge of a fracture point in my life when I left my faculty position to head out on my own. Gardner served as a sort of "wise man in residence" just down the hall from me, and we had a few conversations about where I might channel my intellectual curiosity. I was struggling with whether to pursue a traditional academic path or to carve an independent path. Gardner didn't tell me what to do, but he sensed that I would never happily adapt to the strictures and internal politics of university culture. He was right.

"How do you know when it might be time to make a life change?" I asked.

"As soon as you start asking the question," he replied.

I would have eventually left Stanford anyway, but Gardner's gentle prodding helped me make a full commitment to go over the cliff and never look back. Joanne and I call it our "Thelma and Louise" moment, invoking the image in the movie where the two main characters drive hurtling toward a chasm, hands clasped together. Though in our case, unlike the movie, we wanted to make it to the other side. Fortunately, we did.

However, the biggest impact Gardner had on me related not to a career decision but to the creation of this book. Gardner encouraged me to one day apply my love of big projects to the question of self-renewal, which he felt deserved more research. Gardner's encouragement became the third seed.

As you well know by now, the study became much larger in scope than the topic of self-renewal. In fact, I learned that the entire question of self-renewal largely melts into the background of the main findings in this book. For the most part, the people in our research *did* achieve self-renewal—exuding ageless zeal, expanding their capabilities, and sustaining meaningful engagement. They did so not as an explicit goal but as a residual effect of living in accordance with the larger set of findings in this book. And while I originally envisioned this work being relevant mainly to people seeking to remain vibrant in the second half of life, it became at least as relevant to people navigating the fog of youth and to those working through inevitable cliffs through the midstream of life.

One might expect that I'd wrap up a book like this with a set of recipes for living or a list of ten steps to a better life or a bevy of helpful prescriptions. The findings of the research and the ethos of this book stand against the very idea of doing that. You might have come to greatly admire many of the people in this study (as did I), but that doesn't mean you should try to become exactly like any of them. Don't confuse admiration with prescription, role models with cookie-cutter templates.

The Self-Knowledge Imperative Never Ends

I believe questions can be even more powerful than answers. As I indicated at the very beginning, this is a self-knowledge book, not a self-help book. It is a call to "Know Thyself"—and to bring that knowledge to life in the choices you make—not a prescription. Questions are the seeds of discovery, and the spirit of discovery is at the very core of this work. Not only about discovering shared patterns across the vastly different lives in this study, but also about making discoveries pertinent to our own lives. I've created a set of catalytic questions I hope you might be inspired to consider. Some of these questions might feel particularly pertinent to the moment, whereas others might become more pertinent at a different time in your life.

Catalytic Questions to Consider

Suppose you were to complete the following sentence by replacing X with a single word: "What I most want is a(n) X life." What, for you, is X?

What encodings have you discovered within? What do people who know you well see as your encodings?

What proportion of your energy is expended in frame with your encodings? What can you do—and what can you stop doing—to increase the proportion so that you might come more fully into frame?

What are your encoded operating modes, perhaps idiosyncratic to you, that make you particularly effective?

If you're struggling to get into frame, how would you allocate 100 points between the following two buckets? Bucket 1: You haven't yet *discovered* your encodings. Bucket 2: You don't yet *trust* your encodings enough to reshape your life around them.

What activities ignite the inner fire so strongly, and what activities do you so love doing, that you're willing to pay a hefty Stress and Drudgery Tax to do them?

Which subset of the 12 economic streams can you draw upon to successfully flip the arrow of money?

Have you found a hedgehog—an arena of activity that meets *all three* of the following tests? (1) You're encoded for it, (2) you flip the arrow of money in doing it, and (3) it focuses your inner fire. If so, what is the One Big Thing you've committed to channel a huge chunk of your energy toward and to organize your life around?

How have your cliffs (current or previous) reframed your life and exposed previously hidden encodings?

Can you see a cliff looming, and if so, what can you do to preclear some of the fog—what simplex stepping can you do before the cliff arrives?

If you're in the fog, what might be your next simplex steps, even if you don't know where you are going?

Reflect on the NATILIE moments in your life; assess how well you seized the NATILIE moments. What do your reflections teach you about making more of the next NATILIE moments when they come?

What is your record at getting a high *return* on luck (what luck, who luck, and zeit-luck), and how might you improve your record in the future?

What are you doing to Extend Out/Circle Back, pushing out the edges and doing new things while also returning to prior experiences and capabilities?

What seeds from earlier in life have lain dormant—interests you've always had, but for whatever reason your life went a different direction? How can you water those seeds as a method of Extend Out/Circle Back?

What responsibilities will you freely choose—whether they be public or private, professional or personal—and that might not otherwise happen but for you? What are your responsibilities beyond self?

On a scale of one to ten, how well do you live the Mothershead Mantra, pointed ever forward in the saddle? If your score is below ten, what do you need to do *and* stop doing to get your score higher?

What are your leadership encodings that help you with the art of getting people to want to do what must be done?

If you build teams or lead organizations, how can you do better at discovering other people's encodings and fire, and then aligning their responsibilities with their encodings and fire?

Whom in the study did you fall in love with? Which stories and lives most resonated with you, and why?

What beliefs about life were challenged or upended by reading this book?

Circling back to the first question, how can you harness the findings in this book to make a(n) X life?

What is the best practical suggestion I can give you for how to make use of this book? My answer is this: Engage with these questions and engage in conversation. The very process of engaging in good conversation with other people, combined with your own self-reflections on these questions, is perhaps the single most powerful mechanism for gaining clarity about how these findings apply specifically to you. Never underestimate the transformative power of meaningful conversation.

My Thinking Has Evolved... and My Hopes

Throughout the book I've shared that this entire project had a transformative effect upon me, intellectually and emotionally. Every chapter in this book has insights that I'd not had before I started this research, some substantially altering my prior beliefs about how life works. Nearby, I've delineated some of the ways my thinking has evolved in doing the research and writing this book.

I USED TO BELIEVE	I NOW BELIEVE
I used to believe in the primacy of "find and follow your purpose."	I now believe more in the primacy of "discover and trust your encodings."
I used to believe in the primacy of having a long-term life plan.	I now believe much more in the organic, unplanned, simplex-stepping nature of how great lives unfold.

I used to believe that some lives unfold without cliffs.	I now believe the search for a cliffless life is fruitless.
I used to believe successful people get where they are going by having clear vision.	I now believe that even the most successful people can spend months or years wandering in the fog.
I used to believe that people need to find their thing in life (a hedgehog) by age 30.	I now believe people can find it well past age 30, and still have an exceptionally meaningful life.
I used to believe that self-actualization means discovering the *one* thing you are made for and committing to pursue it with excellence.	I now believe that a single person can achieve self-actualized excellence in multiple radically different things across the long arc of a single life.
I used to believe that we are fully masters of our own fate, creators of our own destiny.	I now believe that the roulette wheel of life plays a huge (if not definitive) role in the paths our lives take.
I used to believe that luck mainly comes in the form of "what luck" and "who luck."	I now believe luck also comes in the "zeit-luck" of big forces that might swirl around us.
I used to believe more in radical self-reinvention and jettisoning the past to create the future.	I now believe more in the organic and continuous looping process of Extend Out/Circle Back.
I used to believe that effective leadership required taking in proven methods and practices of others.	I now believe that effective leadership flows first and foremost from one's own leadership encodings.
I used to believe in thinking about "legacy" and how one might be remembered.	I now believe in remaining focused on the life and work right at hand.
I used to believe that "giving" primarily means giving money and volunteering.	I now believe that the highest form of giving is to give of one's encodings.
I used to believe our most potent creativity happens when we are young.	I now believe we can hit peak creativity well past the midpoint of life.
I used to believe that life can be organized into a stage model, that there are common stages of life to follow.	I now believe that the organic, iterative, adaptive, layered unfolding of life defies stage models.
I used to believe freedom means lack of constraint.	I now believe freedom means choosing responsibilities.

This study changed my views on happiness. I used to view the pursuit of happiness as essentially irrelevant to becoming successful in life, perhaps even detrimental. I always wondered (or worried), "If you become happy, do you lose your drive?" The people in this study changed my mind. Their lives demonstrated that happiness happens for many successful people, even if they're not explicitly seeking happiness as a primary life goal. Most of the people in this study spoke little of happiness as a primary life goal, if they spoke about it at all. But equally, the evidence led me to conclude that most had extended phases of what we might call happiness as a residual result, a marvelous *side benefit*, of the way they went about their lives.

A friend once said of my earlier work that I wrote with a signature of "well-founded hope." The mountains of systematic research, combined with my dedication to drawing insights from the evidence, provided the "well-founded" part. "But the message is always hopeful," he said. "You demonstrate with evidence that good can become great, that people can build organizations worthy of lasting, that strong values can win in a hypercompetitive world." Well-founded hope. This study only added to that signature for me. It made me feel even *more* hopeful and optimistic, not directly about the world at large, but about *people*. And people, after all, make the world.

I emerge from this project with *hopes for myself*, hopes born of ways this study transformed me. I hope to retain my feelings of gratitude for what people are, rather than feeling chronically frustrated with what they are not. I hope to never again mentally sort people on a "worthiness hierarchy" that prioritizes big visible impact, success, and recognition. I hope to retain the humility of knowing that people often have invisible (or less visible) responsibilities in their lives, both difficult and wonderful, and that it is the height of arrogance to judge when you cannot ever see the whole picture. I hope to never again underestimate people, and to instead wonder what spectacular encodings they carry within. I hope to refrain from assessing (much less judging) a life still in progress, including my own life, and to remain always open to the possibility that what comes next will be a big wondrous surprise. Perhaps most of all, I hope to further cultivate the compassion that built up inside me for people going through the inevitable cliffs and fog of life.

Closing the Circle with My Father

I return, finally, to the most profound transformation of all, to my changed relationship with my late father.

My father lived through a huge cliff early in his life, with the death of *his* father in a test piloting accident. My grandfather Jimmy Collins (my namesake) became one of the early "right stuff" aviators. He and my grandmother met in Wichita, Kansas, when my grandfather stopped for fuel on a cross-country flight at a landing strip where my grandmother worked. Jimmy, the dashing and daring test pilot, and Delores, the beautiful Oklahoma farm girl who would one day sing in the Rainbow Room at Rockefeller Center, fell instantaneously in love. They married four days later.

Jimmy wrote one of the early memoirs of flying, *Test Pilot*, published initially as articles in outlets such as *The Saturday Evening Post*. He told my grandmother that if anything ever happened to him, he'd already written the last chapter. She could find it in his desk, add it to the existing chapters, and publish the book as a whole.

At age 30, in 1935, my grandfather tested a Grumman biplane fighter developed for the Navy, executing a series of power dives above Long Island. The aircraft failed, and my grandfather died.

When my grandmother pulled the last chapter out of the desk, she read its title with shock: "I Am Dead." My grandfather, knowing well the risks of his profession, had written his own last chapter about the death of the test pilot. The last words of the book, written in my grandfather's own hand, read, "The cold but vibrant fuselage was the last thing to feel my warm and living flesh. The long loud diving roar of the motor, rising to the awful crashing crescendo of its impact with the earth, was my death song. I am dead now." My grandmother published the book in its entirety. It got made into the 1938 movie *Test Pilot*, wherein Clark Gable played a character based on my grandfather and Myrna Loy played the role of his wife, my grandmother.

When my grandmother was in her 90s, I asked her to tell me the story of Jimmy's crash and its aftermath.

"I'd never done that before," she said, wiping away tears that had flowed as she told me about that awful time in her life. "Thank you."

"Done what?" I asked.

"Allowed myself to cry about losing Jim."

"You've *never* cried about it?"

"No. When Jim died, I sat at the service, gripped the arms of the chair, and willed myself to hold it together. It was the middle of the Depression. I had two children. I was alone. I had to hold it together. I *had* to."

My God, I thought to myself, *she'd held it in for seven decades*.

My grandmother gave me a photo of my grandfather and father next to a test plane, with my father as a young boy. My grandmother told me that the photo captured them the day before my grandfather crashed. Now, when I look at that photo, I realize that my grandmother had gone through a horrendous cliff and carried her children into the fog with her. Her ferocious will to survive (*seven decades* holding in the tears!) cast the landscape for my father growing up.

As I now reflect on my father's life, I realize that he'd been in the fog through his entire youth, and that he never really got out of it. He never flourished by discovering a beautiful confluence of encodings, economics, and fire, and he never found a way to turn fully forward in the saddle and choose responsibilities beyond himself. I believe now that if he'd changed the frame from how hard his mother had made his life (as she tried to survive) to the question of "What responsibilities do I want to choose with my life, responsibilities beyond myself?" he would have had a better chance of exiting the fog and maybe even having a wonderful life. And I might have had a father.

Writing these words 50 years after I got back on that Greyhound bus in New Mexico, shot through the heart with the knowledge that there would never be a father there, I no longer feel the furious condemnation that drove me so hard. I now see that he simply didn't know the right questions to ask, the questions for fully seizing the amazing gift of his one life to live. I wish I could go back in time and give him those questions before it was too late. But alas, I cannot. So instead, I offer them here to you. And I take them for my own.

Acknowledgments

Across the 12 years of working on this book—ten years of research and two years of writing—more than 100 people contributed to its creation. As I sifted through my notes and memories to assemble a list of people to recognize, I felt a huge surge of gratitude for those who lent me a good portion of their inner fire. Some invested summers in college or graduate school to join the research team; some joined the project full time for one or more years after graduation; some served in core roles supporting my research and teaching lab; some freely volunteered for critical reading and intellectual challenge; some played other vital roles in my life as I burrowed ever deeper in the creative cave, overwhelmed by the magnitude of this project. With these acknowledgments, I imagine having them all in a room together, handing each of them a personalized copy of the book with a warm clasp of hands and saying, "You are part of this, thank you." And then, getting the entire room to revel in the best party imaginable: a giant, raucous conversation about the findings and study subjects and their feelings about having been part of a grand adventure of discovery. I hope that the final work meets with their approval and, even more, that the stories and insights in *What to Make of a Life* will return the favor of their contributions by enhancing their lives and sparking glowing conversations with people they love.

I could not have done this project without my team of research assistants. They constantly challenged me not only to sharpen my conceptual understanding of the subjects of the book, but also to reflect on my own life. They absolutely, without a doubt, changed this book and me for the better, never hesitating to offer constructive criticism when they felt I'd not quite gotten something right in the research, synthesis, or writing. They are curious, disciplined, brilliant, and wonderfully irreverent. It is a great chosen responsibility in my life that I might play a small part in their emerging from the fog of youth, discovering their encodings, making the most of their luck events, and deploying themselves into the world in ways that feed their inner fire.

Research Team Members for *What to Make of a Life*:

Amelie Bauer	Ahnika LeRoy	Maia Parkin
Hannah Davinroy	Mary Grace Lewis	Brandon Reed
Kate DesCombes	Lorilee Linfield	Peytra Seybold
Jeffrey K. Erickson	Anne Lonowski	Jesse Shapiro
Madeline Garrett	Julia McCue	Midori Skold
Caitlin Davis Guerrie	Sam McMeley	Garrett Stoll
Kate Harris	Reid Morgan	Torrey Udall
Gage Hornung	Nate Nickrent	Camryn Woodworth
Wallace Kalkin	Amy Hodgkinson Nutting	Maren L. York
Noha Kikhia		

What to Make of a Life benefitted tremendously from the input of critical readers who invested themselves in reviewing the first draft of the manuscript. Many of the best changes in the final book flowed directly from their incisive commentary and willingness to embrace the *critical* aspect of being a critical reader, pushing me to make the book the best of which I am capable. While identifying flaws and offering constructive suggestions, they also gave me encouragement that the overall effort had the potential to be life-changing. Every one of these people helped the book become better: Ron Adner, Gideon Argov, Meredith Benjamin, Steve Bottoms, John P. Burke, Tania Burke, Terrence

Cummings, Eric Deardorff, Kate DesCombes (OPUR Chaos), Lori Dulberg, Jim Dunckley, LTC Mike Erwin, Andrew Feiler, Mark M. Ferrara, Christopher Forman, Sean Freitag, John Geisse, Aaron Greenblatt, Eric Hagen, Morten T. Hansen, Lane Hornung, Andy Jassy, Rob Kaufman, Will Kaufman, Alan Khazei, Steven Kyker, Kyle Lefkoff, Angel R. León, Caryn Marooney, Marissa Metz, Simon P. Newman, Keith Norsym, Keith Peters, Jerry Peterson, Tim Phillips, Todd Platt, Jim Reid, Michael J. Ricci, Peter Salvati, Charles A. Seybold, Dave Sheanin, William F. Shuster, Kara Henderson Snead, Roy Spence, Tom Tierney, Michael Wayne Wadsworth, and David Wilkie. Samantha Klein, Lauren Little, Ben Sheanin, and Nathan Sheanin played a vital role in collating and coding the critical reader manuscripts and forms, enabling me to systematically digest the feedback. A number of critical readers identified and suggested what turned out to be the book title, which had been awaiting discovery in the text of the draft manuscript: Tania Burke, Kate DesCombes, Rob Kaufman, Steven Kyker, Tim Phillips, and Dave Sheanin all saw the title before I did.

We have an incredible team at The Good to Great Project LLC, a small bus filled with people who see their work not as a "job," but as a set of responsibilities they choose to carry with such care that I never need to "manage" them. In the final push on the book, this exceptional team made sure that we never missed a beat in sustaining strong relationships with students of my work, ensuring that we made good on every commitment with supreme excellence, and handling all the other demands on our system: Judi Dunckley (forensic accounting Ginger), Catherine T. Gorman (sidecar and checklist champion), Melissa Rutty (who makes friends, learns voraciously, and helps me think), and Dave Sheanin (chief of staff and finder and coach of great people for the bus). Earlier in the project, other team members contributed to the superb running of our system so that I could focus on what only I can do: Alexis Bentley, Rebekkah Erks, Amy Humble, Sam McMeley, Amy Hodgkinson Nutting, Sara Raver, Brandon Reed, Erin Stenhouse, and Torrey Udall.

The book also benefited from a number of other people who contributed to its development in a variety of ways: Pat Adams (for enduring my verbal wanderings trying to make sense of the study lives), Dean Augustad (for lending an ear for me to read draft text out loud and make revisions), Dennis Bale (for providing a space to do my creative work while moving to and from), Janet Brockett (for as-ever brilliant visual creativity), Timothy Curran (for suggesting the term "feeding the inner fire"), Marc Ginsberg (for being Cyber Sherlock and keeping our connected systems secure and humming), Paul Gurien and Sean Jacobson (for consistently coming through in a pinch), James Kilgore (for finding network nodes), Cindy Knight (for giving of her research resources expertise), Lynn Krogh and his entire team (for keeping safety first, so I need never worry and thereby sustain my focus), Alexander Sammells (for efficiently and effectively getting the numbers right), Jane Schwartzberg (for pushing me to "have fun" as an explicit goal in bringing this book into the world), Les Snead (for belief), KR Sridhar (for the rocket ship orbital analogy that appears in chapter 10), brothers JT and JR (ever supportive believers in me for more than five decades), and Michael Weatherwax (for his years of partnership that enabled me to focus less on accounting and more on creative work).

In addition to those mentioned above, a number of people joined in gatherings of current and former team members to engage in spirited dialogue and debate about emerging findings in the research. Multiple portions of this book directly reflect moments of epiphany or challenge from those gatherings, including the entire creation of the analysis behind chapter 4 when a group of them rose up in spirited revolt against my initial framing of the personal economics of the lives in the study. In addition to many of the team members mentioned above, participants included: Brian Bagley, Robyn K. Bitner, Kyle Blackmer, Bradley Caldwell, Scott Cederberg, Anthony Chirikos, Lauren Cujé, Duane Duffy, Michael Graham, Ryan Hall, Beth Hartman, Christine Jones, Scott R. Jones, Stefanie Judd, Deborah Knox, Michael Lane, Weijia (Eve) Li, Nicholas Osgood, Catherine Patterson, Alyson Sinclair, Adam Stack, Matthew Unangst, Peter Van Genderen, Leigh Wilbanks, and Nathaniel (Natty) Zola.

As always, I'm grateful for my enduring partnerships in publishing. My agent, Peter Ginsberg, has worked with me on every one of my published titles going back more than three decades; not only has Peter represented the best interest of my books, he has done so with a strategic acumen and inspired imagination that has opened distinctively creative paths for the ultimate success and impact of my work. Peter Moldave, my trusted legal counsel for all aspects of intellectual property and literary agreements, proves himself repeatedly to be the type of attorney who crafts paths to "Yes" while building durable contracts. Hollis Heimbouch, my long-time working partner at HarperCollins Publishers, has always encouraged me to take whatever time I need to create a new book, showing full confidence that the best work requires years to bake. Once Hollis had this book in hand, we collaborated closely on the entire publication and launch process, and she assembled a passionate team of talents dedicated to the book: Kirby Sandmeyer, David Koral, Bonni Leon-Berman, Olivia McGiff, and Joanne O'Neill blended creativity and careful attention to detail in the editing, design, and production of the book; Tina Andreadis, Leslie Cohen, Jessica Gilo, Amanda Pritzker, and Leah Wasielewski, along with Aileen Boyle of Audere Media, dedicated themselves with drive and precision to bringing *What to Make of a Life* to a vastly new readership. Nigel Wilcockson, my longtime publishing partner in the U.K., proved himself yet again to be a writer's editor with whom I can engage intellectually and philosophically. Early in our working friendship, Nigel grasped that my work was never fundamentally about business and leadership, but about the study of *people* and exceptional human endeavor, and he encouraged me to boldly break out of the limiting circle of being defined as a business and leadership author.

I would like to thank my mother, Faith, and my brother, Michael, for reviewing the text of my own stories that open and close the book, fact-checking my memories with their recollections of those painful episodes, and lending me their perspective on what we lived through. As a wonderful side benefit, this sparked conversations that we'd never had before. I'm truly grateful that, at age 91, my mom finally wanted to have the conversation about my father that we'd avoided for five decades. I'm equally grateful that my brother and I used this as an opportunity to continue to build something largely missing for much of our lives: an ever-deepening relationship as true brothers who like, love, and respect each other.

Finally, I would like to make special note of three people who supported me and this work by challenging me over the long course of this project from its very inception.

Bill Meehan, intellectual provocateur and caring friend, encouraged and challenged me to widen and deepen the scope of what this book is all about. "Don't waste your time—or your words—on the little questions," he'd hammer at me. "Go for the big questions, the questions of truth and wisdom and meaning. You need to be more of a poet and less of an analyst, more of a philosopher and less of a strategist." I've always built my books on a foundation of rigorous research and empirical evidence, and *What to Make of a Life* is no exception. But throughout the ten years of research, Bill kept pushing me to use the data to explore and discover what really matters in life. Sadly, we lost Bill in early 2023, just as I finished the research and began the process of synthesis and writing. I put a Post-it note on the cover of my home laptop, "Rem Bill Meehan," to keep Bill's searing (and loving) provocations in mind. I hope that this book in its final form came somewhat close to living up to Bill's challenges.

Tom Tierney encouraged and challenged me every step of the way through the long process of research and writing. In the early phases of this work more than twelve years ago, Tom and I would have long conversations about how to rigorously examine such elusive topics as "self-renewal" and then to eventually tackle the much larger questions of life. Over the course of the study, I estimate that we likely spent something on the order of a hundred hours in various conversations—iterating, exploring, sharpening, reframing, testing, expanding, focusing, and always keeping me pointed toward discovering what is timeless and true. Tom is, and will always be, a core member of my Personal Band of Brothers.

Joanne, my wife and life partner of now 45 years, never waivered in her faith that I would somehow get through the mountain of research and discover a powerful set of ideas. Even more, she made monumental contributions to the intellectual framing of the entire study, challenging me to question and set aside my own assumptions as I studied the lives in the research. Joanne's sharp, piercing intellect has influenced all of my books and guided my big strategic choices. I like to say that while I am the creative propulsion machine, Joanne is the strategic guidance mechanism. Without her fierce protective instinct that compels her to correct my direction when needed, I would have likely spent my life expending huge amounts of energy without meaningful result or, worse, have crashed spectacularly in ill-conceived adventure. Anyone who knows me well understands that it is "Jim and Joanne"—equal partners—always, and in everything.

APPENDIX 4.1

Personal Economics Analysis

This appendix captures the definitions and nuances of coding economic streams. We required either direct evidence or strong inference from the overall evidence in making economic coding determinations.

Mastering Scarcity

Mastering Scarcity Definition: The person went through a phase of scarcity of economic resources while in pursuit of a hedgehog. The phase required some combination of sacrifice, creativity, resourcefulness, living lean, and/or sheer work ethic to meet basic material needs while simultaneously being fully committed to pursuit of a hedgehog.

IN CONTEXT
1. When Maurice White committed to music, he struggled economically. White reflected in his memoir, "No money, many days hungry, I was dropping weight.... Every day I would go down to this Greek restaurant.... They had this great deal: pita bread, some veggies, and a piece of meat, all for $1. I ate that way for a few months, one meal a day, one dollar a day." White's ability to master scarcity sustained him as he developed his early career in music.
2. Michael J. Fox spent years as a struggling actor in Hollywood, cobbling together a series of small roles, before catching his big break. He lived in a tiny apartment. The phone company cut off his phone service. He even began selling off his furniture, at one

point selling off chunks of his sectional sofa, piece by piece, just to keep going. Mastering scarcity allowed Fox to pursue acting while meeting his economic needs.

CODING NOTES AND CLARIFICATIONS

1. If the person endured a scarcity phase but did so only at a point in life when not in pursuit of a hedgehog, then it would not count as mastering scarcity.
2. Scarcity, as opposed to modesty or frugality, is defined by a state that required significant sacrifice, creativity, resourcefulness, living lean, and/or sheer work ethic in order to meet the person's basic needs, such as food or housing.
3. If the person had to master scarcity to get an education that later proved integral to pursuit of a hedgehog, then we count this as mastering scarcity even if the person was not yet in pursuit of that future hedgehog.

Family Wealth

Family Wealth Definition: The person came from a family with substantial economic wealth that directly enabled full commitment to a hedgehog with little (if any) worry about personal economics.

IN CONTEXT

1. Lucy Burns and Alice Paul both came from wealth (their fathers were successful bankers), which enabled them to pursue the cause of women's suffrage and the fight for the 19th Amendment. Because both women received financial support from their families, they could focus on their activism rather than generating income.

CODING NOTES AND CLARIFICATIONS

1. Family wealth is coded as an economic source only if the person's family had such significant wealth that economics were

never a concern when pursuing a hedgehog. The person might have made money from another source but would not have been prohibited from pursuing the hedgehog without that other source of income.

Spousal Economics

Spousal Economics Definition: The person's spouse provided substantial economics (in the form of income that the spouse generated or by inheriting assets from a deceased spouse) that partly or fully supported pursuit of a hedgehog.

IN CONTEXT

1. Despite having graduated near the top of her class, Sandra Day O'Connor struggled to find a paying job practicing law. When she and her husband moved to Arizona, he brought in the bulk of the family's income. Meanwhile, Sandra took steps that kept her connected to the law, but with minimal pay. Having spousal economics allowed the O'Connors to stay afloat as Sandra Day O'Connor iterated back to a full-time career in law.

CODING NOTES AND CLARIFICATIONS

1. Any inherited spousal asset that became an integral part of solving the economic circle of the hedgehog counts for this category. The inheritance could have come in a range of possible forms, including insurance and other payouts that came from the death of a spouse.
2. Spousal economics can qualify as an economic source even if the person did not need to draw substantially upon spousal economics through the entire duration of a hedgehog. Spousal economics might have played an integral role only to start a hedgehog, or for only a portion of time while pursuing a hedgehog.

3. In cases where the person had a financially successful spouse, yet the evidence strongly suggests that spousal economics played no significant role in fueling pursuit of the hedgehog, we do not count as spousal economics.

Funding for Education/Training

Funding for Education/Training Definition: The person received financial or material support for education that proved directly beneficial to the pursuit of a hedgehog. Education/training has a wide definition here, from traditional schooling to direct training for skills and craft.

IN CONTEXT

1. The U.S. government funded Gordon Cooper's advanced training as a military jet fighter pilot, test pilot, and astronaut. It would have been impossible for Cooper to pay for this skill development, but the funding he received for education/training enabled him to learn how to fly fighter jets, test advanced supersonic aircraft, and orbit Earth in a space capsule.

CODING NOTES AND CLARIFICATIONS

1. Support can have come from a range of possible sources, including family, scholarships, government, military, and others.
2. This category can be met by funding support for skills development or vocational training.
3. Funding for education/training is coded as an economic source only if the training or schooling contributed to laying the foundations for or the direct pursuit of a hedgehog.
4. Funding for education/training can be coded as an economic source if the person did not know at the time of getting the education that it would be directly useful to a future hedgehog.

Cross Funding

Cross Funding Definition: The person did non-hedgehog work for a period of time to bring in money while simultaneously pursuing a hedgehog.

IN CONTEXT

1. Meryl Streep waited tables and took a job typing plays while attending drama school. Streep cross funded by working outside her hedgehog so that she could sustain herself through acting school.
2. Carlos Santana worked as a dishwasher in the early phase of his music career before he could make enough money on music alone. Santana's income from dishwashing helped partially sustain him until his music career could.

CODING NOTES AND CLARIFICATIONS

1. Cross funding only counts if it came from non-hedgehog activities.
2. Cross funding is coded as an economic source only if the person used it as economic support while in full pursuit of a hedgehog.
3. Cross funding is coded as an economic source only if it was an integral part of solving the economics circle of getting into and actualizing a hedgehog, and not if it simply provided excess wealth or financial cushion not used in pursuit of a hedgehog.
4. If a person had an overlap period from one hedgehog to another, and where economics from the first hedgehog helped fund transition into the second hedgehog, it does not count as cross funding because the source of economics still derived from a hedgehog.

Salaried Hedgehog

Salaried Hedgehog Definition: The person pursued a hedgehog that came in the form of a salaried position, a "job" that the person was encoded for, that fed the inner fire, and that came with a paycheck.

IN CONTEXT

1. George C. Marshall spent most of his career serving as a military officer, for which he received a salary. Marshall made his personal economics work through a salaried hedgehog.

CODING NOTES AND CLARIFICATIONS

1. If the person was self-employed or an entrepreneur, or if the person drew economics principally from ownership stake in a business flywheel, then we do not code as a salaried hedgehog even if the person drew a salary from the business.
2. To count as a salaried hedgehog, the salary must come from a role that is a hedgehog, not one that is ancillary to a hedgehog or one that led to a hedgehog without yet being a hedgehog. The point of this caveat is to capture cases where the person did hold a salaried job at one point, but where the essence of the person's hedgehog required *not* being in a traditional salary/job structure.
3. Salaried hedgehog is coded as an economic source only if the person's income derived primarily from doing one distinct job/position that had a consistent salary structure.

Creative Flywheel

Creative Flywheel Definition: The person created a self-reinforcing positive loop of creative work, wherein doing successful and financially viable creative work (such as acting, writing, music, architecture, design) then generated more opportunities for financially viable creative work.

IN CONTEXT
1. Toni Morrison built her writing career step by step. Her first two novels gained a relatively small readership upon initial publication. Her third novel won the National Book Critics Circle Award for Fiction, and her readership grew. She attributed the success of her fourth book to "a very active and enthusiastic readership" that she'd built with her first three books. Morrison sustained a perpetual cycle of successful writing and publishing for another three decades. Her creative flywheel built momentum that sustained her financially.

CODING NOTES AND CLARIFICATIONS
1. A creative flywheel can (but is not required to) have coexisted with or fed into a business flywheel.

Business Flywheel

Business Flywheel Definition: The person created, co-created, and/or controlled a business entity that generated profits and cash flow that could go back into fueling the business and where the activities of the business were directly in line with the person's hedgehog.

Note: I have written extensively about the elements of building business flywheels in my prior work. To learn more, see *Good to Great* (chapter 8) and the companion monograph, *Turning the Flywheel*. From an entrepreneurial perspective, see *Beyond Entrepreneurship 2.0*, co-authored with Bill Lazier.

IN CONTEXT

1. Vera Wang founded the Vera Wang Bridal House and the Vera Wang company. After initial seed capital from her father, Wang began a multiyear process to grow the company into a self-sustaining flywheel. As she began to generate more cash flow, Wang reinvested back into the company and creating new fashion designs, which in turn generated more economic fuel to further reinvest. Turn upon turn, push upon push, the flywheel gained increasing momentum, enabling her to pursue and expand her hedgehog in fashion design.
2. There are many permutations of business flywheels in this study. Examples include Benjamin Franklin's publishing and printing flywheel, I. M. Pei's architecture firm flywheel, and the business aspect of the Led Zeppelin flywheel.

CODING NOTES AND CLARIFICATIONS

1. To qualify, the business must be an organization or entity largely owned and/or controlled by the person under study.
2. To qualify, the activities of the business must be directly in line with the person's hedgehog. If the person operated a business flywheel that generated economics useful in the pursuit of a hedgehog but where doing the business was not integral to the hedgehog itself, then it would be categorized under cross funding.
3. If the person converted creative talent in a hedgehog into a related business flywheel, then the person would have both a creative flywheel and a business flywheel.
4. If the person created a profitable business (whether a corporate entity or a sole proprietorship) that principally involved rendering services by that person, and where those services were directly in line with the person's hedgehog, then it counts as a business flywheel. That the business might not have survived if the person stopped doing the business does not disqualify it from being counted in this category.

Social Cause Flywheel

Social Cause Flywheel Definition: The person created or co-created a social cause organization (directly in line with the person's encodings) that attracted and/or generated funding to be deployed into creating impact, which then attracted/generated more funding to create even more impact, in a continuous reinforcing loop of funding and impact.

Note: I have written about the elements of building social cause flywheels in my prior work. To learn more, reference the monographs *Good to Great and the Social Sectors* and *Turning the Flywheel*.

IN CONTEXT

1. Michael J. Fox founded The Michael J. Fox Foundation for Parkinson's Research to support work on behalf of those who suffer from Parkinson's disease. The foundation's flywheel gained momentum year upon year, raising funds and reallocating them to the most promising scientific work. After two decades, the foundation funded $1 billion in scientific research, becoming the second-largest funder of research on Parkinson's disease. Fox's social cause flywheel generated resources to support his work with the Parkinson's community.

CODING NOTES AND CLARIFICATIONS

1. The idea here is that for the person to have fully pursued a social cause hedgehog through the platform of a social cause organization, the organization must have had sustainable funding economics.
2. Having a social cause flywheel as an economic source does not require that the person's personal life was primarily funded by the social cause organization.

Earned Earlier

Earned Earlier Definition: The person generated and saved substantial economics earlier in life and then drew upon those assets to further pursue an existing hedgehog or to start a new one.

IN CONTEXT

1. Benjamin Franklin's first hedgehog as a business entrepreneur generated substantial wealth that enabled him to retire from the day-to-day running of his printing and publishing operations and redeploy his prodigious energies into science and invention. His accumulated assets and investments continued to provide a portion of his economic foundation late in life when he became a visionary public leader in the revolution and formation of the United States. Because Franklin had resources earned earlier, he was able to explore other endeavors that were financially supported by his previous earnings.

CODING NOTES AND CLARIFICATIONS

1. Earned earlier is coded as an economic source only if the resources that were earned earlier became an integral part of doing the hedgehog later. If the person saved substantial economic resources earlier in life but did not draw upon those resources to pursue a hedgehog, then this does not count as earned earlier. This caveat helps to capture the difference between economics saved and used for non-hedgehog activities (like retirement or non-hedgehog philanthropy) and economics used for hedgehog activities.
2. The form of the saved economic asset that the person drew upon need not have been as simple as a cash bank account. Permutations that would count as earned earlier:
   - If the person invested money earned earlier into assets that later generated cash flow the person drew upon to pursue a hedgehog (for

example, bonds, stocks, real estate, and direct investments in business ventures).
- If the person used money earned earlier to buy tangible assets that were later directly used as part of pursuing a hedgehog (for example, a piece of real estate that the person converted to a studio working space for doing hedgehog work).
- If the person drew upon a substantial pension or similar payout from earlier work to pursue a hedgehog.
- If the person created or co-created an asset earlier in life and that person held a contractual claim or ownership stake in that asset, such that the asset created cash flow later in life that the person drew upon to pursue a hedgehog. Note for clarity: If the income fell under the creative flywheel—such as royalties from books, films, and music—it would be categorized not as earned earlier but, rather, under creative flywheel, even if some of those royalties derive from work that was done earlier in life (such as royalties that flowed to the person for decades from a book published early in life).

Direct Personal Support

Direct Personal Support Definition: The person drew support from people in the immediate community (such as friends, family, acquaintances, mentors, neighbors, or other community members) while in pursuit of a hedgehog; this support came in the form of money or donation of goods and services that would otherwise cost money.

IN CONTEXT

1. When Cardiss Collins moved to Washington, D.C., to become a member of the U.S. House of Representatives, her mother helped take care of her son in Chicago. Collins's mother provided direct personal support, mitigating the need to find and pay for child care.

CODING NOTES AND CLARIFICATIONS

1. This category captures material support or support in the form of services that the person would have otherwise needed to pay for.

Special Sources

Special Sources Definition: The person drew upon some other economic resource that does not fit neatly into one of the other 11 categories; this includes such resources as government housing, financial settlements from lawsuits, and prize money from scientific and literary awards.

IN CONTEXT

1. Dolores Huerta won a lawsuit settlement that had a payout of $825,000 paid in increments of $2,000 a month, related to a near-fatal beating at a protest that sent her to the hospital with a damaged spleen and several broken ribs. After the settlement, this special source of income partially sustained Huerta through her activism.
2. Gerald R. Ford and Jimmy Carter's housing costs were covered by living in the White House while they served as president.
3. Barbara McClintock received fellowships and prize money for her scientific work, including a MacArthur Fellowship and a Nobel Prize.

CODING NOTES AND CLARIFICATIONS

1. If there is no other category that the source fit into, it goes into this category.

APPENDIX 6.1

Cliff Scoring Rubric

MAGNITUDE OF THE CLIFF

We assess the magnitude of the cliff based on three dimensions:
1. The extent of life change brought about by the cliff.
2. The extent to which the cliff was beyond the person's control.
3. The extent to which the cliff was unforeseen and/or uncertain before it happened.

Extent of Life Change

High: The cliff creates a demarcation of the end of one major phase of life and/or career identity. The activities and objectives toward which the person principally channels life energies are forced by the cliff to be substantially different in the post-cliff life from in the pre-cliff life. A cliff need not be instantaneous in its effect to be of a high magnitude; while there is a specific cliff marker in every case (the period in time best seen as marking the onset of the cliff), the full form of the cliff and its transformative impact might unfold over a period of time. Any clear and dominant personal or professional identity that existed pre-cliff will henceforth be in the past, even if that past identity remains heavily associated with the person's professional reputation and personal history. Any case where the person holds a life/career-defining role/title that comes to a clear and distinct termination would qualify as an *H*.

Medium: The cliff creates a demarcation of the end of one major phase of life and/or career identity. However, unlike cases that receive an *H*, the person is able to continue substantial effort toward the primary activities and objectives in the post-cliff life that were pursued in the pre-cliff life, and the person is able to sustain those activities for an indefinite time beyond the cliff. Any clear and dominant personal or professional identity that existed pre-cliff will change in some significant way, but it will also have some substantial carryover from pre-cliff to post-cliff. A cliff that substantially diminishes the opportunities the person has in a primary activity—but where the person nonetheless remains able to continue to channel energy heavily into that pre-cliff activity—would fall here.

Low: The cliff is a major event or episode that impacts the person's personal and/or professional life, but the cliff does not substantially alter the activities and/or objectives toward which the person principally channels life energies. This can be a negative event, such as a significant career setback or personal loss that must be worked through, or it can be a positive event that serves as a significant marker in one's personal or professional life trajectory.

Beyond the Person's Control

High: Whether or not the cliff happens is almost entirely out of the person's control, and there is very little choice the person has as to the speed/timing of the cliff or how the cliff itself unfolds.

Medium: Whether or not the cliff happens is almost entirely out of the person's control; however, unlike an *H*, the person has some choice/influence as to the speed/timing of the cliff and/or how the cliff itself unfolds. There are also some situations where the person plays a role in creating or triggering the cliff, yet the cliff nonetheless remains in a category where the person is not the primary decider as to whether or not the cliff ultimately happens.

Low: Whether or not the cliff happens is largely within the person's control. It is essentially a self-generated choice to step or jump off the cliff.

Unforeseen/Uncertain

High: The cliff is unforeseen by the person before it hits; it comes as a complete surprise.

Medium: There are two possible ways to get an *M*: (1) The person sees an increasing likelihood of the cliff before it happens, but there remains considerable uncertainty as to whether the cliff will actually happen; (2) the person knows for certain that the cliff will happen, but there is considerable uncertainty as to the precise timing and/or form of the cliff.

Low: The person knows for certain that the cliff will happen, and there is near certainty as to when the cliff will happen and the form it will take.

Conversion into Numeric Score

We place the most emphasis on dimension No. 1 (the degree of life change), using the following scoring methodology:
- The extent of life change brought about by the cliff: High (H) = 6; Medium (M) = 4; Low (L) = 2.
- The extent to which the cliff is beyond the person's control: High (H) = 2; Medium (M) = 1; Low (L) = 0.

- The extent to which the cliff is unforeseen/uncertain: High (H) = 2; Medium (M) = 1; Low (L) = 0.

The magnitude score for the cliff is the sum of the scores across the three dimensions.

We will define categories of magnitude as follows:
- Mega Cliff: A score of 8 to 10
- Major Cliff: A score of 6 to 7
- Minor Cliff: A score of 5 or below

Sources

The following pages provide the sources used for the facts contained in each chapter. These are not the only sources used in doing the research for this study; there are thousands of additional sources that I read, watched, and listened to in forming my insights and conclusions for this book. If I'd included a listing of the entire mountain of research materials processed on the study subjects, not to mention the thousands of further materials used in constructing the study set, it would have roughly *tripled* the page count of this book! I've therefore limited what follows to materials that undergird the text of each chapter. Sources are organized by chapter into five categories: (1) Books; (2) Videos and Audio; (3) Newspapers and Magazines; (4) Websites and Online Articles; and (5) Other. The use of an asterisk indicates that the source contains a quotation from a study subject in that person's own voice. My primary objective is to credit the sources that underpin each chapter. I also hope for a second objective: that you might find materials you'd like to read, watch, or listen to yourself, to continue your own exploration of the lives of the people you've come to know in reading *What to Make of a Life*.

Chapter 2: One Big Thing
BOOKS
*Beyer, Kurt W. *Grace Hopper and the Invention of the Information Age.* Cambridge, Mass.: MIT Press, 2009. Kindle.
Billings, Charlene W. *Grace Hopper: Navy Admiral and Computer Pioneer.* Hillside, N.J.: Enslow, 1989.
Comfort, Nathaniel C. *The Tangled Field: Barbara McClintock's Search for the Patterns of Genetic Control.* Cambridge, Mass.: Harvard University Press, 2003. Kindle.
*Fine, Edith Hope. *Barbara McClintock: Nobel Prize Geneticist.* eFrog Press, 2012. Kindle.

Heiligman, Deborah. *Barbara McClintock: Alone in Her Field.* New York: W. H. Freeman, 1994. Kindle.
*Keller, Evelyn Fox. *A Feeling for the Organism: The Life and Work of Barbara McClintock.* New York: Henry Holt, 1983.
Marx, Christy. *Grace Hopper: The First Woman to Program the First Computer in the United States.* New York: Rosen, 2003.
*McGrane, Bill. *All Rise: The Remarkable Journey of Alan Page.* Chicago: Triumph Books, 2010. Kindle.
*Mompoullan, Chantal. *Voice of America Interviews with Eight American Women of Achievement.* University of Michigan Libraries.
Spangenburg, Ray, and Diane Kit Moser. *Barbara McClintock: Pioneering Geneticist.* New York: Chelsea House Publishers, 2008. Kindle.
Twain, Mark. *The Wit and Wisdom of Mark Twain: A Book of Quotations.* Mineola, N.Y.: Dover Publications, 1998.
Vare, Ethlie Ann, and Greg Ptacek. *Mothers of Invention: From the Bra to the Bomb: Forgotten Women and Their Unforgettable Ideas.* New York: Quill William Morrow, 1989.
Williams, Kathleen Broome. *Grace Hopper: Admiral of the Cyber Sea.* Annapolis, Md.: Naval Institute Press, 2004.

VIDEOS AND AUDIO

*"Alan Page." *A Football Life.* NFL Films, Oct. 16, 2015.
*"Alan Page on Leadership (The Mary Hanson Show)." *Mary Hanson,* Sept. 24, 2001.
"Alan Page on Twin Cities Live 4.2.14." Page Education Foundation, April 9, 2014.
Beyer, Kurt W. "The Invention of the Information Age." Talks at Google, May 19, 2010.
"Carl Eller Interview—Vike Fans—Part 1 of 2." tdb8420. www.youtube.com /watch?v=iM3j59C4Vfs.
*"Grace Hopper: She Taught Computers to Talk." *60 Minutes,* March 6, 1983.
"Grace Hopper Is The Computer Queen." *Letterman,* Oct. 2, 1986.
"Grace Hopper Lecture." MIT Lincoln Laboratory, April 25, 1985.
"Honorable Alan Page Visited STA." Saint Thomas Academy, Feb. 3, 2016.
*Jacobs, Gillian, dir. "The Queen of Code." ESPN Films, Feb. 2, 2015.
*"Justice Alan Page Interview." Walden University, Oct. 10, 2018.
"A Look Back at Former Minnesota Vikings Defensive Tackle Alan Page's 1971 Season." USA AS. www.youtube.com/watch?v=ZKJzoTSg7iM.
Rath, Arun. "Grace Hopper, 'the Queen of Code,' Would Have Hated That Title." *All Tech Considered,* NPR, March 7, 2015.

NEWSPAPERS AND MAGAZINES

Belson, Ken. "Carl Eller, ExViking, Is Using the Super Bowl as a Platform." *New York Times,* Feb. 2, 2018.

Byrd, David. "Courting Alan Page." *National Journal*, Dec. 12, 1998, 50.
"Computer Programing Pioneer Promoted by Remington Rand." *New York Times*, Aug. 18, 1961, 31.
Grow, Doug. "If 'Moose' Roared, Would They Listen?" *Star Tribune*, Jan. 9, 2005, 1.
Ketcham, Diane. "About Long Island: A Very Private Legend." *New York Times*, July 26, 1992, 13.
Kolata, Gina. "Dr. Barbara McClintock, 90, Gene Research Pioneer, Dies." *New York Times*, Sept. 4, 1992, 1.
Lassiter, Jim. "Carl Eller Has a New Habit Fighting Drugs." *Oklahoman*, Feb. 27, 1985.
"Prep Athletes Get Some Help from Carl Eller." *Los Angeles Times*, March 17, 1985.
*"Quotation of the Day." *New York Times*, Oct. 11, 1983, B1.
Raghavendran, Beena. "Alan Page Welcomes Minneapolis Students to the School Now Bearing His Name." *TCA Regional News*, Sept. 2, 2017, 1.
Schaap, Jeremy. "Now He Tackles Injustice." *Washington Post*, May 15, 1994, AA12.
*Smith, William D. "Pioneer in Computers: Navy Officer Likes to Rock the Boat." *New York Times*, Sept. 5, 1971, F5.
Swift, E. M. "Don't Kick Sand in His Face." *Sports Illustrated*, July 16, 1979, 6.
Teltsch, Kathleen. "Award-Winning Scientist on L.I. Prizes Privacy." *New York Times*, Nov. 18, 1981.
*"They're Helping Teenagers to Stay Sober." *Hartford Courant*, July 30, 1989, SM5.
*Wilford, John Noble. "A Brilliant Loner in Love with Genetics: Barbara McClintock." *New York Times*, Oct. 11, 1983, C7.

WEBSITES AND ONLINE ARTICLES

"About RPA: Our Mission." Retired Players Association. nflretiredplayers association.org/about-rpa.asp.
"About Us: Our Founders Diane and Alan Page." Page Education Foundation.
"Alan C. Page: Justice." Minnesota State Law Library.
"Alan Page." Pro Football Hall of Fame.
*"Alan Page: Enshrinement Speech." Pro Football Hall of Fame, July 30, 1988.
Bailey, Frank J. "Justice Alan Page's Search for Justice from the Football Hall of Fame to the Minnesota Supreme Court." American Bar Association, Nov. 11, 2024.
"Barbara McClintock." Cold Spring Harbor Laboratory. www.cshl.edu/personal -collections/barbara-mcclintock.
"Barbara McClintock: About." Cold Spring Harbor Laboratory. facultyprofiles .cshl.edu/barbara.mcclintock.
*"Barbara McClintock: Biographical." Nobel Prize, 1983. www.nobelprize.org /prizes/medicine/1983/mcclintock/biographical.

"Barbara McClintock: Publications." Cold Spring Harbor Laboratory. faculty-profiles.cshl.edu/barbara.mcclintock/publications.

"Barbara McClintock Life Sciences Lecture Series: About Barbara McClintock." Cornell University.

"Biography of Grace Murray Hopper." Yale University: Office of the President.

"Carl Eller." Pro Football Hall of Fame.

*"Carl Eller: Enshrinement Speech." Pro Football Hall of Fame, Aug. 8, 2004.

"Carl Eller Set to Showcase Art in New Vikings Stadium." Pro Football Hall of Fame.

Chomet, Paul, and Rob Martienssen. "Barbara McClintock's Final Years as Nobelist and Mentor: A Memoir." *Cell* 170, no. 6 (2017).

Conklin, Richard. "Alan Page: He Dedicated His Life to Education." *Strong of Heart*, University of Notre Dame, 2011.

"Controlling Elements: Cold Spring Harbor, 1942–1967." National Library of Medicine.

"Detroit Lions at Minnesota Vikings—December 11th, 1971: Scoring." Pro Football Reference, Dec. 11, 1971.

"Harvard IBM Mark I—Crew." Harvard University: Collection of Historical Scientific Instruments.

"Higher Level Languages." Computer History Museum.

Isaacson, Walter. "Grace Hopper, Computing Pioneer." *Harvard Gazette*, Dec. 3, 2014.

Jones, Susie. "Fmr. MN Viking Helps Players Adjust to Life After Football." CBS Minnesota, Jan. 20, 2013.

Kaplan, Emily. "That '70s Strike." *Sports Illustrated*, July 31, 2014.

*McClintock, Barbara. "Barbara McClintock: Banquet Speech." Nobel Prize, Dec. 10, 1983. www.nobelprize.org/prizes/medicine/1983/mcclintock/speech.

"NFL MVPs: Complete List of Award Winners by Year." Fox Sports, May 30, 2024.

"The Nobel Prize in Physiology or Medicine 1983." Nobel Prize. www.nobelprize.org/prizes/medicine/1983/summary.

"Retired Players Association: Official Page." Facebook.

"60 Heroes: The Fight Continues." NFL Players Association.

Williams, Ellis. "Lunchbreak: Alan Page's Continuing Quest for Justice." Minnesota Vikings, Feb. 22, 2024.

OTHER

Hearing Before the Select Committee on Narcotics Abuse and Control. U.S. House of Representatives, 99th Cong., 1st Sess., July 16, 1985.

*Hopper, Grace Murray. "Technology: Future Directions." Conference '74 Data Processing Institute, June 1974.

McClintock, Barbara. "Letter from Barbara McClintock to Charles R. Burnham," Sept. 16, 1940. National Library of Medicine.

Mitchell, Carmen L. "The Contributions of Grace Murray Hopper to Computer Science and Computer Education." PhD diss., *University of North Texas*, 1994.

Chapter 3: A Constellation of Encodings
BOOKS
Burgess, Colin. *Faith 7: L. Gordon Cooper Jr. and the Final Mercury Mission*. Cham: Springer, 2016. Kindle.

Carpenter, M. Scott, L. Gordon Cooper Jr., John H. Glenn Jr., Virgil I. Grissom, Walter M. Schirra Jr., Alan B. Shepard Jr., and Donald K. Slayton. *We Seven*. New York: Simon & Schuster Paperbacks, 2010.

*Cooper, Gordon. *Leap of Faith: An Astronaut's Journey into the Unknown*. With Bruce Henderson. New York: Open Road Integrated Media, 2018. Kindle.

*Denard, Carolyn C., ed. *Toni Morrison: Conversations*. Jackson: University Press of Mississippi, 2008.

*Glenn, John. *John Glenn: A Memoir*. With Nick Taylor. New York: Bantam Books, 1999. Kindle.

Glenn, John. *John Glenn Jr. Debriefed*. International Space Business Council, 2015.

Kennedy, Robert F. *Thirteen Days: A Memoir of the Cuban Missile Crisis*. New York: W. W. Norton, 1999. Kindle.

Kramer, Barbara. *Toni Morrison: A Biography of a Nobel Prize–Winning Writer*. Berkeley Heights, N.J.: Enslow, 2013.

McGrane, Bill. *All Rise: The Remarkable Journey of Alan Page*. Chicago: Triumph Books, 2010. Kindle.

Mitchell, Don. *Liftoff: A Photobiography of John Glenn*. Washington, D.C.: National Geographic Society, 2006.

*Morrison, Toni. *The Source of Self-Regard: Selected Essays, Speeches, and Meditations*. New York: Alfred A. Knopf, 2019.

*Taylor-Guthrie, Danille, ed. *Conversations with Toni Morrison*. Jackson: University Press of Mississippi, 1994.

*Tuchman, Barbara W. *Bible and Sword: England and Palestine from the Bronze Age to Balfour*. New York: Random House Trade Paperbacks, 2014.

*Tuchman, Barbara W. *The Guns of August: The Outbreak of World War I*. New York: Random House Trade Paperbacks, 2014. Kindle.

Tuchman, Barbara W. *Notes from China*. New York: Random House, 2017.

*Tuchman, Barbara W. *Practicing History: Selected Essays*. New York: Random House Trade Paperbacks, 2014.

*Tuchman, Barbara W. *The Proud Tower: A Portrait of the World Before the War, 1890–1914*. New York: Random House Trade Paperbacks, 2014.

*Wolfe, Tom. *The Right Stuff*. New York: Picador, 1979. Kindle.

VIDEOS AND AUDIO
*Arnold, Elizabeth. "Senator John Glenn to Retire." *Morning Edition*, NPR, Feb. 20, 1997.
Greenfield-Sanders, Timothy, dir. *Toni Morrison: The Pieces I Am*. Magnolia Pictures, 2019.
Gross, Terry. "'I Regret Everything': Toni Morrison Looks Back on Her Personal Life." *Fresh Air*, NPR, Aug. 24, 2015.
*"May 16, 1963—President John F. Kennedy's Phonecall to Astronaut Major Gordon Cooper." HelmerReenberg. www.youtube.com/watch?v=isi7n8ET2Gc.
Rose, Charlie. "John Glenn." *Charlie Rose*, Dec. 23, 1999.
Rose, Charlie. "Toni Morrison." *Charlie Rose*, May 7, 1993.
*Rose, Charlie. "Toni Morrison." *Charlie Rose*, Jan. 19, 1998.
Rose, Charlie. "Toni Morrison." *Charlie Rose*, Nov. 10, 2008.

NEWSPAPERS AND MAGAZINES
*Als, Hilton. "Ghosts in the House: Profiles." *New Yorker*, Oct. 27, 2003.
Balz, Dan. "John Glenn." *Washington Post*, Jan. 15, 1984.
Baum, Geraldine. "A Hero Gets Back to Business." *Los Angeles Times*, June 2, 1998.
Bennett, Charles G. "City to Give Cooper Ticker-Tape Parade." *New York Times*, May 18, 1963, 1.
*Birmingham, Stephen. "Barbara Tuchman: The Lady Is an Historian." *Cosmopolitan*, Nov. 1971.
Bollen, Christopher. "Toni Morrison's Haunting Resonance." *Interview*, May 1, 2012.
Childs, Marquis. "Euphoria Among the Democrats." *Washington Post*, Oct. 8, 1974, A21.
*Darling, Lynn. "Echoes and Omens: Barbara Tuchman's Travels in the Past." *Washington Post*, Oct. 5, 1978, B1.
*Davis, Christina. "Interview with Toni Morrison." *Présence Africaine*, n.s., no. 145 (1988): 141–50.
De Witt, Karen. "Song of Solomon." *Washington Post*, Sept. 30, 1977.
DiPietro, Edward. "Friendship Lives for John Glenn." *Atlanta Constitution*, Feb. 20, 1972, 1E.
Dowling, Colette. "The Song of Toni Morrison." *New York Times*, May 20, 1979, SM110.
*Dreifus, Claudia. "Chloe Wofford Talks About Toni Morrison." *New York Times*, Sept. 11, 1994, A73.
"Former Astronaut Gordon Cooper Helps Send Disneyland Visitors out of This World." *People*, Aug. 29, 1977.
Frankel, Erwin. "Barbara Tuchman: History Meant to Be Read." *Jerusalem Post*, March 10, 1966.

*Fuller, Edmund. "A Conversation with Barbara W. Tuchman." *Wall Street Journal*, Sept. 28, 1978, 22.
"Gordon Cooper." *Time*, May 24, 1963.
"John Glenn: One Machine That Worked Without Flaw." *Newsweek*, March 5, 1962, 19.
"John Glenn Again Seeks Nomination." *Globe and Mail*, Dec. 11, 1973.
Kelly, Harry. "Sky Is Limit for Politician John Glenn." *Chicago Tribune*, July 23, 1975.
Kennedy, Eugene. "John Glenn's Presidential Countdown." *New York Times*, Oct. 11, 1981.
Kissel, Howard. "Barbara Tuchman: Holding the Mirror Up to Human Nature." *Women's Wear Daily*, Oct. 10, 1978, 30.
Kluger, Jeffrey. "John Glenn: Back to the Future." *Time*, Aug. 17, 1998.
*Lohman, Patricia. "Barbara Tuchman: The Disciplined Writer." *Hartford Courant*, July 29, 1979, 10H.
MacDonald, Marianne. "Interview: Toni Morrison." *Observer*, March 29, 1998.
*May, Ernest. "A Conversation with Barbara Tuchman." *Nieman Reports*, 1981.
McCullough, David. "Can John Glenn Be President?" *Boston Globe*, June 13, 1982, SMA4.
Miller, Zeke J. "A Life of Public Service." *Time*, 2016, 49–51.
*Newcott, William R. "John Glenn: Man with a Mission." *National Geographic*, June 1, 1999, 60.
*Nordell, Roderick. "Mrs. Tuchman and Her Best Seller." *Christian Science Monitor*, May 17, 1962, 7.
Parsons, Cynthia. "Barbara Tuchman Reads Before She Writes." *Christian Science Monitor*, Nov. 2, 1962.
Pollock, Ellen Joan, and Carlos Tejada. "Down to Earth: An Astronaut's Fame Draws Desperate Cities into Risky Investments." *Wall Street Journal*, Nov. 7, 1997.
*Robertson, Nan. "Barbara Tuchman: A Loner at the Top of Her Field." *New York Times*, Feb. 27, 1979, C10.
Rybak, R. T. "Alan Page: 'Purple People Eater' Now Pursues Compromise." *Minneapolis Star and Tribune*, Sept. 1, 1986, 1C.
Sawyer, Kathy. "John Glenn, Time Traveler; The First American to Orbit the Earth Is Making History Again, as the Oldest." *Washington Post*, Oct. 8, 1998, D01.
*Schappell, Elissa, and Claudia Brodsky Lacour. "Toni Morrison: The Art of Fiction No. 134." *Paris Review* (Fall 1993).
Shribman, David. "An Interview with John Glenn, Senator and Former Astronaut." *New York Times*, Dec. 27, 1983, B7.
Smith, Dinitia. "Toni Morrison's Mix of Tragedy, Domesticity, and Folklore." *New York Times*, Jan. 8, 1998, 1.

Stansky, Peter. "Variegated Tuchman." *New York Times*, Sept. 27, 1981, BR2.
*Sutton, Rebecca. "Toni Morrison: Write, Erase, Do It Over." *NEA Arts Magazine*, Feb. 2015.
Wald, Matthew L. "Gordon Cooper, Astronaut, Is Dead at 77." *New York Times*, Oct. 5, 2004.

WEBSITES AND ONLINE ARTICLES
"Barbara Tuchman: Historian and Author." Kansas State University.
Brockes, Emma. "Toni Morrison: 'I Want to Feel What I Feel. Even if It's Not Happiness.'" *Guardian*, April 13, 2012.
Diemer, Tom. "Metzenbaum, Howard Morton." In *Encyclopedia of Cleveland History*. Case Western Reserve University.
*Elkann, Alain. "Toni Morrison." Alain Elkann Interviews, Oct. 14, 2018.
"John H. Glenn: Former NASA Astronaut." National Aeronautics and Space Administration.
"Leroy Gordon Cooper Jr.: Former NASA Astronaut." National Aeronautics and Space Administration, Oct. 2004.
"Nobel Prize in Physiology or Medicine 1983: Press Release." Nobel Prize. www.nobelprize.org/prizes/medicine/1983/press-release.
"Senate Election Results and Data: 1974–1992." Ohio Secretary of State.
"Toni Morrison: Literary Icon: Children's Books." Cornell University Library.

OTHER
Bakerman, Jane. "The Seams Can't Show: An Interview with Toni Morrison." *Black American Literature Forum* 12, no. 2 (Summer 1978): 56–60.
*Frías, María, Wayne Pond, and Trudier Harris. "An Interview with Toni Morrison, and a Commentary About Her Work." *Atlantis* 16, no. 1/2 (Nov. 1994): 273–83.
*"Gold Star Mother Speech." Ohio State University Libraries, May 4, 1974.
Hindley, Meredith. "The Dramatist: Barbara Tuchman Saw History as a Grand Tragedy." *Humanities* 33, no. 5 (Sept./Oct. 2012).
*McKay, Nellie. "An Interview with Toni Morrison." *Contemporary Literature* 24, no. 4 (Winter 1983): 413–29.

Chapter 4: Flipping the Arrow of Money
BOOKS
Beyer, Kurt W. *Grace Hopper and the Invention of the Information Age*. Cambridge, Mass.: MIT Press, 2009. Kindle.
Page, Jimmy. *Jimmy Page: The Anthology*. Surrey, England: Genesis, 2020.
Power, Martin. *No Quarter: The Three Lives of Jimmy Page*. New York: Omnibus Press, 2016. Kindle.
*Rees, Paul. *Robert Plant: A Life*. New York: HarperCollins, 2013. Kindle.

Salewicz, Chris. *Jimmy Page: The Definitive Biography*. New York: Da Capo Press, 2019. Kindle.

Thompson, Dave. *Robert Plant: The Voice That Sailed the Zeppelin*. Milwaukee, Wis.: Backbeat Books, 2014. Kindle.

VIDEOS AND AUDIO

*Allison. "Episode #62: Carol Heiss Jenkins, Part 1." *Manleywoman SkateCast*, Dec. 31, 2012.

Beyer, Kurt W. "The Invention of the Information Age." Talks at Google, May 19, 2010.

"Jimmy Page & Robert Plant—the Truth Explodes (Yallah) Morocco 1994." Mark Zep. www.youtube.com/watch?v=EowrUGm4gU0.

*Montagne, Renee. "Interview: Musician Robert Plant Discusses His Work on the New CD 'Festival in the Desert.'" *Morning Edition*, NPR, Dec. 8, 2003.

"Robert Plant | Zirka Part 4 | Malian Journey to and from Festival in the Desert 2003." Robert Plant.

*"Robert Plant Interviewed by George Stroumboulopoulos." CBC Television, Sept. 20, 2010.

Rodley, Chris, dir. *Robert Plant: By Myself*. BBC, 2010.

Siegel, Robert, David Greene, and Melissa Block. "Robert Plant: Born in England, Made in America." *All Things Considered*, NPR, Sept. 20, 2010.

"Tenley Albright, M.D., Interview." Academy of Achievement, June 21, 1991.

NEWSPAPERS AND MAGAZINES

"Carol Heiss to Enroll at N.Y.U. This Fall." *New York Times*, Aug. 24, 1957, 9.

"Carol Heiss Wed to Hayes Jenkins: Skating Champions Are Married in St. Thomas Church." *New York Times*, May 1, 1960.

*Christian, Frederick. "Carol Heiss." *Washington Post*, Sept. 25, 1960, AW4.

Craigue, Paul V. "A World Champion of 17 First in the Hearts of the Newtons: Tenley Albright Gets Big Welcome Home." *Daily Boston Globe*, Feb. 24, 1953, 1.

de los Reyes, Gastón. "Manter School Endures." *Harvard Crimson*, Nov. 13, 1993.

De Witt, Karen. "Song of Solomon." *Washington Post*, Sept. 30, 1977.

*Dwyer, Michael. "Robert Plant on Life After Led Zeppelin (Don't Expect a Memoir Any Time Soon)." *Sydney Morning Herald*, Jan. 22, 2018.

*Edwards, Mark. "Hush the Talk of Reunions, Please." *Sunday Times*, Sept. 12, 2010, 26.

*Fricke, David. "Robert Plant: The Rolling Stone Interview." *Rolling Stone*, March 24, 1988.

*Fricke, David. "Robert Plant Channels 'Zep III' on Latest Solo Album." *Rolling Stone*, Aug. 5, 2010, 24.

Greene, Andy. "Robert Plant Slams Idea of Zeppelin Tour: 'I'm Not Part of a Jukebox.'" *Rolling Stone*, May 8, 2014.

Hanc, John. "Carol Heiss, New York's First Olympic Figure Skating Champion, Was . . . a Blue-Collar Star in a Sequin-Spangled Sport." *Newsday*, March 13, 2002, B06.

"Heiss Captures Gold Medal: Fans Stand, Cheer First U.S. Victory." *Washington Post*, Feb. 24, 1960, C1.

Hunter-Tilney, Ludovic. "Jimmy Page: Rock Legend." *Financial Times*, Oct. 31, 2014.

Jaffee, Irving. "Carol Heiss Figure Skating Victory Reward for Dedication." *Hartford Courant*, March 3, 1957, 5D1.

Kachka, Boris. "Who Is the Author of Toni Morrison?" *New York*, May 7, 2012.

*Lagemann, John Kord. "Who Says I'm Lucky?" *New York Herald Tribune*, March 15, 1959, F4.

*"Leads Olympic Figure Skating: Carol Heiss Can Win Title Today." *New York Herald Tribune*, Feb. 23, 1960, 31.

Martin, Gavin. "Stairlift to Heaven: Robert Plant Has Left the Sex and Drugs but Not the Rock 'n' Roll Behind." *Daily Mirror*, Nov. 14, 2003.

*McCormick, Neil. "Robert Plant Interview: 'Re-Form Led Zeppelin? You Can't Ever Really Go Back.'" *Telegraph*, Oct. 12, 2017.

McNair, James. "Robert Plant: Searching for Strange Sensations." *Independent*, Nov. 7, 2003.

"Merry-Go-Round Ride for Miss Carol Heiss." *Christian Science Monitor*, Jan. 9, 1960.

"Mother's Devotion Is Recalled as Carol Heiss Retains Title." *New York Times*, March 3, 1957, 187.

Richards, Chris. "Kennedy Center Honors Recipients Jimmy Page, Robert Plant, and John Paul Jones on Led Zeppelin's Fabled Chemistry and Unwritten Future." *Washington Post*, Nov. 30, 2012.

Rodrick, Stephen. "Robert Plant's Mystical Mountain Hop." *Rolling Stone*, Jan. 20, 2011.

*Scaggs, Austin. "Q&A: Robert Plant." *Rolling Stone*, May 19, 2005.

*Scaggs, Austin. "Whole Lotta Sand." *Rolling Stone*, March 6, 2003, 24.

Schappell, Elissa, and Claudia Brodsky Lacour. "Toni Morrison: The Art of Fiction No. 134." *Paris Review* (Fall 1993).

Shadwick, Keith. "Stairway to Heaven: Out of the Ashes of the Yardbirds Rose the Biggest, Loudest, Most Successful Rock Band in the World." *Independent*, Nov. 25, 2005.

*Shearer, Lloyd. "Carol Heiss: Hollywood's New Sonja Henie Has a Real Career Problem." *Boston Globe*, Feb. 5, 1961, A10.

*Simmons, Sylvie. "'This Is Very Present Tense': Robert Plant Has a New Band, an Acclaimed Album, and a Bright Future. But It's Not Enough to Banish the Ghost of Led Zeppelin." *Guardian*, Oct. 14, 2005, 3.

Sinclair, Ed. "Carol Heiss, at 15, Eyes Mid-Atlantic Skate Title." *New York Herald Tribune*, Jan. 28, 1955, 20.

"Skater Knows Where She's Going: College, Home Mean More Than Medals to Carol Heiss." *New York Times*, Feb. 28, 1959, 16.

"Space Triumph: Key Moments in the Historic Flight of Astronaut Gordon Cooper." *New York Times*, May 19, 1963, E1.

Strauss, Neil. "Getting the Led Out of Led Zeppelin." *New York Times*, Oct. 30, 1994.

*Thrills, Adrian. "My Screaming Led Zep Days Are Over." *Daily Mail*, Oct. 8, 2010, 64.

Welles, Margery Miller. "Olympic Heights for Carol Heiss?" *Christian Science Monitor*, Dec. 30, 1955, 17.

Williams, Richard. "Robert Plant: 'The First Led Zeppelin Practice . . . You Couldn't Walk Away'—Classic Interview." *Guardian*, Sept. 10, 2014.

WEBSITES AND ONLINE ARTICLES

"Alan C. Page: Justice." Minnesota State Law Library.

"Carol Heiss." Team USA. www.teamusa.com/hall-of-fame/hall-of-fame-members/carol-heiss.

"Discovery: Celebration Day." LedZeppelin.com.

"The Festival." Festival au Désert. www.festival-au-desert.org/index.cfm?m=0&s=2.

"Grammy Awards: Robert Plant." Recording Academy.

"Hall of Fame: Tenley Albright." United States Olympic & Paralympic Museum.

"Hollis L. Albright, MD '31, Symposium." Harvard Medical School.

"Mythbusters: Carol Heiss-Jenkins." Benjamin Rose Institute on Aging, Sept. 30, 2008.

"Pierre Brunet: Biography." International Olympic Committee. olympics.com/en/athletes/pierre-brunet.

"Tenley Albright, M.D." Academy of Achievement.

"Tenley E. Albright, MD." My Name Is Tenley.

OTHER

McClintock, Barbara. "Letter from Barbara McClintock to Charles R. Burnham," Sept. 16, 1940. National Library of Medicine.

"U.S. Figure Skating: Records & Results Through 2023–24 Season." U.S. Figure Skating.

Chapter 5: Focus the Fire
BOOKS
Cannell, Michael. *I. M. Pei: Mandarin of Modernism*. New York: Carol Southern Books, 1995.

McGrane, Bill. *All Rise: The Remarkable Journey of Alan Page.* Chicago: Triumph Books, 2010. Kindle.
*Mompoullan, Chantal. *Voice of America Interviews with Eight American Women of Achievement.* University of Michigan Libraries.
Rees, Paul. *Robert Plant: A Life.* New York: HarperCollins, 2013. Kindle.
*Stevens, Doris. *Jailed for Freedom.* New York: Liveright, 1920.
Vaillant, George E. *Adaptation to Life.* Cambridge, Mass.: Harvard University Press, 1977.
Walton, Mary. *A Woman's Crusade: Alice Paul and the Battle for the Ballot.* New York: St. Martin's Press, 2010. Kindle.
*Zahniser, J. D., and Amelia R. Fry. *Alice Paul: Claiming Power.* New York: Oxford University Press, 2014. Kindle.

VIDEOS AND AUDIO

"Alan Page." *A Football Life.* NFL Films, Oct. 16, 2015.
"[CoSI Lecture] Dr. Tenley Albright: From Olympic Figure Skating to Tackling National . . . (Part 1/2)." MIT Sidney-Pacific Committee on Scholarly Interactions, May 7, 2015.
*"[CoSI Lecture] Dr. Tenley Albright: From Olympic Figure Skating to Tackling National . . . (Part 2/2)." MIT Sidney-Pacific Committee on Scholarly Interactions, May 7, 2015.
"Heart of a Hall of Famer Powered by Extreme Networks ft. Alan Page (2014)." Pro Football Hall of Fame, Jan. 5, 2021.
*"My Name Is Tenley." Thom Dunn. youtu.be/YwZKv9skLHg?si=mXBEWc-jzOtmp4oVg.
*"Tenley Albright, M.D., Interview." Academy of Achievement, June 21, 1991.

NEWSPAPERS AND MAGAZINES

"Alice Paul Describes Her Life in a Cell: Complains Bitterly Because She Is Denied Fresh Air." *Los Angeles Times*, Nov. 19, 1917, 12.
"Alice Paul Returns Home: No Suffragettes to Greet Girl Released from English Jail." *New York Times*, Jan. 21, 1910.
*Bernstein, Richard. "I. M. Pei's Pyramid: A Provocative Plan for the Louvre." *New York Times*, Nov. 24, 1985.
Daley, Robert. "Tenley Albright in Long Workout." *New York Times*, Jan. 24, 1956, 34.
De Witt, Karen. "Song of Solomon." *Washington Post*, Sept. 30, 1977.
*Dreifus, Claudia. "Chloe Wofford Talks About Toni Morrison." *New York Times*, Sept. 11, 1994, A73.
English, Bella. "For Dr. Albright, Being Gold-Medal Winner Simply a Footnote." *Boston Globe*, Sept. 21, 2015.
Finan, Eileen, and Steve Dougherty. "Meet the First U.S. Woman to Win

Olympic Gold in Figure Skating, Who Is Now 82 and a Doctor!" *People*, Jan. 31, 2018.

Goldberger, Paul. "I. M. Pei, Master Architect Whose Buildings Dazzled the World, Dies at 102." *New York Times*, May 16, 2019.

*Greenburg, Steve. "I'm a Runner: Alan Page." *Runner's World*, Nov. 2007, 136.

*Helfgott, Hali. "Tenley Albright, Figure Skater January 30, 1956." *Sports Illustrated*, Nov. 5, 2001.

*Hunt, Dennis. "Jimmy Page, Unlikely Guitar Hero." *Los Angeles Times*, July 3, 1988.

Kleiman, Dena. "Alice Paul, a Leader for Suffrage and Women's Rights, Dies at 92." *New York Times*, July 10, 1977.

*Klemesrud, Judy. "Skating and Medicine: Is There a Link?" *New York Times*, Nov. 30, 1971.

Luther, Claudia. "I. M. Pei, 1917–2019: Famed Architect's Designs on Display Around the Globe." *Los Angeles Times*, May 17, 2019.

*MacDonald, Marianne. "Interview: Toni Morrison." *Observer*, March 29, 1998.

"Miss Alice Paul on Hunger Strike: Suffragist Leader Adopts This Means of Protesting Against Washington Prison Fare." *New York Times*, Nov. 7, 1917.

"Miss Paul Describes Feeding by Force." *New York Times*, Dec. 10, 1909.

Murray, William D. "Judging from His Past Page Will Achieve Goal." *Chicago Tribune*, Sept. 20, 1987.

*"1956 Olympic Skating Champion: Dr. Tenley Albright Thinks Peggy Fleming 'Wonderful.'" *Washington Post*, Feb. 10, 1968, D3.

Pollitzer, Anita. "Woman's Party Launches Campaign Through South." *Jackson (Miss.) Daily News*, Nov. 23, 1921, 6.

*Rosen, Karen. "Meet Tenley Albright and Carol Heiss, the Figure Skaters Who Started Team USA's History of Olympic Gold 60 Years Ago." United States Olympic Committee, Feb. 2, 2016.

Smith, William D. "Pioneer in Computers: Navy Officer Likes to Rock Boat." *New York Times*, Sept. 5, 1971, F5.

"Vikings' Alan Page Turns Cook at Home, Forgets Grid Wars." *Chicago Defender*, Nov. 13, 1971, 35.

*Von Eckardt, Wolf. "Celebrated Non-Celebrity: The Architect Who Understands Social and Visual Dynamics." *Washington Post*, May 14, 1978, F2.

"Women Face a Fight: Opposition to the Alice Paul Constitutional Amendment." *St. Joesph News-Press*, Dec. 23, 1921, 20.

WEBSITES AND ONLINE ARTICLES

"Changing Strategies of NAWSA and NWP: The Infamous Kaiser Wilson Banner." Library of Congress.

*"Dr. Tenley E. Albright: Biography." *Changing the Face of Medicine*, U.S. National Library of Medicine, June 3, 2015.

"History of the DSO." Dallas Symphony.
"The History of the Equal Rights Amendment (ERA)." Alice Paul Center for Gender Justice.
Michals, Debra. "Alice Paul (1885–1977)." National Women's History Museum, 2015.
"New Models: Overview." MIT Collaborative Initiatives.
"The Packer Collegiate Institute: A Story of Education in Brooklyn: Lucy Burns Class of 1899." Brooklyn Public Library.
"Timeline: A Chronology of Key Events in the History of the National American Woman Suffrage Association (NAWSA)." Library of Congress.

OTHER
*Bland, Sidney R. "'Never Quite as Committed as We'd Like': The Suffrage Militancy of Lucy Burns." *Journal of Long Island History* 17, no. 2 (July 1981).
"Detailed Chronology: National Woman's Party History." American Memory, Library of Congress.
"Tenley E. Albright, M.D." MIT Collaborative Initiatives, Oct. 2014.

Chapter 6: Cliffs
VIDEOS AND AUDIO
Collins, Cardiss. "Balancing a Child and Politics." National Visionary Leadership Project, April 27, 2010.
Collins, Cardiss. "Entering Congress After My Husband's Death." National Visionary Leadership Project, Oct. 18, 2013.
Collins, Cardiss. "Political Changes in Chicago/Political Changes for My Husband." National Visionary Leadership Project, April 27, 2010.

NEWSPAPERS AND MAGAZINES
"Alabama Voters to Go to Polls Tuesday for Three Runoffs." *Los Angeles Times*, Sept. 25, 1978, B6.
*Allen, Maryon. "Free at Last!" *Washington Post*, Jan. 21, 1979.
Allen, Maryon Pittman. "Maryon Allen's Washington." *Washington Post*, 1979–81.
Cherokee, Charlie. "Charlie Cherokee Says." *Chicago Defender*, Nov. 22, 1973, 16.
*Christy, Marian. "She Battled Wallace." *Boston Globe*, Feb. 25, 1979, C1.
*Crimmins, Jerry. "'I Answer Only to Jesus,' Says Cardiss Collins." *Chicago Tribune*, April 19, 1973, 12.
Edwards, Audrey. "Cardiss Collins Do Our Votes Count?" *Essence*, Nov. 1980, 84.
"In Brief: Sen. Allen Loses." *Boston Globe*, Sept. 27, 1978, 2.
"In 7th District House Race: Mrs. Collins Wins Seat." *Chicago Tribune*, June 6, 1973, 15.

Ingraham, Christopher. "Interactive: When Women Inherit Their Husbands' Congressional Seats." *Washington Post*, March 18, 2014.
Jarrett, Vernon. "Cardiss Collins Speaks Sharply." *Chicago Tribune*, Sept. 26, 1979, C4.
King, Seth. "Black Woman Backed by Daley Sweeps Primary in House Race." *New York Times*, April 19, 1973, 26.
Lewis, Pat. "Sen. Maryon Allen: 'She Has a Will of Iron,' Her Son Sandy Says." *Atlanta Constitution*, June 15, 1978, 6A.
Malcolm, Andrew H. "Illinois Elects Its First Black Woman to Congress, on 92% of Vote." *New York Times*, June 7, 1973, 11.
*McClory, Robert. "Rep. Collins' Widow Reveals Aims." *Chicago Daily Defender*, Jan. 17, 1973, 1.
"Mitchell Heads Black Caucus." *Oakland Post*, Dec. 19, 1976, 2.
"Mrs. Allen Decides to Return to Alabama." *Montgomery Advertiser*, July 9, 1981, 9.
*Poinsett, Alex. "The New Cardiss Collins." *Ebony*, Dec. 1979.
*Quinn, Sally. "Maryon Allen—the Southerngirl in the Senate." *Washington Post*, July 30, 1978.
Quinn, Sally. "Nobody Can Run Over This 'Southerngirl.'" *Boston Globe*, Aug. 16, 1978, 37.
Reynolds, Barbara. "Collins to Head Black Caucus." *Chicago Tribune*, Jan. 25, 1979, 4.
*Reynolds, Barbara. "Column 1: Rep. Collins Speaking Out Louder Now but She May Collide with Chicago Machine." *Chicago Tribune*, Feb. 8, 1979, 1.
Roberson, Peggy. "Mrs. Allen Blames Many for Senate Loss." *Alabama Journal*, Jan. 19, 1979, 1.
*Trescott, Jacqueline. "The Coming Out of Cardiss Collins." *Washington Post*, Sept. 21, 1979.
Walker, Jennifer A. "Wed to Tradition." *Montgomery Advertiser*, April 26, 1996.
Williams, Marjorie. "The 'Widow's Mandate.'" *Washington Post*, Oct. 27, 2000, A35.

WEBSITES AND ONLINE ARTICLES
"Allen, Maryon Pittman." *Biographical Directory of the United States Congress*.
"Collins, Cardiss." History, Art & Archives: United States House of Representatives.
"Collins, George Washington." *Biographical Directory of the United States Congress*.
Ellaby, Liz. "All Dolled Up: Former Alabama Senator Maryon Allen Restores WPA Handicrafts." Birmingham History Center, Nov. 8, 2011.

OTHER
Aircraft Accident Report: File No. 1-0048. National Transportation Safety Board, Aug. 29, 1973.

Guthrie, Benjamin J. *Statistics of the Congressional Election of November 4, 1974.* Washington, D.C.: U.S. Government Printing Office, 1975.

Chapter 7: Fog
BOOKS
*Denard, Carolyn C., ed. *Toni Morrison: Conversations.* Jackson: University Press of Mississippi, 2008.
*Fox, Michael J. *Lucky Man: A Memoir.* Hyperion e-books, 2010. Kindle.
*Fox, Michael J. *No Time Like the Future: An Optimist Considers Mortality.* New York: Flatiron Books, 2020. Kindle.
Glenn, John. *John Glenn: A Memoir.* With Nick Taylor. New York: Bantam Books, 1999. Kindle.
Kramer, Barbara. *Toni Morrison: A Biography of a Nobel Prize–Winning Writer.* Berkeley Heights, N.J.: Enslow, 2013.
Thompson, Dave. *Robert Plant: The Voice That Sailed the Zeppelin.* Milwaukee, Wis.: Backbeat Books, 2014. Kindle.
Walton, Mary. *A Woman's Crusade: Alice Paul and the Battle for the Ballot.* New York: St. Martin's Press, 2010. Kindle.
*White, Maurice. *My Life with Earth, Wind & Fire.* With Herb Powell. New York: Amistad, 2016. Kindle.
Zahniser, J. D., and Amelia R. Fry. *Alice Paul: Claiming Power.* New York: Oxford University Press, 2014. Kindle.

VIDEOS AND AUDIO
"Earth, Wind & Fire Performing One of Their Illusions During a 1979 Concert in Japan." FunkSoulBluesJazzRockPop Live Music. www.youtube.com/watch?v=oxwO8YgU2GQ.
"Earth, Wind & Fire's Acceptance Speech—Rock & Roll Hall of Fame Induction Ceremony (2000)." Maurice White, March 6, 2000.
*"Michael J Fox/Barbara Walters Interview." That's Entertainment. www.youtube.com/watch?v=NLunLKp4Mg0.

NEWSPAPERS AND MAGAZINES
"Actor Michael J. Fox Has Parkinson's Disease." *Washington Post,* Nov. 26, 1998, C6.
Als, Hilton. "Ghosts in the House: Profiles." *New Yorker,* Oct. 27, 2003.
Epstein, Dan. "Earth, Wind, and Fire Founder Stricken with Parkinson's Disease." *Rolling Stone,* Feb. 29, 2000.
Gundersen, Edna. "Elements of R&B Style Set the Tempo for a Rockin' Night." *USA Today,* March 8, 2000.
*Hiatt, Brian. "Michael J. Fox: The Toughest Man on TV." *Rolling Stone,* Sept. 26, 2013, 1–15.

*Houpt, Simon. "Globe Exclusive: Interview Michael J. Fox Happy Man." *Globe and Mail*, April 4, 2009, R1.

Paoletta, Michael. "White Juiced About Concord." *Billboard*, Aug. 2005.

Schneider, Jason. "Robert Plant: The Mighty Rearranger." *Exclaim!*, Sept. 25, 2010.

*Schwartz, Tony. "Power of Positive Singing." *Newsweek*, March 6, 1978, 107.

*Smith, Kyle, and Julie Jordan. "Michael J. Fox: The Fight of His Life." *People*, Dec. 7, 1998.

*Spelling, Ian. "Out of the Woods." New York Times News Service, July 6, 1996.

"Tenley Albright Quits as Skater to Prepare for Medical School." *New York Times*, Jan. 20, 1957.

*Wolf, Jeanne, and Shep Morgan. "The Gig That Sent Michael J. Fox Back to Television." Entertainment News Service, July 19, 1996, 43.

WEBSITES AND ONLINE ARTICLES

"Billboard Hot 100: Earth, Wind & Fire." *Billboard*.

"Gold & Platinum: Earth, Wind & Fire." Recording Industry Association of America.

"Grammy Awards: Earth, Wind & Fire." Recording Academy.

"Historical Overview of the National Womans Party." Library of Congress.

*"History: Biography." Earth, Wind & Fire. www.earthwindandfire.com/history/biography.

"History: Members." Earth, Wind & Fire. www.earthwindandfire.com/history/members.

"Home." Michael J. Fox Foundation.

"Michael's Story." Michael J. Fox Foundation.

Michals, Debra. "Alice Paul (1885–1977)." National Women's History Museum, 2015.

"National Woman's Party." Alice Paul Institute for Gender Justice.

"Tenley E. Albright MD." My Name Is Tenley.

"Who Was Alice Paul?" Alice Paul Center for Gender Justice.

Chapter 8: Simplex Stepping

BOOKS

Bradlee, Ben. *A Good Life: Newspapering and Other Adventures*. New York: Touchstone, 1996. Kindle.

Collins, Jim, and Jerry I. Porras. *Built to Last: Successful Habits of Visionary Companies*. New York: Harper Business, 2002.

*Graham, Katharine. *Personal History: A Memoir*. New York: Alfred A. Knopf, 1997. Kindle.

McGrane, Bill. *All Rise: The Remarkable Journey of Alan Page*. Chicago: Triumph Books, 2010. Kindle.

Rees, Paul. *Robert Plant: A Life*. New York: HarperCollins, 2013. Kindle.
Zahniser, J. D., and Amelia R. Fry. *Alice Paul: Claiming Power*. New York: Oxford University Press, 2014. Kindle.

VIDEOS AND AUDIO
"Alan Page." *A Football Life*. NFL Films, Oct. 16, 2015.
"1981 American Express Commercial with Georgia Frontiere." GoodOld TVCommercials. www.youtube.com/watch?v=5eSvukTGpto.
*Pachter, Marc. "Living Self-Portrait: Katharine Graham." National Portrait Gallery, Jan. 12, 2018.
Rose, Charlie. "Katharine Graham." *Charlie Rose*, Feb. 5, 1997.

NEWSPAPERS AND MAGAZINES
*Forbes, J. B. "It Wasn't a Dream: Frontiere Rivaled Jones in Stunning Finish." *St. Louis Post-Dispatch*, Feb. 1, 2000, 41.
Goldstein, Richard. "Georgia Frontiere, 80, First Female N.F.L. Owner, Is Dead." *New York Times*, Jan. 19, 2008.
*Green, Ted. "Georgia Ends Her Silence." *Los Angeles Times*, April 29, 1981.
*Green, Ted. "Georgia Meets the Press and Says She'll Hang Tough." *Los Angeles Times*, Aug. 24, 1979, 43.
Green, Ted. "It's No Song and Dance Routine." *Los Angeles Times*, May 17, 1981, 63.
Green, Ted. "Now There Are 7 Answers to 'Who's Advising Georgia?'" *Los Angeles Times*, Aug. 13, 1981.
Green, Ted. "Ram Family Comes Apart: Steve Rosenbloom Is Out." *Los Angeles Times*, Aug. 17, 1979, 29.
*Green, Ted. "Rams' New Owner Was Groomed by an Expert." *Los Angeles Times*, July 29, 1979, 55.
Greenberg, Alan, and Mike Goodman. "Georgia Rosenbloom: Widow Who's in Command of the Rams." *Los Angeles Times*, Oct. 3, 1979.
*Hall, John. "So Help Me." *Los Angeles Times*, Aug. 15, 1979, 56.
*"The Kay We Loved." *Newsweek*, March 13, 2010.
McGrory, Mary. "Evolution of a Newspaperwoman." Graham Holdings Company, July 19, 2001.
*Oates, Bob. "Rosenbloom Legacy Lives in New Ram Leadership." *Los Angeles Times*, May 8, 1979, 27.
O'Neil, Tim. "The New Frontiere." *St. Louis Post-Dispatch*, Oct. 22, 1995.
Peltz, Jim. "Georgia Frontiere, Who Moved Rams to St. Louis, Dies." *Los Angeles Times*, Jan. 19, 2008.
*Simers, T. J. "Moving Is an Option, but Rams Not for Sale." *Los Angeles Times*, Dec. 24, 1993, 33.
Simers, T. J. "No Dumb Blond Jokes About Georgia Here." *Los Angeles Times*, Jan. 20, 2008.

*Simers, T. J. "Rams Owner May Sell Part of Team." *Los Angeles Times*, May 9, 1994, 99.

*Zimmerman, Paul. "L.A. Goes Marching Behind Georgia." *Sports Illustrated*, Aug. 13, 1979.

WEBSITES AND ONLINE ARTICLES

Buffett, Warren E. "Kay Graham's Management Career." Graham Holdings Company.

"Past Stadiums: Anaheim Stadium." Stadiums of Pro Football.

Small, Evelyn. "Katharine Graham at 100: Inside the Making of One of the Greatest Washington Memoirs Ever." *Washington Post*, June 15, 2017.

Smith, J. Y., and Noel Epstein. "Katharine Graham Dies at 84." Graham Holdings Company.

*Woodward, Bob. "Hands Off, Mind On." Graham Holdings Company, July 23, 2001.

Chapter 9: The Roulette Wheel of Life

BOOKS

Alter, Jonathan. *His Very Best: Jimmy Carter, a Life*. New York: Simon & Schuster, 2020. Kindle.

*Cannon, James. *Gerald R. Ford: An Honorable Life*. Ann Arbor: University of Michigan Press, 2013. Kindle.

*Carter, Jimmy. *Faith: A Journey for All*. New York: Simon & Schuster, 2018. Kindle.

*Carter, Jimmy. *A Full Life: Reflections at Ninety*. New York: Simon & Schuster, 2015. Kindle.

*Carter, Jimmy. *White House Diary*. New York: Farrar, Straus and Giroux, 2010.

Carter, Jimmy. *Why Not the Best?* Fayetteville: University of Arkansas Press, 1996.

*Carter, Jimmy, and Rosalynn Carter. *Everything to Gain: Making the Most of the Rest of Your Life*. New York: Random House, 1987.

Collins, Jim, and Morten T. Hansen. *Great by Choice: Uncertainty, Chaos, and Luck—Why Some Thrive Despite Them All*. New York: Harper Business, 2011.

*DeFrank, Thomas M. *Write It When I'm Gone: Remarkable Off-the-Record Conversations with Gerald R. Ford*. New York: G. P. Putnam's Sons, 2007. Kindle.

*Ford, Gerald R. *A Time to Heal*. New York: Harper & Row, 1979.

Fox, Michael J. *Lucky Man: A Memoir*. Hyperion e-books, 2010. Kindle.

Glenn, John. *John Glenn: A Memoir*. With Nick Taylor. New York: Bantam Books, 1999. Kindle.

Graham, Katharine. *Personal History: A Memoir*. New York: Alfred A. Knopf, 1997. Kindle.

*Hersey, John. *The President: A Minute-by-Minute Account of a Week in the Life of Gerald Ford*. New York: Vintage Books, 1975. Kindle.

*Kaufman, Scott. *Ambition, Pragmatism, and Party: A Political Biography of Gerald R. Ford*. Lawrence: University Press of Kansas, 2017. Kindle.

McGrane, Bill. *All Rise: The Remarkable Journey of Alan Page*. Chicago: Triumph Books, 2010. Kindle.

Mompoullan, Chantal. *Voice of America Interviews with Eight American Women of Achievement*. University of Michigan Libraries.

*Page, Jimmy. *Jimmy Page: The Anthology*. Surrey, England: Genesis, 2020.

Power, Martin. *No Quarter: The Three Lives of Jimmy Page*. New York: Omnibus Press, 2016. Kindle.

*Rumsfeld, Donald. *When the Center Held: Gerald Ford and the Rescue of the American Presidency*. New York: Free Press, 2018. Kindle.

Salewicz, Chris. *Jimmy Page: The Definitive Biography*. New York: Da Capo Press, 2019. Kindle.

Thompson, Hunter S. *Fear and Loathing in Las Vegas: A Savage Journey to the Heart of the American Dream*. New York: Vintage Books, 1998.

*Wenner, Jann S. *Fear and Loathing at "Rolling Stone": The Essential Writing of Hunter S. Thompson*. New York: Simon & Schuster Paperbacks, 2011. Kindle.

*White, Maurice. *My Life with Earth, Wind & Fire*. With Herb Powell. New York: Amistad, 2016. Kindle.

VIDEOS AND AUDIO

Collins, Cardiss. "Entering Congress After My Husband's Death." National Visionary Leadership Project, Oct. 18, 2013.

"From the Archives: Jimmy Carter Inaugural Address: Jan. 20 1977." CBS News.

Kopple, Barbara, dir. *Desert One*. History Films, 2019.

*Rose, Charlie. "Jimmy Carter." *Charlie Rose*, Dec. 4, 2001.

Rose, Charlie. "Jimmy Carter." *Charlie Rose*, March 25, 2014.

NEWSPAPERS AND MAGAZINES

Barrell, Tony. "Hits and Myths." *Sunday Times*, Aug. 22, 2010, 22.

Ford, Gerald, and Jimmy Carter. "A Time to Heal Our Nation." *New York Times*, Dec. 21, 1998, A29.

Fricke, David. "The Rolling Stone Interview: Jimmy Page." *Rolling Stone*, Dec. 6, 2012.

Roselle, Laura. "Consultation Produces Imaginative Ideas for Arms Control." *Carter Center News* (Fall 1985): 1–3.

Safire, William. "Et Tu, Gerry?" *New York Times*, April 11, 1974, 35.

"We're Not Worthy! The Exclusive Interview with Jimmy Page." *Guitar World*, May 1993.

WEBSITES AND ONLINE ARTICLES
*"Barbara McClintock: Biographical." Nobel Prize, 1983. www.nobelprize.org/prizes/medicine/1983/mcclintock/biographical.
"The Best and the Brightest by David Halberstam." Penguin Random House.
*Carter, Jimmy. "Former U.S. President Jimmy Carter's Remarks at the Funeral Service for President Gerald R. Ford." Carter Center, Jan. 2, 2007.
Clement, Brooke. "Ford in Focus: Squeaky." National Archives, Sept. 5, 2023.
"Health Programs." Carter Center. www.cartercenter.org/health/index.html.
Isaacson, Walter. "Grace Hopper, Computing Pioneer." *Harvard Gazette*, Dec. 3, 2014.
"Jordan: Waging Peace." Carter Center. www.cartercenter.org/countries/jordan.html.
*Klosterman, Chuck. "Jimmy Page and the Grouses of the Holy." *GQ*, Dec. 1, 2014.

OTHER
Aircraft Accident Report: File No. 1-0048. National Transportation Safety Board, Aug. 29, 1973.
Carter, Jimmy. "Common Sense on Competitiveness: Conference Report Series." Carter Center, April 1988.

Chapter 10: Extend Out/Circle Back
BOOKS
Carlson, Erin. *Queen Meryl: The Iconic Roles, Heroic Deeds, and Legendary Life of Meryl Streep*. New York: Hachette Books, 2019. Kindle.
Graham, Katharine. *Personal History: A Memoir*. New York: Alfred A. Knopf, 1997. Kindle.
Michener, James A. *The World Is My Home: A Memoir*. New York: Dial Press, 2015. Kindle.
Rees, Paul. *Robert Plant: A Life*. New York: HarperCollins, 2013. Kindle.
Schulman, Michael. *Her Again: Becoming Meryl Streep*. New York: HarperCollins, 2016. Kindle.
*Winger, Debra. *Undiscovered*. New York: Simon & Schuster, 2008. Kindle.

VIDEOS AND AUDIO
*Arquette, Rosanna, dir. *Searching for Debra Winger*. Lionsgate Entertainment, 2002.
Babenco, Hector, dir. *Ironweed*. TriStar Pictures, 1988.
*"Debra Winger Is Obsessed with Catholic Saints." *Late Show with Stephen Colbert*, May 5, 2017.

"An Evening of Conversation with Meryl Streep & Jane Pauley (2010)." Meryl Streep Archives.
*"Indiana University Meryl Streep 2010." simplystreep. www.youtube.com/watch?v=oYliSTRcbmc.
*"Meryl Streep, Barnard Commencement Speaker 2010, Columbia University." Columbia University, May 18, 2010.
*Rodley, Chris, dir. *Robert Plant: By Myself.* BBC, 2010.
Rose, Charlie. "John Glenn." *Charlie Rose*, Dec. 23, 1999.
Rose, Charlie. "'Raising Sand.'" *Charlie Rose*, Nov. 14, 2007.

NEWSPAPERS AND MAGAZINES

*Bhattacharji, Alex. "Meryl Streep: A League of Her Own." *Wall Street Journal*, July 28, 2016.
*Burns, Ken. "Meryl Streep." *USA Weekend*, Nov. 29, 2002, 7.
"Debra Winger." *People*, Dec. 26, 1983.
"Debra Winger: High Ideals of a Hell-Raiser." *Observer*, March 6, 1994, 23.
*Dicker, Ron. "Debra Winger: Some Things Unexplainable." *Hartford Courant*, March 29, 2002, D3.
*Dreifus, Claudia. "Meryl Streep: Why I've Taken a Year Off for Motherhood." *Ladies' Home Journal*, April 1984, 48.
Farber, Stephen. "Where There's Smoke, There's a Fiery Actress Named Debra Winger." *New York Times*, July 6, 1986.
*Gaber, C. L. "When Debra Winger Isn't on Set, She's at Home on Her Farm." *Las Vegas Review-Journal*, May 20, 2017.
*Green, Jesse. "What, Meryl Worry?" *New York Times*, July 25, 2004.
*Groen, Rick. "Catching Debra on the Wing at the Festival." *Globe and Mail*, Sept. 13, 1993.
Gussow, Mel. "The Rising Star of Meryl Streep." *New York Times*, Feb. 4, 1979.
*Harris, Mark. "Debra Winger Drops Back In." *New York Times Magazine*, Nov. 5, 2010.
*Hiscock, John. "Debra Winger: A Star Is Re-Born." *Telegraph*, Dec. 19, 2018.
*Hoffman, Jan. "Debra Winger, Caught on a Winter Afternoon." *New York Times*, Jan. 9, 1994, H11.
*Italie, Hillel. "Debra Winger Sums Up Her Life: 'No Regrets.'" *Los Angeles Times*, Dec. 28, 1990, 10.
*Johnstone, Iain. "Funny Side of Meryl Streep." *Times Media Limited*, Nov. 29, 1992.
Kennedy, Dana. "Back from a Long Break, but on Her Own Terms." *New York Times*, Feb. 17, 2002.
Kennedy, Dana. "Winger Returns to Work on Her Own Terms." *News & Observer*, May 17, 2002, 7E.
Lester, Peter. "Two Sexy 'Urban Cowgirls'—One Called Debra Winger—Give Travolta a Run for His Movie." *People*, Aug. 18, 1980.

*May, Ernest. "A Conversation with Barbara Tuchman." *Nieman Reports*, 1981.
Millea, Holly. "Does Debra Winger Still Have Legs?" *New York*, Feb. 25, 2002.
*Mottram, James. "Streep Life." *Belfast Telegraph*, Jan. 31, 2009, 12.
*Oldenburg, Ann. "An Evening with Meryl Streep." *USA Today*, Feb. 19, 2002, 11.
Olsen, Mark. "Midlife Axis: Embracing the Mystique of Debra Winger." *Los Angeles Times*, May 5, 2017, E1.
O'Neil, Tim. "The New Frontiere." *St. Louis Post-Dispatch*, Oct. 22, 1995.
*Parker, Jerry. "Debra Winger: The Wing-a-Ding Wow." *Cosmopolitan*, June 1983.
Pearce, Garth. "Why I Quit Hollywood." *Guardian*, Aug. 1, 2002.
*Pearlman, Cindy. "Meryl Streep: Actress Sheds Cerebral Image for Physical Role." *Record*, Sept. 29, 1994, D3.
Peltz, Jim. "Georgia Frontiere, Who Moved Rams to St. Louis, Dies." *Los Angeles Times*, Jan. 19, 2008.
*Persall, Steve. "Meryl Streep: Mother of Invention." *St. Petersburg Times*, Sept. 8, 1998, 1D.
*Riley, Jenelle. "Without Limits: Debra Winger Brings Her Frank, Refreshing Voice to the Big Screen." *Back Stage East*, Oct. 2, 2008, 14.
*Rosenfield, Paul. "The Movie Star Series: Hollywood and the Exercise of Power." *Los Angeles Times*, Aug. 28, 1988, 4.
*Simmons, Sylvie. "'This Is Very Present Tense': Robert Plant Has a New Band, an Acclaimed Album, and a Bright Future. But It's Not Enough to Banish the Ghost of Led Zeppelin." *Guardian*, Oct. 14, 2005, 3.
Siskel, Gene. "Debra Winger: Vulnerable, Sexy, Tough—and a Fine Actress." *Chicago Tribune*, Nov. 27, 1983, K16.
*Skow, John. "What Makes Meryl Magic: Actress Streep Brings Passion and Skill to Her Richest Role Yet." *Time*, Sept. 7, 1981, 41.
Snow, Shauna. "Splittsville." *Los Angeles Times*, Dec. 19, 1989.
Solomon-Schwartz, Benjamin P. "Winger Trades Silver Screen for Section." *Harvard Crimson*, Sept. 28, 1999.
"START: Fast Chat Debra Winger." *Newsday*, Feb. 24, 2002, D03.
*Strauss, Bob. "Terms of Endurance." *Daily Mail*, March 3, 2002, U4.
*"Talking with Meryl Streep." *Redbook*, Sept. 1989.
Thomson, David. "Debra Winger: Earthy & Real on Film." *Philadelphia Daily News*, Nov. 29, 1983, 39.
Vida, Vendela. "An Interview with Debra Winger." *Believer*, March 1, 2011.
Wallenberg, Christopher. "Debra Winger Has No Regrets for the Road She's Taken." *Boston Globe*, May 4, 2017.
Waxman, Sharon. "Mother Knows Best." *Washington Post*, Sept. 19, 1998, B01.
Weinraub, Bernard. "Her Peculiar Career: Meryl Streep." *New York Times*, Sept. 18, 1994.
*Willens, Michele. "Still on Her Terms." *Los Angeles Times*, March 3, 2002, F3.
Woods, Vicki. "Meryl Streep: Force of Nature." *Vogue*, Dec. 12, 2011.

WEBSITES AND ONLINE ARTICLES
"Debra Winger." IMDb.
"Full Length Plays: The Idiots Karamazov." Christopher Durang.
"Grammy Awards: Robert Plant." Recording Academy.
"Meryl Streep." IMDb.
"Most Oscar-Nominated Actors." IMDb.
"Search by Nominee: 'Debra Winger.'" Academy of Motion Picture Arts and Sciences. awardsdatabase.oscars.org.
"Search by Nominee: 'Meryl Streep.'" Academy of Motion Picture Arts and Sciences. awardsdatabase.oscars.org.

Chapter 11: Choosing Responsibilities
BOOKS
Aitken, Jonathan. *Charles W. Colson: A Life Redeemed.* Colorado Springs: Waterbrook Press, 2005. Kindle.
*Colson, Charles W. *Born Again.* Grand Rapids: Chosen Books, 1976. Kindle.
*Colson, Charles W. *The Good Life.* Carol Stream, Ill.: Tyndale House Publishers, 2005. Kindle.
*Colson, Charles W. *Life Sentence.* Old Tappan, N.J.: Fleming H. Revell, 1979.
Colson, Charles W. *My Final Word.* With Anne Morse. Grand Rapids: Zondervan, 2015. Kindle.
Ehrlichman, John. *The China Card.* New York: Simon & Schuster, 1986.
Ehrlichman, John. *The Company.* New York: Simon & Schuster, 1976.
Ehrlichman, John. *The Whole Truth.* New York: Simon & Schuster, 1979.
*Ehrlichman, John. *Witness to Power: The Nixon Years.* New York: Simon & Schuster, 1982.
*Taylor-Guthrie, Danille, ed. *Conversations with Toni Morrison.* Jackson: University Press of Mississippi, 1994.

VIDEOS AND AUDIO
*Block, Melissa, and Michele Norris. "Jeb Stuart Magruder, Charles Colson, and William Ruckelshaus Discuss the Revelation of Deep Throat's Identity." *All Things Considered*, NPR, June 1, 2005.
Edwards, Bob. "Interview: Professor Stanley Kutler from the University of Wisconsin Talks About John Ehrlichman, Who Died Sunday." *Morning Edition*, NPR, Feb. 16, 1999.
*Guggenheim, Davis, dir. *Still: A Michael J. Fox Movie.* Apple Original Films, 2023.
Hagerty, Barbara Bradley. "Watergate Figure, Evangelist Chuck Colson Dies at 80." *All Things Considered*, NPR, April 21, 2012.

*"SYND 22 6 74 COLSON STATEMENT AFTER BEING SENTENCED FOR OBSTRUCTION OF JUSTICE." AP Archive. www.youtube.com /watch?v=FDeHu-7pr98&ab_channel=APArchive.

Wertheimer, Linda. "Profile: John Ehrlichman, President Nixon's Domestic Policy Adviser and Figure in the Watergate Scandal, Dead at the Age of 73." *All Things Considered*, NPR, Feb. 15, 1999.

NEWSPAPERS AND MAGAZINES

*Albright, Tenley. "Family: Growing Up with a Doctor in the House Makes a Lasting Impression." *Harvard Medicine* (Autumn 2013).

Bennett, Tom. "John Ehrlichman: Watergate Conspirator." *Atlanta Journal-Constitution*, Feb. 16, 1999, A4.

Berck, Martin. "Colson's Role: Dirty Tricks?" *Newsday*, May 9, 1973, 11.

*Beyette, Beverly. "John Ehrlichman—from the Power Elite to the Simple Life." *Los Angeles Times*, Feb. 5, 1982.

*Colson, Charles W. "Despair: A Trigger of Jail Rioting." *New York Times*, Oct. 13, 1985, E21.

"Colson Steps Down as Fellowship Chief." *Chicago Tribune*, Oct. 27, 2006, 13.

Condon, Richard. "Hail to the Chiefs." *Harper's Magazine*, Aug. 1, 1976, 253.

Dilulio, John J. Jr. "Chuck Colson and Second Chances." *Wall Street Journal*, April 23, 2012.

Dobbs, Michael. "Charles Colson, Nixon's 'Dirty Tricks' Man, Dies at 80." *Washington Post*, April 21, 2012, A1.

Dudar, Helen. "John Ehrlichman's Latest Chapter." *Chicago Tribune*, May 6, 1979, J20.

Ehrlichman, John. "Reagan's Challenge in China." *New York Times*, March 30, 1984, A31.

*Ehrlichman, John. "The Taste of Ashes: A Nixon Adviser Reflects on Reagan Under Siege." *Newsweek*, Dec. 8, 1986, 51.

Ehrlichman, John. "Trout Fishing in the Rockies." *Washington Post*, June 5, 1983, E2.

"Former Nixon Adviser Dies." *BBC News*, Feb. 16, 1999.

Garment, Leonard. "John Ehrlichman's Other Legacy." *New York Times*, Feb. 17, 1999, A15.

Houston, Jack. "'Finding Christ' No Copout, Colson Says." *Chicago Tribune*, Nov. 22, 1979, A3.

Jackson, Harold. "John Ehrlichman Obituary: The Watergate Plumbers' Mate." *Guardian*, Feb. 16, 1999.

Jones, Cass. "Charles Colson Dies Aged 80." *Guardian*, April 21, 2012.

Lowry, Rich. "Chuck Colson, Once Disgraced, Is Now a Mentor." *Daily News*, April 8, 2012.

Morton, Tom. "Colson: U.S. Threatened by Loss of Moral Values." *Colorado Springs Gazette-Telegraph*, July 21, 1990, D3.

Nyhan, David. "Charles Colson: Nixon's Tough Guy Moves to Defense." *Boston Globe*, Sept. 16, 1973, A1.

O Connor, Fionnuala. "Chuck Colson: A Born-Again Watergate Christian Who Still Believes in Nixon." *Irish Times*, Nov. 13, 1976, 6.

Phelps, Timothy M. "Charles Colson, 1931–2012: Watergate Felon and Prison Reformer." *Los Angeles Times*, April 22, 2012, A33.

Reeves, Richard. "What Ehrlichman Really Thought of Nixon." *New York*, May 10, 1976, 42.

Rubin, Alissa J. "Nixon Loyalist Ehrlichman Is Dead at 73." *Los Angeles Times*, Feb. 16, 1999.

Schell, Orville. "Boy Gets Girl, Changes World History: The China Card." *New York Times*, June 22, 1986, BR13.

Sherrill, Robert. "White House Conspiracy: The Whole Truth." *Washington Post*, April 29, 1979, M1.

Stern, Laurence. "Ehrlichman at the Helm: The Company." *Washington Post*, June 20, 1976, 107.

*Treadwell, David. "Colson's 'Born-Again' Faith Real, His Critics Agree." *Los Angeles Times*, Aug. 21, 1980, C1.

"Watergate Figure, Christian Leader Chuck Colson Dies." CNN, April 21, 2012.

Weil, Martin. "Key Nixon Advisor John D. Ehrlichman Dies at 73." *Washington Post*, Feb. 16, 1999.

Weiner, Tim. "Charles W. Colson, Watergate Felon Who Became Evangelical Leader, Dies at 80." *New York Times*, April 21, 2012.

"The White House in Turmoil: John Ehrlichman and H. R. Haldeman." *Newsweek*, May 7, 1973.

*"Why Charles Colson's Heart Is Still in Prison." *Christianity Today*, Sept. 16, 1983.

Witcover, Jules. "Reputed Dirty Tricks Man Colson Finds Career on the Line." *Washington Post*, Sept. 25, 1973, A14.

Wunderink, Susan. "Charles Colson." *Christianity Today*, Feb. 2009, 15.

WEBSITES AND ONLINE ARTICLES

"About Chuck Colson." Colson Center. colsoncenter.org/about.

"Charles W. Colson (White House Special Files: Staff Member and Office Files)." Richard Nixon Presidential Library and Museum.

Delaney, Bill. "Prisoners Riot Against Conditions in Attica." EBSCO Information Services, 2023.

Eye of the Storm Documentary Film Collection. Special Collection Libraries, University of Georgia.

"John D. Ehrlichman (White House Special Files: Staff Member and Office Files)." Richard Nixon Presidential Library and Museum.

*"Richard Nixon's Political Scandal: Researching Watergate in the Manuscript Collections at the Library of Congress." Library of Congress.

*Schulz, Kathryn. "From the White House to the Jailhouse to the Pulpit: Chuck Colson on Being Wrong." *Slate*, Oct. 20, 2010.

"Who We Are." Prison Fellowship International.

"The World's Most Interesting Prize." Templeton Prize.

OTHER

"Charles 'Chuck' Wendell Colson Part 01 (Final)." Federal Bureau of Investigation Records: The Vault.

"John Ehrlichman Part 02." Federal Bureau of Investigation Records: The Vault.

"John Ehrlichman Part 03." Federal Bureau of Investigation Records: The Vault.

Chapter 12: Feeding the Inner Fire (and Doing Great Work Late)

BOOKS

Boardman, Roger Sherman. *Roger Sherman: Signer and Statesman*. Philadelphia: University of Pennsylvania Press, 1938.

*Boutell, Lewis Henry. *The Life of Roger Sherman*. Chicago: A. C. McClurg, 1896.

Brands, H. W. *The First American: The Life and Times of Benjamin Franklin*. New York: Vintage Books, 2000. Kindle.

Collier, Christopher. *Roger Sherman's Connecticut: Yankee Politics and the American Revolution*. Middletown, Conn.: Wesleyan University Press, 1971.

Comfort, Nathaniel C. *The Tangled Field: Barbara McClintock's Search for the Patterns of Genetic Control*. Cambridge, Mass.: Harvard University Press, 2003. Kindle.

Franklin, Benjamin. *The Autobiography of Benjamin Franklin*. New York: P. F. Collier & Son Company, 1909. Kindle.

*Hall, Mark David. *Roger Sherman and the Creation of the American Republic*. New York: Oxford University Press, 2013. Kindle.

Hall, Mark David, ed. *Collected Works of Roger Sherman*. Indianapolis: Liberty Fund, 2016.

*Isaacson, Walter. *Benjamin Franklin: An American Life*. New York: Simon & Schuster Paperbacks, 2003. Kindle.

Labunski, Richard. *James Madison and the Struggle for the Bill of Rights*. New York: Oxford University Press, 2006. Kindle.

*Van Doren, Carl. *Benjamin Franklin*. New York: Viking Press, 1938.

VIDEOS AND AUDIO
*Burns, Ken, dir. *Benjamin Franklin*. Season 1, episode 1, "Join or Die (1706–1774)." Aired April 4, 2022, on PBS.
Burns, Ken, dir. *Benjamin Franklin*. Season 1, episode 2, "An American (1775–1790)." Aired April 5, 2022, on PBS.

NEWSPAPERS AND MAGAZINES
Mitgang, Herbert. "Handwritten Draft of a Bill of Rights Found." *New York Times*, July 29, 1987, A1.

WEBSITES AND ONLINE ARTICLES
"Articles of Confederation (1777)." National Archives.
"Benjamin Franklin: First American Diplomat, 1776–1785." United States Department of State Office of the Historian.
"Benjamin Franklin: Man of Business and Science." Library of Congress.
"Benjamin Franklin in London." George Washington's Mount Vernon. www.mountvernon.org/library/digitalhistory/digital-encyclopedia/article/benjamin-franklin-in-london.
*"Benjamin Franklin's Famous Quotes." Franklin Institute.
"Boston Tea Party Facts." Boston Tea Party Ships & Museum.
"Closing Speech at the Constitutional Convention (1787)." National Constitution Center.
"Connecticut: Roger Sherman." U.S. Capitol Visitor Center.
"The Constitution: How Was It Made?" National Archives.
"Convict Labor During the Colonial Period." Virginia Humanities.
"Creating the United States: Creating the Bill of Rights." Library of Congress.
"Declaration of Independence (1776)." National Archives.
"Declaring Independence: Drafting the Documents." Library of Congress.
"Felons and Rattlesnakes, 9 May 1751." National Archives.
"From Benjamin Franklin to Josiah Quincy Sr., 15 April 1776." National Archives.
*"From Benjamin Franklin to William Franklin, 7 October 1769." National Archives.
"Grammy Awards: Robert Plant." Recording Academy.
"Instructions and Commission from Congress to Franklin, Charles Carroll, and Samuel Chase for the Canadian Mission, 20 March 1776." National Archives.
Mangan, Gregg. "Roger Sherman, Revolutionary and Dedicated Public Servant." ConnecticutHistory.org, Oct. 10, 2020.
"Nobel Prize in Literature 1993: Press Release." Nobel Prize, Oct. 7, 1993. www.nobelprize.org/prizes/literature/1993/press-release.
"Roger Sherman." Bill of Rights Institute.
"Roger Sherman: Connecticut." U.S. Army Center of Military History.

"Roger Sherman Statue." Architect of the Capitol.
"1774 Articles of Association." National Archives Foundation.
"1721–1793 Roger Sherman." Descendants of the Signers of the Declaration of Independence.
"Signers of the Declaration of Independence." National Archives.

OTHER
*Allison, Robert J. *The Age of Benjamin Franklin*. Chantilly, Va.: Great Courses, 2018.
Gerber, Scott. "Roger Sherman and the Bill of Rights." *Polity* 28, no. 4 (1996): 528, 531.
Guelzo, Allen C. *America's Founding Fathers*. Chantilly, Va.: Great Courses, 2017.
"Thomas Jefferson: Original Rough Draft of the Declaration." Library of Congress.

Chapter 13: Questions Are Better Than Answers
BOOKS
Collins, Jimmy. *Test Pilot*. Garden City, N.Y.: Doubleday, Doran, 1935.
Corn, Joseph J. *Into the Blue: American Writing on Aviation and Spaceflight*. New York: Literary Classics of the United States, 2011.

Appendix 4.1: Personal Economics Analysis
BOOKS
Cooper, Gordon. *Leap of Faith: An Astronaut's Journey into the Unknown*. With Bruce Henderson. New York: Open Road Integrated Media, 2018. Kindle.
Fox, Michael J. *Lucky Man: A Memoir*. Hyperion e-books, 2010. Kindle.
Fox, Michael J. *No Time Like the Future: An Optimist Considers Mortality*. New York: Flatiron Books, 2020. Kindle.
Isaacson, Walter. *Benjamin Franklin: An American Life*. New York: Simon & Schuster Paperbacks, 2003. Kindle.
Pogue, Forrest C. *George C. Marshall: Education of a General, 1880–1939*. Plunkett Lake Press, 2020. Kindle.
Santana, Carlos. *The Universal Tone: Bringing My Story to Light*. With Ashley Kahn and Hal Miller. New York: Little, Brown, 2014. Kindle.
Thomas, Evan. *First: Sandra Day O'Connor*. New York: Random House, 2019. Kindle.
Walton, Mary. *A Woman's Crusade: Alice Paul and the Battle for the Ballot*. New York: St. Martin's Press, 2010. Kindle.
*White, Maurice. *My Life with Earth, Wind & Fire*. With Herb Powell. New York: Amistad, 2016. Kindle.

Zahniser, J. D., and Amelia R. Fry. *Alice Paul: Claiming Power.* New York: Oxford University Press, 2014. Kindle.

VIDEOS AND AUDIO

Collins, Cardiss. "Entering Congress After My Husband's Death." National Visionary Leadership Project, Oct. 18, 2013.

NEWSPAPERS AND MAGAZINES

Bulseco, Donna. "Vera Wang's Wedding Belles." *Women's Wear Daily*, Aug. 30, 1990, 7.

"Farm Workers' Story Is Hers: Supporters Say Credit Overdue for Dolores Huerta." *Chicago Tribune*, May 28, 1995, G8.

Goudreau, Jenna. "Michael J. Fox Foundation Cofounder Creates the Match.com of Clinical Trials." *Forbes*, Feb. 24, 2012.

Gussow, Mel. "The Rising Star of Meryl Streep." *New York Times*, Feb. 4, 1979.

Italie, Hillel. "Toni Morrison: A Black Woman in Paradise." *Los Angeles Sentinel*, Feb. 11, 1998, B7.

Karimzadeh, Marc. "The Transformation of Vera Wang." *Women's Wear Daily*, Nov. 16, 2005.

MacDonald, Marianne. "Interview: Toni Morrison." *Observer*, March 29, 1998.

*McDowell, Edwin. "Behind the Best Sellers: Toni Morrison." *New York Times*, July 5, 1981, A18.

McElwaine, Sandra. "Hero Grandmother Dolores Huerta Honored with Medal of Freedom." *Daily Beast*, May 18, 2012.

Morain, Dan. "Police Batons Blamed as UFW Official Is Badly Hurt During Bush S.F. Protest." *Los Angeles Times*, Sept. 16, 1988, 3.

Stober, Dan. "Huerta Calls on Women's Voices." *Mercury News*, March 3, 1991, 1B.

"Vera Wang's Business Is No Longer All Dressed in White." *New York Times*, Dec. 15, 2005.

Witchel, Alex. "From Aisle to Runway: Vera Wang." *New York Times*, June 19, 1994, SM22.

WEBSITES AND ONLINE ARTICLES

"Company." Vera Wang. www.verawang.com/company.

"FAQ: Getting Involved: Donations." Michael J. Fox Foundation.

"Marshall and Taxes." George C. Marshall Foundation, April 15, 2016.

Index

Page numbers followed by an *n* indicate notes.

Adams, John, 293, 296, 305
Adaptation to Life (Vaillant), 133–34
adversity, 235–36. *See also* cliffs; "roulette wheel of life"
Aiken, Howard, 27, 28
Albright, Tenley
   choosing responsibility and, 275
   economic circumstances and, 106–7
   fog of retirement and, 179
   fog of success and, 178
   Heiss and, 104–7
   inner fire and figure skating, 113–16, 118, 120
   inner fire and surgery career, 116–19
   polio and, 104–5, 117, 119
Alice Paul: Claiming Power (Zahniser and Fry), 128
Allen, James Browning, 147
All Rise: The Remarkable Journey of Alan Page (McGrane), 41
All the President's Men (Woodward and Bernstein), 191
Alter, Jonathan, 238
Ambition, Pragmatism, and Party (Kaufman), 221
arrow of money, flipping of
   Albright and, 104–7
      Curse of Competence Loop and, 111
      economic circumstances and, 101–7
   as element of One Big Thing, 22, 26, 34, 47
   Heiss and, 102–7
   Hopper and, 31, 34, 99–100
   McClintock and, 22, 24, 34, 99
   Page and, 101
   Plant and, 90–95, 97–98, 100–101
   relationship between work and money, 99

Back to the Future (film), 156, 233–34
bad luck. *See* "roulette wheel of life"
Baker v. Carr, 225, 233
Bancroft, George, 296
Beck, Jeff, 210
Beloved (Morrison), 73, 79, 290
Benjamin Franklin: An American Life (Isaacson), 303
Berlin, Isaiah, 25
Bernstein, Carl, 191, 272
Beyer, Kurt W., 29, 99–100
BHAG (Big Hairy Audacious Goal), decline after achievement of, 177–78
Bible and Sword (Tuchman), 78, 79
Bland, Sidney R., 130
Blatz, Kathleen, 41
Bluest Eye, The (Morrison), 73, 76, 79

Bogle, Jack, 313–16
Bonham, Jason, 96, 97
Bonham, John (Bonzo), 4, 91–96, 172, 202, 210, 262
Born Again (Colson), 269
Bradlee, Ben, 188, 189, 194
Brands, H. W., 302
Bridges of Madison County, The (film), 246, 249
Brown v. Board of Education, 38
Brunet, Pierre, 102, 103–4
Buffett, Warren, 192–93, 194, 195, 231
Built to Last (Collins and Porras), 6, 178, 183
Burns, Lucy, 4
  choosing responsibility and, 275
  cliffs, preclearing the fog and, 201
  inner fire and suffrage fight, 124, 125, 126–27, 129–30, 170
  personal economics and, 338
business empire heir, fog of youth and, 172–74
business flywheel economic stream, 110, 175, 343–44
"but for" test, 276, 321

Cannell, Michael, 122–23
Cannon, James, 221
Carlton, Richard P., 198
Carter, Jimmy, 149, 224–25
  campaign for president, 224–27
  Carter Center and life after presidency, 236–39, 291
  choosing responsibility and, 274
  inner fire and, 291
  luck and, 231–32, 233
  in Navy, 222–24
  personal economics and, 348
  as president, 228–29, 239–40
Carter, Rosalynn, 237–38
Celebration Day (album and film), 97, 101
Chicago Tribune, 282
China Card, The (Ehrlichman), 282
Clapton, Eric, 90, 210
cliffs
  C. Collins and, 145–50, 151, 152
  cliff of success and, 78–79, 154–55, 177
  defined, 142–43
  Ernst and, 139–42
  as inevitable part of life, 153–55
  matched pairs and, 144–45
  navigating fog and, 8
  Pittman Allen and, 145, 147–48, 150–52
  as primary lens for study, 3–6, 142
  ranges of positive and negative, 143, 154–55
  "roulette wheel of life" and, 216
  scoring rubric, 349–52
  study methodology and, 143–45
CMT Crossroads (music show), 262
Collins, Cardiss, 4, 146
  husband's death and service in Congress, 145–50, 151, 152
  inner fire and, 291
  personal economics and, 347
  "roulette wheel of life" and, 214, 235
Collins, Delores (author's grandmother), 325–26
Collins, George, 145, 146, 148
Collins, Jim (author)
  bug book of, 180–84
  evolution of beliefs and hopes of, 322–25

Extend Out/Circle Back and, 264–66
his father and, 1–2, 172, 317, 325–27
study's transformation of, 9–11, 206–8, 324
Collins, Jimmy (author's grandfather), 325–26
Colson, Charles
Ehrlichman and, 279, 282–84
Prison Fellowship ministry and choosing responsibility, 268–73, 276, 278
responsibility, not legacy and, 288
role in Nixon White House, 267, 273
sentenced to prison, 267, 268
Colson, Patty, 270
"coming into frame," defined, 8
Company, The (Ehrlichman), 281, 282
computers. *See* Hopper, Grace
Congressional Black Caucus, C. Collins and, 149, 291
Cooper, Gordon, 315
arrow of money and, 100
cliff after space program and, 65–68, 69
encodings and, 55–60, 65–70
luck and, 232
personal economics and, 340
similarities to Glenn, 55–56
Crawling King Snakes, 91
creative flywheel economic stream, 109–10, 167, 342–43
credibility equity, age and inner fire, 308–9
cross funding economic stream, 109, 341
CrushPod cycling team, 286

Cry in the Dark, A (film), 245, 249, 254
cumulative experience, age and inner fire, 307–8
Curse of Competence Doom Loop, 111

Daley, Richard, 145
Dantzig, George, 185
Death Becomes Her (film), 245, 249
Declaration of Independence
Franklin and, 295, 304, 308
Sherman and, 292, 294, 295, 304
Deer Hunter, The (film), 244, 248, 254
DeFrank, Thomas M., 220–21
Desert One (documentary), 228–29
Devil Wears Prada, The (film), 246, 249, 251
direct personal support economic stream, 110, 347–48
disappointment, fog of, 174–76
discipline, love as greater than, 135–36
Doubt (film), 246, 249

earned earlier economic stream, 110, 346–47
Earth, Wind & Fire, 162–66, 167, 175–76, 235
economic circumstances
Albright and figure skating, 104–7
Heiss and figure skating, 102–7
ways to manage, 107–10
see also personal economic analysis

education/training economic stream, funding for, 109, 340
Ehrlichman, John
  after-prison writing and choosing responsibility, 281–84
  Colson and, 279, 282–84
  prison sentencing and term, 278, 281
  Watergate and Nixon White House, 278, 280, 283
Eisenhower, Dwight D., 64, 310
Eller, Carl, 4
  arrow of money and, 100
  choosing responsibility and, 274
  commonalities and differences with Page, 46–47
  football career and later ceramic artistry, 37, 38, 43–46
encodings
  age and inner fire, 307
  as deeper than strengths, 59–60
  as element of One Big Thing, 22, 23–24, 47
  enhanced operating modes and, 70, 71–77, 77–84
  "in frame" and, 49, 51, 67–68, 149, 307
  hedgehog mode and, 26
  as new lens on leadership, 309–12
  self-awareness and, 68–70
  trusting of one's own, 85–89
Equal Rights Amendment, 129
Ernst, Joanne, 6, 9–10, 183, 288, 317, 318
  cliffs and, 139–42
  coaching and choosing responsibility, 285–87

Ertegun, Ahmet, 96, 97
Everything to Gain (Carter and Carter), 238
Extend Out/Circle Back, inner fire and, 118–19, 243–66
  element of fun and, 264–66
  encoding and, 247–48
  Plant and, 261–62
  Streep and, 243–52, 260, 264
  Winger and, 252–60

family and relationships, inner fire and, 132–34
Family Ties (television program), 156, 159, 167, 233–34
family wealth economic stream, 107, 109, 338–39
Fear and Loathing in Las Vegas (Thompson), 226
Feeling for the Organism, A (Keller), 18
"First Who" principle, 189
Florence Foster Jenkins (film), 250, 264
fog, 156–84
  bug book of J. Collins and, 180–84
  defined, 157
  fog of disappointment, 174–76
  fog of retirement, 179–80
  fog of success, 176–78
  fog of youth, 169–74
  Fox and, 156–62, 166–67, 168
  as inevitable part of life, 166–69
  interative steps and, 184
  White and, 162–68, 175–76, 178
  see also simplex stepping
Ford, Betty, 222, 239
Ford, Gerald R., 203
  after presidency, 239–40

assassination attempts on,
    221–22
choosing responsibility and, 274
in Congress, 219–20, 222
early life, college, and law
    school, 217–18
luck and, 231, 232
in Navy, 218–19
as Nixon's vice president,
    220–21
personal economics and, 348
as president, 221–22
Fox, Michael J., 201, 316
    choosing responsibility and,
        274
    fog of success and, 178
    luck, "roulette wheel of life"
        and, 214, 231
    NATILIE moments, 233–34
    One Big Thing and, 166–67
    Parkinson's diagnosis and
        responses to, 156–62, 163,
        166
    personal economics and,
        337–38, 345
Frankfurter, Felix, 208
Franklin, Benjamin, 291, 306, 316
    as ambassador to France, 304–5
    curiosity and experimental
        inventing, 300–301
    leadership encodings and,
        308–11
    personal economics and, 344,
        346
    role in founding of U.S.,
        293–95, 301–7, 311
    as writer and businessman,
        299–300, 303
Frontiere, Georgia
    Extend Out/Circle Back and,
        263

preclearing fog and, 200–201,
    202–3
"roulette wheel of life" and, 235
similarities and differences with
    Graham, 200–201, 204–5
simplex stepping out of fog,
    199–204
Fry, Amelia R., 128
Full Life, A (Carter), 223

Gardner, John W., 250, 252,
    317–18
Gerald R. Ford (Cannon), 221
Glenn, John, 172, 291, 315
    arrow of money and, 100
    cliff after space program
        and U.S. Senate service,
        60–65, 69
    encodings and, 50–55, 59–60,
        67–70
    Extend Out/Circle Back and, 262
    fog of retirement and, 179
    luck, "roulette wheel of life"
        and, 211, 232
    run for president, 63–64
    similarities to Cooper, 55–56
Good Life, The (Colson), 282
Good to Great (Collins), 6, 109n,
    343n
*Grace Hopper and the Invention
    of the Information Age*
    (Beyer), 29
Graham, Katharine, 290
    Extend Out/Circle Back and,
        263
    luck, "roulette wheel of life"
        and, 211, 214, 231, 235
    pressmen's strike and, 193–94
    publishing decisions at *The
        Washington Post*, 151,
        189–92, 195

Graham, Katharine (*cont.*)
   similarities and differences with Frontiere, 200–201, 204–5
   simplex stepping out of fog, 186–96, 198–99
Graham, Philip, 186–87, 194, 263
Grant, Bud, 38
Great by Choice (Collins and Hansen), 230
Guns of August, The (Tuchman), 78, 79, 85–86

Halberstam, David, 225
Haldeman, H. R., 280, 282
Hansen, Morten, 230, 233
hedgehog mode
   difference between *the* hedgehog and *a* hedgehog, 214
   Eller and, 43–46
   finding personal, 25–26
   Glenn, Cooper, and encodings, 69–70
   Hopper and, 34, 36, 47
   McClintock and, 26, 34, 36, 47
   Morrison and, 74
   Page and, 37–43
   "roulette wheel of life" and, 211–16
   single and serial hedgehogs, 37
Heiss, Carol
   Albright and, 105–7
   economic circumstances and figure skating, 102–7
   luck and, 231
Henry, Patrick, 293
Hewlett-Packard Co. (HP), 180–82
His Very Best (Alter), 238
Hopper, Grace, 315
   arrow of money and, 31, 34, 99–100
   choosing responsibility and, 274
   commonalities and differences with McClintock, 27, 28, 30, 31, 32–37
   encodings and, 28, 30, 32, 36
   hedgehog mode and, 34, 36, 47
   inner fire and, 28, 31, 34, 121
   luck, "roulette wheel of life" and, 211, 232, 235
   pioneering computer work in academia, Navy, and business, 26–32, 121
Huerta, Dolores, 153, 348
Hutchinson, Thomas, 302

I. M. Pei: Mandarin of Modernism (Cannell), 122–23
Idiots Karamazov, The (musical), 244, 245
inner fire, 113–36
   Albright and, 113–18, 120–21
   Burns and, 124, 125–27, 129–30
   as element of One Big Thing, 22, 25, 47
   Extend Out/Circle Back and, 118–19, 265–66
   family and relationships and, 132–34
   freely chosen responsibilities and, 119–20
   hedgehog mode and, 26
   Hopper and, 28, 31, 34, 121
   love of the doing and, 115–18, 134–36
   McClintock and, 22, 25, 34, 123
   Paul and, 124–29, 130, 133
   relentlessness and, 124–25, 127–30
   side passions and, 131–32

Stress and Drudgery Tax and, 121–24
see also inner fire, feeding long and late
inner fire, feeding long and late, 9, 290–316
   credible equity and, 308–9
   cumulative experience and, 307–8
   encoding as new lens on leadership, 309–12
   Franklin and U.S. founding, 290–95
   Sherman and U.S. founding, 291–99
Iran, hostage crisis, 228–29
Iron Lady, The (film), 247, 249
Ironman World Championship, Ernst and, 139–41, 183, 286
Ironweed (film), 245, 249, 254
Isaacson, Walter, 303
iterative steps, out fog, 171, 179, 184, 185, 199, 202, 207, 258, 271. *See also* simplex stepping

Jay, John, 305
Jazz (Morrison), 79, 290
Jefferson, Thomas, 293, 295, 298, 304, 308
Jenkins, Carol Heiss. *See* Heiss, Carol
Jenkins, Hayes Alan, 106n
John Ehrlichman: In the Eye of the Storm (documentary), 279, 282
John Glenn, A Memoir (Glenn), 53
Jones, John Paul, 92, 93, 96, 210, 262

Kaufman, Scott, 221
Keller, Evelyn Fox, 18
Kennedy, John F., 58, 60–61, 85–86, 100
Kennedy, Robert, 85
Khazei, Alan, 286–87
"Know Thyself," 3, 68–69, 319. *See also* self-knowledge
Kooser, Ted, 258
Kramer vs. Kramer (film), 244, 248, 251, 254
Krauss, Alison, 97, 261–62

Late Night with David Letterman (television program), 31, 35
Lazier, Bill, 10, 343
leadership, encodings as new lens on, 309–12
Leap of Faith (Cooper), 57
Led Zeppelin, 4, 93–98, 101, 178, 202, 210–11, 261–62, 344
"legacy," dangers of focusing on, 288–89
Los Angeles Rams, Frontiere's successful management of, 199–205
Louvre Museum, Pei and, 122–23
love of the doing, inner fire and, 115–18, 134–36
luck. *See* "roulette wheel of life"
Lucky Man (Fox's memoir), 156, 158, 161

Madison, James, 293, 297, 298, 308, 311
Mamma Mia! (film), 246, 249, 251
Marshall, George C., 153, 342
Marshall, Thurgood, 38
mastering scarcity economic stream, 108–9, 337–38
McClintock, Barbara, 123, 291, 315

arrow of money and, 22, 24, 34, 99
commonalities and differences with Hopper, 27, 28, 30, 31, 32–37
encodings and, 22, 23–24, 69–70, 87–88
fog of success and, 178
genetics research and career path, 17–25, 26
hedgehog mode, 26, 36, 47
inner fire and, 22, 25, 34
personal economics and, 348
"roulette wheel of life" and, 211, 215, 235
McGrane, Bill, 41
Metzenbaum, Howard, 61–62
Michael J. Fox Foundation for Parkinson's Research, 156–57, 161, 345
Michener, James A., 245
Minnesota Vikings. *See* Eller, Carl; Page, Alan
MIT Collaborative Initiatives, Albright and, 119–20
money. *See* arrow of money; personal economic analysis
Morrison, Toni, 171, 290, 315
choosing responsibility and, 133, 273
cliff of success and, 78–79
economic circumstances and, 112
encoded operating modes of writing, 71–77, 84
fog of success and, 177
personal economics and, 343
similarities and differences with Tuchman, 78–81, 84
Mothershead, John L., Jr., 277–78

Mothershead Mantra, 277–78, 284, 321
My Fifth Super Bowl (film), 44
My Life with Earth, Wind & Fire (White), 166
Myers, Rochelle, 181

naps, "second mornings" and, 182
NATILIE moments
evaluating of own, 320
extending out/circling back and, 253
"roulette wheel of life" and seizing of, 233–34
Newsweek, 188, 189, 280
New York Times, 64, 190, 203, 282
Nixon, Richard M., 191
Colson and Watergate, 267–68, 278–79
Ehrlichman and Watergate, 278–80, 282–84
Ford and, 220–21
Nobel Prize
McClintock and, 17, 21–22, 24, 87–88, 178, 348
Morrison and, 79, 177, 290
No Quarter: Jimmy Page and Robert Plant Unledded (album), 95

O'Connor, Sandra Day, 153, 339
Officer and a Gentleman, An (film), 253–54
Olympic Games. *See* Albright, Tenley; Heiss, Carol
"One Big Thing," 17–47
elements of, 22–25
Eller's football and ceramic work, 38, 43–47
Hopper's computer work and, 26–32
McClintock's research and, 17–25

Page's football, legal, and
    educational work, 37–43
personal hedgehogs and,
    25–26, 37

Page, Alan, 4
    arrow of money and, 100
    commonalities and differences
        with Eller, 46–47
    Extend Out/Circle Back and, 263
    football career, law career, and
        educational work, 37–43,
        70, 202
    luck and, 231
    side passions, inner fire and,
        131–32
Page, Diane, 41–42, 46, 131
Page, Jimmy, 4, 316
    arrow of money and, 101
    luck, "roulette wheel of life"
        and, 209–11, 215, 231
    music and, 90, 92–93, 95–97,
        121–22
    Stress and Drudgery Tax and,
        121–22
Page Education Foundation,
    41–42, 46
parents, fog of youth and, 171–74
Parkinson's disease. *See* Fox,
    Michael J.; White, Maurice
Paul, Alice, 4, 133, 201, 316
    fog of youth and, 169–71
    inner fire and, 124–29, 130
    luck, "roulette wheel of life"
        and, 211, 232
    personal economics and, 338
Pei, I. M., 153, 291, 344
    Stress and Drudgery Tax and,
        122–23
Pentagon Papers, Graham's decision
    to publish, 189–91, 195, 198,
    199

Perry Mason (television program),
    38–39, 263
personal economic analysis, 337–48
    business flywheel, 110, 343–44
    creative flywheel, 109–10,
        342–43
    cross funding, 109, 341
    direct personal support, 110,
        347–48
    earned earlier, 110, 346–47
    education/training funding,
        109, 340
    family wealth, 109, 338–39
    mastering scarcity, 108–9,
        337–38
    salaried hedgehog, 109, 342
    social cause flywheel, 110, 345
    special sources, 110, 348
    spousal economics, 109, 339–40
Personal History (Graham's
    memoir), 187, 196, 198
Pierce, William, 305
Pittman Allen, Maryon, 4, 145,
    151–52
    Congress and, 147–48, 150–51
Plant, Karac, 94
Plant, Robert, 4, 171–72, 290,
    315–16
    arrow of money and, 95, 97–98,
        100–101
    choosing responsibility and, 275
    Extend Out/Circle Back and,
        261–62
    fog of success and, 178
    life of musical adventure and,
        90–95
    Page and, 96–97, 210
    side passions, inner fire and, 131
    simplex stepping, 202
polio, Albright and, 104–5, 117,
    119
Pollan, Tracy, 159

Porras, Jerry, 178, 183
Powell, Herb, 166
Practicing History (Tuchman), 80

Rachel Getting Married (film), 257
Raising Sand (album), 97, 261
responsibilities, inner fire and freely chosen, 119–20, 267–89
    Albright and, 275
    beyond self and, 284–88
    Colson and, 267–74, 278, 283–84
    dangers of focus on "legacy" and, 288–89
    Ehrlichman and, 278–84
    Fox and, 274
    Mothershead Mantra and, 277–78, 284
    personal core values and, 275
retirement, fog of, 179–80
return on luck, 229–34
Rickover, Hyman, 223–24, 231, 233
River Wild, The (film), 245–46, 249
Robert Plant: A Life (Rees), 91
Rock & Roll Hall of Fame, 96, 162, 164
Rockefeller, Nelson, 222
Rolling Stone magazine, 226, 227
Rosenbloom, Carroll, 200–201, 203, 204, 205
"roulette wheel of life," 209–40
    bad luck, adversity, and "fortunate enough," 235–36
    finding hedgehog and, 211–16
    luck's role and Carter, 216, 222–29, 236–40
    luck's role and Ford, 216–22, 239–40
    NATILIE moments and, 233–34
    Page and, 209–11
    return on luck and, 229–34
    three tests of "luck events," 230
Rumsfeld, Donald, 219–20

salaried hedgehog economic stream, 109, 342
Santana, Carlos, 153, 341
Scanlon, Paul, 225–26
Searching for Debra Winger (documentary), 257
self-awareness and self-knowledge
    bug book and, 182–84
    catalytic questions to consider, 319–22
    encodings and, 68–70, 89
Self-Renewal (Gardner), 250, 317
Sherman, Roger, 316
    leadership encodings and, 297, 310–11
    role in founding of U.S., 291–99, 305, 308–9, 311
    traits and encodings of, 295–96, 308–9
side passions, inner fire and, 131–32
Silkwood (film), 244–45, 248, 254
"simplex algorithm," Dantzig and, 185
simplex stepping, 184, 185–208
    in anticipation of cliffs, 201–2
    clarity for making decisions and, 199
    Collins's management transformation and, 206–8
    Frontiere and, 199–205
    Graham and, 186–99, 204–5
    Winger and, 258
Sipple, Oliver, 222
Small, Evelyn, 196
social cause flywheel economic stream, 110, 345

Song of Solomon (Morrison), 73, 76, 79
Sophie's Choice (film), 244, 248, 251, 254
space program. *See* Cooper, Gordon; Glenn, John
Space Shuttle *Discovery*, 65
special sources economic stream, 110, 348
Spielberg, Steven, 233
Spin City (television program), 159–61
spousal economics economic stream, 109, 339–40
Stadler, Lewis, 19–20
Stanford University, Collins and
   Graduate School of Business, 10, 181, 183, 285, 317–18
   undergraduate education, 9, 277
Stevens, Doris, 127–28
Still (documentary), 274
Streep, Meryl, 291
   drama school and early acting of, 243–45
   Extend Out/Circle Back and, 243–52, 260, 264
   film career of Winger and, 254
   list of films of, 248–50
   personal economics and, 341
Stress and Drudgery Tax, 121–24
   Fox, White and, 168
   Graham and, 194
   Hopper and, 121
   Page and, 121–22
   Pei, I. M. and, 122–23
   Winger and, 255
success, fog of, 176–78
Suffragist newspaper, 125
Sula (Morrison), 73, 76, 79

Tennyson, Alfred, 40
Test Pilot (Collins), 325
Test Pilot (film), 326
Thompson, Hunter S., 225–27, 231
Tierney, Tom, 276
Tuareg nomads, Plant plays for, 94–95
Tuchman, Barbara, 315
   choosing responsibility and, 274–75
   cliff of success and, 78–79
   encoded operating modes of writing, 77–86
   Extend Out/Circle Back and, 262–63
   similarities and differences with Morrison, 77, 78–81
Twain, Mark, 26

Ulysses (Tennyson), 40
Undiscovered (Winger), 253
United States Athletes Association, 44
University of Michigan, Ford and, 217–18, 232
Urban Cowboy (film), 253, 254
U.S. Congress
   C. Collins and, 145–50, 151, 152
   Ford and, 219–20, 222
   Glenn and, 61–65, 69
   Pittman Allen and, 147–48, 150–51
   widow's mandate and, 145
U.S. Constitution
   Franklin and, 305–6, 311
   19th Amendment to, 4, 124, 127–30, 338
   Sherman and, 292, 293, 297–99, 305, 308–9, 311
U.S. Supreme Court
   Baker v. Carr, 225, 233
   Brown v. Board of Education, 38
USS *Hopper*, 32

USS *Monterey*, 218–19
USS *Nimitz*, 228
USS *Pomfret*, 222–23

Vaillant, George A., 133–34
Van Doren, Carl, 300

Wall Street Journal, 66, 267, 284
Walters, Barbara, 156, 160, 161
Wang, Vera, 153, 344
Washington Post, 63, 149, 151, 263, 272
   Graham's simple stepping and management of, 186–96, 198–99
Washington Post Company, Graham and, 186, 191–92, 195, 211
Watergate
   Carter's election and, 225
   Graham, *The Washington Post* and, 189, 191–92, 195
   see also Colson, Charles; Ehrlichman, John; Nixon, Richard M.
Wedderburn, Alexander, 302
"what luck," 231
"What to make of a life" study
   cliffs as lens for, 3–6, 142–45
   Collins's transformation by, 9–11, 206–8, 324
   economic circumstances and, 107–10
   list of matched-pair study subjects, 12–13
   study methodology and, 2–8, 142–45
When the Center Held (Rumsfeld), 219

White, Maurice, 201
   choosing responsibility and, 275
   fog of disappointment and, 175–76
   fog of success and, 178
   luck, "roulette wheel of life" and, 231, 232, 235
   One Big Thing and, 167, 168
   personal economics and, 337
   Parkinson's diagnosis and responses to, 162–166
White House Diary (J. Carter), 238
Whole Truth, The (Ehrlichman), 282
"who luck," 231
Why Not the Best? (Carter memoir), 224
Wilson, James, 305
Winger, Debra
   acting and reactions to fame, 252–55
   choosing responsibility and, 275
   Extend Out/Circle Back and acting, 257–60
   fade-in and fade-out pattern and move away from Hollywood, 256–58
   film career of Streep and, 254
   NATILIE moments, 253
Witness to Power (Ehrlichman), 280
Wolverhampton Wanderers Football Club, 131
women's suffrage. *See* Burns, Lucy; Paul, Alice
Wonder Woman (television program), 253
Woodward, Bob, 191–192, 272

Woolpert, Bruce, 181
"worthiness hierarchy," 86, 130, 287, 324
Write It When I'm Gone (DeFrank), 220–21

Yale Law School, 218
Yale School of Drama, 244, 260
Yardbirds, 92–93, 210

youth, fog of, 36, 51, 68, 169–74, 180

Zahniser, J. D., 128
"zeit-luck," 231–32
Zemeckis, Robert, 233
"Zen Garden elements," 259–60
Zimmermann Telegram, The (Tuchman), 78, 79

About the Author

JIM COLLINS is a student and teacher of exceptional human endeavor and a Socratic advisor to leaders across all sectors of society.

Having invested more than three decades in rigorous research, he has authored or coauthored a series of books that have sold in total more than 11 million copies worldwide, including the #1 bestseller *Good to Great*, the enduring classic *Built to Last*, and other highly influential writings.

With *What to Make of a Life*, Jim has broadened the scope of his work, extending out from the question of what makes great companies tick to the study of remarkable people and their lives. Through his research, he seeks to uncover timeless principles on which people can reliably depend.

Driven by a relentless curiosity, Jim began his research and teaching career on the faculty at the Stanford Graduate School of Business, where he received the Distinguished Teaching Award in 1992. In 1995, he founded The Good to Great Project LLC in Boulder, Colorado, where he conducts research and engages with leaders from around the world.

Jim has a passion for learning and teaching in the social sectors, including education, healthcare, government, faith-based organizations, social ventures, and cause-driven nonprofits. In 2012 and 2013, he had the honor to serve a two-year appointment as the Class of 1951 Chair for the Study of Leadership at the United States Military Academy at West Point.

He holds a bachelor's degree in mathematical sciences and an MBA from Stanford University, and honorary doctoral degrees from the University of Colorado and the Peter F. Drucker Graduate School of Management at Claremont Graduate University. In 2017, Forbes selected Jim as one of the 100 Greatest Living Business Minds.